Architecture of Sovereignty

In this innovative study, Gita V. Pai traces the history of the Pudu Maṇḍapam (Tamil, 'new hall')—a Hindu temple structure in Madurai—through the rise and fall of empires in south India from the seventeenth century to the present. This wide-ranging work illustrates how south Indian temples became entangled in broader conflicts over sovereignty, from early modern Nāyaka kings, to British colonial rule, to the post-independence government today. Drawing from methodologies in anthropology, religious studies, and art and architectural history, the author argues that the small temple site provides profound insight into the relationship between aesthetics, sovereignty, and religion in modern South Asia.

Gita V. Pai is a cultural historian of South Asia. She is Professor of History and Director of International and Global Studies at the University of Wisconsin-La Crosse.

Architecture of Sovereignty

Stone Bodies, Colonial Gazes, and Living Gods in South India

Gita V. Pai

CAMBRIDGE
UNIVERSITY PRESS

CAMBRIDGE
UNIVERSITY PRESS

University Printing House, Cambridge CB2 8BS, United Kingdom

One Liberty Plaza, 20th Floor, New York, NY 10006, USA

477 Williamstown Road, Port Melbourne, vic 3207, Australia

314 to 321, 3rd Floor, Plot No.3, Splendor Forum, Jasola District Centre, New Delhi 110025, India

103 Penang Road, #05–06/07, Visioncrest Commercial, Singapore 238467

Cambridge University Press is part of the University of Cambridge.

It furthers the University's mission by disseminating knowledge in the pursuit of education, learning and research at the highest international levels of excellence.

www.cambridge.org
Information on this title: www.cambridge.org/9781009150156

First published 2023

Printed in India by Avantika Printers Pvt. Ltd.

A catalogue record for this publication is available from the British Library

Library of Congress Cataloging-in-Publication Data

Names: Pai, Gita V., author.
Title: Architecture of sovereignty : stone bodies, colonial gazes, and living gods in South India / Gita V. Pai.
Description: Cambridge: Cambridge University Press, 2022. | Includes bibliographical references and index.
Identifiers: LCCN 2022022774 (print) | LCCN 2022022775 (ebook) | ISBN 9781009150156 (hardback) | ISBN 9781009150163 (ebook)
Subjects: LCSH: Maturai Aruḷmiku Mīn̲āṭci Cuntarēsvarar Ālayam. | Pudu Maṇḍapam. | Architecture and society--India--Madurai. | Art and society--India--Madurai. | Architecture--Political aspects--India. | Art--Political aspects--India. | BISAC: LITERARY CRITICISM / European / English, Irish, Scottish, Welsh
Classification: LCC BL1243.76.M332 M3765 2022 (print) | LCC BL1243.76.M332 (ebook) | DDC 294.5/35095482--dc23/eng20220721
LC record available at https://lccn.loc.gov/2022022774
LC ebook record available at https://lccn.loc.gov/2022022775

ISBN 978-1-009-15015-6 Hardback

For
Ananda who departed this world,
Anand who entered it, and
Vidya and Vinay who came in between.

Contents

Part III Living Gods

Figures

Acknowledgments

This book began on a humid August day in 2001. Before my stay in Madurai to learn Tamil ended, I wanted to see the royal portrait sculpture located inside the Mīṉākṣī-Sundareśvara temple's Pudu Maṇḍapam, the topic of a paper I wrote for a religion of south India course at the University of California, Berkeley. So I waited near the temple's towering south gateway, clutching a handwritten note for the temple's executive officer. After convincing him to allow me to enter the pillared hall's central portion kept locked throughout the year (except when religious festivals occur within it), I acclimated to its dark cavernous interior, walked across its dusty granite floor, and gazed upward at its stone statues of Madurai's Nāyaka rulers. Surrounded by the bustling noise from the commercial activity encircling this nave, I marveled at the life-size, full-figured images projecting from colossal columns: they were unlike anything I had seen of earlier depictions of south Indian kings. That visit confirmed a fascination in early modern Nāyaka historiography and that paper inspired this book.

My thanks go to my *gurus* involved in the project's initial phase: George L. and Kausalya Hart for their never-ending guidance, warm friendship, and, most importantly, instilling in me a love for Tamil culture; Joanna Williams for mentoring me on art historical matters and for being a caring teacher; Eugene Irschick for advising me on historical concerns; and Lawrence Cohen for encouraging many creative paths and for demonstrating through his example that academia is a noble profession. I am also grateful to several other individuals at UC Berkeley, both in and out of the classroom: Paola Bacchetta, Matthew Baxter, Catherine Becker, Jennifer Clare, Vasudha Dalmia, Prachi Deshpande, Penelope Edwards, Robert and Sally Goldman, Nikhil Govind, Tapati Guha-Thakurta, Alka Hingorani, Usha Jain, Kiran Keshavamurthy, Sonal Khullar, Jinah Kim, Nancy Lin, Layne Little, Preetha Mani, Sujatha Meegama, Carlos Mena, Trinh T. Minh-ha, Minoo Moallem, Geetha Murali, V. N. Muthukumar, Bharathy Sankara Rajulu, Harsha Ram, Raka Ray, Srinivas Reddy, Elizabeth Segran, Kirtana Thangavelu, Charis Thompson, Sylvia Tiwon, Archana Venkatesan, and Alexander von Rospatt. I extend my gratitude to my colleagues in the History Department at the University of Wisconsin-La Crosse for supporting my scholarship, in particular Gerry Iguchi, a dear and treasured friend who has been invariably generous with his erudition and encouragement.

Through the years, I benefitted greatly from the lively intellectual atmosphere and conversations generated in university seminars, conference panels, and writing workshops. I am appreciative of Naman P. Ahuja, Daud Ali, Amy Allocco, Jacqueline Armijo, Maitrii Aung-Thwin, Michael Baltutis, Benjamin Bogin, Crispin Branfoot, Leslie Castro-Woodhouse, Isabelle Clark-Deces, Frank Cody, Whitney Cox, Richard H. Davis, Sangeetha Desai, Michael Di Giovine, Diana Dimitrova, Polina Dimova, Joyce Flueckiger, Zeynep Gürsel, Brian Hatcher, Padma Kaimal, Omar A. Khan, Esther Klein, Sunil Kumar, Chiara Letizia, Michael Linderman, Boreth Ly, Thomas Metcalf, Anne Monius, Vasudha Narayanan, Isabella Nardi, Anand Pandian, George Pati, Indira V. Peterson, Tracy Pintchman, Tatiana Oranskaia, Leslie C. Orr, Srilata Raman, Sumathi Ramaswamy, Martha Ann Selby, Kavita Singh, Davesh Soneji, Smriti Srinivas, Kara Olsen Theiding, Susan S. Wadley, and Joanne Waghorne.

For the book's research, writing, and image permissions, I have been enormously fortunate to have received financial support from many sources, which include UW-La Crosse's History Department; UW-La Crosse's Faculty Research Grants, International Scholarship Grants, and College of Arts, Social Sciences, and Humanities (CASSH) Small Grants; American Association of University Women (AAUW) American Dissertation Fellowship; U.S. Department of Education's Fulbright-Hays Doctoral Dissertation Research Abroad (DDRA) Fellowship and Foreign Language and Area Studies (FLAS) Fellowships; UC Berkeley's Doreen B. Townsend Center for the Humanities Dissertation Fellowship, Dean's Normative Time Fellowship (DNTF), and Tamil Chair Graduate Student Fellowship; and grants from UC Berkeley's South and Southeast Asian Studies Department, Gender and Women's Studies Department, and Institute for South Asia Studies.

Kindhearted assistance from many institutions and people across the world have enhanced this project. I am immensely grateful to the Alkazi Foundation for the Arts, New Delhi: Jennifer Chowdhry Biswas; American Institute of Indian Studies: Elise Auerbach (Chicago), Purnima Mehta (New Delhi), Bharathy Sankara Rajulu (Madurai); American Institute of Indian Studies Center for Art and Archaeology, Gurgaon: Sushil Sharma, Vandana Sinha; Archives and Historical Research Department, Tamil Nadu Archives, Chennai: Santhana Gopalan, Madan, Ram Prasad, A. Rajappa, Sridhar; British Library, London: Jennifer Howes, Bruna Lago-Fazolo, Malini Roy, its staff and librarians; British Museum, London: Francesca Hillier, Lucia Rinolfi; California State Library-Sutro Library, San Francisco: Diana Kohnke; Hindu Religious and Charitable Endowments Department, Chennai: the many staff members who facilitated my research; French Institute of Pondicherry, Puducherry: Jean-Pierre Muller, Kannan Muthukrishnan, Anurupa Naik, R. Narenthiran, Y. Subbarayalu; J. Paul Getty Museum: Open Content Program; Metropolitan Museum of Art, New York: John Guy, Meredith Reiss, Open Access Initiative; Mīnākṣī-Sundareśvara temple, Madurai: Senthil Bhattar, Shekar Bhattar, Raju Bhattar, Ganesan, Karumuttu T.

and Uma Kannan, N. Natarajan, B. Raja, T. Vijayaraghunathan; Musée National des Arts Asiatiques-Guimet, Paris: Vincent Lefèvre; Pudu Mandapam, Mīnākṣī-Sundareśvara temple, Madurai: Kannan, G. and Bala Ganesh Muthupandi, Pooncholai; Royal Asiatic Society of Great Britain and Ireland, London: Camilla Larsen, Edward Weech; Senthamil College, Madurai: library staff; Society of Antiquaries of London: Adrian James; United States–India Educational Foundation, New Delhi and Chennai: S. K. Bharathi, Girish Kaul, Varrtika Mudaliar, Seethalakshmi Raghavachary, S. Vasudevan; UW-La Crosse: Katy Davidson, Laura Godden (Murphy Library Special Collections/ ARC), Kevin Dinsmore (Interlibrary Loan Services), John Kelly (Geography and Earth Sciences), Linda Levinson (Art), Amy Ticknor (History); Victoria & Albert Museum, London: Nick Barnard, Freya Levett, Revati Mann, Divia Patel, Ekta Sunil Raheja, Nicholas Smith; Wilson Centre for Photography, London: Hope Kingsley; Yale Center for British Art, New Haven: Laura Callery, Chitra Ramalingam, Maria Singer; and in Bengaluru: Kishore and Deepti Jaganath, Sathish Mallya; Chennai: Dilip Kumar, Justice V. and Sarojini Ramaswami, Geetha Toke; Madurai: K. P. Bharathi, Ligi George, G. Vasudevan, V. Vedachalam, R. Venkatraman; New Delhi: Rahul and Sindhushree Khullar; Pondicherry: K. Anupama, Varalakshmi Krishnamoorthy; Tirunagar: Bharathy and Lakshmana Perumal, and R. and Vidya Varadharajan.

At Cambridge University Press, Qudsiya Ahmed, Aniruddha De, Sohini Ghosh, Anwesha Rana, and many others guided the manuscript through the publication process with gentle care and painstaking attention. I am tremendously grateful to them for ushering this book into the world as well as to the anonymous peer reviewers whose incisive and thoughtful comments shaped the manuscript into a much better monograph.

Because this book is also about south India, I mention my parents and role models, Ananda and Syamala Rao, who were born there. Despite facing unfathomable poverty and the demands of running the family coffee stand, performing odd jobs, and providing for his eight siblings as a young man in rural Kerala, my father studied with resolve and earned a scholarship to complete his PhD in biochemistry in the United States. My mother arrived shortly afterwards with a high school education and limited English, but later attended college and became a teacher. While I was working towards my own doctoral degree that would lead to this monograph, my father spent his retirement days picking my two children from school and my mother hosted fun-filled sleepovers for them. I wish my father were alive to read this book: he loved Tamil culture and was thrilled that his daughter studied it. My mother-in-law, Jahnavi Pai, passed away recently too: her afternoon *chai* erased the day's wear and her evening dinners sustained me for late-night writing. I could not have succeeded without them.

Nor could I without my husband, Vivek, who shouldered the extra child-care and household responsibilities, and tolerated my study hours in local coffee shops and absences in other continents with patience and some grumbling. As children and later teenagers, Vidya and Vinay endured those days when deadlines loomed and my office door bore a "Do not disturb" sign. Now thriving and successful adults, they continue to be unfailingly supportive. Vinay even read every chapter multiple times with great sensitivity and critical acumen, helping me to assert my voice. I thank him for putting his time and energy into the spirit of this book. Over the years, my brother Vivek Rao, sister Veena Mitchell, and their spouses cheered from the sidelines. As did Hershey Avula and Rudrani Ghosh, wonderful additions to our family. Last but not least, there is Anand, my adorable grandson born a little over a year after my father—his namesake—passed away and on the very day that Cambridge University Press expressed an interest in this project: being his "Ammama" brings me immense joy.

Notes on Transliteration and Spelling

In general, my transliteration of Tamil words follows the University of Madras' *Tamil Lexicon* scheme. Where a term or name is used in both Sanskrit and Tamil, I opted for Sanskrit in some cases to avoid confusion, for example, *digvijaya* instead of *tikkuvicayam* and *utsavam* rather than *uṟcavam*. For the sake of readability, I rendered frequently appearing words as they are pronounced, not as they are written, for instance, "Pudu Maṇḍapam" for "Putu Maṇṭapam," "Mīnākṣī" for "Mīṉāṭci," and "Pāṇḍyan" for "Pāṇṭiyaṉ." I spelled the names of historical persons, deities, and temples with diacritics, but left modern place and personal names without them. All errors remain my own.

Introduction

Sovereignty's Trace in Architectural Forms

This book begins with a popular legend about an heir apparent, an illness, and a dream. In the seventeenth century, Tirumala Nāyaka, crown prince of the Madurai Nāyaka dynasty in the Tamil region of southeastern India, suffered from chronic catarrh that left him with an upper respiratory infection that neither doctors nor the gods from neighboring temples could cure (Figure I.1). As he journeyed to Madurai for his coronation, Tirumala collapsed from fatigue. That night, goddess Mīnākṣī (Tamil, 'the fish-eyed one,' a manifestation of Pārvatī) and god Sundareśvara ('the beautiful lord,' the local form of Śiva) appeared in his dream: they promised that if Tirumala moved his kingdom's capital from Tiruchirappalli to Madurai, where the deities dwelled in their temple, they would relieve him of his ailment. After consulting with his Brahmins and court ministers, Tirumala accepted the gods' request—he vowed that when cured, he would not only make Madurai his permanent home, he would also spend lavishly on the temple by financing its restoration and sponsoring its rituals. According to legend, Tirumala was immediately restored to health, and as Madurai's ruler from 1623 to 1659, he became Mīnākṣī and Sundareśvara's most ardent devotee.

The setting of this book is one of Tirumala's promised projects: the Pudu Maṇḍapam ('new hall'). Built in the 1630s as a major addition to the Mīnākṣī-Sundareśvara temple complex under Tirumala Nāyaka's patronage, the Pudu Maṇḍapam is one of the best-known monuments from the Nāyaka period (spanning the sixteenth to eighteenth centuries) and one of the largest festival *maṇḍapams* ('pillared halls') in the Indian subcontinent (Figure I.2). While the god's *mūla mūrti*—its immovable 'root or original image'—remains in the temple's *garbhagṛha* (Skt, 'inner sanctum'), the deity also takes the form of a bronze, movable festival image, or *utsava mūrti*, which travels from the temple's main shrine and stays in the *maṇḍapam* during ritual performances. In addition to a stage for religious functions, the Pudu Maṇḍapam boasts massive granite pillars sculpted with gods, mythological figures, and fully modeled portraits of the Nāyaka royal lineage arranged in chronological order—with Tirumala, the patron

Figure I.1 Tirumala Nāyaka, ivory, seventeenth century, Temple Art Museum, Mīnākṣī-Sundareśvara temple, Madurai

Source: Photo by author.

of the project, at the end. The temple and its pillared hall are the religious and cultural hub of Madurai, and a popular site for tourists and Hindu devotees making pilgrimage. Tens of thousands of people visit daily, particularly on Friday (believed to be the goddess's day), and many more arrive during temple festivals—such as the annual Cittirai festival in spring, when over a million devotees throng the temple town to celebrate the celestial wedding between Mīnākṣī and Sundareśvara.

In the Tamil country, perhaps more than any other part of the Indian subcontinent, the king's relationship with the temple was the defining characteristic of sovereign power. Arjun Appadurai's classic history of the Śrī Pārtasārati Svāmi temple in Madras (now Chennai) clarifies the enduring relationship between human kings and temple gods in the pre-colonial period, where the temple served as a sacred domain in which transactional and redistributive roles were performed by ruler and deity, mediated by the ritual exchange of gifts. In the cycle of exchange that defined south Indian temples, the local deity was the "paradigmatic" sovereign whom the king serves; the king, in return, received special honors that defined his participation in the deity's sovereignty.[1] British colonization severed the links between gods and kings, in part, by directly intervening in the indigenous

Figure I.2 Archaeological Survey of India, General view of the Pudu Maṇḍapam from the north-east with the eastern *gōpuram* of the Mīnākṣī-Sundareśvara temple, Madurai, in the background, 24 × 28.5 centimeters, 1899

Source: © The British Library Board, Photo 1008/4(355).

management of temples through bureaucratic apparatuses that interfered with the traditional mechanisms of redistribution. Nicholas Dirks' analysis of the Tamil princely state of Pudukkottai is an important study of how British administrators introduced bureaucratized revenue systems and altered palace rituals that severed the south Indian king from the source of his religious authority, leaving him with a "hollow" crown.[2]

In ancient Tamil, the king (*kō*) was considered a representative of god on earth and lived in a *kōyil* ('palace,' 'residence of a king'). Old Tamil words for a ruler or eminent person, such as *kō* ('king,' 'emperor'), *iṟaivaṉ* ('chief,' 'master', 'superior'), and *āṇṭavan* ('master') are now words for god; the Tamil word for temple has become *kōyil*, which means 'the residence or house of god.'[3] This linguistic mapping links the *ruler*, the *master*, the *palace*, and the *temple*: it emphasizes the central importance of *architecture* in analyzing the problem of sovereignty in the context of ancient and contemporary south India. We can gain profound insight into the configurations of technologies of power by studying the temple, its political and ethical claims, and its aesthetic representational forms. Work on Nāyaka visual culture by Crispin Branfoot and Anna Lise Seastrand illustrate the affective and spatial dimensions of power encoded in temple architecture: temple murals and statues as well as representations of deities that circumambulate during rituals and festivals invoke the "real presence" of the figures depicted, and generate a spontaneous affect and embodied immediacy for the devotee within the temple, turning the temple into a space of kinetic self-transformation modulated by the divine temporality of the sculpture and paintings.[4] Research by Lennart Bes and Velcheru Narayana Rao, David Shulman, and Sanjay Subrahmanyam on the Nāyakas' complex relationship to the Vijayanagara empire offer important insights into the idiosyncrasies of Nāyaka architectural forms;[5] in the corpulent shapes of the figures that line the Pudu Maṇḍapam, we see how the Nāyakas interrupted imaginations of the ideal 'royal body' in south India and produced new conceptualizations of 'kingship' in the seventeenth century.

Colonial representations of the pillared hall—as travel narratives, watercolors, engravings, maps, poems, and photographs—rendered 'Indian civilization' as a curiosity for European scholars and middle-class consumers, and thus produced 'British India' as an object that could be rationally administered from afar. The proliferation of diverse forms of visual and textual representation traces transformations in the material conditions and self-imaginations of both colonial subjects in south India and metropolitan subjects in Britain, whose destinies were intertwined by the mechanisms of empire. The Pudu Maṇḍapam, as a religious architectural site, offers a fertile context for rethinking the concept of 'sovereignty,' not only in south India from the seventeenth century, but also in the global context of postcolonial societies with complex attachments to their former metropoles. The contemporary social sciences are preoccupied with discourses of sovereignty that shaped early modern European forms of government in which "sovereignty" is often reducible to *state* sovereignty, and its genesis as a political question is typically credited to English philosopher Thomas Hobbes, for whom sovereignty is the "soul" of the Leviathan, the supreme authority of the ruler over its subjects.[6] Even popular narratives about sovereignty, which theorize its movement *away* from the nation-state (for example, Michael Hardt and Antonio Negri's thesis that state sovereignty has evolved into a global empire[7]), nevertheless fail to detach the concept from a distinctly European, state-centric historical context. A proper genealogy of sovereignty requires analyzing configurations of power outside the dominant Eurocentric scene, before colonization transplanted the European forms across the globe, and it must contemplate more seriously the complex ways the European forms were, in turn, profoundly changed by the colonial encounter.

Today, the Pudu Maṇḍapam is the site of renewed political conflict as Madurai's elites seek to convert the pillared hall into a museum, and thus remake Madurai into an appealing global tourism destination. The Pudu Maṇḍapam may appear, to different observers at different times, as a resting place for a revered goddess, a historical archive of a royal genealogy, a performance of a sacred scripture, a crowded and dirty marketplace, or a lucrative real estate investment. In the pillared hall, each observer *sees* something entirely different—the complex and antagonistic political claims about the Pudu Maṇḍapam must be analyzed in terms of the aesthetic representations that render those claims intelligible. "Aesthetics," in a simple sense, refers to what we deem *beautiful* or *desirable*, the criteria according to which we make such judgments, and the media through which these judgments are exercised and shared. Aesthetic representations function in a cyclical relation to the exercise of power: power relations constrain the objects we consider beautiful and desirable, and representations of desire and beauty constrain the forms of power we consider legitimate and acceptable. The realm of aesthetics intimately informs how we become *subjects* of political claims, how we understand our relation to rule and recognize our obligation to it. A sanitary exhibition of sculptures encased in glass is beautiful to some; the crowd and cacophony of petty merchants is beautiful to others. Which of these forms the Pudu Maṇḍapam will take in the future is a question in which aesthetics and power are interconnected.

This study is informed by recent work on the "scaffolding of sovereignty," which focuses on the aesthetic dimensions of power and rule.[8] Here, the "aesthetics" of sovereignty refers to an anthropological category that encompasses both the phenomenology of power (the *sensations* and *experiences* in which power relations become embedded) and the art of power (the *rituals*, *customs*, and *symbols* through which power relations are mediated). In tracing the aesthetic contours of "sovereignty," we search for the scenes in which power is expressed not as brute force and naked coercion, but as "regimes of truth": the mechanisms by which certain statements are accepted as 'true' or 'false,' and the practical obligations set in motion when a certain discourse is acknowledged as authority.[9] Ritual performances of power in South and Southeast Asia have long been a source of fascination for anthropologists, such as Clifford Geertz's "theatre state" in Bali—in which kings were "impresarios," priests were "directors," and peasants were "supporting cast, stage, crew, and audience."[10] However, where this anthropological tradition starts with the identification of dominant customs and symbols, and then describes the social phenomena that gave them 'meaning,' my investigation follows the inverse path, by concentrating on the 'meaning-giving' forces and disciplines that give certain customs and symbols an authoritative status.[11] The emphasis of this work is on the *media* through which power relations are inscribed and ethical commitments are defined. In the Tamil context, the *temple* offers a site of 'meaning-ful' conflict and contestation, in which diverse aesthetic representations were formed and acquired the status of 'truth.'

This book is a contribution to the genealogy of technologies of power in a global context, through an analysis of formally and temporally diffuse aesthetic representations. My aim is not to excavate the 'true' identity of the Madurai temple, nor to reclaim some transcendental religious meaning that was 'lost' to the violence of colonization. Rather, I will demonstrate through several scenes how aesthetic considerations about a pillared hall in a small temple town informed the practical exercise of power within much broader dynamics of empire—first the south Indian kings who shared the 'world empire' of Vijayanagara, then the British empire and its global networks of labor and capital, and finally the postcolonial state and its nationalisms formed by the twin legacies of colonization and globalization. The Pudu Maṇḍapam, as a living temple and an architectural monument, provides a context for rethinking the demands, entitlements, and constraints of power from the early modern to colonial to post-independence rule in south India, offering insight into unfolding transformations in relationships between aesthetics and politics over the long duration of South Asian history.

A brief history of Madurai and its temple

Madurai is one of the oldest urban settlements in South Asia, located about 300 miles southwest of Chennai, the capital of the modern state of Tamil Nadu in south India.[12] The densely populated core of the city lies on the southern banks of the Vaigai, the river that flows eastward from the Western Ghats to the Bay of Bengal (Figure I.3). The story of Madurai is intertwined with the stories of the *talapurāṇam* ('place-history') that describe Śiva's "sacred games," the deity's exploits that formed the city and molded its various features: its hills, rivers, ponds, and temples. According to popular legend, Madurai was once a forest of *kaṭampu* trees, where Lord Indra traveled in search of purification for his sins; there, Indra discovered a stone *liṅgam*, the aniconic representation of Śiva, beside a golden pond, in which Indra bathed and collected lilies to decorate the *liṅgam*. In an early chapter of Parañcōti Muṉivar's seventeenth-century version of *Tiruviḷaiyāṭal Purāṇam* ('Story of Śiva's sacred games'), a merchant stumbles upon this same *liṅgam* by chance, and informs the Pāṇḍyan king Kulacēkaraṉ of his discovery—the king orders the forest cleared, and a temple constructed around the *liṅgam*. Later chapters describe how Śiva dons myriad disguises and intervenes in the lives of rulers and inhabitants of the city; eventually, Śiva himself becomes king of Madurai after being married to the Pāṇḍyan princess Mīnākṣī. Śiva created the Vaigai, it is said, by asking the Gaṅgā river in his hair to quench the thirst of

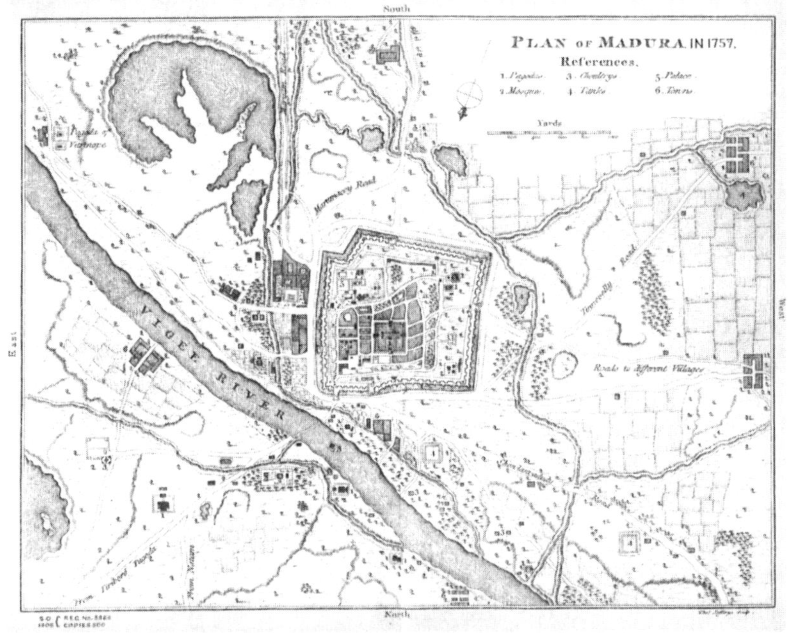

Figure I.3 Plan of Madura in 1757

Source: W. Francis, *Madras District Gazetteers: Madura*, vol. I (Madras: Printed by the Superintendent, Government Press, 1906), between pages 264 and 265.

a guest at their wedding. It is impossible to identify a precise 'origin' for these ancient stories, which appear in various Sanskrit and Tamil *purāṇa*s—however, some scholars suggest the tale of a Pāṇḍyan princess who married a deity was recorded as early as the fourth century BCE, by the Greek traveler Megasthenes. Tamil-Brahmi cave inscriptions from the second century BCE refer to *matir-ay*, translated as 'walled city.' The name "Madurai" may alternately derive from a story in the *purāṇam*s of Śiva purifying and blessing the new town by showering drops of nectar full of sweetness (Tamil, *maturam*; Skt, *madhura*) from his matted locks.

The ancient city of Madurai was the seat of the Pāṇḍyan dynasty, a line of kings referenced in Greco-Roman texts as early as the fourth century BCE, which survived in the southeastern region of the Indian peninsula, with varying periods of dominance and decline, until the sixteenth century.[13] Greek and Latin accounts, including the works of Strabo (64 BCE–24 CE), Pliny the Younger (61–113 CE), and Ptolemy (100–170 CE), describe imports of pearls and textiles from Madurai and the reception of a Pāṇḍyan assembly by Augustus Caesar. Ancient Tamil literature from the early centuries CE name Madurai as a meeting place of poets in legendary scholarly assemblies called Tamil Saṅgam. Along with the Cōḻas and Cēras, the Pāṇḍyas were one of three royal lineages of ancient south India, comprising a triumvirate of rival dynasties known as the Mūvēntar, or 'Three Crowned Kings.' The Pāṇḍyas practiced Jainism, but later became devotees of Śiva, as recorded in seventh-century hymns by itinerant poet-saints who sang of Hindu shrines in Madurai. In the late twelfth century or early thirteenth century, the Pāṇḍyan king Kulacēkaraṉ (r. 1190–1216 CE) constructed the current Mīnākṣī-Sundareśvara temple as an abode for the Pāṇḍyan queen who became a goddess after her marriage to Śiva. The Venetian explorer Marco Polo wrote a vivid description of Madurai and the Mīnākṣī temple during his visit in the thirteenth century.

In the early fourteenth century, Muslim invaders from northern India ransacked Madurai and its temple, and established a Madurai sultanate.[14] During this period, the Moroccan Arab explorer Ibn Baṭṭūṭah visited Madurai en route to China, and his *Riḥla* (Arabic, 'journey') documents a great plague and the exceptional tyranny of a short-lived sultan who died of poisoning by aphrodisiac. By the end of the century, an army from Vijayanagara captured Madurai again, and restored worship in Hindu temples and the kingly tradition of temple patronage. Vijayanagara (Skt, 'city of victory') was a city in the Deccan Plateau in modern-day Karnataka, founded by brothers Harihara and Bukkarāya, that grew into a formidable empire spanning the southern peninsula. The Vijayanagara emperors managed the far-flung territories under their rule through a system of subordinate 'kings' engaged in a delicate balance of power. In the Tamil region to the south, they appointed Nāyakas, Telugu-speaking outsiders, as their regional military and administrative governors. The Vijayanagaras encouraged rivalries and destructive wars between the Muslim kings of the five Deccan sultanates bounding the empire's northern territory, but this condition did not last: in 1565, the sultanates formed an alliance and destroyed the Vijayanagara capital in Hampi. Seizing upon Vijayanagara's weakness, the Madurai Nāyakas severed themselves from the empire in the early seventeenth century. During this period, the rulers of Madurai invented novel expressions of independent Nāyaka kingship, which included major expansions to the Mīṉākṣī-Sundareśvara temple.

In the tumultuous late seventeenth century, as the army of the Mughal empire appeared poised to conquer the southern peninsula, the Madurai Nāyakas escaped Mughal invasion by paying tribute to Aurangzeb and supporting his capture of Senji from the Marāṭhās. The waning rulers of Madurai, already tributaries of the Mughal subordinate ruler, were wiped out by the Nawāb of Arcot in 1736. The next several decades were a period of intense struggle over the southern peninsula, entangling the Nawāb, the English East India Company, the French East India

Company, and the Marāṭhās, during which time Madurai changed hands multiple times. After falling heavily into debt, the last independent Nawāb of Arcot, Muḥammad 'Alī Khān Wallajah, assigned revenues from his territory to the British in 1781 to defray the cost of a 1780 war against Mysore ruler Haider 'Alī Khān and the French—for the first time, there was a British revenue collector in Madurai. After Haider 'Alī Khān's son, Tipū Sultān, was killed in the last Anglo-Mysore war at the 1799 siege of Seringapatam in the southern part of modern-day Karnataka, Madurai was captured by the English East India Company in 1801 and annexed to its Madras Presidency.

The British instituted ambitious programs of urban redevelopment in Madurai (now called "Madura") in the early nineteenth century. Collector John Blackburne, who administered the Madura Collectorate from 1835 to 1848, demolished the old Pāṇḍyan forts, laid down new roads, and expanded the city. A railway line was opened connecting Madurai to Tiruchirappalli in 1857, the same year as the Sepoy Mutiny, which caused the British crown to abolish Company rule and assume direct control of India's administrative and taxing authorities. Madurai was constituted in 1866 as a municipality under the Town Improvement Act of 1865, which created a system of municipal taxes for services like street lighting, water supply, and sewage; the Act was amended in 1871 to include issues like birth and death registration, sanitation, and vaccination. Under pressure from Christian missionaries, the British had initially resisted active involvement in the affairs of the Mīnākṣī temple—now they invalidated temple land grants made under the *iṇām* (Arabic, 'gift') system and passed a law stipulating that temple oversight be given to local management committees, which were broadly perceived as corrupt institutions. In 1937, the provincial government in Madras assumed supervision of the temple through the Hindu Religious Endowments (HRE) Board, tasked with handling widespread mismanagement. After India's independence in 1947, Madurai became a major district and the third most populous city in the postcolonial state of Tamil Nadu—the colonial institutions were reconfigured for use by the independent government. The city of Madurai is now administered by the Madurai Corporation, an upgrade of the municipal institution formed under British rule. The Hindu Religious and Charitable Endowment (HR & CE) Department, which replaced the old Board, now controls the Mīnākṣī temple administration as a branch of the Tamil Nadu state government in Chennai.

The power of place

The Tamil *talapurāṇam* is a history (*purāṇam*) of a specific sacred place or a pilgrimage site (*talam*). Many sculptures and paintings in the Mīnākṣī temple and its Pudu Maṇḍapam are recreations of stories from Śiva's "sacred games" in

Madurai, narrated in Parañcōti Muṉivar's seventeenth-century *Tiruviḷaiyāṭal Purāṇam*, Perumpaṟṟapuliyūr Nampi's thirteenth-century *Tiruvālavāyuṭaiyār Tiruviḷaiyāṭaṟpurāṇam*, and other Tamil and Sanskrit *purāṇa*s. The earliest references to Madurai as a temple site can be found in the sixth- to eighth-century tradition of Śaiva *Tēvāram* poetry, where traveling saints praised shrines visited in *tala yāttirai* ('a tour of sacred places').[15] British academic interventions in India were guided by a belief that narrative genres like the *purāṇa*s indicated an absence of historical consciousness, and India thus lacked 'history'—indeed, several chapters in this book focus on the archival technologies introduced by the British in order to ameliorate this 'lack,' which sought to extract India's 'lost' history from visual records of its religious architecture.[16] In navigating the divine temporality of the *purāṇa*s, the historiographic interventions of European scholars, and my own ethnographic research in Madurai, I am writing the history of the Pudu Maṇḍapam as a critical geography of a place. The task of a geographer and historian is to map the domain of these social constructions: to scrutinize the dominant meta-narratives about a place, the local and everyday uses of a place, and all the (often fleeting) representations that fall in between.[17]

The multifarious perspectives on the Pudu Maṇḍapam are significant to understanding the broader political and cultural history of south India, from the Nāyaka period to the present. This book delves into the concept of 'sovereignty' through the lens of the pillared hall by examining its aesthetic representations and ethnographic narratives. I am indebted to a tradition of "humanistic geography," which analyzes geographical phenomena not only in terms of their physical attributes, but also in terms of the human meanings and values ascribed to them.[18] I also utilize J. Nicholas Entrikin's definition of "place" as a site socially constructed within a particular context and period, where 'meaning' is produced by the particular concerns of the *subjects* of that place.[19] From this perspective, the "place" is inseparable from the "thoughts, feelings and experiences that make up the consciousness of inhabitants…place is not so much a location as a setting, less a thing than a relationship."[20] My task is to navigate the web of "relationships" bundled at the Mīnākṣī temple through the Śaiva poets who made pilgrimage there, the Nāyaka kings who left their likenesses there, the British travelers who captured photographs there, the petty merchants who traded their wares there, and so on. This book traces transformations of societies—both the present-day south Indian state of Tamil Nadu and its distant British colonial metropole—through the complex, and often contradictory, texts reflecting diverse experiences and relationships with the Pudu Maṇḍapam. This history is told through an analysis of letters, travelogues, bronze models, paintings and drawings, photographs, temple manuscripts and legends, physical architecture, sculpture, ritual, and tourism. Deliberating on these disparate forms, this book explores the ways various people experienced the site over several centuries.[21]

Using a variety of research methods taken from geography, art history, gender studies, and ethnography, this book illustrates how varied religious, economic, domestic, and foreign influences converge in shaping and conceptualizing the Pudu Maṇḍapam as a place, and India as an object and problem of government. My analysis draws from the genealogical approach of Michel Foucault.[22] Inspired by Friedrich Nietzsche, Foucault resisted an approach to history based on linear and evolutionary tropes; instead, he sought to unearth transformations in *power relations* by examining the silences and discordances in often contradictory texts and historical narratives.[23] This book understands the Pudu Maṇḍapam not as a discreet or singular object that persists through many periods of history, but as various related yet different things appearing at a certain intersection—a 'place.' Consequently, this book embraces discontinuities, shifts, ruptures, and transformations as it documents how various groups in divergent contexts and historical circumstances have understood and experienced the Pudu Maṇḍapam.[24] Foucault wrote that the historian possesses in him or herself not "an immortal soul but many mortal ones," and in each of these souls, "history will not discover a forgotten identity, eager to be reborn, but a complex system of distinct and multiple elements, unable to be mastered by the powers of synthesis."[25] In other words, the function of genealogy is not to discover some transcendental 'origin,' or to identify some fixed or permanent object that can be extended through time, but rather to commit ourselves to the *dissipation* of identity: "to make visible all of those discontinuities that cross us." The Pudu Maṇḍapam, as a site of great political, cultural, and religious contestation, offers a rich semantic web for studying the history of South Asia in the past centuries.[26]

Framework of the book

The first two chapters of the book address important concepts relating to Nāyaka rule in Madurai from the sixteenth century. In chapter 1 ("Constructing Kingship: Nāyaka Rule in Early Modern Madurai"), I discuss how Tirumala Nāyaka used temple patronage to articulate a mode of independent kingship outside the dominant tropes of Vijayanagara subordination. Through new genres of prose poetry connected to temple rituals, the Nāyaka king was celebrated not for his valor in combat, but for his devotion and piety. The statues he erected in the temple's new hall radically reconfigured concepts of masculinity relating to sovereignty: in place of the perfect, svelte *kṣatriya* kings, the Nāyaka statues are corpulent and full-bodied, indicating a revision of the dharmic norms regulating kingship. Chapter 2 ("Co-opting a Local Goddess in Madurai: From Warrior Queen to Śiva's Consort to Political Pawn") describes the apotheosis of goddess Mīnākṣī through an analysis of religious mythological texts, sculptural reliefs, and religious festivals connected to the Pudu Maṇḍapam. I focus on the novel ritual functions introduced at the temple by Tirumala Nāyaka, and their associated social meta-narratives about gender, agriculture, and fertility. Tirumala Nāyaka's patronage is illustrative of a distinctive form of sovereignty in south India in which local rituals became intimately linked with kingly authority.

Chapters 3 through 6 follow the British colonial encounter with south India, and its ramifications upon the Madurai temple. In chapter 3 ("Imagining Civilization: Antiquarian Curiosities in Madura"), I examine civil and military servants who arrived in India with the East India Company, and their attachments to private literary and scholarly societies in London and British India, most notably the Society of Antiquaries and the Asiatick Society of Bengal. The colonial antiquarians operated within a tradition of liberal humanism, and they regarded the Madurai temple as a source of great "curiosity"—they were motivated by a civilizational logic that aimed at improving humanity by seeking the common origins of art and scientific knowledge. As the British expanded their reach from footholds in Calcutta and Bombay into the interior of the subcontinent, burgeoning scientific interest in the colonizing mission helped to define 'India' as an object that could be rationally analyzed, and thus disassembled and reassembled in the image (and name) of Enlightenment. In chapter 4 ("Tracing the Vernacular: Drawing Madura into Debates over Language in British India"), I discuss how the British aesthetic inquiry into south Indian art and architecture, specifically the Madurai temple and its Pudu Maṇḍapam, became entangled in critical imperial debates over the government of the British colony as a whole—in particular, arguments over the methods of colonial education and decisions about the official languages of colonial administration.

Chapter 5 ("Illustrating Madura: Art as 'History' and State-Building") evaluates an important mechanism of British knowledge production in south India: the use of native informants. I explore the methods of East India Company surveyor Colin Mackenzie and Royal Asiatic Society scholar Ram Raz, who each produced their own detailed architectural drawings of the Pudu Maṇḍapam in the nineteenth century, to consider the colonial government's co-optation of Indian intellectuals in service of the British governing project. Chapter 6 ("Photographing Madura: The Living Temple as a Site of Ruin") ponders the emergence of photography in British India, which rapidly replaced the costly drafting techniques of Mackenzie and others. Through stylized and edited images,

British photographers helped recast living temples as archaeological ruins in the imagination of the British public. By erasing the colonized subject from these images, the temple could become a 'pure' artifact of ancient architecture; British paternalism in India depended fundamentally on this aesthetic maneuver of reconstituting India as a 'dying civilization.'

Through these differing artistic and political interventions, we begin to see how British colonization depended on the aesthetic erasure of the spiritual geography of the Madurai temple—this trajectory has culminated in the present moment with the *actual* erasure of the temple's spiritual functions through the Tamil Nadu government's attempts to convert the temple into a museum and tourist destination. Chapter 7 ("Producing Heritage: Culture as Commodity in Contemporary Madurai") documents the efforts of private investors and state bureaucrats to reconfigure the everyday life of the temple to accommodate a globalized format of heritage tourism, which accompanies a fundamental economic restructuring of the city of Madurai itself, in a bid to attract capital to the city. These programs are supported by the educated middle and upper classes of Madurai grappling with the contradictions of decolonization and the 'backward' status of their ancestral traditions within modernity's conceptual frameworks. The epilogue ("Rejecting the State: Priestly Devotion and Protest in Modern Madurai") discusses the embodied spirituality of the temple priests, who imagine their devotional practices as resistance to and rejection of the modern state apparatus—an attempt to hold onto the configurations of sovereignty that preceded colonization.

This book uses the Madurai temple, a site of extraordinary political contestation over the past several centuries, as an illustration of the fundamental link between technologies of *representation* and technologies of *government*. Sovereign forms have continually reoriented and rematerialized the south Indian temple complex according to the aesthetic demands of government. The Pudu Maṇḍapam is a small place—and yet, in reading the histories of this small place, the ways in which it has been adorned and decorated, and its various forms of representation and reproduction, we can gain profound insight into the commitments of early modern rulers, the mechanisms of colonization, the logic of colonial government, and the enduring attachments between the colonial state and the post-independence government of India.[27] Although the temple's sacred hall is in the "same" place it was centuries ago, a complex and diffuse network of actors have repurposed and reworked its meaning, experience, and practice according to a constantly shifting game of sovereignty. By closely studying this small place, and the multivalent web in which it is imagined, inhabited, and transformed, we can better understand our *own* place in the complex global politics that comes 'after' colonization.

Notes

1. Arjun Appadurai, *Worship and Conflict under Colonial Rule: A South Indian Case* (Cambridge: Cambridge University Press, 1981).
2. Nicholas B. Dirks, *The Hollow Crown: Ethnohistory of an Indian Kingdom* (Cambridge: Cambridge University Press, 1987).
3. George L. Hart, *The Poems of Ancient Tamil: Their Milieu and Their Sanskrit Counterparts* (New York and New Delhi: Oxford University Press, 1999 [1975]), 13.
4. Crispin Branfoot, *Gods on the Move: Architecture and Ritual in the South Indian Temple* (London: The Society for South Asian Studies, 2007); Anna Lise Seastrand, "Praise, Politics, and Language: South Indian Murals, 1500–1800" (PhD diss., Columbia University, 2013).
5. Lennart Bes, *The Heirs of Vijayanagara: Court Politics in Early Modern South India* (Leiden: Leiden University Press, 2022); Velcheru Narayana Rao, David Shulman, and Sanjay Subrahmanyam, *Symbols of Substance: Court and State in Nāyaka Period Tamilnadu* (Delhi and Oxford: Oxford University Press, 1998).
6. For example: James Bryce, "The Nature of Sovereignty," in *Studies in History and Jurisprudence*, vol. II (New York: Oxford University Press, 1901), 503-555; Carl Schmitt, *Political Theology: Four Chapters on the Concept of Sovereignty*, trans. George Schwab (Chicago and London: The University of Chicago Press, 2005 [1922]); F. H. Hinsley, *Sovereignty*, 2nd ed. (Cambridge: Cambridge University Press, 1986); Michel Foucault, *Discipline and Punish: The Birth of the Prison* (New York: Vintage, 1995); Clifford Geertz, "What Is a State If It Is Not a Sovereign?: Reflections on Politics in Complicated Places," *Current Anthropology* 45, no. 5 (December 2004): 577–593; Giorgio Agamben, *State of Exception*, trans. Kevin Attell (Chicago and London: The University of Chicago Press, 2005); James J. Sheehan, "The Problem of Sovereignty in European History," *American Historical Review* 111, no. 1 (February 2006): 1–15; Hent Kalmo and Quentin Skinner, eds., *Sovereignty in Fragments: The Past, Present and Future of a Contested Concept* (Cambridge: Cambridge University Press, 2010); Philip J. Stern, *The Company-State: Corporate Sovereignty and the Early Modern Foundations of the British Empire in India* (Oxford and New York: Oxford University Press, 2011); and Brian Goldstone, "Life After Sovereignty," *History of the Present* 4, no. 1 (Spring 2014): 97–113.
7. Michael Hardt and Antonio Negri, *Empire* (Cambridge, MA: Harvard University Press, 2000).
8. Zvi Ben-Dor Benite, Stefanos Geroulanos, and Nicole Jerr, eds., *The Scaffolding of Sovereignty: Global and Aesthetic Perspectives on the History of a Concept* (New York: Columbia University Press, 2017).

9. "Truth is a thing of this world: it is produced only by virtue of multiple forms of constraint. And it induces regular effects of power. Each society has its régime of truth, its 'general politics' of truth: that is, the types of discourse which it accepts and makes function as true; the mechanisms and instances which enable one to distinguish true and false statements, the means by which each is sanctioned; the techniques and procedures accorded value in the acquisition of truth; the status of those who are charged with saying what counts as true." Michel Foucault, *Power/Knowledge: Selected Interviews and Other Writings, 1972–1977*, ed. Colin Gordon (New York: Pantheon Books, 1980), 131.
10. Clifford Geertz, *Negara: The Theatre State in Nineteenth-Century Bali* (Princeton: Princeton University Press, 1980), 13.
11. Talal Asad, "The Construction of Religion as an Anthropological Category," in *Genealogies of Religion: Discipline and Reasons of Power in Christianity and Islam* (Baltimore: Johns Hopkins University Press, 1993), 27–54.
12. Information for this section was culled from A. V. Jeyechandrun, *The Madurai Temple Complex (With Special Reference to Literature and Legends)* (Madurai: Publications Division, Madurai Kamaraj University, 1985); Burton Stein, *Vijayanagara*, The New Cambridge History of India I.2 (Cambridge: Cambridge University Press, 1989); C. J. Fuller, *Servants of the Goddess: The Priests of a South Indian Temple* (Cambridge: Cambridge University Press, 1984); D. Devakunjari, *Madurai through the Ages: From the Earliest Times to 1801 A.D.* (Madras: Society for Archaeological, Historical, and Epigraphical Research, 1979); Holly Baker Reynolds, "Madurai: *Kōyil Nakar*," in *The City as a Sacred Center: Essays on Six Asian Contexts*, ed. Bardwell Smith and Holly Baker Reynolds (Leiden and New York: E. J. Brill, 1987), 12–44; Iravatham Mahadevan, ed. and trans., *Early Tamil Epigraphy from the Earliest Times to the Sixth Century A.D.* (Cambridge: Harvard University Press, 2003); J. H. Nelson, *The Madura Country: A Manual Compiled by Order of the Madras Government* (Madras: Asylum Press by W. Thomas, 1868); K. A. Nilakanta Sastri, *A History of South India from Prehistoric Times to the Fall of Vijayanagar*, 2nd ed. (London: Oxford University Press, 1958 [1955]); K. A. Nilakanta Sastri, *The Pāṇḍyan Kingdom from the Earliest Times to the Sixteenth Century* (London: Luzac & Co., 1929); William P. Harman, *The Sacred Marriage of a Hindu Goddess* (Bloomington: Indiana University Press, 1989); and W. Francis, *Madras District Gazetteers: Madura*, vol. 1 (Madras: Printed by the Superintendent, Government Press, 1906).
13. Pāṇḍyan rule in Madurai, which waxed and waned because of the Kaḷabhras and Cōḻas, transpired in three major phases: (*a*) Saṅgam Age to 250 CE, (*b*) First Empire (590–925 CE), and (*c*) Second Empire (1190–1311 CE).

14. During my 2017 visit, temple priests showed me the damage to what is believed to be the duplicate *liṅgam* that was installed to save the real *liṅgam* during Malik Kāfūr's fourteenth-century southern campaign on behalf of the Delhi sultanate.
15. Indira V. Peterson, "Singing of a Place: Pilgrimage as Metaphor and Motif in the Tēvāram Songs of the Tamil Śaivite Saints," *Journal of the American Oriental Society* 102, no. 1 (January–March 1982): 69–90.
16. Rama Mantena, "The Question of History in Precolonial India," *History and Theory* 46, no. 3 (October 2007): 396–408.
17. Jon Goss, "The Built Environment and Social Theory: Towards an Architectural Geography," *Professional Geographer* 40, no. 4 (November 1988): 392–403, 398. Michel de Certeau's writings on spatial practices help distinguish place from space. Place, according to de Certeau, refers to the locational instantiation of what is customary, proper, or even pre-established. Conversely, space is composed of the "intersections of mobile elements" that are ambiguous and at times in conflict. Space is produced when place is activated in practice, or as de Certeau writes, "space is practiced place." See Michel de Certeau, *The Practice of Everyday Life,* trans. Steven F. Rendall (Berkeley and Los Angeles: University of California Press, 1984), 117–118.
18. Yi-Fu Tuan, "Humanistic Geography," *Annals of the Association of American Geographers* 66, no. 2 (June 1976): 266–276; Yi-Fu Tuan, "Experiential Perspective," in *Space and Place: The Perspective of Experience* (Minneapolis: University of Minnesota, 2014 [1977]), 8–18.
19. J. Nicholas Entrikin, *The Betweenness of Place: Towards a Geography of Modernity* (Baltimore: Johns Hopkins University Press, 1991), 5.
20. Stephen Daniels, "Arguments for a Humanistic Geography," in *The Future of Geography*, ed. R. J. Johnston (London and New York: Methuen, 1985), 143–158, 146.
21. The book's use of transtemporal history draws loosely from historian David Armitage's model of historiography that stresses both enduring and shifting social, economic, and cultural realities over long spans of history. See David Armitage, "What's the Big Idea? Intellectual History and the Longue Durée," *History of European Ideas* 38, no. 4 (2012): 493–507. This approach has been likewise adopted by Jason Freitag, who examines nineteenth-century British political agent James Tod's production of a historical account of the Rājputs, a princely martial caste in Rajasthan, western India, and the reception and influence of Tod's European narrative from his own time through to the period of India's independence to the contemporary heritage construction for the tourism industry. See Jason Freitag, *Serving Empire, Serving Nation: James Tod and the Rajputs of Rajasthan* (Leiden and Boston: Brill, 2009).

22. Michael Mahon, *Foucault's Nietzschean Genealogy: Truth, Power, and the Subject* (Albany: State University of New York Press, 1992), 7–9.
23. Michel Foucault, "Nietzsche, Genealogy, History," in *Language, Counter-Memory, Practice: Selected Essays and Interviews*, ed. D. Bourchard (Ithaca: Cornell University Press, 1977), 139–164.
24. Similarly, Sanjay Subrahmanyam underscores the impossibility of a single narrative about "Europe's India" emerging between 1500–1800, highlighting the multiplicities, fragmentations, contradictions, and ambiguities within and across European constructions of India and Indian culture through texts and drawings produced by multiple actors. See Sanjay Subrahmanyam, *Europe's India: Words, People, Empires, 1500–1800* (Cambridge, MA: Harvard University Press, 2017).
25. Foucault, "Nietzsche, Genealogy, History," 161.
26. Foucault, "Nietzsche, Genealogy, History," 162.
27. In examining the correlation between geography and sovereignty in European empires between the fifteenth and nineteenth centuries, Lauren Benton investigates exceptional places under colonial power, arguing that such spaces, generally thought to be external to or beyond the law, were indeed sites closely linked with the imperial enterprise. See Lauren Benton, *A Search for Sovereignty: Law and Geography in European Empires, 1400–1900* (Cambridge: Cambridge University Press, 2010).

Part I

Stone Bodies

1

Constructing Kingship

Nāyaka Rule in Early Modern Madurai

Introduction

The Nāyaka warriors migrated to the Tamil region in the fourteenth century, where they ruled first as subordinate governors on behalf of the Vijayanagara empire, then as autonomous kingdoms after the empire's collapse. As their ties to Vijayanagara waned, the Nāyakas began to redefine kingship in early modern south India through literary and architectural traditions that challenged norms of sovereignty and the royal body. The consolidation of Nāyaka rule corresponded to a shift in discourses of kingship from narratives of valor, loyalty, and conquest to narratives of devotion and spirituality. This chapter presents a brief overview of Nāyaka history, drawing focus upon Nāyaka patronage of the Mīnākṣī-Sundareśvara temple and its Pudu Maṇḍapam, a major architectural project of Tirumala Nāyaka (r. 1623–1659 CE). Tamil chronicles, missionary reports, temple manuscripts, and epigraphical records illustrate how the Nāyaka rulers, and Tirumala Nāyaka in particular, became central to the history and identity of the Madurai temple. Tirumala's contributions to the temple were celebrated in prose poetry that lauded the king not as a soldier but as a great devotee: the corpulent statues that line the Pudu Maṇḍapam, in turn, reflect transformations in the aesthetics of sovereignty that accompanied transformations in political relations in south India.

Beginnings of Nāyaka rule in Madurai

The Nāyakas were warrior-peasants from Andhra territory who penetrated the Tamil country beginning in the fourteenth century. The word *nāyaka* referred to military officers in command of troops with prebendal rights over land. There are several speculated reasons for their southward migration: an opportunity to display their military prowess and expand their wealth; the promise of plentiful, thinly populated tracts of black soil for cultivation; or a desire to escape tax and conscription by the Bahmani and Golconda sultanates.[1] Among the early Nāyaka settlers were Telugu soldiers who settled in the Tamil country during general

Kumāra Kampaṇa's campaigns to extend the Vijayanagara empire in the late fourteenth century.[2] Another early settlement was populated by the 1,400 bowmen, soldiers, and retainers who accompanied Eṭṭappa Nāyaka when he left his natal home of Candragiri in 1423 to settle in Madurai.[3] During this period, merchants and artisans also journeyed from the north[4] and settled in the arid and black-soil land peripheral to fertile areas.[5] Telugu warriors, as *nāyaka*s ('leaders'), initially served as local governors or intermediary authorities between the Vijayanagara overlords and peasants, but later ascended to political prominence as the imperial center disintegrated in the sixteenth century. They established kingdoms in Senji, Tanjavur (Cōḻa capital), and Madurai (Pāṇḍya capital), while maintaining nominal subordination to the Vijayanagara emperors (Figure 1.1).

A handful of texts offer narratives on the origins of the Nāyaka kings in Madurai. An early eighteenth-century Telugu text, *Tañjāvūri Āndhra Rājula Caritra* ('Story of Tanjavur's Andhra rulers'), is a popular reference and a likely source for the Tamil chronicle translated by William Taylor in 1835.[6] These texts recount the heroic legend of Viśvanātha Nāyaka (r. 1529–1564 CE), son of Nāgama Nāyaka, an officer and revenue collector for the Vijayanagara empire.[7] In these stories, a childless Nāgama Nāyaka bathes in the Gaṅgā river for forty days, until Śiva visits him in a dream with a prophecy of Viśvanātha's birth. When Viśvanātha is a youth, a strong buffalo is caught for the annual Navarātri festival sacrifice in the Vijayanagara capital, but the emperor, Kṛṣṇadevarāya, is worried that the buffalo cannot be beheaded in a single blow, and he fears an omen of catastrophe if the sacrifice fails. Goddess Durgā visits Viśvanātha in a dream, and advises him to volunteer to perform the sacrifice using a special sword from the royal armory; when Viśvanātha succeeds, the emperor invites the young man into his service and promises him a kingdom of his own. One day, Vīracēkaraṉ, the Cōḻa king of Tanjavur, invades the Pāṇḍya country and usurps the throne from Cantiracēkaraṉ, the Pāṇḍyan king of Madurai. Although the Vijayanagara emperor reigned over the southern peninsula from the capital in Hampi, he left the Pāṇḍyas and Cōḻas to preside over these remote lands, the ancestral territories of the lesser kings.[8] At the Pāṇḍyan king's request for aid, the emperor dispatches Viśvanātha's father, Nāgama, to defeat the invading Cōḻas and make peace—however, rather than restore the kingdom to the Pāṇḍyan king, Nāgama declares himself ruler in Madurai and reorganizes the territory's administration under his own men in order to collect revenue and recover the costs of war.[9] When Kṛṣṇadevarāya assembles his courtiers to bring back Nāgama's head, Viśvanātha volunteers: he tells the emperor that his duty to his king supersedes his loyalty to his father. Viśvanātha travels to Madurai and delivers a proposal to his father:

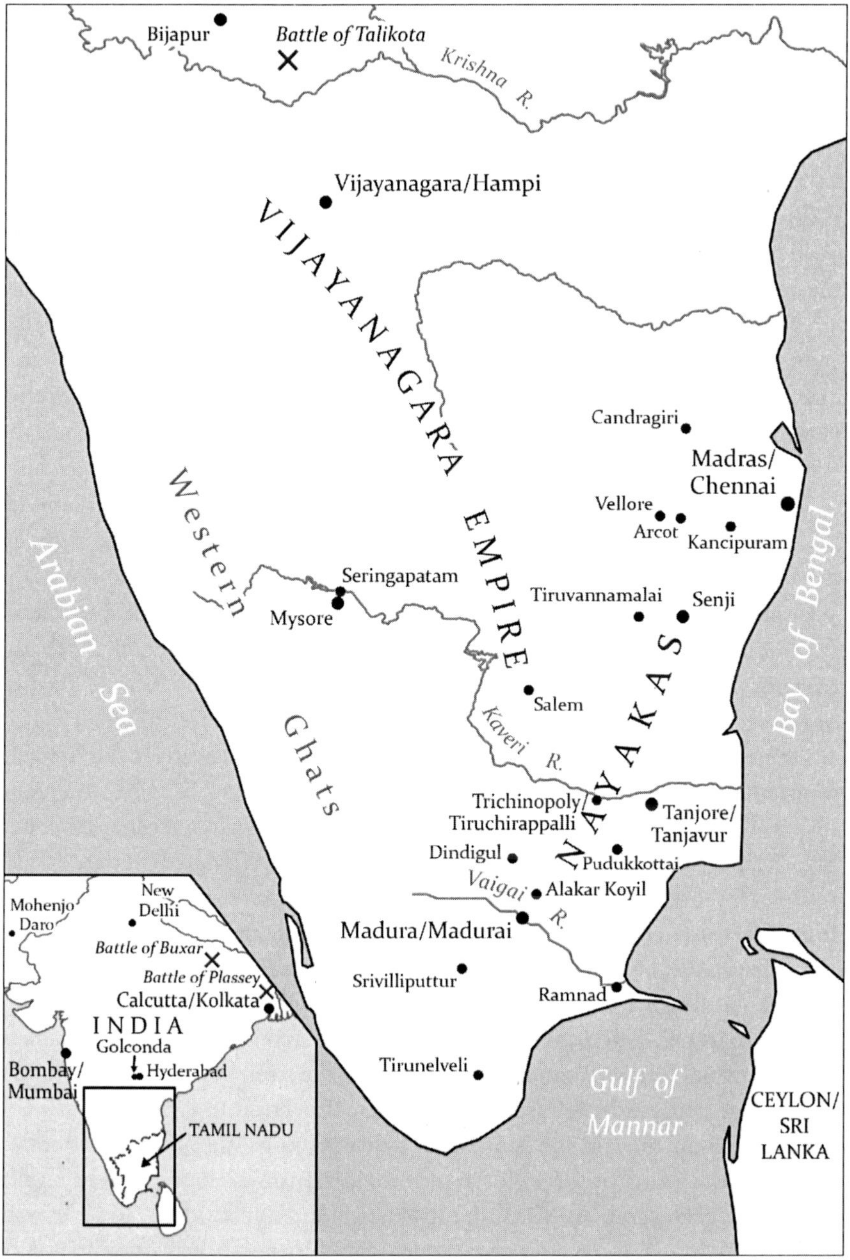

Figure 1.1 Map of south India

Source: Map prepared by John Kelly.

Note: Map not to scale and does not represent authentic international boundaries.

if Nāgama restores the kingdom to the rightful Pāṇḍyan king, Viśvanātha will ask the emperor to spare Nāgama's life. Nāgama refuses the offer and informs his son that he conquered Madurai for his son's benefit, so they could rule together; Viśvanātha ignores the overtures, subdues his father, and returns to Kṛṣṇadevarāya. The emperor is impressed with Viśvanātha's loyalty, and he spares Nāgama's life. The Pāṇḍyan king has no heir, and the Vijayanagara emperor makes good on his promise—he appoints Viśvanātha as Madurai's ruler, inaugurating the new Nāyaka dynasty in 1529.[10]

There are many accounts of Viśvanātha's ascendence to the throne that contradict the narrative in *Tañjāvūri Āndhra Rājula Caritra* and its derivatives:[11] one Telugu text claims that the Pāṇḍyan king adopted Viśvanātha as his son after Nāgama's defeat; another text asserts that Nāgama killed the Pāṇḍyan king and the throne was passed on to Viśvanātha. A Dutch East India Company document from 1677, referencing the alleged testimonies of some Madurai Brahmins, contends that there was no relation between Nāgama and Viśvanātha at all. According to the Dutch report, a wealthy merchant ruled Madurai and loaned money to the Vijayanagara court, and his son Nāgama was given the title of Nāyaka. Nāgama, so the story goes, fell out of favor with the imperial court, and upon his death, the emperor placed his loyal servant on the throne, Viśvanātha, who received the title of Nāyaka through marriage.

In spite of the discordances and contradictions in these narratives, they contain several distinct motifs, as detailed in Lennart Bes' historiography of Nāyaka origin stories.[12] Viśvanātha's lineage is never traced back more than one generation, and his legitimacy as ruler has little to do with his paternity. Viśvanātha's right to rule is tied to his loyalty and service to the Vijayanagara emperor, and his extraordinary feats of heroism and conquest. In addition to his military victories, these stories often emphasize Viśvanātha's physical prowess and aptitude for combat: a young Viśvanātha slaughters a strong buffalo whose horns "bended backwards and reached to its tail,"[13] and as ruler of Madurai, he overcomes a band of rebel chiefs, relatives of the former Pāṇḍyan king, by killing the strongest amongst them in a one-on-one struggle. In almost every case, there is an effort to establish continuity between Viśvanātha and the Pāṇḍyan line that preceded him: through adoption by the Pāṇḍyan king or through the ceremonial transmission of Pāṇḍyan regalia, the scepter of the goddess Mīnākṣi, the Pāṇḍyan queen considered to be Pārvatī. *Tañjāvūri Āndhra Rājula Caritra* reports that Nāgama Nāyaka was visited by Mīnākṣi in a dream with a prophecy of Viśvanātha's regal destiny; in other stories, Viśvanātha himself is directly descended from Mīnākṣi. The divine authorization of Viśvanātha's rule is self-evident: there is no need for Brahmins in this story, whether as ministers, advisors, or recipients of gifts.

The *Tañjāvūri Āndhra Rājula Caritra* portrays Viśvanātha as a strong and able king, who swiftly secures the territory under his newfound supervision.[14] The Nāyakas' formal relationship with the Vijayanagara center was that of partnership, or *pālu* (Telugu, 'share' or 'parcel'), in the 'world empire' (Skt, *pṛthivī rājyam*) of Vijayanagara, which involved *nāyaṅkara*, an agreement that entitled Nāyakas to collect revenue in their territory and keep a specified share; Nāyakas therefore took an active interest in clearing new lands, encouraging settlement, and cultivating new sources of revenue through the taxation of farms.[15] Accordingly, the chronicle of the Madurai Nāyakas narrates Viśvanātha's efforts to divert water sources for better irrigation, clear jungles, and found new villages that add to the region's population. He demolishes the old Pāṇḍyan rampart around the Mīnākṣi temple, builds a new double-walled fortress, and provides living quarters for Brahmins. Aided by Ariyanātha Mudaliyār, his *taḷavāy* ('military commander') and *piratāṉi* ('financial officer'), Viśvanātha departed from both Pāṇḍyan and Vijayanagara idioms of government by organizing the new Nāyaka state into seventy-two bastions called *pāḷaiyams*, each manned by an administrator, or *pāḷaiyakkārar*.[16] *Pāḷaiyakkārars*, a class of territorial military chiefs, collected taxes, ran the local judiciary, protected civilians from robbers, and maintained troops for the Nāyaka ruler, while paying him a fixed tribute. The chronicle of the Madurai Nāyakas describes Viśvanātha's victorious efforts to suppress revolts by local nobility disempowered by the new *pāḷaiyam* system. In this way, the origin narratives establish two clear 'axes' of Nāyaka legitimacy: 'vertical legitimacy,' the fiscal and symbolic relationship to the Vijayanagara center, and 'horizontal legitimacy,' the conquest and successful defense of territory against rivals.[17]

In the years after Viśvanātha's death in 1564, the Vijayanagara empire suffered precipitous declines. In 1565, the Vijayanagara capital of Hampi was destroyed in a humiliating defeat to the Deccan sultanates in the Battle of Talikota. As Viśvanātha's descendants successfully fended off *pāḷaiyakkārar* rebellions and captured territory stretching to the tip of the southern peninsula, the Madurai Nāyakas retained their loyalty to Vijayanagara's Aravīḍu line of kings, which succeeded the Tuḷuva line of Kṛṣṇadevarāya. Nevertheless, there was a clear shift in the dynamics between the Nāyaka rulers and the imperial center; the institution of *nāyaṅkara* declined, and fewer and fewer resources were transferred from the Nāyaka localities.[18] During a Vijayanagara succession struggle and civil war beginning in 1614, the Madurai Nāyakas were emboldened: Muttu Vīrappa Nāyaka (r. 1609–1623 CE) seized the opportunity to "discard the phantom of imperial sovereignty" and halted tribute payments to Vijayanagara.[19] The Tanjavur and Madurai Nāyakas were divided in their loyalties in the Vijayanagara civil war, and Muttu Vīrappa transferred his capital from Madurai to Tiruchirappalli, on a high, impregnable rock by the bountiful Kāvēri river, to wage war against Tanjavur.[20] This series of events set the stage for Tirumala Nāyaka to advance the cause of Madurai's independence from Vijayanagara.

The king as god's servant and devotee

Nearly sixty years after Viśvanātha's death, Tirumala Nāyaka ascended the throne: he began his rule in 1623.[21] Tirumala inherited a kingdom that stretched to the southern coast and extended northward into Konganadu.[22] He relocated the capital back to Madurai, perhaps because Madurai was in a more central location relative to the rest of the kingdom, and it was more distant from the encroachments of an invading Mysore king, buffered by the citadels in Tiruchirappalli and Dindigul. In the popular legend, Tirumala fell gravely ill in Tiruchirappalli, and while traveling to Madurai, he was visited by Mīnākṣi and Sundareśvara in a dream: he was told that if he moved the capital to Madurai and restored the temple there, he would be cured of his disease.[23] Madurai was the home of the Mīnākṣī-Sundareśvara temple, a pilgrimage site of great spiritual significance. Tirumala vowed to serve the deities: he promised a golden ornamental arch (*tiruvāṭci*) to place over processional images of the deities, a jeweled throne for the god, a temple pond for devotional festivals, a pillared hall, and various temple ornaments.[24] In William Taylor's 1835 chronicle "The Accounts of Tirumali-Naicker, and of His Buildings," the pillared hall is the Pudu Maṇḍapam, called by its other name, "Vasanta-Mandabam," referring to Vasantam ('spring'), the Tamil months of Cittirai (April/May)—when Mīnākṣi and Sundareśvara are married—and Vaikāci (May/June)—when metal embodiments of Mīnākṣi and Sundareśvara rest and receive guests inside the hall during ritual functions. Taylor's manuscript, based on undated Tamil texts, names Tirumala Nāyaka as the patron of the Pudu Maṇḍapam, but there are no stone or copperplate inscriptions substantiating this claim, nor any clear references to the hall's construction date.

A possible resource for identifying the hall's origins is *Maturaittala-Varalāṟu* ('History of the place of Madurai'), part of *Śrītāḷa*, the palm-leaf manuscripts at the Madurai temple and later published by the Madurai Tamil Saṅgam. This text provides some of the political history of the temple and traces the succession of monarchs. The entry for Tirumala states:[25]

> On the seventh day of Mārkaḻi in the year of Dundubi,[26]
> Muttutirumalanāyakkar, brother of Muttuvīrappanāyakkar,
> became a great devotee of Mīnākṣi and Sundareśvara by their grace.
> For the god, he

gifted many ornaments,
built the Pudu Maṇḍapam and Teppakkuḷam,
constructed a golden throne, an ivory chariot, a stone seat, and a throne inlaid with precious stones,
ordered construction projects in seven temples,
endowed lands yielding 44,000 *poṉ*s income for daily worship (*pūjā*),[27]
granted tax-free villages for the sustenance of temple employees,
created his own endowment and donated protected villages,
conducted temple festivals in a grand manner,
created a chariot for lord Aḻakar during the sacred day of Cittirai festival,[28] and made places very famous.
Whenever he came for *darśan*, he offered 1,000 *poṉ*s at god's feet for *abhiṣēkam* and *naivēdya*.[29]
When the god was taken in procession on Maci Street, he presented 1,000 *poṉ*s at god's feet.
In this way, he ruled for thirty-six years from the seventh day of Māci in the year of Dundubī until his death on Tuesday night, the fourth day of Māci in the year of Vīlambī.[30]

According to *Maturaittala-Varalāṟu*, Tirumala granted many large estates of crown lands to religious institutions. Epigraphical evidence documents these land grants during the Nāyaka's reign: a 1634 inscription shows that at Tirumala's request, Vijayanagara king Veṅkaṭa II granted the Kuniyur village to Brahmins; a 1635 inscription from Aladiyur, Tirunelveli area, and a 1637 inscription from Kapilamalai, Namakkal district, mention Tirumala's land gifts to local temples.[31] Agricultural output from these land grants provided the economic basis for an endowment, or *kaṭṭaḷai*. Revenues of entire villages were granted to temple personnel such as *bhaṭṭār*s ('priests') either for specific ritual purposes such as a *pūjā* ('worship') or *utsavam* ('festival') or for materials used in rituals.[32] The largest Madurai temple endowment, called Tirumala Nāyaka Kaṭṭaḷai, comprised twenty-one villages in Madakkulam Taluk (including Madurai) that generated a sizable revenue for the temple.[33]

Tirumala's flowing coffers supported many substantial endowments, funded by land tax, income from crown lands, and tribute from *pāḷaiyakkārar*s.[34] Since the time of the Pāṇḍyas, pearl fisheries along the oyster bed coast between Ramnad and Tirunelveli also gave profits for Madurai's rulers, who maintained long-standing associations with the maritime trading community along the Gulf of Mannar by offering special patronage to Christian and Muslim pearl fishermen and traders. According to Augustin Saulière, a missionary who translated Jesuit Baltasar da Costa's 1646 account of the Madurai kingdom, Tirumala had an annual income of millions of *patacas* (the currency used in Portuguese territories).[35] Tirumala conferred upon a prominent pearl trader (Mudaliyār Piḷḷai Maraikkāyar) "kingly" honors and gave him authority over the local pearling population.[36] Nāyaka iconography reveals a penchant for pearls;[37] pearls can be seen in crowns and ornaments for royalty and for the gods—such as the pearl turban (*muttu talaippākai*) for Sundareśvara and the pearl crown (*ambāḷ tirumuṭiccāttu*) and pearl dress (*muttu kavacam*) for Mīnākṣi—and on temple canopies.[38] *Maturaittala-Varalāṟu* describes Tirumala's gifts of ornaments to the temple deities possibly embellished with pearls.

Another Tamil temple manuscript, *Tiruvālavāyuṭaiyārkōyil Tiruppaṇimālai* ('Garland of sacred works at the Madurai temple') details Tirumala's specific contributions to the Mīnākṣi-Sundareśvara temple, as part of a record of all the kings, nobles, and merchants who donated to the temple. The document is attributed to Tāṇṭavamūrttīppaṇṭāram, but Madurai temple historian A. V. Jeyechandrun suggests that the style and vocabulary of the 106 verses cannot be credited to a single poet.[39] These verses, a form of prose poetry, are sung when processional deities stop in festival *maṇḍapams.*[40] *Tiruvālavāyuṭaiyārkōyil Tiruppaṇimālai* was a new genre during the Nāyaka period, in which the patron's devoted service to the temple's god is lauded in verses celebrating the financing of temple construction, additions, renovations, or repairs.[41] *Tiruvālavāyuṭaiyārkōyil Tiruppaṇimālai* praises Tirumala Nāyaka as the temple's main financier, and the text devotes more passages to him than to any other patron of the Madurai temple. Verses 80 to 86 of *Tiruvālavāyuṭaiyārkōyil Tiruppaṇimālai* specify Tirumala Nāyaka's "sacred works":

> 80. King Tirumalai,[42] the garlanded, bejeweled, and most eminent king, and son of the benevolent king Muttukṛṣṇappa whom other kings respected, built the everlasting Pudu Maṇḍapam like the renowned Mount Mēru who took many forms and came before god after doing penance, and featuring one hundred and twenty-four pillars, sculpted images, and two smaller *maṇḍapams* that flank the great *maṇḍapam* as garlands, so Mīnākṣi with *kuravam* flowers in her dark hair and Sundareśvara with *koṉṟai* blossoms can rest together during the good Vasantam festival he initiated.
>
> 81. King Tirumalai, son of the pleasant and victorious Muttukṛṣṇappa with mighty mountain-like shoulders, constructed a new temple pond (*teppakkuḷam*) as splendorous as the ocean for the fame of Madurai's ruler, featuring an excellent *maṇḍapam* at its center that resembles golden Mēru and earth's nine continents in the middle of indescribable seven seas because the ocean shattered into pieces, burned, dropped its level, dried up, and became flat, causing it to suffer and lose its significance when Rāma shot arrows at the sea god's fish-filled waters, sage Agastya swallowed the

sea in one handful, the anklet-wearing Pāṇḍyan king (*māṟaṉ*) halted the sea god's downpour, Viṣṇu took the fish *avatāram*, and Subrahmaṇya threw his spear (*vēl*).[43]

82. King Tirumalai should receive all merit for performing several hundred *crores* of good deeds to repair Mīnākṣi's temple properly so it survives through time. For the goddess, he generously gave money to have broken stone pillars and beams replaced, decayed mortar removed, and strong, indestructible mortar of mixed lime, jaggery juice, and twice-ground paste of gallnut, gooseberry, *tāṉṟikkai*,[44] and black gram soaked in good water applied on laid-down bricks.

83. King Tirumalai of Kacci granted land for cultivating dry crops and gained fame for ensuring that the daily distribution of food from the temple kitchen would occur on earth for temple employees and those who came to the choultry to be fed while in the presence of the goddess with sharp, spear-like eyes.

84. King Tirumalai of ever-increasing fame and the son of Muttukṛṣṇappa on whom Lakṣmī resides, gold-plated the flagpole and sacrificial altar (*balipīḍam*) in front of the shrine to Sundareśvara, our lord of Madurai.

85. King Tirumalai, given by god's grace, ruler of Madurai, and seeker of pleasures, also renewed with gold the excellent flagpole and sacrificial altar of the goddess with a beautiful forehead, so she will be praised well.

86. King Tirumalai, adorned with gold ornaments and garlanded shoulders, made copper guardian deities (*dvārapālas*) that received god's sweet grace for Sundareśvara with matted *jaṭā* locks on his six-legged throne and the resplendently beautiful Mīnākṣi on her six-legged throne.[45]

These verses celebrate Tirumala's construction of the Pudu Maṇḍapam with two water-filled trenches for cooling deities during the Vasantam festival; the Māriyammaṉ Teppakkuḷam, the artificial pond for the Teppam ('float') festival for Mīnākṣi and Sundareśvara; the replacement and renovation of dilapidated elements of the goddess's shrine; the gilded and beautified structures in and around the shrines; and, importantly, the endowment of agricultural lands to sustain temple workers and their families. Both *Maturaittala-Varalāṟu* and *Tiruvālavāyuṭaiyārkōyil Tiruppaṇimālai* record Nāyaka benefactions to the Madurai temple through a network of individual patrons, documenting the contributions of each donor to the temple. They speak of transactions with the Madurai temple as either pious donations (such as endowment of lamps, creation of flower gardens for *pūjā*s, and gifting ornaments for the idols), land tenurial arrangements that subsidized the temple (such as transfer of tax revenue from an assigned parcel of land), or building construction and renovation.

While the laudatory temple manuscripts appear documentary in nature, their remaking of ideal narratives involves an imaginative refashioning of Nāyaka identity in Madurai. There is a striking absence of any remark about Nāyaka temple donations in the *Maturaittala-Varalāṟu* before Tirumala's rule. We find parallels in *Tiruvālavāyuṭaiyārkōyil Tiruppaṇimālai*, where Tirumala's ancestors are characterized in fantastic, heroic terms. For example, verse 49 describes Viśvanātha as "famous and victorious with a cloud-like generosity, the great one who restored the country to the Pāṇḍyan and took tribute when he came and fought,"[46] referring to the legend of Viśvanātha removing his father from the Pāṇḍyan throne. Later verses identify Viśvanātha's son Kṛṣṇappa Nāyaka as one who "fights in wars," "is adept in using bows to conquer in wars," and "kicks the golden crowns of enemy kings who tremble before him."[47] Such heroic panegyrics are virtually absent in the verses dedicated to Tirumala Nāyaka. The *Maturaittala-Varalāṟu* and *Tiruvālavāyuṭaiyārkōyil Tiruppaṇimālai* shower effusive praise on a munificent king: the texts render the ruler not as a valiant war hero, but as god's most devout servant and devotee.

Although the temple manuscripts make little reference to Tirumala Nāyaka's martial attributes, the king spent much of his reign engaged in war.[48] Tirumala inherited a wealthy kingdom saddled by constant conflict at its borders: he successfully fended off invasions from Mysore in the north, he invaded a defiant Travancore to the southwest, and he allied with the Portuguese to quash a revolt by a neighboring Sētupati vassal in Ramnad, backed by the Dutch, in the southeast. A weak Vijayanagara had failed in its commitments to protect Madurai from northern invasion, and Tirumala refused to pay tribute, much like his predecessor Muttu Vīrappa Nāyaka.[49] Veṅkaṭa III, the Aravīḍu king of Vijayanagara, accepted this state of affairs until his death in 1642, but his successor Śrīraṅga III demanded payment of debts, and he marched southward to provoke a confrontation. Tirumala proposed an alliance with the Nāyakas in Tanjavur and Senji, but he was betrayed when the Tanjavur ruler revealed the plot to the Vijayanagara king. Tirumala then turned to the Golconda sultan for aid—with Tirumala's encouragement, the sultan attacked Vellore, a Vijayanagara stronghold, to divert the emperor and halt his progress. The maneuver was successful, and the Vijayanagara army was defeated at Vellore—but the Golconda sultan was emboldened, and with the aid of the Bijapur sultan, he marched on Senji and captured the Nāyaka territory in 1649. The Muslim armies subsequently advanced on Tanjavur and Madurai, but were routed by Tirumala's army with the support of Kaḷḷar soldiers. The Vijayanagara king made a final effort to reinstate his kingdom by forming a partnership with Mysore, but Tirumala incurred a massive debt to buy the protection of the Bijapur sultan, and the plot was extinguished. The Vijayanagara empire was finished, and the Madurai Nāyakas' independence preserved—at great cost.

Tirumala's strenuous efforts to support temple endowments, both inside and outside Madurai, must be interpreted in terms of the inherent fragility of his rule in a time of political volatility and threats to Nāyaka sovereignty. From the earliest days of his reign, Tirumala was concerned with the interconnected problems of northern invasion and independence from a weakened Vijayanagara court. Indeed, before his coronation, the deities instructed the crown prince to move the capital from Tiruchirappalli, a fortress at greater risk of northern penetration, and restore the Madurai temple, to cure his illness and restore himself to strength. The relationship between his illness, his devotion, and the security of his kingdom could not have been lost on Tirumala and his advisors. As Caleb Simmons observes in his study of nineteenth-century Mysore kings, religious devotion "provided a unique idiom in the face of change that could work to bridge previous forms of sovereignty into new realities," especially in periods of uncertainty and unrest.[50] Land endowments simultaneously generated sources of agricultural revenue and cultivated local allegiances,[51] while the temples they supported provided ritual contexts for performing novel, public imaginations of kingship. The collective memory of Tirumala's rule was shaped by his patronage and the rituals celebrating these achievements. The gifts of temple construction, maintenance, and preservation, and the cyclical performance of those gifts at mass religious festivals attended by pilgrims from far and wide, articulated a form of kingly valor in the Nāyaka state that conquest narratives and martial attributes could not.

Nāyaka aesthetics of sovereignty

The Mīnākṣi-Sundareśvara temple boasts twelve *gōpurams* ('tall pyramidal gateways'), some as high as 52 meters, and a golden-sculptured *vimāṉam* ('tower') over each sanctum to the two main deities. It has four main entrances facing the four cardinal directions, an uncommon configuration for many Tamil temples. The temple complex is divided into many concentric quadrangular enclosures that comprise several shrines (including those for Mīnākṣi and Sundareśvara), a temple tank, numerous *prākārams* ('large enclosure corridors'), and several columned halls or *maṇḍapams* (Figure 1.2). The Madurai temple was built during Pāṇḍyan rule, but most major improvements and renovations occurred in the Nāyaka era, spanning the reigns of Viśvanātha and Tirumala. Chief additions during this period include the south and north outer monumental *gōpurams*, several inner *gōpurams* near Sundareśvara and Mīnākṣi's shrines, temple outer walls, steps for Poṟṟāmaraikkuḷam ('golden lotus tank'), Māriyammaṉ Teppakkuḷam (a huge

Figure 1.2 View of the Mīnākṣī-Sundareśvara temple, Madurai, from the south *gōpuram*

Source: American Institute of Indian Studies.

artificial pond located away from the temple), several *prākārams*, and many *maṇḍapams* including the Āyirakkāl Maṇḍapam ('thousand pillar hall') and the Pudu Maṇḍapam.[52]

The Pudu Maṇḍapam was built in a phase of major expansion during Tirumala's rule. Temple manuscripts do not provide concrete dates of the hall's completion; architectural historian George Michell infers from the documented dates of Tirumala's rule that the Pudu Maṇḍapam was finished in the year 1635.[53] Tirumala relocated priests' homes to near the north *gōpuram* (where they still stand), to align the Pudu Maṇḍapam axially with the eastern *gōpuram* between East Cittirai and East Avani Mula Streets.[54] Tirumala's unfinished Rāya ('king') Gōpuram near the Pudu Maṇḍapam's eastern entrance, if completed, would have expanded the temple complex much farther. According to legend, Tirumala took an active interest in the Pudu Maṇḍapam's construction. Once, when he visited to check the hall's progress, he rolled some betel leaves for Cumantira Mūrti Ācārya, the chief sculptor and principal architect, who was deeply engrossed in his work. The *sthapati* did not realize that the king had prepared the betel, and he hurriedly ate it without waiting for the king, a sign of disrespect. When the architect realized what he had done, he cut off the two fingers with which he had placed the betel in his mouth; moved by this action, Tirumala rewarded the sculptor with a gift of cloth and gold.[55]

The *maṇḍapam* is a stone pillared hall in a Tamil temple complex. One type of *maṇḍapam* is an attached hall: either an *ardhamaṇḍapam* ('half-*maṇḍapam*') that directly connects to the main shrine, or a *mahāmaṇḍapam* ('large *maṇḍapam*') that sits beyond the *ardhamaṇḍapam*. The other type of *maṇḍapam* is a detached structure used to celebrate and perform festival (*utsavam*) rituals.[56] While the development of the separate festival *maṇḍapam* dates to the twelfth century, it was not until the early sixteenth century that it became a central component of later Tamil Drāviḍa (south Indian) temple-building tradition.[57] The purpose of festival *maṇḍapams*, reflected in the Pudu Maṇḍapam's design, is to house the deity's movable metal image during Hindu festivals after it leaves the main shrine to travel outside the temple to receive worshippers in the hall near the east gateway. The Pudu Maṇḍapam's pronounced axial interior emphasizes a single line of approach leading to the central nave, whose western end has the black granite throne platform used to conduct rituals to the sacred image. There is also a concentric processional aisle for the deity's circumambulation, and lower trenches for water once used to cool the god during the hot summer months.

The Pudu Maṇḍapam is one of the largest festival *maṇḍapams* on the Indian subcontinent. The precise dimensions of the hall vary depending on who performed the measurement and when the measurement was taken. The Pudu Maṇḍapam measures 340 feet long by 127 feet wide according to nineteenth-century Archaeological Survey of India superintendent Henry Hardy Cole; 330 feet long by 105 feet wide according to historian D. Devakunjari; or 328 feet long by 82 feet wide according to art historian Crispin Branfoot.[58] The decreasing length and width is explained in part by the many shops and stalls that had encroached into the Pudu Maṇḍapam's processional space over the years.[59]

One hundred and twenty-four granite piers rich with sculptural detail support the hall's flat roof. Figural columns are concentrated at the east and west entrances of the *maṇḍapam*, along the processional aisle, and in the central nave. These large, nearly 2-meter tall sculptures that project from the monolithic columns are carved in the round and mounted high so they are on level with the gods' processional festival images when carried on bearers' shoulders. The Pudu Maṇḍapam showcases sculptures of deities and mythological figures that appear in the local Tamil myths of the Madurai temple: Parañcōti Muṉivar's seventeenth-century *Tiruviḷaiyāṭal Purāṇam*, or 'Story of Śiva's sacred games,' in Madurai.[60]

Figure 1.3 Central nave, Pudu Maṇḍapam, seventeenth century, Mīnākṣī-Sundareśvara temple, Madurai

Source: Photo by author.

The Pudu Maṇḍapam's most distinctive feature is the sculpted dynastic history of the Madurai Nāyakas, located in the central nave (Figure 1.3). The massive granite pillars of the huge rectangular hall include portraits of the Nāyaka lineage with joined palms in a gesture of reverence, facing the center aisle, and arranged in chronological order—Tirumala Nāyaka, the sponsor of the project, stands at the end.[61] They are situated at an elevated height: when strong temple personnel walk through the corridor holding the processional icons of the gods aloft, the deities are on the same level as the royal statues. This style of sculptural composition on piers, the ability to liberate the stone carvings from their supports, and the development of full-bodied, formal portraiture into a temple art form are Nāyaka-period innovations.[62] The ten stone portrayals that construct the Nāyaka family genealogy show the kings accompanied by diminutive consorts on the sides (Figure 1.4). Although all figures stand with splayed bare feet, pressed palms, and a rigid formality lacking suggestion of age or mood, the kings are adorned with various forms of headwear (conical or cloth-wraps), textile fabrics (plain or patterned), decorative ornaments, and body bulk (Figures 1.5 and 1.6). Tirumala is the most elaborately sculptured: unlike his bare-chested ancestors, he is clothed in a dense paisley-patterned garment, with several rows of beads or pearls, and

Figure 1.4 Madurai Nāyaka portraits, south side, Pudu Maṇḍapam

Source: Photo by author.

a knotted red cloth that holds his gathered hair to one side in a chignon (the standard headdress of later Nāyaka monarchy) (Figure 1.7).[63] Colorful coats of paint give Tirumala special prominence within the hall. Directly opposite him is a figure believed to be Viśvanātha, the first Madurai Nāyaka king, who wears a less ostentatious, diaphanous, and thinly patterned loincloth (Figure 1.8).[64]

The Nāyaka kings are reproduced with paunches, a major departure from the stereotypical images of perfect *kṣatriya* kings. Where earlier depictions of south Indian monarchs—such as the Vijayanagara likeness of Kṛṣṇadevarāya in low relief on the Naṭarāja temple's north *gōpuram* in Cidambaram and as a free-standing metal statue within the Tirumala Veṅkaṭeśvara temple's Pratimā Maṇḍapam in Tirupati (Figures 1.9 and 1.10)—exhibited 'ideal' and streamlined bodies, paradigms of divinely perfection with wide, elephant trunk-like shoulders and tapered, lion-like waistlines, Nāyaka rulers received full-sized, portly presentations. While Nāyaka men typically had ample proportions with swelling stomachs and

Figure 1.5 Nāyaka ruler, Pudu Maṇḍapam

Source: Photo by author.

heavy hips, Tirumala is portrayed as extraordinarily plump (Figure 1.7). One of his necklaces hangs to his protruding abdomen, drawing the viewer's eye to his large belly that bulges out of the lower waistband. His clasped hands and arms form a triangle whose sides frame his broad girth.

The sculptural emphasis on Tirumala's well-fed stomach suggests the importance of food to Nāyaka political philosophy, in which political authority was signified primarily by gift-giving and expenditure of wealth, rather than traditional norms of *varṇa* or caste. Madurai rulers were of likely Balija heritage, merchant-warriors proud of their *śūdra* status, who came from the relatively less-stratified arid zones of the Andhra region, where wealth and influence were wielded by families who built up factions of clients in positions as village headmen and accountants.[65] The practice of giving gifts—of food, of titles and emblems, of privileges to use land, of special rights to rule—played a principal role in defining the sovereignty of south Indian kings, especially in the "shared" sovereignty of Vijayanagara and the Nāyakas.[66] Nicholas Dirks considers the *pūjā*, the ritual of

Figure 1.6 Nāyaka ruler, Pudu Maṇḍapam

Source: Photo by author.

worship, as the "root metaphor" and "cultural mechanism" for all political relations in the Nāyaka kingdom, in which the taking and eating of food given by the deity (*prasādam*) signifies a privileged relationship with the god. The gift (a second meaning of *prasādam*) can trump even kinship ties—indeed, in *Tañjāvūri Āndhra Rājula Caritra,* when the Vijayanagara king asks why Viśvanātha has volunteered to subdue his own father, he replies that he has "eaten the king's food."[67]

Wealth had two primary functions in Nāyaka political life, both symbolically connected to food: gift-giving and enjoyment (Skt, *bhoga*). This sentiment is captured by a popular Telugu verse: "Giving gifts [*dānamu*], enjoyment [*bhōgamu*], loss [*nāśamu*]: there are only these three paths for money on this earth. The ignorant fool who does not take the first two paths will see his money take the third."[68] The semantic scope of *bhoga* underwent numerous transformations in Indian courts from the early centuries CE, as the concept came to encompass enjoyment of sensual pleasures, enjoyment of one's possessions, 'enjoyment' of a sovereign domain, and eventually a vast range of privileges and entitlements

Figure 1.7 Tirumala Nāyaka and his consorts, Pudu Maṇḍapam

Source: Photo by author.

in the arts of government.[69] The theme of *bhoga* was prominent in the Telugu genre of *abhyudayamu* poetry, popular in the Nāyaka Tanjavur court, which relayed the Nāyaka kings' highly ritualized and strictly patterned daily routines, dominated by sensual scenes of bathing, dressing, eating, and lovemaking.[70] Such displays are also visible on *kalamkāri* textiles and ivory panels attributed to Nāyaka-period Madurai.[71] Even the Tamil temple document discussed earlier describes Tirumala as a "seeker of pleasures" (*pōkam*).[72] The Nāyaka kings seemed especially concerned with the public performance of such experiences—a significant part of Tirumala's daily routine was to *show himself* to the public, by way of massive royal processions, accompanied by courtiers, nobles, and soldiers.[73] The temple, where a manuscript reports Tirumala's daily distribution of food, was an important space for such performances.[74]

The humanizing and individualized representation of corpulent Nāyaka kings in the Pudu Maṇḍapam bears a marked contrast with bronze statues of earlier

Figure 1.8 Viśvanātha, founder of the Madurai Nāyakas, Pudu Maṇḍapam

Source: Photo by author.

Figure 1.9 Vijayanagara king Kṛṣṇadevarāya, sixteenth century, north *gōpuram*, Naṭarāja temple, Cidambaram

Source: Photo by author.

Figure 1.10 Vijayanagara king Kṛṣṇadevarāya and his consorts, copper, sixteenth century, Pratimā Maṇḍapam, Veṅkaṭeśvara temple, Tirumala hill, Andhra Pradesh

Source: Private collection.

Vijayanagara kings. As Vidya Dehejia wrote of Kṛṣṇadevarāya and his two queens depicted in Tirupati, the Vijayanagara trio appear as "generic idealized aristocratic images that could equally well be portraits of any royal or aristocratic group."[75] By contrast, Henry Heras, a Spanish Jesuit priest and historian living in India, proclaimed the sculptures in Tirumala Nāyaka's pillared hall as "true" and "not idealized" portrayals.[76] Every Nāyaka portrait in the Pudu Maṇḍapam is unique with physiognomic and sartorial specificity: each statue is not only labeled with the ruler's name, but also contains distinguishing, readily identifiable idiosyncrasies (in terms of anatomy, facial detail, headgear, attire, and ornament), rendering each king discernible as a particular king, rather than an abstract 'ruler.' The distinctive Nāyaka form—large-scale, three-dimensional figures sculpted from monolithic columns lining corridors and filling *maṇḍapams*—departs from prior ones carved in low relief in shallow architectural niches or smaller-than-life-size bronze images installed in halls. Branfoot observes an inherent dynamism in Nāyaka figural columns not present in previous Tamil temples: the individual images of deities and rulers emerge from the column as "expanding form," they "spread forwards and sideways, becoming larger and more active until they are visually dominant, hardly appearing to be attached to the column at all."[77]

The royal genealogical portraiture in Madurai traces the changing relationship between the Nāyaka governors and the waning Vijayanagara empire. In 1565, the Vijayanagara emperor suffered a devastating defeat to the Deccan sultanates in Talikota, and the sacking of the royal capital in Hampi set into motion the gradual disintegration of Vijayanagara power. As indicated by the Madurai Nāyaka origin narratives, the Nāyaka kings were linked inextricably to the Vijayanagara court, and Viśvanātha's loyalty to Kṛṣṇadevarāya—now, a weakened reigning center produced a basic contradiction in the ideological form of Nāyaka sovereignty. The Pudu Maṇḍapam genealogy illustrates this shift: on the south side of the central nave, four of the first five carvings exhibit early Nāyaka rulers wearing tall conical cloth hats, or *kuḷḷāyi*, common in the Vijayanagara court,[78] signaling their allegiance to the Vijayanagara regime. On the north side, four of the last five carvings exhibit later Nāyaka rulers sporting tight-fitting cloth caps, the customary Nāyaka court headdress, reflecting their political (and vestiary) distance from the declining authority of the final Aravīḍu dynasty of Vijayanagara kings.

Imperial inscriptions chart the transition from subservience to autonomy in Nāyaka statecraft: a 1535 village grant introduces Viśvanātha Nāyaka as the Vijayanagara king's officer, a 1634 grant states that Tirumala Nāyaka requested the Vijayanagara king to bestow land and provides both dynastic genealogies, and a 1653 land grant records Tirumala Nāyaka's tour of his kingdom with no Vijayanagara allusion.[79] As Phillip Wagoner observes of this period of transition in Nāyaka history:

> Nayaka power was real, but ideologically dependent, while Vijayanagara's power, even though remaining ideologically absolute, had all but vanished in any real sense. With the legitimacy of their legitimizing overlord now itself in question, Madurai's rulers were confronted with a serious dilemma that could be resolved only by means of a thorough transformation of the ideological system on which all political relations were based.... Eventually, the dilemma would be resolved by a simple but drastic solution: with the final collapse of Vijayanagara authority, the rulers of Madura would themselves rise to assume the role of great kings, no longer "looking upward" for legitimation of their power, but now beginning to constitute their authority by "looking downward" to their own subordinates, the chiefly Palaiyakkars, who would themselves be elevated to the status of little kings.[80]

This "looking downward," the political ascension of the Nāyaka kings, is architecturally represented in the elevated position of the Nāyaka statues in the

Figure 1.11 Mīnākṣī's metal image travels in front of Tirumala Nāyaka's stone image, Pudu Maṇḍapam, 2009

Source: Photo by author.

Pudu Maṇḍapam. In other temples, Tirumala's stone images—attached to the granite column, life-size with erect frontality, stout physique with distended stomach, waistband with dangling dagger, head with a lopsided cloth covering, and hands joined in devotion—are on a low plinth closer to ground level, as seen near the inner sanctum at the Subrahmaṇyam Cave temple in Tirupparankunram and in the Tirumala Nāyaka Maṇḍapam at the Kaḷḷaḻakar temple in Alakar Koyil.[81] In the region surrounding Madurai and beyond, such as in Srivilliputtur and Srirangam, such portraits can serve as visual records of the Nāyaka ruler's patronage when donative inscriptional evidence engraved on temple walls and copperplates is absent.[82] The royal devotional statuary in the Pudu Maṇḍapam, however, appear on raised platforms, so that their feet rest at the level of worshippers' heads, standing eye-to-eye with the *utsava mūrtis*, the movable metal processional forms of the gods that travel through the hall during religious festivals (Figure 1.11).[83] By elevating the corpulent, relatively 'authentic' and recognizable dynastic portraits to the same level as the deities at the Mīnākṣi-Sundareśvara temple, the Nāyaka kings transcended their former subordination, and articulated a relationship of parity with the gods themselves.

Notes

1. Burton Stein, *Vijayanagara*, The New Cambridge History of India I.2 (Cambridge: Cambridge University Press, 1989), 46.
2. Cynthia Talbot, *Precolonial India in Practice: Society, Region, and Identity in Medieval Andhra* (Oxford and New York: Oxford University Press, 2001), 197.
3. David Ludden, *Peasant History in South India* (Princeton: Princeton University Press, 1985), 51.
4. Ludden, *Peasant History in South India*, 51.
5. Burton Stein, *Peasant State and Society in Medieval South India* (Delhi: Oxford University Press, 1980), 394–396.
6. Vēṭūri Prabhākaraśāstri, ed., *Tañjāvūri Āndhrarājula Caritra* (Telugu) (Haidarābādu: Maṇimañjari Pracuraṇa, Vēṭūri Prabhākaraśāstri Memōriyal Ṭrasṭ, 1984). See William Taylor, "History of the Carnataca Governors Who Ruled over the Pandiya Mandalam," in *Oriental Historical Manuscripts, in the Tamil Language*, vol. II, ed. and trans. William Taylor (Madras: Printed and Published by Charles Josiah Taylor, 1835), 3–49, and R. Sathyanatha Aiyar, *History of the Nayakas of Madura*, introduction by S. Krishnaswami Aiyangar (Madras: Oxford University Press, 1924), 34–35.
7. Taylor, "History of the Carnataca Governors Who Ruled over the Pandiya Mandalam," 3–15; V. Rangachari, "The History of the Naik Kingdom of Madura," *The Indian Antiquary, A Journal of Oriental Research* 43 (September 1914): 187–192, 191–192; V. Rangachari, "The History of the Naik Kingdom of Madura," *The Indian Antiquary, A Journal of Oriental Research* 43 (December 1914): 253–262, 253–257.
8. Pāṇḍyas, Cōḻas, and Cēras were three royal lineages of south India known as the Mūvēntar, or 'Three Crowned Kings.'
9. Epigraphical data of Nāgama Nāyaka is meager. One 1483 inscription written in Tamil located in Tirukachur (Chingleput), and under Narasiṅgarāya's rule, states a private individual founded a village for the merit of the king and Nāgama Nāyaka, the foremost of his servants. It also mentions taxing the village's *kaikkōḷars* and other weavers as well as several professional classes. See *Annual Report on Epigraphy 1909–1910* (Madras: Government of Madras Public Department, G.O. No. 665, July 28, 1910), 27: 318 of 1909. Another example is a 1482 inscription from Tittakkudi (Vriddhacalam, South Arcot), which states that Nāgama's agent settled a dispute between two factions. See *Annual Report on Epigraphy 1902–1903* (Madras: Government of Madras Public Department, G.O., etc., Nos. 655–656, July 24, 1903), 20: 6 of 1903.
10. It is possible that Cantiracēkaraṉ did not die but was merely incompetent or had died but was not the last of his dynasty, that Kṛṣṇadevarāya was not the presiding monarch in Hampi when Viśvanātha was sent to Madurai, and 1529

was not the inaugural year of the Nāyaka dynasty. See Rangachari, "The History of the Naik Kingdom of Madura" (December 1914): 255, 257–260. This book follows Aiyar who assigns a 1529 date. See Aiyar, *History of the Nayaks of Madura*, 39–48.

11. Lennart Bes, *The Heirs of Vijayanagara: Court Politics in Early Modern South India* (Leiden: Leiden University Press, 2022), 78–79.
12. Bes, *The Heirs of Vijayanagara*, 75–81.
13. Taylor, "History of the Carnataca Governors Who Ruled over the Pandiya Mandalam," 5.
14. Taylor, "History of the Carnataca Governors Who Ruled over the Pandiya Mandalam," 15–23.
15. Christopher Chekuri, "A 'Share' in the 'World Empire': Nayamkara as Sovereignty in Practice at Vijayanagara, 1480–1580," *Social Scientist* 40, no. 1/2 (January–February 2012): 41–67.
16. V. Rangachari, "The History of the Naik Kingdom of Madura," *The Indian Antiquary, A Journal of Oriental Research* 44 (April 1915): 69–73, 69–70, 71–73; Aiyar, *History of the Nayaks of Madura*, 58–62. Other spellings include *poligar*, *polygar*, and *palegar*. The *pāḷaiyam* system of shared sovereignty may have originated with Pratāparudra, the Kākatīya ruler in the Andhra area from 1289 to 1323 CE, who similarly divided his kingdom into a political network of seventy-plus subordinates. See Talbot, *Precolonial India in Practice*, 201–202.
17. Velcheru Narayana Rao, David Shulman, and Sanjay Subrahmanyam, *Symbols of Substance: Court and State in Nāyaka Period Tamilnadu* (Delhi and Oxford: Oxford University Press, 1998), 258–259.
18. Chekuri, "A 'Share' in the 'World Empire'," 61.
19. Aiyar, *History of the Nayaks of Madura*, 108.
20. Aiyar, *History of the Nayaks of Madura*, 103.
21. Horace Hayman Wilson, "Historical Sketch of the Kingdom of Pándya, Southern Peninsula of India," *Journal of the Royal Asiatic Society of Great Britain and Ireland* 3, no. 2 (1836): 199–242, 230. Wilson describes Tirumala's reign as "a period of chronological certainty" in his historical account of the Nāyakas. Temple documents, not epigraphical evidence or Jesuit accounts, support a February 19, 1623, accession date. See Aiyar, *History of the Nayaks of Madura*, 110–113.
22. M. Arokiaswami, *The Kongu Country: Being the History of the Modern Districts of Coimbatore and Salem from the Earliest Times to the Coming of the British* (Madras: University of Madras, 1956), 336–338.
23. William Taylor, "The Accounts of Tirumali-Naicker, and of His Buildings (As Extracted, for Information, from Written Authorities)," in *Oriental Historical Manuscripts, in the Tamil Language*, vol. II, ed. and trans. William Taylor

(Madras: Printed and Published by Charles Josiah Taylor, 1835), 147–155, 147–149. Taylor extracted from *Mṛtyunjaya MSS* of the Mackenzie Collection. See William Taylor, "Carnataca Dynasty, sec. 9," in *Oriental Historical Manuscripts, in the Tamil Language*, vol. II, ed. and trans. William Taylor (Madras: Printed and Published by Charles Josiah Taylor, 1835), 146.

24. Taylor, "The Accounts of Tirumali-Naicker, and of His Buildings," 149.
25. *Maturaittala-Varalāṟu*, in *Tiruvālavāyuṭaiyārkōyil Tiruppaṇimālai* (Tamiḻ), Centamiḻp Piracuram-27, ed. Po. Pāṇṭitturaittēvar (Maturai: Maturait Tamiḻccaṅka Muttirācālai, 1929 [1909]), 3–13, 4–5 (my translation).
26. Fifty-sixth year of the Jupiter cycle.
27. Type of gold currency (its exact value is unknown) and worship.
28. Local incarnation of Viṣṇu near Madurai and Tamil month from mid-April to mid-May.
29. Beholding of a deity and receiving a blessing, pouring libations on the image of the deity being worshipped, and food offered to the Hindu deity as part of worship.
30. Tamil month from mid-February to mid-March and thirty-second year of the Jupiter cycle.
31. "No. 34. Kuniyur Plates of the Time of Venkata II," in *Epigraphia Indica and Record of the Archæological Survey of India*, vol. III—1894–1895, ed. E. Hultzshe (Calcutta: Office of the Superintendent of Government Printing, India, 1894–1895), 236–258; Robert Sewell, *Archaeological Survey of Southern India, Lists of the Antiquarian Remains in the Presidency of Madras: Compiled under the Orders of Government*, vol. I (Madras: E. Keys, at the Government Press, 1882), 309, 203. J. H. Nelson states that Tirumala frequently granted large land grants to support temples without "materially impairing his resources." See J. H. Nelson, *The Madura Country: A Manual Compiled by Order of the Madras Government* (Madras: Asylum Press by William Thomas, 1868), Part III: 152–153.
32. Carol Appadurai Breckenridge, "The Śrī Mīṉākṣī-Sundarēsvarar Temple: Worship and Endowments in South India, 1833 to 1925" (PhD diss., University of Wisconsin-Madison, 1976), 261–262. See chapter 5 for an extensive discussion on temple endowments at the Mīnākṣi-Sundareśvara complex. Endowments originally established by the Nāyaka kings are now controlled by the Tamil Nadu government's Hindu Religious and Charitable Endowments (HR & CE) Department, which appoints the temple's executive officer, who heads the *dēvastānam* (temple's administration). While funds are controlled by this administration, the concept of separate endowments still persists.
33. Breckenridge, "The Śrī Mīṉākṣī-Sundareśvara Temple," 273–277. In addition to designating economic resources through cash or land, the donor also specified and sponsored particular rituals; a discussion of this component of temple endowment appears in chapter 2.

34. Nelson, *The Madura Country*, Part III: 149–153. Nelson draws from missionary accounts. Tirumala inherited the Telugu warrior conception of kingdom from Viśvanātha. Taylor lists the bastions under Tirumala's rule. See William Taylor, "A List of the Seventy-Two Palliyams Appointed to Guard the Bastions of the Pandion Capital," in *Oriental Historical Manuscripts, in the Tamil Language*, vol. II, ed. and trans. William Taylor (Madras: Printed and Published by Charles Josiah Taylor, 1835), 161–168.
35. A. Sauliere, "The Revolt of the Southern Nayaks," part 1, *Journal of Indian History* 42, no. 1 (April 1964): 89–105, 91.
36. Susan Bayly, *Saints, Goddesses, and Kings: Muslims and Christians in South Indian Society, 1700–1900* (Cambridge: Cambridge University Press, 1989), 323–324. The Sētupatis, prominent feudal chieftains, or *pāḷaiyakkārar*s, in Ramnad under the Madurai Nāyakas, established similar forms of patronage with pearling specialists. See James Hornell, *Report to the Government of Madras on the Indian Pearl Fisheries in the Gulf of Mannar* (Madras: Printed by the Superintendent, Government Press, 1905), 11.
37. Jean-François Hupré, "The Royal Jewels of Tirumala Nāyaka of Madurai (1623–1659)," in *The Jewels of India,* ed. Susan Stronge (Bombay: Marg Publications, 1995), 63–80, 68–69, 74–75, 78.
38. K. Rajaram, *History of Thirumalai Nayak* (Madurai: Ennes Publications, 1982), 58; D. Devakunjari, *Madurai through the Ages: From the Earliest Times to 1801 A.D.* (Madras: Society for Archaeological, Historical, and Epigraphical Research, 1979), 258–259 and four images of temple crowns and ornaments between pages 224–225.
39. A. V. Jeyechandrun, *The Madurai Temple Complex (With Special Reference to Literature and Legends)* (Madurai: Publications Division, Madurai Kamaraj University, 1985), 32–33.
40. Ta. Kurucāmi, "Maturai Tirukkōyilil Tirumuṟai Viṇṇappikkum Varalāṟu," in *Maturait Tirukkōyil: Tirukkuṭa Naṉṉīrāṭṭup Peruviḻā Malar* (*The Madurai Temple Complex: Kumbabhisheka Souvenir*) (Tamiḻ and English), ed. A. V. Jeyechandrun (Maturai: Aruḷmiku Mīṉāṭci Cuntarēcuvarar Tirukkōyil, 1974), 267–270, 268.
41. David Dean Shulman, *The Wisdom of Poets: Studies in Tamil, Telugu, and Sanskrit* (New Delhi: Oxford University Press, 2001), 90–91.
42. In the poem, the spelling of Tirumala Nāyaka appears as Tirumalai Nāyakkar, which is an alternate pronunciation of the ruler's name.
43. This verse alludes to several stories that deal with the sea/ocean. In Kampaṉ's twelfth-century *Rāmāyaṇa*, the demon king Rāvaṇa kidnaps Sītā and takes her to his island kingdom of Lanka. Rāma, Sītā's husband and the king of Ayodhya, prays to Varuṇa to permit him and his army to cross the ocean (in what is now

Rameswaram, about 200 kilometers southeast of Madurai) so he can rescue his wife. When days pass with no response, Rāma unleashes his weapons, which burn the sea and its creatures, until the sea god allows a bridge to be built. See "Placating Varuna," in *Kamba Ramayanam: Yuddha Kandam Part-1*, trans. P. S. Sundaram (Tamil Nadu: Department of Tamil Development-Culture, Government of Tamil Nadu, 1994), 97–110. Also in Kampaṉ's *Rāmāyaṇa*, *rishi* Agastya drank the ocean so that the Dēvas could kill the Asuras, who lay hidden within it. See verse 37. 2758 of "Paṭalam Three: Agastya," in *The Forest Book of the Rāmāyaṇa of Kampaṉ*, trans. George L. Hart and Hank Heifetz (Berkeley and Los Angeles: University of California Press, 1988), 62–73, 68. In Parañcōti Muṉivar's seventeenth-century *Tiruviḷaiyāṭal Purāṇam* I.13, the fourth Pāṇḍyan king, Ukkira, throws his spear at Varuṇa sent by an envious Indra, and prevents the sea god from destroying Madurai with its torrential rain. In *Tiruviḷaiyāṭal Purāṇam* 1.14, the lack of rains causes the Tamil country to suffer. See R. K. K. Rajarajan and Jeyapriya Rajarajan, *Mīnākṣī-Sundareśvara: Tiruviḷaiyāṭaṟ Purāṇam in Letters, Design and Art* (Delhi: Sharada Publishing House, 2013), 25. In *Bhāgavata Purāṇa*, Satyavrata, the king of Drāviḍa performs water rites in the Kṛtamālā river (identified as a tributary of Madurai's Vaigai river) when a small fish swims into his cupped palms and pleads for its life. The king places the fish first in a water vessel, and later in a pond, then a lake, and finally the sea, as it grows larger and larger. The fish reveals himself to be god Viṣṇu and instructs the king to build a boat to house all flora and fauna to save them from an impending deluge. See "The Matsya Avatara," in Ramesh Menon, *Bhagavata Purana* (New Delhi: Rupa & Co., 2007), 580–586. In Aruṇakirinātar's fifteenth-century *Vēl Viruttam*, the sharp spear (*vēl*) of Siva's son Murukaṉ (Subrahmaṇya) sucks all the ocean's waters and dries its beds so Gaṅgā and other rivers could once again flow after a demon (transformed into a mango tree and positioned himself in the middle of the ocean) had obstructed their journey. See verse 1 of Aruṇakirinātar, *Aruṇakirinātar Aruḷiya Vēl Viruttam, Mayil Viruttam, Cēval Viruttam* (Tamiḻ), Commentary by Va. Cu. Ceṅkalvarāya Piḷḷai (Ceṉṉai: Tirunelvēlit Teṉṉintiya Caivacittānta Nūṟpatippuk Kaḻakam, 1971), 2.

44. Belleric myrobalan.
45. *Tiruvālavāyuṭaiyārkōyil Tiruppaṇimālai* (Tamiḻ), Centamiḻp Piracuram-27, ed. Po. Pāṇṭitturaittēvar (Maturai: Maturait Tamiḻccaṅka Muttirācālai, 1929 [1909]), 22–25 (my translation).
46. *Tiruvālavāyuṭaiyārkōyil Tiruppaṇimālai*: v. 49, pp. 13–14.
47. *Tiruvālavāyuṭaiyārkōyil Tiruppaṇimālai*: vv. 51–55, pp. 14–15.
48. The Vijayanagara empire's declining power after the Deccan sultanates' victory in the 1565 Battle of Talikota left the southern peninsula in a confused state

and provided an opportunity for Nāyaka ambitions. Tirumala augmented his army to improve his kingdom's defense and to remove Vijayanagara's hold, as the empire could no longer provide the security Tirumala needed from invading armies. He accepted the emperor in name only, but withheld the requested tribute. So Śrīraṅga III (r. 1642–1652 CE), the last Vijayanagara king, marched southwards to end Tirumala's independence around 1642. Tirumala formed an alliance with the Senji and Tanjavur Nāyakas. When Senji fort was seized and the panic-stricken Tanjavur Nāyaka betrayed his allies, Tirumala sought the Golconda sultanate's assistance. Golconda troops defeated the enemy by attacking Vellore, a Vijayanagara capital, but they also turned on the Senji Nāyakas. Tirumala, now aligned with the Bijapur sultanate, saved Senji fort temporarily and also defeated Śrīraṅga III and Kaṇṭhīrava Narasa Rāja, the Mysore king, who provided aid and asylum to the Vijayanagara emperor. Tirumala preserved his realm, but he isolated himself from Senji and Tanjavur and tolerated a hefty tribute to the Bijapur sultan.

Tirumala Nāyaka also faced rebellions from neighboring feudatories. In the early years of his reign, Tirumala encountered an invasion by Chāmarāja Uḍaiyār of Mysore and engaged in a counterattack of Mysore with the help of his able general Rāmappaiya. In 1634, Tirumala ordered the invasion of Travancore that forced its chiefs to pay a tribute and reduced the Travancore king as a vassal and subordinate of Madurai. Towards the end of his reign, Tirumala endured another conflict with Mysore: Kaṇṭhīrava Narasa Rāja, who sought revenge for his defeat by capturing Coimbatore, which threatened Madurai's safety. Tirumala's devoted vassal, Raghunātha Sētupati of Ramnad, helped to vanquish the Mysorean army: for the Sētupati's efforts, Tirumala honored him with gifts and the title of Tirumalai Sētupati, and he terminated the tribute payment. The Sētupati's loyalty stemmed from Tirumala's earlier help in the 1630s that installed his own nominee and Raghunātha's relative to the Ramnad throne rather than the rival aspirant. During that dispute with the wayward chieftain, Tirumala relied on support from the Portuguese. Sauliere, "The Revolt of the Southern Nayaks," part I; A. Sauliere, "The Revolt of the Southern Nayaks," part 2, *Journal of Indian History* 44, no. 1 (April 1966): 163–180; V. Rangachari, "The History of the Naik Kingdom of Madura," *The Indian Antiquary, A Journal of Oriental Research* 45 (October 1916): 161–171, 166–171, (November 1916): 178–188, (December 1916): 196–204, 196–202.

Taylor's "History of the Carnataca Governors Who Ruled over the Pandiya Mandalam" fixates on this politically unstable time for Tirumala. After two sentences about Tirumala's building projects, the part of the text devoted to Tirumala delves on the rebellious Sētupati, the warring Mysorean ruler, and the loyal Sētupati from Ramnad whom Tirumala honored for his indispensable military service. Furthermore, while Viśvanātha's exploits fill five sections in the chronicle (he appears as a larger-than-life figure: his miraculous birth, extraordinary feats, and physical exploits helped him establish a dynasty in Madurai), Tirumala requires only one, suggesting that he pales in comparison to his heroic forefather. See Taylor, "History of the Carnataca Governors Who Ruled over the Pandiya Mandalam," 29–33.

49. Narayana Rao, Shulman, and Subrahmanyam, *Symbols of Substance*, 107.
50. Caleb Simmons, *Devotional Sovereignty: Kingship and Religion in India* (New York: Oxford University Press, 2020), 18. Simmons observes a turn to "devotion" in his study of Kṛṣṇarāja III (r. 1799–1868 CE) who succumbed to British control: stripped of his political power as administrative and revenue collection transferred to the colonial state, the Woḍeyar king paid increased attention to Mysore's centers of religious power. See Simmons, *Devotional Sovereignty: Kingship and Religion in India*, 4–5, 17–20, 133–167.
51. Noboru Karashima, "Nāyakas as Lease-Holders of Temple Lands," *Journal of the Economic and Social History of the Orient* 19, no. 2 (1976): 227–232, 232.
52. For a list of temple projects and their donors, see Sri K. Palaniappan, *The Great Temple of Madurai* (Madurai: Sri Meenakshisundareswarar Temple Renovation Committee, 1970 [1963]), 70–78, and Rajarajan and Rajarajan, *Mīnākṣī-Sundareśvara,* 115–119. These lists demonstrate that Tirumala's predecessors Kṛṣṇappa (r. 1564–1572 CE) and Vīrappa (r. 1572–1595 CE) contributed towards temple improvements more than any other Nāyaka and that wealthy patrons also supported the Madurai temple. For descriptions of the various temple components, see Jeyechandrun, *The Madurai Temple Complex*, 164–188, and Devakunjari, *Madurai through the Ages*, 220–250.
53. George Michell, *Architecture and Art of Southern India*, The New Cambridge History of India I.6 (Cambridge: Cambridge University Press, 1995), 104.
54. A. Ki. Parantāmaṉār, *Tirumala Nāyakkar Varalāṟu* (Tamil) (Ceṉṉai: A. Cō. Cantāṉa Ilakkumi, 1995), 96.
55. Taylor, "The Accounts of Tirumali-Naicker, and of His Buildings," 149–151.
56. Crispin Branfoot, *Gods on the Move: Architecture and Ritual in the South Indian Temple* (London: The Society for South Asian Studies, 2007), 252.
57. Branfoot, *Gods on the Move*, 138. For a general discussion about the Tamil Drāviḍa tradition in south Indian temple architecture, see G. Jouveau-Dubreuil, *Dravidian Architecture*, ed. S. Krishnaswami Aiyangar (Madras: S.P.C.K. Press, 1917). Briefly, the main components are: *vimāṉam*, or shrine portion that houses the deity and its superstructure, *gōpuram*, or gateway with pyramidal tower, and *maṇḍapam*, or columned hall either attached or detached for festival celebrations.
58. H. H. Cole, "Appendix U: Great Temple to Siva and His Consort at Madura," in *Preservation of National Monuments. Third Report of the Curator of*

Ancient Monuments in India, for the Year 1883–84 (Calcutta: Printed by the Superintendent of Government Printing, 1885), cliii–clvii, clvii; Devakunjari, *Madurai through the Ages*, 244; Crispin Branfoot, "Tirumala Nayaka's 'New Hall' and the European Study of the South Indian Temple," *Journal of the Royal Asiatic Society* 11, no. 2 (2001): 191–217, 193.

59. A discussion about commerce in the Pudu Maṇḍapam follows in chapter 7.
60. Discussed in chapter 2.
61. Although the statues of the first ten Madurai Nāyakas are not inscribed, modern-day, painted labels installed above each portrait by temple authorities in the mid-twentieth century provide some identification: (*a*) Viśvanātha Nāyakkar, (*b*) Kumāra Kṛṣṇappa Nāyakkar, (*c*) Pěriya Vīrappa Nāyakkar, (*d*) Kṛṣṇa Vīrappa Nāyakkar (peeled paint), (*e*) Liṅgama Nāyakkar, (*f*) Kṛṣṇappa Nāyakkar, (*g*) Kastūri Raṅgappa Nāyakkar, (*h*) Muttu Kṛṣṇappa Nāyakkar, (*i*) Muttu Vīrappa Nāyakkar, and (*j*). Tirumalai Nāyakkar. These names (as well as the number of rulers) do not completely line up with lists in William Taylor's 1835 *Oriental Historical Manuscripts*, J. H. Nelson's 1868 *Madura Country*, Robert Sewell's 1884 *Lists of Inscriptions, and Sketch of the Dynasties of Southern India*, R. Sathyanatha Aiyar's 1924 *History of the Nayaks of Madura*, H. Heras' 1925 "The Statues of the Nayaks of Madurai in the Pudu Mandapam," A. V. Jeyechandrun's 1985 *The Madurai Temple Complex*, or temple manuscripts, *Stāṉikar Varalāṟu* (a historical account of the Madurai temple priests) and *Sthala Varalāṟu* (an account of the temple's political history). The disparity in the genealogy reflects the paucity of inscriptions from the Nāyaka period that has contributed to inconsistencies in the historical account, making definitive identities about the Madurai Nāyakas in the Pudu Maṇḍapam challenging, except for the last figure, Tirumala.
62. Branfoot, *Gods on the Move*, 165–242.
63. Hupré, "The Royal Jewels of Tirumala Nāyaka," 68.
64. It is possible that the first ruler directly opposite Tirumala is not Viśvanātha, as is commonly believed and labeled as such, but Nāgama, Viśvaṇātha's father. Jeyechandrun cites the palm-leaf manuscript from the Vētanārāyaṇa Perumāḷ temple, Tirunarayanapuram (Tiruchirappalli district), that mentions the custom of beginning the Madurai Nāyaka dynasty with Nāgama, the founder's father. See Jeyechandrun, *The Madurai Temple Complex*, 309–310. This view was first proposed in 1954. See R. Sathianathaier, *Tamilaham in the 17th Century* (Madras: University of Madras, 1956), 23–25. Lending credence to this interpretation is the Tamil Nadu Department of Archaeology's 2007 discovery of engravings of two Nāyaka rulers on two pillars at the Nellaiyappar temple in Tirunelveli. The inscription above identifies them as Nāgama Nāyaka and Viśvanātha Nāyaka. See "Images of Nayak Kings Found in Sri Nellaiyappar

Temple," *The Hindu*, June 6, 2007, https://www.thehindu.com/todays-paper/tp-national/tp-tamilnadu/Images-of-Nayak-kings-found-in-Sri-Nellaiyappar-Temple/article14773856.ece, accessed December 14, 2021. Furthermore, the first portrait does not wear the tall conical *kuḷḷāyi*, a common Vijayanagara-period headdress, unlike the second through fifth Nāyaka portraits, conveying themselves as the Vijayanagara king's loyal servants, which Nāgama supposedly was not.

65. Narayana Rao, Shulman, and Subrahmanyam, *Symbols of Substance*, 170. G. S. Ghurye claims that the Madurai and Tanjavur Nāyakas were Balijas. See *Caste and Race in India* (London: Kegan Paul, Trench, Trubner & Co., Ltd, 1932), 96. Balijas are an agricultural/merchant/trading/warrior caste primarily from the Andhra region.
66. Nicholas B. Dirks, *The Hollow Crown: Ethnohistory of an Indian Kingdom* (Cambridge: Cambridge University Press, 1987), 47.
67. Dirks, *The Hollow Crown*, 101–102.
68. Narayana Rao, Shulman, and Subrahmanyam, *Symbols of Substance*, 80–81.
69. Daud Ali, *Courtly Culture and Political Life in Early Medieval India* (Cambridge: Cambridge University Press, 2004), 98–99.
70. See the discussion of *abhyudayamu* in chapter 3 of Narayana Rao, Shulman, and Subrahmanyam, *Symbols of Substance*, 57–112.
71. For example, "Painted Canvas Depicting a Court Scene," cotton (painted and resist dyed) textile, 155 x 202 centimeters, seventeenth century, MA 5678 (AEDTA 2221) Musée National des Arts Asiatiques–Guimet, Paris, https://www.guimet.fr/collections/textiles/toile-peinte-representant-une-scene-de-cour/, accessed December 14, 2021, and "Panel from a Box," ivory plaque, 15.2 x 31.4 centimeters), seventeenth century, 80.171 Virginia Museum of Fine Arts, Richmond, https://www.vmfa.museum/piction/6027262-12968824/, accessed December 14, 2021. The Coromandel Coast was a major textile production center.
72. *Tiruvālavāyuṭaiyārkōyil Tiruppaṇimālai*: v. 85, p. 24.
73. Jesuit missionary Baltasar Da Costa, translated from Portuguese in Narayana Rao, Shulman, and Subrahmanyam, *Symbols of Substance*, 87, states:

> Almost every day he appears on the terrace surrounded by his courtiers, while in front of them his elephants are drawn up in two rows, the space between them being occupied by three or four hundred Turks (*Turcos*), who form his bodyguard. When he comes out of the fortress to visit some pagodes, as he is wont to do on days of festivals, he is surrounded with great pomp. Sometimes he rides in a palanquin, at other times he mounts an enormous elephant.... Next come the elephants in a long file, mounted by his nobles and chief captains, preceded by the arms and insignia of the Nāyaka. Then the cavalry and the rest of the troops follow.

74. *Tiruvālavāyuṭaiyārkōyil Tiruppaṇimālai*: v. 83, p. 24.
75. Vidya Dehejia, "The Very Idea of a Portrait," *ARS Orientalis* 38 (1998): 40–48, 45. An inscription in Telugu on each figure's shoulders identifies them as Kṛṣṇadevarāya and his two queens, Tirumaladēvi and Ciṉṉadēvi. See T. G. Aravamuthan, *Portrait Sculpture in South India*, foreword by Ananda K. Coormaswamy (London: The India Society, 1931), 46–47.
76. Henry Heras, "The Statues of the Nayaks of Madura in the Pudu Mantapam," *Quarterly Journal of the Mythic Society* 15, no. 3 (April 1925): 209–218, 209. Heras' paper is perhaps the earliest analysis of the hall's Nāyaka lineage.
77. Crispin Branfoot, "'Expanding Form': The Architectural Sculpture of the South Indian Temple ca. 1500–1700," *Artibus Asiae* 62, no. 2 (2002): 189–245, 201.
78. Phillip B. Wagoner, "'Sultan among Hindu Kings': Dress, Titles, and the Islamicization of Hindu Culture at Vijayanagara," *The Journal of Asian Studies* 55, no. 4 (November 1996): 851–880. One cap has a slight forward projection.
79. *Annual Report on Epigraphy 1908–1909* (Madras: Government of Madras Public Department, G.O. No. 538, July 28, 1909), 17: 113 of 1908, explanation on p. 118; Hultzshe, *Epigraphia Indica and Record of the Archæological Survey of India*, 236–258; Robert Sewell, *Archaeological Survey of Southern India, List of Inscriptions, and Sketch of the Dynasties of Southern India. Compiled under the Orders of Government*, vol. II (Madras: E. Keys, at the Government Press, 1884), 14: no. 92. For an analysis of this shift in inscriptions, see Dirks, *The Hollow Crown*, 45–47.
80. Phillip B. Wagoner, *Tidings of the King: A Translation and Ethnohistorical Analysis of the Rāyavācakamu* (Honolulu: University of Hawaii Press, 1995), 30.
81. A devotional statuette of Tirumala Nāyaka accompanied by his queen is located inside the Kaḷḷaḻakar temple, Alakar Koyil; while elevated with a modern-day label, it is not life size and was most likely added to the original structure by Tirumala for whom the temple was important.
82. Anna Lise Seastrand, "Text, Image, and Portrait in Early Modern South Indian Murals," *Artibus Asiae* 78, no. 1 (2018): 29–60, 33–35. See also Crispin Branfoot, "Royal Portrait Sculpture in the South Indian Temple," *South Asian Studies* 16, no. 1 (2000): 11–36, 12–23.
83. According to Crispin Branfoot, bases for the Pudu Maṇḍapam's family portraits measure between 145 to 163 centimeters in height. As a comparison, the bases for the Senji Nāyaka genealogical portraits in the Bhū Varāha temple, Srimushnam, are about 1 meter (100 centimeters) high. See Crispin Branfoot, "Dynastic Genealogies, Portraiture, and the Place of the Past in Early Modern South India," *Artibus Asiae* 72, no. 2 (2012): 323–376, 326, 331.

2

Co-opting a Local Goddess in Madurai

From Warrior Queen to Śiva's Consort to Political Pawn*

Introduction

Madurai's most famous temple is dedicated to Mīnākṣī ('the fish-eyed one'), a queen of Madurai's Pāṇḍyan kingdom who is regarded as a manifestation of the pan-Indian goddess Pārvatī. The temple also houses her consort, Sundareśvara ('the beautiful lord'), similarly understood to be a local version of the pan-Indian deity Śiva. Every Cittirai month (April/May) in the Tamil Hindu calendar, more than one million devotees descend upon the temple town to witness the reenactment of the gods' sacred union in a twelve-day celebratory marriage festival. The crowd watches as metal embodiments of the divine couple, dressed in colorful silks and floral garlands, marry on a flower-decked stage and commemorate their nuptials by circumambulating the temple in gigantic wooden chariots through Madurai's streets.

The temple sits on the flat, sandy plain along the river Vaigai. It occupies the geographic and ritual center of Madurai, a city laid out in the shape of a square with a series of concentric streets radiating from the temple like petals around a lotus flower. Mīnākṣī is one of the few Hindu female deities to have a major temple devoted to her: the fish-eyed goddess never blinks, and devotees consider her to provide constant, watchful protection of the town. As a major pilgrimage site, the temple attracts 15,000 visitors on average days, approaching twice that number on Friday, the goddess's sacred day.[1]

The Mīnākṣī-Sundareśvara temple premises, in particular the Pudu Maṇḍapam at the complex's east gateway, represent a critical intersection of architecture and sovereignty in early modern south Indian government. Temple ceremonies for Mīnākṣī helped Madurai's seventeenth-century ruler Tirumala Nāyaka establish

* An earlier version of this chapter, "From Warrior Queen to Śiva's Consort to Political Pawn: The Genesis and Development of a Local Goddess in Madurai," was originally published in Diana Dimitrova and Tatiana Oranskaia, eds., *Divinizing in South Asian Traditions* (London and New York: Routledge, 2018), 59–70.

himself as the goddess's designated heir, by crafting a political identity around rituals that performed a relationship of partnership, interdependence, and exchange between the goddess and the king. Tirumala altered sacred prescriptions and reconstituted ritual traditions into vehicles for his own royal self-fashioning through mass public performances linked to the rhythms and cycles of seasonal labor in the Tamil region. Mythological texts, sculptural reliefs, and religious festivals connected to the Madurai temple help us trace Mīnākṣī's transformation from soldierly heir to her father's throne, to submissive wife of her god-husband, to political pawn of a devout king.

The emergence of a local goddess in Madurai

Goddess worship is a vital aspect of Hindu religious life, involving devotion to female village deities, pan-Indian goddesses, and esoteric, tantric figures. Mīnākṣī was an autochthonous deity to the community that inhabited Madurai village;[2] usually associated with life, fertility, healing, and protection, *grāmadevatās* (Skt, 'village goddesses') the Tamil area are generally unmarried and independent, and frequently referred to as *amma<u>n</u>*, literally 'mother.' During the early medieval period of Hinduism, Mīnākṣī became a form of Pārvatī—a brahmanic deity or Great Goddess (Mahādevī)—as regional identities were assimilated with those of pan-Indian gods.[3] Often finding a home within Śaivism, the goddess-centered (Śākta) tradition worships the god's consort in her various forms as Pārvatī, Durgā, and Kālī personifying female divine energy (*śakti*).

The Śākta-oriented Mīnākṣī-Sundareśvara temple is popularly known as the Mīnākṣī temple or Mīnākṣī Amma<u>n</u> temple. Despite her marriage to Śiva, the goddess Mīnākṣī's ritual precedence is unequivocal: all the various titles for the temple retain the goddess's name. Although Sundareśvara has the central shrine that aligns with the eastern axis, custom dictates that a worshipper enter the doorway on the left of the east gateway called Amma<u>n</u> Ca<u>n</u><u>n</u>iti, and then walk through the Aśṭa Śakti Maṇḍapam ('hall of eight goddesses'), past the Po<u>r</u><u>r</u>āmaraikkuḷam ('golden lotus tank') along the corridor that leads directly to the goddess's shrine; after praying there, the visitor turns left and strolls towards the Śiva shrine—a small distance away—to venerate the god before exiting through the grand eastern gateway (Figure 2.1).[4]

Every major south Indian temple town has its own textual tradition that tells the story of a specific shrine and explains why the temple and its deities came to be situated at that particular place. Parañcōti Mu<u>n</u>ivar's seventeenth-century *Tiruviḷaiyāṭal Purāṇam* ('Story of Śiva's sacred games') documents the local Tamil myths of the Madurai temple; its 3,363 verses in continuous narrative

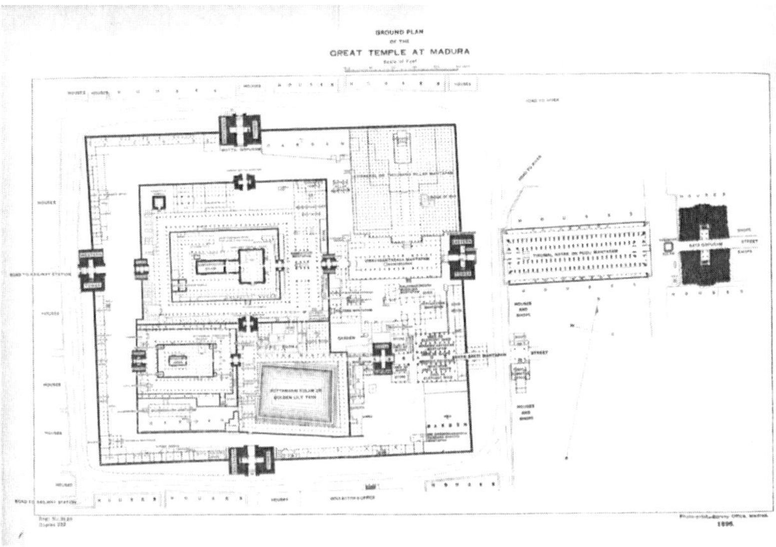

Figure 2.1 Ground plan of the Great Temple at Madura, Survey Office, Madras, 1896

Source: W. Francis, *Madras District Gazetteers: Madura*, vol. I (Madras: Printed by the Superintendent, Government Press, 1906), between pages 266 and 267.

are an example of a *talapurāṇam*, or 'place-history.' *Tiruviḷaiyāṭal Purāṇam* is divided into three parts titled after the city's three names: (I) *Maturaikkāṇṭam*, (II) *Kūṭaṟkāṇṭam*, and (III) *Tiruvālavāykkāṇṭam*. Etymologically, 'Madurai' is derived from *maturam* (Tamil, 'sweetness'; Skt. *madhura*), alluding to the story of Śiva purifying and sanctifying the city by dripping sweet nectar from his hair. 'Kūṭal' ('junction') suggests the story of Śiva saving Madurai by forming four tower-like clouds to shield the city from a disastrous deluge. 'Tiruvālavāy' ('poisoned-mouth one', that is, snake) is the serpent deployed by Śiva to trace the city's perimeter. Parañcōti Muṉivar's poem celebrates the city and its sacred landscape, the backdrop for Śiva's sixty-four divine sports (*tiruviḷaiyāṭal*) centering on themes of protection and aid.

Brightly colored scenes of the temple's *talapurāṇam* have been painted along the long wall that flanks the Poṟṟāmaraikkuḷam tank that leads directly to the goddess's shrine. These paintings (still unfinished) follow the Tamil pictorial idiom: boxed registers divide the narrow strips crowded with figures, one above the other, with the narrative proceeding from left to right, and then alternating right to left. Against an orange-red background, the figures are shown in profile, filled with white, green, and golden-brown colors, and depicted with projecting eyes, sharp noses, and pointed chins. Thin black strokes detail costume, jewelry, and headdress. The original paintings in this corridor date back to the Nāyaka period, and later pieces commissioned for the 1876 Kumbābhiṣēkam ('temple consecration ceremony') were removed, retouched, and displayed on wooden boards in the Temple Art Museum during the twentieth century.[5]

The Pudu Maṇḍapam contains stone renderings of primary figures from *Tiruviḷaiyāṭal Purāṇam*. According to a well-known account, Parañcōti Muṉivar, a Śaiva Veḷḷāla (dominant peasant caste) from Vedaranyam in Tanjavur district, frequently witnessed the Pudu Maṇḍapam's construction while walking to the Śaiva *maṭam* ('monastery') at the corner of East Cittirai and Sundaresvara Sannathi Streets. One day, as he lingered inside the pillared hall, an elderly ascetic gave Parañcōti Muṉivar palm leaves inscribed with instructions about *tiruviḷaiyāṭal* ('sacred play') that inspired him to write his own composition about Śiva (or Sundareśvara, as he is known in Madurai) influenced by the sculptures he saw in the hall.[6] Parañcōti Muṉivar's work is the most prevalent version of Madurai's sacred history.

The stories of Mīnākṣī's birth, coronation, battles, and marriage occur in the fourth and fifth chapters of *Tiruviḷaiyāṭal Purāṇam* I, *Maturaikkāṇṭam*. A life-size depiction of Taṭātakai (Mīnākṣī's birth name) appears in the hall's southeast interior aisle near the main entrance (Figure 2.2): she is poised for battle, standing with splayed legs and brandishing a *vēl* ('lance').[7] Taṭātakai has three breasts; her curious anatomy is explained by a story in *Tiruviḷaiyāṭal Purāṇam* I.4. The legend begins with Malayattuvacaṉ, the son of Kulacēkaraṉ Pāṇḍya, Madurai's founder and the first Pāṇḍyan king.[8] Desiring a son, the childless king Malayattuvacaṉ and his wife Kāñcaṉamālai perform the necessary son-producing sacrifice (*makavēḷvi*); to their surprise, a three-breasted toddler girl materializes out of the sacrificial fire and lands in the queen's lap.[9] A heavenly voice consoles the distraught parents: it instructs the Pāṇḍyan king to treat his daughter like a son,[10] and promises that the child's third breast will vanish when the princess meets her future husband.[11] Malayattuvacaṉ trains Taṭātakai as his male heir, teaching her such skills as archery and equestrianism[12] and, when he feels too old to rule, he crowns his daughter as his successor, dying shortly after installing her on the imperial throne.[13] The end of chapter 4 relays how Pārvatī took the form of Taṭātakai as a boon granted to her devotee Viccāvati: pleased with Viccāvati's penance, Pārvatī agreed to be born as Viccāvati's daughter in her next life as Kāñcaṉamālai.[14] These verses indicate that the locally entrenched goddess had become substantially identified with the pan-Indian goddess of Sanskritic Hinduism by the time Parañcōti Muṉivar composed his *purāṇam* in the seventeenth century.

Two sculptures illustrate the moment Taṭātakai encounters Īśāna, a form of Śiva, as narrated in *Tiruviḷaiyāṭal Purāṇam* I.5. Chapter 5 opens with

Figure 2.2 Taṭātakai, Pudu Maṇḍapam

Source: Photo by author.

Kāñcaṉamālai bemoaning her daughter's unmarried status. Taṭātakai reassures her mother that marriage will happen at the right time; first, the young queen must embark on a tour to establish her sovereignty in the eight quarters of the world.[15] After a string of victories and plundering vanquished foes, she arrives with her army at Śiva's abode, Mount Kailāsa, to do battle with his warriors.[16] Finally, when Taṭātakai confronts Śiva himself on the battlefield, her third breast disappears.[17] Some scholars interpret Mīnākṣī's extra breast as a phallus, and its loss as a form of castration.[18] The sight of Śiva renders her a blushing, bashful bride who is now unambiguously female.[19] Īśāna stands with bow drawn opposite Taṭātakai's image in the Pudu Maṇḍapam's northeast section (Figure 2.3); he is regarded as the guardian of the northeast direction.[20] Taṭātakai's transformation into Mīnākṣī, a consort deity (*mahādevī*) married to a male supreme god, reflects a more general historical process by which local Tamil religiosity assimilated pan-Hindu forms. Early medieval Tamil temple myths, in particular, tend to feature themes of conflict, accommodation, and ultimately divine marriage.[21]

Figure 2.3 Īśāna, Pudu Maṇḍapam

Source: Photo by author.

From warrior queen to Śiva's consort

Tiruviḷaiyāṭal Purāṇam is primarily focused on Śiva's exploits, but its most popular component is the story of Mīnākṣī's marriage to Śiva. The birth and marriage myths convey how the goddess drew the god to the temple site, how they were "rooted there" by marriage, and how they came to rule and protect Madurai together.[22] Although Mīnākṣī loses her independence, bellicosity, and her singular political influence in *Tiruviḷaiyāṭal Purāṇam*, she also gains by meeting and marrying Śiva: she transforms into a mature and complete woman—first as a bride, then as a wife, and later as a mother—and attains divine power to become a goddess.[23] Śiva, in his local incarnate as Sundareśvara, acquires not only a companion, but also a kingdom and a place on the Pāṇḍyan throne in Madurai.[24]

After their initial encounter, Śiva directs Mīnākṣī to leave for Madurai, where he will join her in eight days for their wedding.[25] *Tiruviḷaiyāṭal Purāṇam* I.5 describes a wedding ceremony celebrated with great pomp. Mīnākṣī returns to a jubilant city as the citizens rejoice and prepare for her upcoming nuptials.[26] Śiva arrives with his wedding party, which includes Viṣṇu and Brahmā; women swoon when they catch sight of the devastatingly handsome god.[27] Kāñcaṉamālai greets the bridegroom with a welcoming ritual, and Śiva ascends the jeweled marriage throne and waits for Mīnākṣī as she gets dressed and adorned for

Figure 2.4 Mīnākṣī Kalyāṇam ('Mīnākṣī's marriage'), Pudu Maṇḍapam

Source: Photo by author.

the ceremony.[28] When Mīnākṣī arrives, Viṣṇu enacts *kaṉṉikātāṉam*, the initial rituals traditionally performed by the bride's father, gifting (*tāṉam*, Skt. *dāna*) the daughter (*kaṉṉikā*) to the groom's family. Viṣṇu washes the groom's feet and places the bride's hand in Śiva's hand.[29] *Kalyāṇasundaram* ('Marriage of the beautiful one') is a pan-Indian myth; however, Viṣṇu's presence points to a regional Tamil story. The people of Madurai consider Viṣṇu as Mīnākṣī's sibling: in the matrimonial scene, Viṣṇu (as the goddess's brother) officiates by pouring a lustration blessing (*abhiṣēkam*) over the couples' open hands from a pot. This episode in Mīnākṣī and Sundareśvara's marriage is duplicated sculpturally in the Pudu Maṇḍapam near the western entrance and inside the main temple in front of Śiva's inner sanctum (Figures 2.4 and 2.5). Mīnākṣī's *tirukkalyāṇam* ('sacred marriage') is also recreated in a seventeenth-century painting on the Rāṇi Maṅgammāḷ Maṇḍapam's ceiling (named after the Nāyaka queen regent) and a twentieth-century painting on the wall along the Poṟṟāmaraikkuḷam (Figures 2.6 and 2.7).

Sculptures of Ṛṣis Vyāghrapāda and Patañjali are located in the central nave and face in the direction of the marriage scene, so the sages can be in attendance when Mīnākṣī and Sundareśvara unite in holy wedlock. In *Tiruviḷaiyāṭal*

Figure 2.5 Mīnākṣī Kalyāṇam, Kampattaṭi Maṇḍapam

Source: Photo by author.

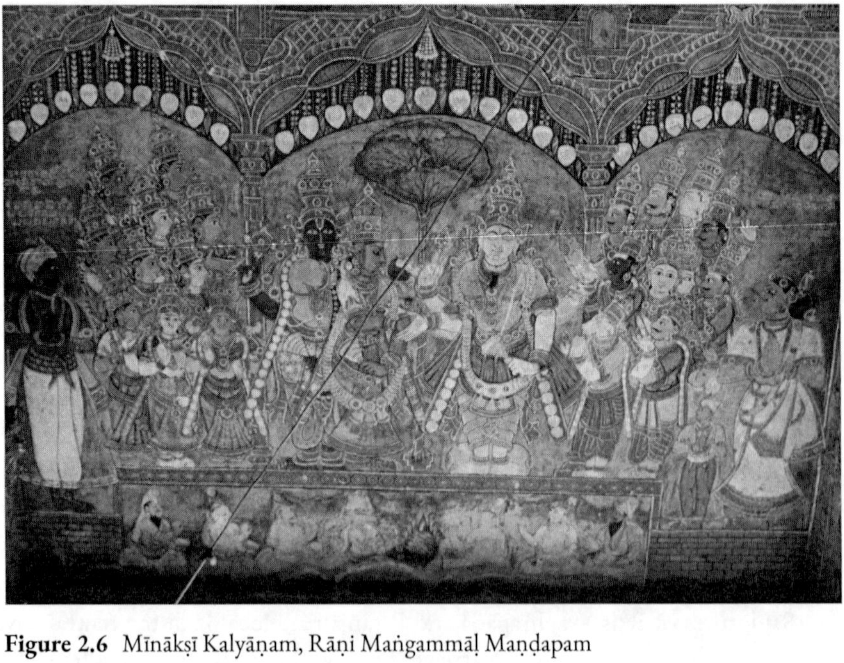

Figure 2.6 Mīnākṣī Kalyāṇam, Rāṇi Maṅgammāḷ Maṇḍapam

Source: Photo by author.

Figure 2.7 Mīnākṣī Kalyāṇam, Poṟṟāmaraikkuḷam

Source: Photo by author.

Purāṇam I.6, these sages would eat food only after seeing Naṭarāja's divine dance at Cidambaram; thus, on his wedding day, Śiva danced for them as Naṭarāja ('lord of dance') on the *veḷḷiyampalam* ('silver hall') in the Madurai temple.[30] The western outer end of the pillared hall includes a multiarmed dancing Śiva, in the *ūrdhva tāṇḍava* (Skt, 'ferocious dance') pose, with his right leg raised over his head. This sculpture is placed across the aisle from the eight-armed Kālī, possibly referring to Śiva defeating the goddess during a dance competition in Cidambaram.[31]

Other visual depictions of Śiva in the Pudu Maṇḍapam are extracted from *Tiruviḷaiyāṭal Purāṇam*'s second part, *Kūṭaṟkāṇṭam*, portraying the deity in the various disguises he donned in Madurai after his marriage. The hall's eastern entrance is flanked by sculptures of Sundareśvara as a sow suckling piglets, discussed in *Tiruviḷaiyāṭal Purāṇam* II.45 as the story of Śiva feeding twelve orphaned children that an ascetic cursed into pigs in a previous life; in chapter 46, they transform into men with pig faces and become the Pāṇḍyan king's ministers.[32] In another sculpture on the entrance's other side, Śiva is a tigress with an anthropomorphic head, holding a tiger in the left hand and a deer in the other, a reference to a story that does not exist in *Tiruviḷaiyāṭal Purāṇam* but is mentioned in an older Tamil *purāṇam*. In chapter 53 of Perumpaṟṟapuliyūr Nampi's thirteenth-century *Tiruvālavāyuṭaiyār Tiruviḷaiyāṭaṟpurāṇam*, Śiva feeds milk to a distressed deer left orphaned after a hunter shoots its mother in Kaṭampavaṉam ('forest of *kaṭampu* trees').[33] At that very same moment, Kulacēkaraṉ Pāṇḍya (Mīnākṣī's grandfather) comes to the forest in search of a Śiva *liṅgam*; he built the temple and city of Madurai in the same location, as recounted in *Tiruviḷaiyāṭal Purāṇam* I.3.[34]

Two more Śaiva myths are replicated in the western end of the central nave. In *Tiruviḷaiyāṭal Purāṇam* II.47, Sundareśvara teaches a small *karikkuruvi* bird a *mantra* to overcome some pestering crows.[35] In *Tiruviḷaiyāṭal Purāṇam* II.21, a Pāṇḍyan king challenges a proud *cittar* (Sundareśvara in disguise as a holy person) to make a stone elephant eat sugarcane; at the mere sight of Śiva, the stone elephant comes alive and accepts the offering.[36] Upon the advice of his Brahmin advisor, Tirumala Nāyaka initiated the practice of dramatizing these (and other) Śaiva stories at the Madurai temple during calendrical festivals;[37] he may have been drawn to stories that emphasize Śiva's compassionate and protective nature because he strove to be viewed similarly as king. The story of Śiva feeding an elephant takes place on the first day of Tai (January/February), known as Poṅgal, the much-celebrated Tamil harvest festival, while the story of Śiva teaching a bird occurs during Āvaṇi (August/September).

As in nearly all Śaiva temples, the god's *mūla mūrti* (immovable 'root or original image') is the stone cylindrical pillar or *liṅgam*, the aniconic symbol of Śiva, housed in the *garbhagṛha* (Skt, 'womb chamber' or sanctum sanctorum). Mīnākṣī's main *mūla mūrti* is an anthropomorphic figure of the goddess constructed of green stone. Adorned with a crown, jewelry, and *sārī*, she stands by herself with her left hand resting at her side and her upraised right hand holding a lotus bud, on which a green parrot is perched. In certain rituals and processions, the deities appear as metal movable *utsava mūrti*s, or 'festival images.' Mīnākṣī's *utsava mūrti* is a smaller replica of her portrayal in her inner sanctum; Sundareśvara's processional icon is Sōmāskanda ('Śiva with Ūma and Skanda') where Śiva sits beside his wife with a small figure of their son Skanda in between them. The image of Mīnākṣī shows her alone and can be worshipped as such, whereas the image of Sundareśvara not only incorporates the goddess, but is also always accompanied by her solo one (Figure 2.8). A single, minor religious festival involves only Sundareśvara, while the rest of the temple's festivals involve the divine couple together or Mīnākṣī on her own.[38] Despite her subordinate status to Śiva in the temple legend, Mīnākṣī maintains ritual dominance in the temple town: she is inherently and immensely powerful on her own given her origins as a local independent goddess.

Figure 2.8 Mīnākṣī (*left*) and Sundareśvara's Somāskanda (*right*), Mīnākṣī-Sundareśvara temple, Madurai, 2009

Source: Photo by author.

The queen as pawn of Nāyaka rule

A life-size, devotional stone sculpture of Tirumala Nāyaka stands directly facing Mīnākṣī's shrine, with palms pressed together in veneration (Figure 2.9). Tirumala portrayed himself as the legitimate inheritor of the Pāṇḍyan regent through seasonal temple rituals that performed an exchange and share of sovereignty between the goddess and the king. Episodes from *Tiruviḷaiyāṭal Purāṇam* are reenacted annually at the temple over twelve days every Cittirai (April/May).[39] Tirumala expanded the wedding festival by including a re-creation of Mīnākṣī's royal coronation (*paṭṭābhiṣēkam*) in front of the goddess's shrine on the eighth day of the festival and by participating in it (Figure 2.10). The king arrived at the temple from his palace in a grand manner, after the priests finished the *pūjā* ('worship') and adorned Mīnākṣī's portable metal image with her coronation crown and the royal scepter (*cenkōl*) (Figure 2.11). Echoing the ceremonies in which Tirumala's Nāyaka ancestors linked themselves to the Pāṇḍyan kings they supplanted, the priests handed Tirumala the *cenkōḷ*, the symbol of Mīnākṣī's divine rule. Tirumala carried the scepter to his palace in a splendorous procession seated

Figure 2.9 Tirumala Nāyaka and his consorts, Mīnākṣī-Sundareśvara temple, Madurai

Source: Photo by author.

Figure 2.10 Mīnākṣī's royal coronation (*paṭṭābhiṣēkam*), 2018

Source: Photo from Chairman Meenakshi Amman Kovil, Karumuttu T. Kannan.

Figure 2.11 Mīnākṣī-Sundareśvara temple's chairman of the Board of Trustees (*left*), who has replaced the Nāyaka king during Mīnākṣī's *paṭṭābhiṣēkam*, receives the *cenkōl*, 2018

Source: Photo from Chairman Meenakshi Amman Kovil, Karumuttu T. Kannan.

on a caparisoned elephant, and placed the scepter on his own throne. There, the scepter was propitiated before returning to the temple the following morning.[40]

The ritual spectacle creatively merged the mythic time of the *talapurāṇam* with the mundane time of the king's embodied performance.[41] Mīnākṣī occupies a unique position as both a queen and a goddess; she is a historical monarch of Madurai and an eternal, transhistorical deity who channels her divine powers to protect her domain.[42] She is unlike Cāmuṇḍā, for example, the local goddess whom seventeenth-century Woḍeyar kings of Mysore in Karnataka reinvented as a royal *purāṇic* goddess to be co-opted as a figure of the state.[43] Through a ritualized theatrical exhibition, Tirumala proclaimed to rule on behalf of the queen; Mīnākṣī directly conferred her sovereignty by 'bestowing' her imperial insignia upon him during her own crowning. This ritual established a cyclic, performative relationship between the king and the goddess.[44] As a member of the Pāṇḍyan lineage, Mīnākṣī was already royalty and thus already occupied the throne. Tirumala's rituals regarded her as the 'true' sovereign:[45] not only because she (not Sundareśvara) receives the crown and *cenkōl* during the coronation ritual in Cittirai,[46] but also because of her strong territorial rootedness as a Madurai-born goddess whose legend is intrinsic to the founding of the city. Tirumala was granted the right to rule Mīnākṣī's land and people on her behalf, through his own implantation in the ritual enactment of power and authority. The ritual exchange, the 'circling' of Mīnākṣī's scepter between the temple and the throne, marked a privileged relationship between king and goddess, involving interdependency and reciprocity: to protect her dominion and to ensure its prosperity, Mīnākṣī depended on Tirumala, whose political status in turn depended on divine authorization for his rule.

On the ninth day, Mīnākṣī's processional image enacts her conquest of the world (*digvijaya*): holding a bow and arrow atop her chariot, she journeys outside her temple compound through Madurai's streets to 'battle' the lords of the eight cardinal directions (Figure 2.12). Resting on the shoulders of strong men, the image of Mīnākṣī, with bow in hand, advances toward an image of each deity at the appropriate directional point on Maci Street. Mīnākṣī and her adversaries engage in the dance of battle: the god retreats before rushing forward, Mīnākṣī flees and returns again, until he finally withdraws. After Mīnākṣī successfully subdues her enemies, she travels to where North and East Maci Streets converge. When she meets Śiva[47] in this northeast corner, she does not fight him. Instead, priests remove her bow, and the two images go back to the temple together.[48]

Mīnākṣī and Sundareśvara are married on the tenth day of the Cittirai festival (Tirukkalyāṇam). Draped in resplendent silks and gold ornaments, metal embodiments of the god and goddess sit on a decorated stage in the open

Figure 2.12 Mīnākṣī's conquest of the world (*digvijaya*), 2017

Source: Photo by author.

Figure 2.13 Mīnākṣī and Sundareśvara's sacred marriage (*tirukkalyāṇam*), 2018

Source: Photo from Chairman Meenakshi Amman Kovil, Karumuttu T. Kannan.

courtyard near the temple's west gate that is packed with spectators (Figure 2.13).[49] Within the two festival images of Sōmāskanda and Mīnākṣī seated side by side, the goddess appears twice, signifying two movements: a local female deity being absorbed into the supra-local through a wedding, and a powerful goddess already 'wedded' to her particular locale. Before them, priests wearing elaborate headgear worn by courtly elites—a tradition started during Tirumala's reign[50]—wave lamps and chant Sanskrit verses. They then exchange the couple's floral garlands and tie silk scarves on the gods' behalf. At the auspicious moment, the *nāgasvaram* (wind instrument) music typically played in south Indian weddings grows louder as a priest, acting the role of Śiva, ties the matrimonial necklace (*tāli*) around Mīnākṣī's neck. Later that evening, Mīnākṣī and Sundareśvara process as a married couple through the four Cittirai Streets that encircle the temple complex. On the eleventh day, *utsava mūrti*s of the divine pair ride in towering wooden chariots (*tēr*s) on Madurai's Maci Streets before huge crowds who have thronged the city to catch a glimpse of the Tēr Tiruviḻā, or 'chariot festival' (Figure 2.14).

Tirumala Nāyaka's alterations to the annual reenactment of the celestial wedding were in direct contradiction to the ritual prescriptions of sacred texts.[51] He fused the observance of the Śaiva marriage (the wedding of Śiva to a manifestation of Pārvatī) with a separate (but related) Vaiṣṇava festival: the journey of Viṣṇu, known locally as Aḻakar, to the Vaigai riverbed from his temple 12 miles north, to attend Mīnākṣī's

Figure 2.14 Tēr Tiruviḻā ('chariot festival'), 2017

Source: Photo by author.

wedding ceremony.[52] In the Vaiṣṇava narrative, Viṣṇu travels to Madurai for his sister Mīnākṣī's marriage to Sundareśvara on the twelfth day of the ceremony; although he arrives late and misses the nuptials, he is nevertheless featured in sculptural and pictorial representations of the event (always shown standing with the bride and groom). According to Madurai temple priests, Tirumala's court poet and minister Nīlakaṇṭha Dīkṣita advised the king to inaugurate new temple festivals and ease conflict between Śaivas and Vaiṣṇavas.[53] A Tamil document alludes to dimensions of sectarian rivalries in Madurai of Tirumala's time, recounting a dispute between Śaivas and Vaiṣṇavas over an image of Ekapādamūrti (the one-legged form of Śiva with Brahmā and Viṣṇu), which may have implied Śiva's supremacy (when the disagreement dragged on for months, Tirumala was forced to appoint an arbitrator for each side before the sculpture could be installed in the Pudu Maṇḍapam).[54] Tirumala's alteration to the wedding ritual incorporated a festival symbolizing the identity of the Ambalakkārar division of the Kaḷḷar, a martial caste closely identified with the journey of Aḻakar,[55] that controlled powerful *pāḷaiyams* ('subordinate bastions') in the country outside Madurai.[56] The Kaḷḷar had been troublesome to obtain allegiance and incorporate into the Nāyaka orbit since the days of the Nāyaka founder, Viśvanātha.[57] Tirumala's relationship with Kaḷḷar communities was likewise fractious and unstable: a popular Tamil folk ballad, *Maturaivīracuvāmi Katai*, narrates Tirumala's efforts to protect Madurai's marketplace from Kaḷḷar bandits,[58] while copperplate charters issued from 1645 to 1656 document the imperial title, land gifts, royal regalia, and collection rights he delivered to a Kaḷḷar leader in Dharmathupatti near Tirumangalam.[59] Such efforts to cultivate relations were well rewarded when, in the same decade, Kaḷḷar soldiers helped the Nāyaka king fend off an invading Muslim army.[60]

The drama that unified Viṣṇu and Śiva into one family represented another political opportunity for the Nāyaka king, who was able to postpone the festival from Māci month (February/March) to the hot season of Cittirai month: by moving the gods' marital rites to after the end of the harvest season, he increased the available manpower for pulling the processional images of the royal couple in enormous chariots during post-wedding celebrations on the eleventh day. In so doing, Tirumala preserved the agrarian labor necessary for a productive harvest and more effectively capitalized on the ritual spectacle as a performance of divine authority. Arjun Appadurai described the significance of this form of 'authority' to Hindu kingship:

> Authority is the capacity to mobilize collective ritual deference to a sovereign deity in such a way that the mobilizing actor partakes of divine authority in relation to those human beings who are either the instruments or beneficiaries of such worship. More simply still, authority is the capacity to command collectivities in the homage of the deity. Of course, given the sociological complexities of the ritual process and the incomplete jural capacities of the deity (whatever its "power" in indigenous eyes), such authority can never be monopolized by any one individual or group and must always be shared.[61]

Appadurai observes that there was not a "Weberian model" of a single, centralized, permanent bureaucracy in South Asia; rather, there was a *fragmented* state: a "temporary affiliation of a number of local groups, constituted by, or in the name of, the king and empowered to make public decisions on specific matters."[62] Tirumala Nāyaka's interventions recall what Valerie Stoker labels "manipulative pluralism" in sixteenth-century Vijayanagara ruling polity, to clarify how king Kṛṣṇadevarāya circumscribed diverse entities (such as state agents, agriculturalists, merchants, spiritual leaders, and craftspeople) for intersectarian purposes, by using religious patronage to create contexts where shared religious identities could be enacted.[63] The topic of *pūjā* as both metaphor and vehicle for shared sovereignty was examined in the previous chapter—Nicholas Dirks has analyzed how, with the decline of Vijayanagara and the ascendance of the Nāyaka kings by the early seventeenth century, the *pāḷaiyakkārar*s (who controlled forts and protected specified parts of the kingdom) were themselves invited to partake in Nāyaka sovereignty through temple rituals and the exchange of gifts, thus becoming "little kings."[64] Concomitant with this process—the gradual disappearance of Vijayanagara and the diffusion and dislocation of the exchange of sovereignty—Nāyaka kings increasingly identified themselves directly with the divine authority that guided their rule.

The Nāyaka king's involvement in the Śrī Mīṉāṭci Putu Maṇṭapam Eḻuntaruḷi Eṇṇaik Kāppu Tirumañcaṉam Cēvai (translated as 'the oil anointing ceremony and bathing ritual for Mīnākṣī in the Pudu Maṇḍapam') gives some clues as to the specific problems of government motivating his interventions in temple rituals. This Eṇṇai Kāppu Utsavam ('oil anointing festival') is a *maṇṭapappaṭi*, a ceremony embedded within a periodical festival (*utsavam*) that takes place in a *maṇḍapam*. Mīnākṣī's Eṇṇai Kāppu Utsavam is performed for nine days in Mārkaḻi month (December/January) before the presence of the *tiruvātirai* star. While visiting the Madurai temple, nineteenth-century Sanskritist Monier Monier-Williams "happened accidentally" to stumble upon this religious festival for Mīnākṣī, which he defines by its Sanskrit term, "Tailotsava," or 'oil festival':

> A coarse image of the goddess, profusely decorated with jewels and having a high head-dress of hair, was carried in the centre of a long procession on a canopied throne borne by eight Brāhmans to a platform in the magnificent hall or Maṇḍapa of the Tirumell Nāyak opposite the temple. There the ceremony of undressing the idol, removing its ornaments, anointing its head with oil, bathing, redecorating and redressing it was gone through amid shouting, singing, beating of tom-toms, waving of lights and cowries, ringing of bells, and deafening discord from forty or fifty so-called musical instruments, each played by a man who did his best to overpower the sound of all others combined. At the head of the procession was borne an image of Gaṇeśa. Then followed three elephants, a long line of priests, musicians, attendants bearing cowries and umbrellas, with a troop of dancing girls bringing up the rear.[65]

During each of the first eight days of the annual Eṇṇai Kāppu Utsavam, the bronze image of Mīnākṣī leaves her stone temple and processes to the Pudu Maṇḍapam.[66] For these first several days, Mīnākṣī's *utsava mūrti* is brought in procession every evening around six o'clock, preceded by a bullock, Pārvatī the temple elephant, and statues of Vināyaka (Gaṇeśa), and Caṇḍeśvara (form of Śiva). Accompanied by several cart pullers, three priests (*bhaṭṭār*s), four musicians, and one temple staff

Figure 2.15 Mīnākṣī enters the Pudu Maṇḍapam, 2009

Source: Photo by author.

member, it crosses East Cittirai Street, travels down Amman Sannathi Street, and turns left on East Avani Mula Street, before entering the Pudu Maṇḍapam (Figure 2.15). (Today, the long line of priests, attendants, and dancing girls described by Monier-Williams are absent, as are the shouting, singing, and "deafening discord."[67]) Once inside, the Mīnākṣī idol is placed onto the ornate black granite stage at the western end of the central space. After priests arrange the necessary items for the ritual, musicians perform.

Before a predominantly female audience, priests complete the elaborate preliminary ceremonies for the ritual bath (*tirumañcaṉam*) that occurs on the ninth day (Figure 2.16). First, the priest waves an oil lamp and a camphor-flamed lamp (*dīpārādhana*) before holding a mirror in front of Mīnākṣī. He washes her face with water, offers her a drink of water from a silver cup, and cleans her teeth with a silver toothbrush. He gives another drink of water, presents betel leaf, provides more water, and places a mirror before her (Figure 2.17). The priest waves the lamps again, removes the flower garlands around Mīnākṣī's neck, and spreads out her wig of hair. He gently rubs oil onto her hair with a flower, trims it with a razor, and combs it with a silver comb, and then he allows Mīnākṣī to admire her beauty in a mirror. This sequence of washing and grooming is repeated two more times before Mīnākṣī is dressed behind a screen and adorned with a crown. More lamps

Figure 2.16 A female audience gathers to watch Mīnākṣī's Eṇṇai Kāppu Utsavam ('oil anointing festival'), Pudu Maṇḍapam, 2009

Source: Photo by author.

Figure 2.17 The priest holds a mirror before Mīnākṣī, Pudu Maṇḍapam, 2009

Source: Photo by author.

Figure 2.18 Mīnākṣī processes through the Pudu Maṇḍapam, 2009

Source: Photo by author.

are shown, and Mīnākṣī's processional image is removed from the granite stage, placed on a cart, and carried through the Pudu Maṇḍapam's corridor followed by a bull and an elephant, circumambulating clockwise (*pradakṣiṇa*) three times (Figure 2.18). By now, the shops have closed to make room for the procession; sometimes, the procession stops to accept offerings from stall keepers who sponsored that day's ritual.

Mīnākṣī finally goes back to the granite stage in the hall's central nave where priests feed her behind a cloth screen. When the screen is lifted, lamps are waved, and a temple servant brings the camphor flame to devotees while the priest distributes *vibhūti* ('sacred ash') and flowers. During the first seven days of the festival, Mīnākṣī returns to the temple after traveling on Cittirai Street. On the eighth day, she processes in a *kōratam* ('cow car') on Avani Mula Street. On the ninth and final day, Mīnākṣī arrives in the Pudu Maṇḍapam during the early morning for her ritual bathing that entails an *abhiṣēkam* ('pouring libations on the deity') of several substances in a specific sequence: rice, incense, turmeric powder, milk, yogurt, *pañcāmirtam* (combination of milk, sugar, yogurt, clarified butter, honey, and *tulasī* leaves necessary for *pūjās*), honey, unripe coconut water,

Figure 2.19 Mīnākṣī sits in her golden palanquin, 2009

Source: Photo by author.

sandalwood paste, rose water, and holy water. Afterwards, she rests for an entire day draped in a loose red *sārī*. In the evening, after her *vastiram* ('dressing'), *alaṅkāram* ('adornment'), and *naivēdya* ('feeding'), Mīnākṣī sits in an elaborate golden palanquin (reserved for the last day) and departs for her stone temple (Figure 2.19).

Madurai temple priests characterize Eṇṇai Kāppu Utsavam as the preparation and beautification of the goddess before her marriage to Sundareśvara a few months later during Cittirai.[68] Indeed, *Tiruviḷaiyāṭal Purāṇam* I.5 dedicates several verses to Mīnākṣī's elaborate bridal makeover.[69] The local population, however, has a different understanding of the ritual: many people in Madurai consider the nine-day festival, and the one-day Poṉṉūñjal ('golden swing') festival that follows, to be a celebration of Mīnākṣī's first menstruation.[70] The fertility of the goddess is indicated by her initial menstrual flow; a menstruating woman is perceived as 'unclean' in Tamil culture, which may explain why the sacred Śaiva hymns *Tēvāram* are not sung at the temple during the ten days Mīnākṣī is believed to have her menstrual period. A menstruating woman must confine herself to a separate, closed room, thus Mīnākṣī's Eṇṇai Kāppu Utsavam takes place not in her sanctum but in the Puḍu Maṇḍapam, situated outside the east gateway of the temple complex.

In Tamil culture, the goddess's first menses is also a harbinger of agricultural success. The Pŏṉṉūñjal ritual illustrates the interconnectedness between fertility

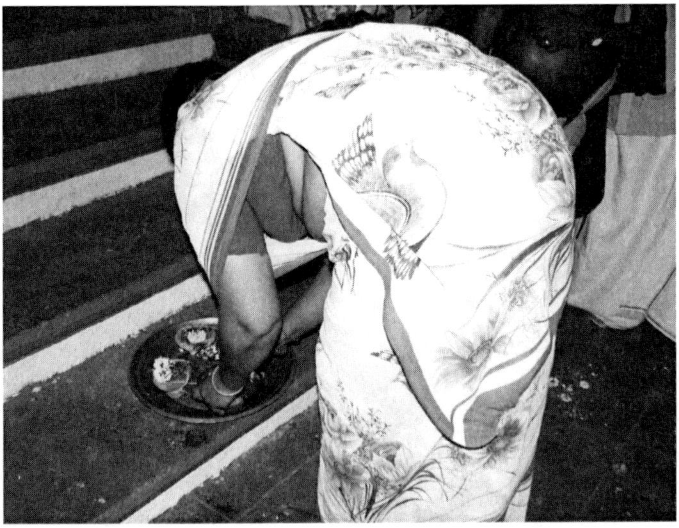

Figure 2.20 A married woman (*cumaṅkali*) sows seeds in bowls of sand, 2009

Source: Photo by author.

and farming: in Mīnākṣī's presence, *cumaṅkali*s ('married women') sow seeds in bowls of sand, and unhusked paddy, raw rice, and a grinding stone mark the stages of rice's growth, harvest, and preparation (Figures 2.20 and 2.21). C. J. Fuller underscores the gendered politics of these ritual performances: "Agricultural fertility is ritually predicated on the maturation of the goddess. Her maturation—the burgeoning of her sexual powers—is imperative for cultivation, but it is, of course, also dangerous and heating, and must, in the end, be controlled."[71] George L. Hart translated the Tamil concept of *aṇaṅku* as a "latent sacred power" that can be dangerous and thus taboo.[72] A menstruating girl in a 'heated' and impure state is typically rubbed with *ghee* (clarified butter) during her *caṭaṅku*—a puberty ceremony that marks her first menstrual cycle—an act deemed 'cooling,' similar to rubbing the body with oil before bathing.[73]

The Tamil conceptual interconnections of menstrual 'heat' and 'danger' are reiterated and reproduced in Mīnākṣī's Eṇṇai Kāppu Utsavam. In a process similar to the traditional *caṭaṅku*, oil is applied to Mīnākṣī's metal embodiment prior to her ceremonial bathing. The shower of turmeric and sandalwood paste that Mīnākṣī receives on the ninth day 'cools' her during her 'heated' state.[74] After Mīnākṣī rests in the Pudu Maṇḍapam from morning to evening on the last day of her *eṇṇaikkāppu* ritual, she is elaborately dressed and placed in a special palanquin, before traveling through the streets around her temple (Figure 2.19). This procession ends her sexual

Figure 2.21 Bowls of sand with seeds, 2009

Source: Photo by author.

maturation as an adolescent; she is now ready for her marriage to Sundareśvara during Cittirai month. In Tamil culture, a girl's first menstruation is an elaborate and festive celebration; the formal terms for *caṭaṅku—irutu maṅkalasnāṉam* ('puberty auspicious-bath') and *pūppuppuṉita nīraṭṭu viḻā* ('auspicious bathing festival for the one who has flowered')—emphasize the bathing of the pubescent girl. Rituals marking female puberty include not only the girl participating in a turmeric bath, but also processing through neighborhood streets dressed like a bride to announce publicly that she has come of age and is eligible for marriage.[75]

The form of the Eṇṇai Kāppu Utsavam ritual is also bound up in Tirumala Nāyaka's politically motivated reconfiguration of Śaiva and Vaiṣṇava rituals. The Eṇṇai Kāppu Utsavam is a Vaiṣṇava affair connected to Āṇḍāḷ, the poet, goddess, and consort of Viṣṇu in Srivilliputtur, a temple town located about 45 miles from Madurai. Tirumala Nāyaka, a Vaiṣṇava and ardent devotee of Āṇḍāḷ, brought the ritual Śrī Āṇṭāḷ Mārkaḻi Nīrāṭṭa Utsavam ('Āṇḍāḷ's ceremonial bathing festival in Mārkaḻi') to the Madurai temple, making it the only Śaiva site to conduct the oil bathing and beautification ceremony to a goddess.[76] This eight-day festival is performed during the last seven days of Mārkaḻi and the first day of Tai month, which is also the widely held Tamil harvest festival called Poṅgal (Figure 2.22). It was Tirumala's wish to have the *eṇṇaikkāppu* ritual performed for Mīnākṣī

Figure 2.22 Āṇḍāḷ's Nīrāṭṭa Utsavam ('ceremonial bathing festival'), Eṇṇai Kāppu Maṇḍapam, Āṇḍāḷ temple, Srivilliputtur, 2009

Source: Photo by author.

in the Pudu Maṇḍapam;[77] Tirumala personally attended the temple festivals he introduced, and the priests honored him as the festivals' prime benefactor.[78]

Tirumala Nāyaka's transplant of a popular Vaiṣṇava festival onto a Śaiva temple was a political technique with ecological aims. The sign of fertility held powerful sway in a dry region that suffered terrible famines if ever the rains failed, resulting, as one Jesuit missionary reported, in "corpses ... heaped up in huge piles."[79] Dennis Hudson described Mārkaḻi month as symbolizing "the pre-birth period of the universe, the moment of unmanifest plentitude ... recapitulated by every pre-dawn hour."[80] The king sought to ensure the agricultural bounty of the territory, for which plentiful rain was necessary. Tirumala appropriated a ritual from the nearby temple town of Srivilliputtur to celebrate Mīnākṣī's first menstruation in Madurai; the ritual signified the fertility of the goddess, and thus the fertility of the territory. The ruler's intervention sought to manage the harvest season and the flow of rain by managing the goddess's fertility and her flow of blood—because of the inextricable link between the two cycles, "if the rains fail ... royalty can be blamed for neglecting the proper relationships with divine powers that would normally promote fertility."[81] The Eṇṇai Kāppu Utsavam ritual thus stitched together disparate political, social, and temporal sign systems addressed to agriculture, a dominant problem of government in Nāyaka Madurai.[82]

Yoking Nāyaka authority to sacred Madurai

The Pudu Maṇḍapam is a public monument that can be studied not only as an architectural marvel and religious pilgrimage site, but also as the emergence and articulation of a Nāyaka political discourse.[83] Tirumala Nāyaka's generous sponsorship of temple expansions such as the Pudu Maṇḍapam, and the insertion of his family's portraits flanked by sculpted images of Madurai's founding legend, helped him to link Nāyaka rule to the eternal sovereignty of the goddess Mīnākṣī. *Tiruviḷaiyāṭal Purāṇam* is a seventeenth-century *talapurāṇam*, or history (*purāṇam*) of a particular sacred place (*talam*), presumably a reworking of the earlier thirteenth-century text, Perumpaṟṟapuliyūr Nampi's *Tiruvālavāyuṭaiyār Tiruviḷaiyāṭaṟpurāṇam*, by narrating the Śaiva myths chronologically and by including the names of the Pāṇḍyan kings in whose reign the miracle transpired.[84] In Madurai, Śiva is Sundareśvara who married Malayattuvacaṉ Pāṇḍya's daughter, Taṭātakai (Mīnākṣī), to provide divine protection and government of the city. Śiva infiltrates the daily lives of Madurai's rulers and inhabitants: he tricks and teaches, humbles and humiliates them.

Tamil *purāṇams* are premised on the belief that the 'sacred' is revealed in individual, localized, and worldly manifestations—tracing the form and genealogy of these manifestations is the basic subject matter of the Tamil myths.[85] The temporality of the *purāṇams* problematizes conventional notions of 'history' that dominate our contemporary conceptual vocabulary. *Tiruviḷaiyāṭal Purāṇam* appears as a history of a place (Madurai) documenting chronological events, but it concerns a cosmic temporality 'outside' of history, the mythological domain where its divinities reside. Rather than attempt to fit the *purāṇams* within frameworks of 'history' and scientific 'historicity' available in modernity, we should analyze their function from the perspective of the *place*, the Pudu Maṇḍapam. Tirumala Nāyaka and his architects, likely aided by poet and Śaiva theologian Nīlakaṇṭha Dīkṣita, seemed to regard the stories of the *purāṇams* as veridical.[86] The story of Madurai's divine origins, and its links to Pāṇḍyan rulers, are inseparable from the Pudu Maṇḍapam's sculptural layout and corresponding spatial and architectural imagination: the temple itself is a technique of narrative, an extension and interpretation of the *purāṇam*. The processional route that guides the devotee's *movement* through the temple also guides their *reading* of the text encoded in the sacred architecture. Movement, in this way, becomes the mechanism by which the devotee participates in the performance of sovereignty: the temple, and the city built around it, are constructed in concentric rings coinciding with the ritual of circumambulation.

The sacred architecture of the Pudu Maṇḍapam offers profound insight into the political technologies of the Nāyaka historical drama, of which the Nāyaka kings were leading actors. Scenes from *Tiruviḷaiyāṭal Purāṇam* are located on the ceiling of the central nave near the Nāyaka family lineage, in elevated niches along the perimeter of the central nave where Nāyaka-period rituals occur, and in the processional aisle surrounding the nave that the deities circumambulate during Nāyaka-initiated ceremonies. Crispin Branfoot elucidates the triangular axis linking the god, the king, and the devotee at the moment of the festival ritual:

> ... this is a three-cornered relationship between god, king and devotee. Not only do the god and king greet each other, but the priests, devotees or worshippers see both the king and the deity greeting each other when the two are assembled for a festival. A king, a frequently inaccessible figure in his palace, is given permanent presence in the temple in a life-size representation and in locations there that are widely accessible and visible. At festival periods the king's relationship with the temple's deities is seen by worshippers, a relationship crucial to the welfare of the kingdom.... The Nayaka is depicted as the protector, devoted servant and regent of the deities.[87]

The identity of the king is thus yoked to the identity of Madurai itself: between the portraits of Viśvanātha and Tirumala (the founder of the Madurai Nāyakas and the sponsor of the Pudu Maṇḍapam, respectively) is a low-relief ceiling panel with

Figure 2.23 Ceiling panel in the central nave, Pudu Maṇḍapam

Source: Photo by author.

Figure 2.24 A scene from *Tiruviḷaiyāṭal Purāṇam*, Pudu Maṇḍapam

Source: Photo by author.

three images that denote the establishment of the Madurai temple—the Ālavāy snake encircling Mīnākṣī, an enshrined *liṅgam*, and a *kaṭampu* tree (Figure 2.23). In *Tiruviḷaiyāṭal Purāṇam*, Indra discovers a Śiva *liṅgam* in the *kaṭampu* tree forest of Madurai (I.2); Pāṇḍyan king Kulacēkaraṉ (Mīnākṣī's grandfather) constructed a temple encircling this *liṅgam* (I.3), around which a city was built.[88] At the request of the Pāṇḍyan ruler who wanted to know the boundaries of his city, Śiva deployed a serpent to encircle Madurai by bringing its mouth and tail together (III.49).[89] High up along the perimeter of this central nave are sixty-four bas-relief friezes carved in the granite depicting Śiva's cosmic plays (*viḷaiyāṭal*s), his exploits as lord Sundareśvara alongside Pāṇḍyan rulers in Madurai (Figure 2.24).[90] The processional aisle that surrounds this nave exhibits some principal scenes from *Tiruviḷaiyāṭal Purāṇam,* including the battle between Mīnākṣī and Śiva in *Tiruviḷaiyāṭal Purāṇam* I.4 and their marriage in *Tiruviḷaiyāṭal Purāṇam* I.5. Episodes from *Tiruviḷaiyāṭal Purāṇam* are mapped onto the hall as the aesthetic loci of the religio-civic activity of the Madurai Nāyakas.

Tirumala Nāyaka built the Pudu Maṇḍapam for mass public ritual performances among the ubiquitous presence of sculpted stories from the *purāṇam*: since the seventeenth century, bronze images of Mīnākṣī and Sundareśvara are carried past the gallery of stone Nāyaka portraits at the beginning and end of annual festivities, while the Nāyakas symbolically propitiate them from on high. The Nāyakas' shared sovereignty with Mīnākṣī and Sundareśvara entailed a link between the eternal temporality of Mīnākṣī and Sundareśvara and the worldly temporality of Nāyaka kings, mediated by twin cycles: the circumambulation of the immortal gods, and the seasonal festivals in which the living Nāyaka kings performed an active role. Mīnākṣī's Eṇṇai Kāppu Utsavam, a ritual brought by Tirumala Nāyaka to Madurai from Srivilliputtur, and the Poṉṉūñjal that follows in the main temple, became an important mechanism for the king's stewardship of Madurai's environs, and ascribed to him the divine responsibility for the region's agricultural prosperity. In this way, the goddess with localized specificity and significance became a necessary partner for an ambitious monarch. Today, the Pudu Maṇḍapam at the Mīnākṣī-Sundareśvara temple is a living artifact of this game of sovereignty—connecting the present to the seventeenth century, when the Nāyaka king symbolically married his dynasty to Madurai.

Notes

1. P. Jayaraman (joint commissioner and executive officer, Hindu Religious and Charitable Endowments Department, Mīṉākṣī-Sundareśvara temple, Madurai), in interview with author, July 25, 2011.
2. J. P. Lasrado Shenoy, *Madura: The Temple City*, 2nd ed. (Madras: Associated Printers Ltd., 1955 [1937]), 43.
3. For a general discussion of this process, see R. Mahalakshmi, *The Making of the Goddess-Koṟṟavai-Durgā in the Tamil Traditions* (New Delhi: Penguin Books, 2011), 2–36.
4. K. Palaniappan, *The Great Temple of Madurai* (Madurai: Sri Meenakshisundareswarar Temple Renovation Committee, 1970 [1963]), 89–90.
5. A. V. Jeyechandrun, *The Madurai Temple Complex (With Special Reference to Literature and Legends)* (Madurai: Publications Division, Madurai Kamaraj University, 1985), 89.
6. Jeyechandrun, *The Madurai Temple Complex*, 30. In another account, while Parañcōti Muṉivar was visiting the Madurai temple, Mīṉākṣī appeared in a vision and instructed him to praise the holy games of Śiva in verse. See William P. Harman, *The Sacred Marriage of a Hindu Goddess* (Bloomington: Indiana University Press, 1989), 27–28.
7. The etymology is unclear. It could mean "irresistible valor" according to D. Dennis Hudson, "Two Citrā Festivals in Madurai," in *Religious Festivals in South India and Sri Lanka*, ed. Guy R. Welbon and Glenn E. Yocum (New Delhi: Manohar, 1982), 101–156, 109, or refer to the goddess's hand (*kai*), which does not ward off (*taṭu*) her devotees, according to William P. Harman, *The Sacred Marriage of a Hindu Goddess* (Bloomington: Indiana University Press, 1989), 24.
8. The Pāṇḍyan dynasty was one of three royal lineages of south India: the Pāṇḍyas, Cōḻas, and Cēras comprised a triumvirate known as the Mūvēntar, or

'Three Crowned Kings,' in ancient Tamil country. The Pāṇḍyas made Madurai their imperial headquarters.

9. Parañcōti Muṉivar, *Tiruviḷaiyāṭar Purāṇam*: *Maturaikkāṇṭam* (Tamiḻ), ed. and comm. Cokkaliṅkam Ceṭṭiyar (Maturai: Mīṉāṭci Cuntarēcuvarar Tirukkōyil, 1973), I.4: vv. 525–537, pp. 124–126 (hereafter *TVP*).
10. *TVP* I.4: v. 543, p. 128.
11. *TVP* I.4: v. 543, p. 128.
12. *TVP* I.4: v. 553, p. 131.
13. *TVP* I.4: vv. 554–559, pp. 132–133.
14. *TVP* I.4: vv. 582–599, pp. 138–142.
15. *TVP* I.5: vv. 602–604, pp. 143–144.
16. *TVP* I.5: vv. 605–639, pp. 144–151.
17. *TVP* I.5: vv. 640–643, pp. 152–153.
18. David Dean Shulman, *Tamil Temple Myths: Sacrifice and Divine Marriage in the South Indian Śaiva Tradition* (Princeton: Princeton University Press, 1980), 209–211; Wendy Doniger O'Flaherty, *The Origins of Evil in Hindu Mythology* (Berkeley and Los Angeles: University of California Press, 1976), 341–342; and P. Spratt, *Hindu Culture and Personality: A Psycho-Analytic Study* (Bombay: Manaktalas, 1966), 268.
19. For an analysis of the various interpretations of Mīnākṣī's transformation, see Harman, *The Sacred Marriage of a Hindu Goddess*, 49.
20. *Aṣṭadikpāla*s, or eight guardians of the directions, are known in Hinduism as the deities who rule specific directions: north (Kubera), south (Yama), east (Indra), west (Varuṇa), northeast (Īśāna), southeast (Agni), northwest (Vāyu) and Southwest (Nirṛti). The northeast direction represents prosperity and knowledge.
21. Shulman, *Tamil Temple Myths*, 138–294. See also Mahalakshmi, *The Making of the Goddess-Koṟṟavai-Durgā in the Tamil Traditions*, 34.
22. Shulman, *Tamil Temple Myths*, 139.
23. C. J. Fuller, "The Divine Couple's Relationship in a South Indian Temple: Mīnākṣī and Sundareśvara at Madurai," *History of Religions* 19, no. 4 (May 1980): 321–348, 344.
24. *TVP* I.5: vv. 793–795, pp. 197–198.
25. *TVP* I.5: v. 644, p. 153.
26. *TVP* I.5: vv. 645–670, pp. 153–162.
27. *TVP* I.5: vv. 712–714, pp. 176; *TVP* I.5: vv. 722–742, pp. 179–185.
28. *TVP* I.5: vv. 747–770, pp. 186–191.
29. *TVP* I.5: vv. 771–777, pp. 192–193.
30. *TVP* I.6: vv. 799–826, pp. 199–206.

31. See Paul Younger, *The Home of the Dancing Śivan: The Traditions of the Hindu Temple in Citamparam* (New York and Oxford: Oxford University Press, 1995), 90. This kind of depiction is also associated with the Vaṭāraṇyēśvarar temple, Tiruvalangadu, when Kālī lost a dance challenge to Śiva, who retrieved a fallen earring with his toe and affixed it while dancing. Naṭarāja dances on his right foot on a *poṉṉampalam* ('golden hall') at Cidambaram and on his left foot on a *veḷḷiyampalam* ('silver hall') in Madurai. In *TVP* I.24, the Pāṇḍyan king of Madurai pleads with Śiva to switch his dancing leg from right to left, and relieve the left leg by lifting his right leg. See R. K. K. Rajarajan and Jeyapriya Rajarajan, *Mīnākṣī-Sundareśvara: Tiruviḷaiyāṭaṟ Purāṇam in Letters, Design and Art* (Delhi: Sharada Publishing House, 2013), 28.
32. Parañcōti Muṉivar, *Parañcōtimuṉivar Aruḷicceyta Tiruviḷaiyāṭaṟ Purāṇam: Kūṭaṟkāṇṭam* (Tamiḻ), comm. Naṭukkāvēri Mu. Vēṅkaṭacāmi Nāṭṭār (Ceṉṉai: Tirunelvēlit Teṉṉintiya Caivacittānta Nūṟpatippuk Kaḻakam, Limiṭeṭ, 1969 [1928]), II.45: vv. 1–63, pp. 451–477; II.46: vv. 1–18, pp. 478–486.
33. Cellinakar Perumpaṟṟapuliyūr Nampi, *Tiruvālavāyuṭaiyār Tiruviḷaiyāṭaṟpurāṇam* (Tamiḻ), comm. U. Vē. Cāminātaiyar (Ceṉṉai: Kapīr Accukkūṭattiṟ Patippikkappeṟṟatu, 1972 [1906]), 263–266.
34. *TVP* I.3: vv. 472–518, pp. 112–122.
35. *TVP* II.47: vv. 1–23, pp. 487–496.
36. *TVP* II.21: vv. 1–29, pp. 27–40.
37. Jeyechandrun, *The Madurai Temple Complex*, 92–93. The historical chronicle of the priests at the Mīṉākṣī-Sundareśvara temple, Madurai, states that Tirumala Nāyaka, advised by Ayya Dīkṣita, established an endowment so that episodes of the *Tiruviḷaiyāṭal Purāṇam* could be performed. See *Maturai Stāṉikar Varalāṟu* (Tamiḻ), *Centamiḻ* 5 (1906–1907): 87–95, 141–148, 220–222, 261–272, 294–300 (Maturai: Maturait Tamiḻccaṅka Muttirācālai, 1907), 270. It is unclear who Ayya is, although Jeyechandrun identifies him as seventeenth-century poet-philosopher Nīlakaṇṭha Dīkṣita, which aligns with the opinion of the Madurai temple priests.

    For a discussion of how public performances of the *Tiruviḷaiyāṭal Purāṇam*, as interpreted and rendered by various sectarian communities, reveals that Hindu pluralism was predominantly a spatial phenomenon, see "The Language Games of Śiva: Mapping Text and Space in Public Religious Culture," in Elaine M. Fisher, *Hindu Pluralism: Religion and the Public Sphere in Early Modern South India* (Oakland: University of California Press, 2017), 137–182.
38. Fuller, "The Divine Couple's Relationship," 323, 326–332.
39. I witnessed the Cittirai festival from May 5 to 9, 2017.

40. D. Devakunjari, *Madurai through the Ages: From the Earliest Times to 1801 A.D.* (Madras: Society for Archaeological, Historical, and Epigraphical Research, 1979), 303–305; R. Nagaswamy, *Tantric Cult of South India* (Delhi: Agam Kala Prakashan, 1982), 195–197.

 These days, the chairman of the Board of Trustees at the Mīnākṣī-Sundareśvara temple receives the royal scepter from the temple priest. With the *cenkōl* in hand, the temple chairman goes in procession with priests, musicians, and devotees around the second corridor (*prākāram*) of Svāmi Caṉṉiti near Śiva's shrine, before placing the scepter beside the deity, symbolizing the transfer of power from lord Sundareśvara to goddess Mīnākṣī. When I attended Mīnākṣī's *paṭṭābhiṣēkam* on May 5, 2017, Temple Board chairman Karumuttu T. Kannan (industrialist and chief executive officer at Thiagarajar Mills Limited, Madurai) accepted the *cenkōl*.

41. This spectacle of power evokes what Clifford Geertz noted in his examination of nineteenth-century Balinese state polity that emphasized the centrality of ritual displays to sovereignty:

> It was a theatre state in which kings and princes were impresarios, the priests the directors, and the peasants the supporting cast, stage crew, and audience ... court ceremonialism was the driving force of court politics; and mass ritual was not a device to shore up the state, but rather the state ... was a device for the enactment of mass ritual. Power served pomp, not pomp power. (Clifford Geertz, *Negara: The Theatre State in Nineteenth-Century Bali* [Princeton: Princeton University Press, 1980], 13)

 About mythic time and historic time, see Velcheru Narayana Rao, "Purāṇa as Brahminic Ideology," in *Purāṇa Perennis: Reciprocity and Transformation in Hindu and Jain Texts*, ed. Wendy Doniger (Albany: State University of New York, 1993), 85–100.

42. C. J. Fuller, *The Camphor Flame: Popular Hinduism and Society in India* (Princeton: Princeton University Press, 1992), 42.

43. Caleb Simmons, "The Goddess on the Hill: The (Re)Invention of a Local Hill Goddess as Chamundeshvari," in *Inventing and Reinventing the Goddess: Contemporary Iterations of Hindu Deities on the Move*, ed. Sree Padma (Lanham, MD: Lexington Books, 2014), 217–244. Cāmuṇḍā is associated with Kālī, the fierce form of Pārvatī.

44. Ritual performance, as Anne T. Mocko observed in her study of Nepal's Hindu monarchy, has the capacity to announce relationships between the king and the goddess. See chapter 5, "Reinforcement Rituals II: Gaining the Goddess's Blessing," in Anne T. Mocko, *Demoting Vishnu: Ritual, Politics, and the Unraveling of Nepal's Hindu Monarchy* (New York: Oxford University Press, 2016), 120–144.

45. Nagaswamy, *Tantric Cult of South India*, 195, 197.
46. The second most important temple festival after Cittirai is the twelve-day Āvaṇi Mūla during Āvaṇi (August/September), which includes Sundareśvara's coronation on day seven as well as enactments of *Tiruviḷaiyāṭal Purāṇam* on the eighth and ninth days. While both festivals revolve around rulership, Sundareśvara 'becomes' king after his marriage to Mīṉākṣī.
47. Actually, Sōmāskanda.
48. Here, the ritual differs from the text: in *TVP*, Mīṉākṣī returns alone.
49. The original wedding hall, or Tirukkalyāṇam Maṇḍapam, can no longer hold the thousands of people who now attend.
50. Sekhar Bhattar (priest, Mīṉākṣī-Sundareśvara temple, Madurai), in text message to author, January 11, 2021. Priests claim that wearing a headgear during the wedding ceremony began with Tirumala Nāyaka, and therefore perceive the style as Nāyaka. However, the turban appears more like the headgear of the Marāthās, warriors from western India with a powerful presence in south Indian politics from mid-seventeenth to mid-eighteenth centuries. Lennart Bes attributes the shift to Marāṭhā-style clothing to Madurai ruler Muttu Vīrappa Nāyaka III (r. 1682–1689 CE). See Lennart Bes, "Sultan among Dutchmen? Royal Dress at Court Audiences in South India, as Portrayed in Local Works of Art and Dutch Embassy Reports, Seventeenth–Eighteenth Centuries," *Modern Asian Studies* 50, no. 6 (2016): 1792–1845, 1793–1794.
51. Senthil Bhattar (priest, Mīṉākṣī-Sundareśvara temple, Madurai), in interview with author, January 7, 2009.
52. Dennis Hudson, "Śiva, Mīṉākṣī, Viṣṇu—Reflections on a Popular Myth in Madurai," *Indian Economic and Social History Review* 14, no. 1 (January 1977): 107–118. I witnessed Aḻakar's journey on May 9, 2017, as he made his way to Madurai stopping at each *maṇṭapappaṭi* (halting place for a deity in a festival procession) along Alakar Kovil Road to receive and take *darśan* from his devotees (Etir Cēvai), accompanied by beating drums, bursting firecrackers, and enthusiastic dancing.
53. Sekhar Bhattar, in interview with author, June 1, 2017; N. Parameswaran Unni, *Nilakantha Diksita* (New Delhi: Sahitya Akademi, 1995), 15, 18.
54. William Taylor, "The Accounts of Tirumali-Naicker, and of His Buildings (As Extracted, for Information, from Written Authorities)," in *Oriental Historical Manuscripts, in the Tamil Language*, vol. II, ed. and trans. William Taylor (Madras: Printed and Published by Charles Josiah Taylor, 1835), 147–155, 149–150. Vaiṣṇavas felt the image declared Śiva's supremacy over Viṣṇu. Senthil Bhattar, interview, January 7, 2009.
55. Hudson, "Śiva, Mīṉākṣī, Viṣṇu," 112.
56. Parvathi Menon, "Agrarian Economy of the Carnatic in the 17th and 18th Centuries" (PhD diss., Aligarh Muslim University, 1986), 47–48.

57. Nicholas B. Dirks, *The Hollow Crown: Ethnohistory of an Indian Kingdom* (Cambridge: Cambridge University Press, 1987), 45.
58. In the story that purportedly describes events during his reign, Tirumala Nāyaka hires Maturaivīraṉ to subdue the Kaḷḷar. When Maturaivīraṉ succeeds in protecting Madurai's bazaar from Kaḷḷar looters, the Nāyaka king rewards him with dancing girls. Maturaivīraṉ falls in love with one of them and tries to elope with her, disguised as a Kaḷḷar. Failing to recognize Maturaivīraṉ, Tirumala orders his limbs amputated. Once the true identity of the "thief" is known, Tirumala prays to goddess Mīṉākṣī to have the arm and leg restored. After Maturaivīraṉ commits suicide, Tirumala builds a shrine that initiated the worship of Maturaivīraṉ in Madurai. See David [Dean] Shulman, "On South Indian Bandits and Kings," *The Indian Economic and Social History Review* 17, no. 3 (July 1980): 283–306, 283–297, and *The King and the Clown in South Indian Myth and Poetry* (Princeton: Princeton University Press, 1985), 355–366.
59. P. A. Narayani, "King Thirumalai Nayak and the Kallar connection," *The Hindu*, August 24, 2020, https://www.thehindu.com/news/cities/Madurai/king-thirumalai-nayak-and-the-kallar-connection/article32431472.ece, accessed December 14, 2021. Of the three copperplate charters dated 1645, 1655, and 1656, the 1655 grant is most significant. It states that Tirumala Nāyaka awarded a Kaḷḷar leader the name of "Tirumalai," the headmanship of several provinces, and objects related to administering justice: blanket, bronze vessel, and wooden sandals. See Louis Dumont, *A South Indian Subcaste: Social Organization and Religion of the Pramalai Kallar*, trans. M. Moffat, L. and A. Morton (Oxford and New York: Oxford University Press, 1986), 22–23, 155–156, 467–470, and Stuart H. Blackburn, "The Kallars: A Tamil 'Criminal Tribe' Reconsidered," *South Asia: Journal of South Asian Studies* 1, no. 1 (1978): 38–51, 40–41. The Government of Tamil Nadu's Department of Archaeology published details about these three copperplate grants. See Naṭaṉa Kācinātaṉ, Cu. Irācakōpāl, Ve. Vētācalam (eds.), *Tirumalaināyakkar Ceppēṭukaḷ* (Tamiḻ) (Ceṉṉai: Tamiḻnāṭu Aracu Tolporuḷ Āyvutturai, 1994). In 1640, Tirumala Nāyaka granted the Kaḷḷar of Melur (near Madurai) *māṉiyam* (land gift) and the right to collect *kāvali* (protection fees) for their previous service in safeguarding that area from robbery and violence. See J. H. Nelson, *The Madura Country: A Manual Compiled by Order of the Madras Government* (Madras: Asylum Press by William Thomas, 1868), Part II: 47–48.
60. R. Sathyanatha Aiyar, *History of the Nayaks of Madura*, introduction by S. Krishnaswami Aiyangar (Madras: Oxford University Press, 1924), 130. The Nāyakas manned their forces with primarily Kaḷḷar and Maṟava warriors. See Susan Bayly, *Saints, Goddesses, and Kings: Muslims and Christians in South Indian Society, 1700–1900* (Cambridge: Cambridge University Press, 1989), 23.

61. Arjun Appadurai, *Worship and Conflict under Colonial Rule: A South Indian Case* (Cambridge: Cambridge University Press, 1981), 226.
62. Appadurai, *Worship and Conflict under Colonial Rule*, 214–215.
63. Valerie Stoker, *Polemics and Patronage in the City of Victory: Vyāsatīrtha, Hindu Sectarianism, and the Sixteenth-Century Vijayanagara Court* (Oakland: University of California Press, 2016), 142.
64. Dirks, *The Hollow Crown*, 104–106.
65. Sir Monier Monier-Williams, *Brāhmanism and Hindūism; or, Religious Thought and Life in India, as Based on the Veda and Other Sacred Books of the Hindūs*, 4th ed. (London: John Murray, 1891), 442–443.
66. I observed and documented Mīṉākṣī's Eṇṇai Kāppu Utsavam from January 1 to 9, 2009.
67. The Devadasi Abolition Act of 1947 eliminated the dancing performances of *devadāsī*s, or eternally auspicious women (*nittyacumaṅkali*s), who were married to the god. Prior to the 1947 Act, these women's main role was to dance during Mīṉākṣī's principal festivals such as the Āṭi Muḷaikoṭṭu, Navarāttiri Kōlāṭṭa, and Eṇṇai Kāppu as well as in front of halls during processions on the city streets. See C. J. Fuller, *Servants of the Goddess: The Priests of a South Indian Temple* (Cambridge: Cambridge University Press, 1984), 40–41.
68. Senthil Bhattar, interview, January 7, 2009.
69. *TVP* I.5: vv. 754–763, pp. 188–190.
70. The temple festival Āṭi Pūram (which coincides with the Tamil festival Āṭipperakku that celebrates the monsoons and water's life-giving properties) seems to also mark the goddess's menstruation. It is celebrated during Āṭi month (July/August) when the first crop is sown and transplanted, and when the rivers rise in Tamil Nadu. Here, Mīṉākṣī is worshipped as the goddess of rivers and the soil. See Fuller, "Divine Couple's Relationship," 333.
71. Fuller, "Divine Couple's Relationship," 333.
72. George L. Hart III, "Women and the Sacred in Ancient Tamilnad," *Journal of Asian Studies* 32, no. 2 (February 1973): 233–250, 236.
73. Brenda E. F. Beck, "Colour and Heat in South Indian Ritual," *Man* 4, no. 4 (December 1969): 553–572, 562.
74. For a discussion of turmeric and sandalwood paste as cooling, see Dennis B. McGilvray, *Symbolic Heat: Gender, Health & Worship among the Tamils of South India and Sri Lanka* (Ahmedabad: Mapin Publishing Pvt. Ltd.; Boulder: University of Colorado Museum, 1998), 25, 27, 35.
75. See Anthony Good, *The Female Bridegroom: A Comparative Study of Life-Crisis Rituals in South India and Sri Lanka* (Oxford: Clarendon Press, 1991), 97–110, and Karin Kapadia, *Siva and Her Sisters: Gender, Caste, and Class in Rural South India* (Boulder, CO: Westview Press, 1995), 92–123.

76. For a detailed explanation of Śrī Āṇṭāḷ Mārkaḻi Nīrāṭṭa Utsavam, see chapter 8, "Mārgaḻi, Morning Rituals, and Matrimony," in Gita V. Pai, "Kingship, Images, and Rituals: A Nāyaka Monument in South India, 1635–2009" (PhD diss., University of California, Berkeley, 2010): 274–338.
77. Senthil Bhattar, interview, January 7, 2009.
78. Jeyechandrun, *The Madurai Temple Complex*, 119. A discussion about honoring sponsors of temple rituals follows in the Epilogue.
79. Velcheru Narayana Rao, David Shulman, and Sanjay Subrahmanyam, *Symbols of Substance: Court and State in Nāyaka Period Tamilnadu* (Delhi and Oxford: Oxford University Press, 1998), 112.
80. Dennis Hudson, "Āṇṭāḷ's Desire," in *Vaiṣṇavī: Women and the Worship of Krishna,* ed. Steven J. Rosen (New Delhi: Motilal Banarsidass Publishers, 1996), 171–209, 181.
81. William Harman, "How the Fearsome Fish-Eyed Queen Mīṉāṭci Became a Perfectly Ordinary Goddess," in *Goddesses Who Rule*, ed. Elisabeth Benard and Beverly Moon (Oxford and New York: Oxford University Press, 2000), 33–50, 35.
82. Roy A. Rappaport proposes that ritual actions are performed in order to produce a practical result on the "external" or natural world. To him, ritual is "the performance of more or less invariant sequences of formal acts and utterances not entirely encoded by the performers," which nevertheless function to communicate and transmit ideas about ecology and a community's relationship to their environment. An ecology produces various templates of how to live and act in the world, which are circumscribed by social and cultural forms always and already present within that space. Rappaport thus calls the ritual "the social act basic to humanity": the ritual emerges as a necessary mechanism for negotiating the complex interconnections of social and ecological processes. See Roy A. Rappaport, *Ecology, Meaning, and Religion* (Richmond, CA: North Atlantic Books, 1979), 27–42, and *Ritual and Religion in the Making of Humanity* (Cambridge: Cambridge University Press, 1999), 23–68 (In his work on the Maring people of New Guinea, Rappaport theorizes that the Maring maintain balance in their ecosystem through traditional ecological knowledge rooted in ritual regulations. While the Maring people slaughtered pigs within a ritual framework out of an ecological imperative, it is their belief that rituals regulate the environment—not their swine-killing practice—which is important to this chapter.). See also Vijaya Rettakudi Nagarajan, "The Earth as Goddess Bhū Devī: Toward a Theory of 'Embedded Ecologies' in Folk Hinduism," in *Purifying the Earthly Body of God: Religion and Ecology in Hindu India*, ed. Lance E. Nelson (Albany: State University of New York Press, 1998), 269–295 (In her work on women's ritual art tradition in Tamil Nadu called *kōlam*, Nagarajan proposes the concept of

"embedded ecologies" as a way of understanding how beliefs about ecology and practices of relating to ecology become embedded in "social" and "cultural" forms, especially in religious and aesthetic practices and institutions. This concept does not assume a conservationist or "harmonious" relationship with some "idealized" nature—rather, it seeks to illustrate how "ecological practices and beliefs are situated in a matrix of larger cultural ideas and practices" that themselves require careful deconstruction and historical contextualization [280–281].).

83. Here, I draw on geographer Nuala Johnson, "Cast in Stone: Monuments, Geography, and Nationalism," *Environment and Planning D: Society and Space* 13, no. 1 (1995): 51–65, 62.
84. Kamil Veith Zvelebil, *Tamil Literature* (Wiesbaden, Germany: Otto Harrassowitz, 1974), 178–180.
85. Shulman, *Tamil Temple Myths*, 88.
86. For a discussion on Nīlakaṇṭha Dīkṣita, see Fisher, *Hindu Pluralism*.
87. Crispin Branfoot, "Heroic Rulers and Devoted Servants: Performing Kingship in the Tamil Temple," in *Portraiture in South Asia since the Mughals: Art, Presentation and History*, ed. Crispin Branfoot (London and New York: I. B. Tauris & Co., 2018), 165–197, 170, 173.
88. *TVP* I.2: vv. 441–471, pp. 104–111; *TVP* I.3: vv. 472–518, pp. 112–122.
89. Parañcōti Muṉivar, *Parañcōtimuṉivar Aruḷicceyta Tiruviḷaiyāṭaṟ Purāṇam: Tiruvālavāykkāṇṭam* (Tamil), comm. Naṭukkāvēri Mu. Vēṅkaṭacāmi Nāṭṭār; (Tirunelvēli: Tirunelvēlit Teṉṉintiya Caivacittānta Nūṟpatippuk Kaḻakam, Limiṭeṭ, 1965 [1931]), III.49, pp. 1–13.
90. Since these panels have not been well conserved (unlike other parts of the temple), the alcoves of the Kiḷikkūṭṭu Maṇḍapam, located in front of the doorway that leads to the goddess's shrine, depict sculpturally what some of these scenes would have looked like. Sekhar Bhattar, interview, June 1, 2017.

Part II

Colonial Gazes

3

Imagining Civilization

Antiquarian Curiosities in Madura

Introduction

The 1792 edition of *Archaeologia*, the journal of the Society of Antiquaries of London, contained articles on many familiar topics: artifacts discovered at Bath, observations on Canterbury Cathedral, the stalls in Maidstone Church—but the last entry in the issue was an anomalous one. Adam Blackader, a British surgeon working in Madurai (often called "Madura" in colonial records), submitted a letter titled "The Great Pagoda of Madura, and the Choultry of Trimul Naik"—the earliest detailed description of the Mīnākṣī-Sundareśvara temple and its Pudu Maṇḍapam to appear in a British journal, and one of only two Indian architectural subjects recorded by the Society of Antiquaries in the late eighteenth century.[1]

This seminal letter about the temple (labeled a "pagoda" by the British) and its "choultry" (the British name for halls like the Pudu Maṇḍapam), as well as the accompanying drawings and model of the hall, reveal how certain private interests shaped scientific knowledge about India through the formation of academic 'collections' in Britain.[2] The *Archaeologia* issue is one of the first European attempts to analyze the aesthetics of Drāviḍa or south Indian Hindu temple architecture.[3] Blackader's appraisal of the "great choultry of Trimul Naik" contributed to a burgeoning attentiveness towards Indian monuments among wealthy antiquarian enthusiasts during the late eighteenth century that centered on curiosity toward 'exotic' native architecture. Scholars in Britain and military and civil servants in British India expressed fascination, admiration, and respect for India—they were nevertheless involved in the process of *defining* India in such a way that made possible the exercise of power. It was this scientific research that rendered colonization both viable and *rational*, because 'India' became a kind of object that could be rationally analyzed and understood, and thus broken apart, deconstructed, and then reconstructed in the image of the Enlightenment.

Amartya Sen assigned three categories of methods of analyzing India and its traditions.[4] The "exoticist" approach concentrated on the "wondrous aspects" of

India, emphasizing what is *strange* and *unfamiliar*. The "magisterial" approach related directly to the exercise of imperial power, and is concerned with the cultural superiority of British civilization for the purpose of justifying British paternalism and domination. The "curatorial" approach was the classification and exhibition of diverse aspects of Indian culture, without necessarily prioritizing what is 'strange.' All three forms of scholarship—the exoticist, the magisterial, and the curatorial—were evident in eighteenth-century British discourse on the Mīnākṣī-Sundareśvara temple and the Pudu Maṇḍapam; the works of surgeon Adam Blackader, naturalist Joseph Banks, and philologist William Jones illustrate how British social science provided the discursive and ideological scaffolding for colonial rule in south India.

The East India Company and the Society of Antiquaries

Little is known about Adam Blackader, except that he worked in Madurai in the 1780s as a resident surgeon for the English East India Company. The East India Company started in the early seventeenth century as a small trading company searching for a slice of the spice trade in the "East Indies," the archipelagos east of the Indian subcontinent. When the Company encountered opposition from the Dutch, who had firm commercial grasp of the Indonesian islands, the British traders settled in India to move textiles, indigo, saltpeter, and spices. In the mid-eighteenth century, the ambitious company protected its mercantile endeavors and economic investments by operating increasingly as an early modern government: its corporate clients employed direct military action and political interference, penetrated local governing authorities, and acquired more land and territorial control.[5] The East India Company, which laid the foundations of the British empire in India, was organized into three coastal 'presidencies' (administrative units): Bengal, Bombay, and Madras.[6] Calcutta in Bengal was the seat of the governor-general and the Government of India.

With the East India Company's shift to military and political administration, a new cohort of civil servants, army officers, surveyors, engineers, and surgeons voyaged to India to seek their fortune. Blackader was stationed as a surgeon in Madura (the British name for Madurai) in the Madras Presidency, about 300 miles south of the Madras headquarters at Fort St George. He was so completely awed at the temple town's monuments that he felt moved to write a letter to his friend Sir Joseph Banks, a prominent member of the Society of Antiquaries, renowned botanist, world traveler, and Royal Society president.[7] Banks read the letter at the Society of Antiquaries of London meeting on July 2, 1789.[8]

The Society of Antiquaries began as informal meetings among well-heeled and well-educated men who discussed historical and genealogical work in a coffeehouse or tavern; the Society was eventually formalized in 1707. The minutes of the Society's first meeting recorded that the "Business of this Society shall be limited to the subject of Antiquities; and more particularly, to such things as may Illustrate and Relate to the History of Great Britain."[9] Members paid an admission fee and annual contribution, and the Society was comprised of

> nobles and Gentlemen meeting in Order to Improve and Cultivate the History and Antiquities of Great Britain; wherein many most excellent Monuments are still to be found, which for want of due Care, go more and more to decay and Ruin.[10]

By 1717, the Society had expanded its agenda: it would collect, print, disseminate, and keep copies of valuable British relics to preserve them for future generations.[11] In the course of the eighteenth century, while many ancient buildings in London were being razed in the name of urban improvement, antiquarian sentiments prompted the Society to gather and publish engravings and etchings of Great Britain's metropolitan topography for the sake of historical preservation.[12]

The Society operated according to a conceptual framework that located 'history' in the material substance of relics: the impetus for antiquarian activities germinated in a modern industrial society where preserving physical artifacts of 'the past' could work to save the present. As self-proclaimed 'guardians' of ancient artifacts, the Society protected the past by making its material substance visible and permanent in the 'contemporary' imagination. The Society incorporated a Royal Charter in 1751, whose opening lines attempted to more clearly define the study of "antiquity":

> ... Whereas the study of Antiquity, and the History of former times, has ever been esteemed highly commendable and useful, not only to improve the minds of men, but also to incite them to virtuous and noble actions, and such as may hereafter render them famous and worthy examples to late posterity ... there shall be for ever hereafter a Society, which shall be called by the name of *The Society of Antiquaries of London*....[13]

A loose definition of "antiquity" arises from this Charter. They are objects of considerable age and links to the past; the study and knowledge of these antiquities not only advances scientific thought ("improve[s] the minds of men") but also encourages philanthropy ("incite[s] them to virtuous and noble actions"). In accordance with this sentiment, the Society of Antiquaries published in 1770 the first volume of *Archaeologia, or, Miscellaneous Tracts Relating to Antiquity*, a periodical collection of miscellaneous papers presented at its meetings. Richard Gough, the Society's director from 1771 to 1798, oversaw the publication of *Archaeologia*, and in the introduction to the first volume, Gough proposed a conceptual distinction between "history" and "antiquity," which were effectively synonymous in the 1751 charter. Whereas a historian attends to the "arrangement and proper use of facts ... a regular and elaborate inquiry into every ancient record and proof, that can elucidate or establish them," Gough writes, the antiquarian "supplies materials to those who have sagacity or leisure to extract from the common mass whatever may answer useful purposes." Because of this, the antiquarian "will never be deemed an unserviceable member of the community." The point that Gough makes is that since the antiquarian's work advances the whole of civilization and is beneficial to society, it should be seen as a form of 'community service.' A significant component of this service was advancing the civilizational aims of the British empire: the antiquarian's collection will always be a valuable instrument of society "in an age wherein every part of science is advancing to perfection, and in a nation not afraid of penetrating into the remotest periods of their origin."[14]

Archaeologia focused solely on British antiquities until 1785, when the journal first published papers about the popular Hindu and Buddhist rock-cut caverns at Elephanta, Jogeshwari, and Kanheri in the Bombay Presidency.[15] The introduction of Indian antiquities was undoubtedly influenced by Gough, whose father was director of the East India Company: Gough compiled the observations and illustrations of the caves in his 1785 book *A Comparative View of the Antient Monuments of India, Particularly Those in the Island of Salset near Bombay, as Described by Different Writers, Illustrated with Print.* This curiosity in the caverns reflected growing British interest in India beyond commercial ventures: Gough justified his comparative study of Indian monuments in a letter to his publisher by arguing for an expansion of the concept of "British antiquities" to include artifacts from British India. Gough was preoccupied with the British empire's status with respect to the other European powers, and he sought to advance Britain's scholarship on its colonial territories:

> In one instance, however, do me the favour to gratify my wish to serve you, by accepting a little Essay, which, though you may deem it foreign to the plan of a work on *British Antiquities*, is by no means unworthy the attention of *British Antiquities*.... It gives me pain to reflect how little concern our countrymen have given themselves to teach or learn civilization in their East Indian pursuits. Other nations of Europe have produced men ... who, either as missionaries or private gentlemen, have enquired into the manners of the Orientals. How small has been

> the number of Englishmen who have practiced the arts of peace among them! May we at last rejoice that now peace is restored in all our acquisitions, our enquiries may be pursued in a milder manner under the auspices of a governor general who has established a *printing press*, and of a judge who has founded a *literary society* at CALCUTTA....[16]

Here, the "antiquity," the material artifact extracted from the colony, was to become a tool for both *teaching* and *learning* civilization. Gough's celebration of "peace ... in all our acquisitions" likely refers to the 1757 Battle of Plassey and the 1764 Battle of Buxar, decisive victories for the East India Company against local rulers, that established British dominion over the subcontinent and led to the 1765 acquisition of the *dīwānī* ('revenue authority') for Bengal, Bihar, and Orissa. This important passage from Gough's letter presses for the closer study of India's civilization in the relatively tranquil aftermath of these two battles, which allowed foreign philological and literary pursuits to flourish in the subcontinent.

Gough's letter makes allusions to Warren Hastings (1732–1818), the governor-general of Bengal and advocate of Hindu culture and learning, and Sir William Jones (1746–1794), the judge and linguist who founded the Asiatick Society of Bengal in 1784 with Hastings' encouragement. Modeled after the Royal Society of London, the Asiatick Society of Bengal sought to investigate "MAN and NATURE" in Asia: "whatever is performed by the one, or produced by the other." Weekly meetings were held where original papers were shared and deliberated, and "all curious and learned men" were invited to submit their tracts.[17] The launch of the Asiatick Society effectively made the Society of Antiquaries obsolete in generating knowledge about Indian antiquities for a European audience: after its 1785, 1787, and 1792 publication of papers on Indian subjects, *Archaeologia* published only sporadically on India.[18] The emergence of the Asiatick Society highlights an important dynamic of the colonizing mission in the late eighteenth century: once the British solidified their material dominion over the subcontinent, they were able to create major institutions of knowledge-production *within* India, rather than depend on a distant Society located in the colonial metropole.

Blackader's letter

In addition to providing the earliest English-language historical record of the Mīnākṣī-Sundareśvara temple outside British India, Adam Blackader's letter to the Society of Antiquaries offers significant insight into the circulation of knowledge about south India in the early phase of British colonization.[19] Blackader begins his letter with a short description of his overall impressions of Madurai; he was astonished not only by the unique complexity of the architecture, but also by the fact that it was constructed with relatively primitive means:

> In this district there are situated some of the most magnificent buildings now to be met in India, whether we consider their immense size, or the richness of the workmanship; and these edifices are rendered objects of great curiosity to the European observer by the singularity of their architecture, which is different from any thing to be seen in other countries. I was much struck with these remarkable monuments of the Hindoo taste and grandeur. What added to my astonishment was the incredible labour which must have attended their erection, from the ignorance of the natives in the application of the mechanical powers; so that I became particularly solicitous to have it in my power to convey some idea of them to those who make antiquities more particularly their study.[20]

Blackader, as an 'explorer' subject, came across an aesthetic object that exceeded the bounds of his comprehension of standard forms of architectural imagination. In his letter, he regards these monuments as "objects of great curiosity" for his compatriots at home, pointing to the *singularity* of their architectural forms ("different from any thing to be seen in other countries"). Blackader exemplifies the exoticist approach in Sen's schema: his avidity for the 'wondrous' and 'marvelous' is typical of discovery travelogues of the New World. "Wonder" is a human response to the first encounter with the unfamiliar: the phenomenon of "wonder" undermines the integrity of conceptual interconnections and their discursive field, thus problematizing the framework in which actions and judgments are made.[21] This effective disruption of what was familiar made the phenomenon of "wonder" central to the rationalization of empire: "a recognition of distance excites a desire to cross the threshold, break through the barrier, enter the space of the alien."[22] The explorer recognizes the other in the self, yet also perceives the other as "alien"—thus, the other is made into an object of *desire* which must be 'transformed' and 'incorporated.'

Scholarly inquiry into Indian architecture served the agenda of advancing British civilization based on a humanist belief that the radically *other* Indian civilization nevertheless springs from a shared origin as British civilization. In the preface to *A Comparative View of the Antient Monuments of India*, Gough suggests Greco-Roman civilization as a common, unifying source connecting Europe and India.[23] Stephen Greenblatt describes the dual form of "wonder" as a basic mechanism of colonizing logic:

> [T]he path that leads from wonder back out to the web of connections—connections that make descriptions, judgments, and actions possible—branches in two sharply opposed directions. One path leads to ... articulations of the hidden links between

> the radically opposed ways of being and hence to some form of acceptance of the other in the self and the self in the other. The movement is from radical alterity—you have nothing in common with the other—to a self-recognition that is also a mode of self-estrangement: you *are* the other and the other is you. The alternative path leads to ... articulations of the radical differences that make renaming, transformation, and appropriation possible. The movement here must pass through identification to complete estrangement: for a moment you see yourself confounded with the other, but then you make the other become an alien object, a thing, that you can destroy or incorporate at will.[24]

Blackader's reaction to the temple and *maṇḍapam*—astonishment at the wondrous and strange singularity of its architectural forms—led him to share his findings with British antiquities experts, in hopes of informing and advancing British architecture and science. This movement between alterity and identity—from the articulation of difference and 'strangeness' to the articulation of a "hidden link" to a radical other—creates an unintelligibility that must be reconciled through mechanisms of assimilation. Blackader's writings to the Society of Antiquaries, and subsequent involvements of the Asiatick Society, manufactured the 'strangeness' of the new colony, thus producing an object of "great curiosity" ripe for intervention.

Transmission of particles

Blackader spent three years sketching the temple and the pillars in the Pudu Maṇḍapam.[25] One hundred and forty-three pen and ink scaled drawings preserved at London's Victoria and Albert Museum are likely the same illustrations cited in Blackader's letter[26] and comprise the most extensive known series of the Pudu Maṇḍapam.[27] Printed on two sizes of paper (48.5 × 30.5 centimeters and 37.5 × 54 centimeters), they are annotated in pencil with Tamil and English notes, providing architectural descriptions of most pillars (Figures 3.1 and 3.2). The delineations of these pillars captures the copious decorative details from nearly all sides; for example, the troop of soldiers on the *upapīṭha* ('pedestal'), the bevy of women on the *adhiṣṭhāna* ('base'), Tirumala Nāyaka and his consorts on the *stambha* ('pillar'), and the floral motifs on the *prastara* ('entablature') are depicted in bold, dark contour lines (Figure 3.3). Light gray shadows along the edges of the body and face connote volume in the figures, and meandering scroll patterns on the textiles convey the fabrics' rich designs.

Blackader commissioned eighteen bronze models of the choultry's pillars, selected to provide a general impression of the hall and to show its various types of rich carvings: "In the models I have made, the number of columns is eighteen; but

Figure 3.1 *Yāḷi*s and Gajasaṁhāramūrti, ink on paper, architectural drawing of Tirumala Nāyaka's Pudu Maṇḍapam, Madurai, 37.5 × 54 centimeters, c. 1780–1789

Source: AL.7766:137 © Victoria and Albert Museum, London.

these are not taken regularly from one end of the choultry but different pillars are selected from the whole, so as to give all the principal varieties which occurred in the carving."[28] Absent in the model is the compulsion towards completeness and totality found in the drawn version. Blackader writes:

> The whole number is 124, curiously carved with different figures, representing stories connected with their religion, and the family of the founder of the choultry, with a number of devices of the workmen's own invention.... [F]or although no two pillars are exactly alike, the same figures are frequently repeated with trifling variations which make them, with respect to information, mere repetitions. There are, for instance, ten pillars representing the history of the founder and nine rajahs of his family. The pillar of the founder is in the model, the others are left out; and a similar selection made with respect to other pillars.[29]

Of the ten Nāyaka rulers, only the hall's patron, Tirumala, is included in the model. His selection for the model reinscribes his elevated importance among his family members in temple narratives, reminiscent of the laudatory Tamil temple manuscripts as discussed in chapter 1. Certainly, scarcity of resources played a

Figure 3.2 Female *caurī* (flywhisk) bearer and Rāvaṇānugṛhamūrti, ink on paper, 48.5 × 30.5 centimeters, c. 1780–1789

Source: AL.7766:14 © Victoria and Albert Museum, London.

role in Blackader's decision to limit the number of pillars: ink and paper are more accessible than clay and metal, it is far easier to sketch than to shape and mold, and a light stack of papers are much cheaper to transport back to London.

But Blackader's omissions demonstrate more than merely economic limitations: they reflect the explorer's *reproduction* of the temple into a work of 'art' or 'architecture' and corresponding *disintegration* of the site as a space of spiritual worship. The temple site in its totality and lived experience contains a form of *spiritual geography* delineated in some detail in chapters 1 and 2. Blackader's images effectively divorced the temple from its day-to-day functioning (now relegated to marginal notes in drafts and pictures), and converted the temple into *artwork* for the purpose of conveying the temple's 'exoticism.' This method of literally slicing away parts of the temple and sending the fragments back to Britain reminds of a passage from Edward Said's *Orientalism:* "a generalization about 'the Orient' drew its power from the presumed representativeness of everything Oriental; each particle of the Orient told of its Orientalness, so much so that the attribute

Figure 3.3 Tirumala Nāyaka and his consorts, ink on paper, 37.5 × 54 centimeters, c. 1780–1789

Source: AL.7766:87 © Victoria and Albert Museum, London.

of being Oriental overrode any countervailing instance."[30] Blackader extracted a "particle," fragments of the temple, and submitted it to the Society of Antiquaries as an absolutely illustrative representation of "Orientalness"—in the process, the actual spiritual geography of the space is lost, and only its exoticism remains.

A series of bronze pillars are now housed at the Victoria and Albert Museum and the Ashmolean Museum of Art and Archaeology, University of Oxford (Figure 3.4).[31] These pillars appear to have been modeled on the basis of the Victoria and Albert Museum drawings and they seem closely aligned to those pictorial depictions,[32] although in the transference from paper to bronze, there is a distortion and foreshortening of the human figures on the pillars: for example, the metal Tirumala Nāyaka is stouter and more corpulent than his paper image (Figure 3.5).

Blackader's letter unveils a chain of transmissions and a series of transformations of the temple as it traveled from Madurai to London. More than simply replicas and sketches of the temple, the temple *itself* traveled, in the form of physical representations and abstractions of the actual site. First, the 'whole' temple is turned into an illustration, a sort of 'map' reinforced by penciled notes corresponding to each pillar's cardinal direction. Then, the map becomes

Figure 3.4 Model of pillars in Tirumala Nāyaka's Pudu Maṇḍapam, Madurai, copper alloy, 32.5 × 41 × 16 centimeters, c. 1780–1789

Source: 98 to D-1870 ©Victoria and Albert Museum, London.

Figure 3.5 Tirumala Nāyaka and his consorts, copper alloy, 24.5 × 13 × 7 centimeters, c. 1780–1789

Source: 98B/2-1870. Courtesy of the Victoria and Albert Museum, London.

a 'guide' for converting flat 'fragments' of the temple into three-dimensional 'artifacts' (bronze models) for an antiquarian society, which would later become spectacular displays in a museum. This micro-practice of drawing maps of the temple foreshadowed British colonial cartography after the growth of the Madras Presidency's territories between 1790 and 1801—a period which led to "extensive cartographic innovation" in south India.[33] In the same way the Madurai temple was disassembled and analyzed by private scholars, detailed maps of British India were necessary for the colonizing government to observe from afar, to inspect, to dismantle, and then ultimately reassemble the social and political institutions of South Asia (the subject of chapter 5).[34]

Worshipping the feminine

Blackader's writing about the Madurai temple is vivid and perceptive, and most likely inspired by the testimony of informants for details of certain architectural features and religious ceremonies, as he was probably prohibited access to privileged spaces traditionally reserved for Hindu worshippers. Even so, Blackader's observations on the Madurai temple are very clearly informed by British preconceptions (and *mis*conceptions) about Hindu spirituality. After providing basic information about the structure and format of the temple, Blackader introduces the deity whom he (mistakenly) identifies as the most sacred to the temple: Sundareśvara (Śiva) locally known as "Chocalingam." First, he describes the *liṅgam*, the aniconic form of Śiva housed in the inner sanctum (*garbhagṛha*), which is the god's immobile image (*mūla mūrti*):

> The image or representation of the deity is placed in the middle of the apartment facing the door. It is a block of granite, about four feet high, of a conic shape, with the outlines of a human face on the top, and a gold arch over it, carved in open work, resembling the glory. This figure is never moved from its place....[35]

Next, he writes of Sundareśvara's *utsava mūrti*, or processional image:

> ... the bramins [*sic*] upon particular occasions bring out a representation of the deity to gratify the publick, at which time he is supposed to have assumed a human form, of about three feet in height with four arms, made of gold, and in a very singular manner richly ornamented with jewels and silks.
>
> This image is carried on men's shoulders in this form seated on a throne, attended by the bramins [*sic*] as his servants, and seldom appears in public without being accompanied by his wife *Minachie.*[36]

Goddess Mīnākṣī appears only two times in Blackader's account of the temple; by his version, the temple only concerns "Chocalingam," while Mīnākṣī is relegated to the status of a consort. Somehow, Blackader came to believe that Hindus worship only one god, Śiva, and he explains that "the names by which he is known in different districts are very numerous, as are also the various forms under which he is represented." Blackader's description of Hindu 'monotheism' is simplistic and unsophisticated: he leaves "to the more versed in the history of India the explanation of the Hindoo mythology, which is exceedingly obscure, and in general very little understood."[37] The *Monthly Review; or, Literary Journal*'s 1793 review of *Archaeologia* 10 recognized the blatant omission of Mīnākṣī from Blackader's account:

> This temple is delineated with considerable attention, as is also the *choultry* or building annexed, for accommodating the people; the latter was erected 170 years ago by *Trimul Naik*, (that is, by his subjects,) and is said to have cost above a million sterling. To these is annexed an account of the *founder's* pillar, and of some others. Mr. Blackader, together with other historians, speaks of the Hindoos as worshipping *only one God* under different names: but we observe that his wife *Minachie* is introduced in the course of the narration; ignorance and superstition abound with them, as in all other places where unprincipled men are able to maintain a supremacy.[38]

The reviewer accurately identifies a role for Mīnākṣī at the temple. However, in admonishing Blackader, he also disparages Hinduism as a product of "ignorance and superstition," where people worship multiple deities, even the "wife" of a god. Blackader's oversight and the reviewer's comments convey two important, interconnected aspects of gender and empire in late-eighteenth- and early-nineteenth-century British India. First, Blackader cannot fathom the possibility of a goddess dominating the temple site. At this temple, Mīnākṣī has total ritual precedence over Śiva (the subject of chapter 2),[39] but Blackader does not mention Mīnākṣī's shrine, nor does he refer to the temple by its proper name, Mīnākṣī-Sundareśvara temple, nor any of its other popular titles, all of which refer to the goddess. Second, the reviewer, in correcting Blackader's omission of Mīnākṣī, interprets the worship of the feminine as evidence of rule by "unprincipled men"—the clear implication is that British men who believe in only one male God are justified in their aim of colonial domination. Philippa Levine observed that British colonization was a masculine enterprise that envisioned and celebrated white maleness as fundamentally industrious and energetic.[40] Late-eighteenth- and early-nineteenth-century British scholars identified Hindu men as idle, effeminate, and easily conquerable by both Mughals and the British, thereby portraying them as poor stewards of Hindu women.[41] A customary colonial trope characterized the Hindu mind as "female" and "inherently disorderly," in opposition to the West's "masculine, world-ordering rationality."[42] Despite residing in Madurai for several years, Blackader was unable to grasp the basic fact of Mīnākṣī's importance in that city. The reviewer's response to Blackader's letter betrays the logical terminus of colonial reasoning about Hindu worship: polytheistic veneration of the feminine divine becomes a justification for the enlightened despotism of the colonizing mission.

"Ridiculous and absurd notions"

Blackader obtained versions of the temple myths by asking for translations of temple records, and he displayed patronizing disdain for the Hindu conceptions of 'time' and the 'history' they entailed, which were totally antithetical to the antiquarians' materialist understanding of history. "I took the trouble of procuring copies of the descriptions of the different columns, as registered in the accounts of the temple, and of having them literally translated," he wrote; he planned to record descriptions of the pillars "as affording a specimen of their ridiculous and absurd notions respecting religious history."[43] In this passage, Blackader boasts of his own impeccable attention to detail, which then serves to justify and reinforce his claim about the natives' "ridiculous" and "absurd" perceptions of religious history. The discourse of "curiosity" in colonial writing often involved an obsession with empiricism, which sought to 'explain' strange and spectacularly exotic cultures through precise reproduction and translation; this allowed the curious writer to take on the "disinterestedness of the scientist."[44] These writers proliferated exhaustive and encyclopedic knowledge on obscure topics to fabricate a veneer of "privileged, rarefied, and authoritative judgment," which in turn allowed them to appear as "mediators of the occult."[45]

Blackader's role as a "mediator" to the strange and foreign forms of the Madurai temple complex gives insight into the modes of subjectivation of the colonizing subject, or the mechanisms by which the colonizer came to understand the project of colonization and *realize* it in their regular conduct. Michel Foucault defined subject formation as "the way in which the individual establishes his relation to the rule and recognizes himself as obligated to put it into practice."[46] Blackader's paternalism was presented as a form of imperial humanism; Barbara M. Benedict described this discursive move as a form of self-imagination that entailed *correcting* an Indian civilization irreconcilable with 'enlightened' British norms:

> The scientific urge to dissect and classify the physical universe marks a new subjectivity: a selfhood projected outward, explaining phenomena beyond the inquiring self, not reflective except insofar as the self can be objectified as an item

> for analysis. The self thus expands to occupy the world, and to obsess narrative: it consumes novelty, information, experience, and, to many, seems consumed itself and thus transformed into something dehumanized.[47]

The novel cultural knowledge Blackader seeks to produce is unsettling and unfamiliar; so, he expresses his profound estrangement in a crude denunciation of Hindu beliefs. Though he finds the temple's architectural forms wondrous and spectacular, he cannot reconcile the temple's extraordinary beauty with the foreign spiritual discourses and practices that circulate the temple. Vijay Mishra interprets this dual emotional quality of attraction and fear as "pleasurable alienation"—the combination of *pleasure* and *anxiety* generates a moment of *sublime awe,* "a mental violence to the imagination" in which reason and imagination come into direct conflict.[48] The physical architecture of the temple, which can be rationally analyzed and reproduced, is in immediate antagonism with the abstract architecture of the temple's spiritual geography, which escapes Blackader's imagination. Blackader's text reflects a struggle to resolve the fuzzy boundary between two forms of aesthetics: the immediately apparent attributes of an architectural object, and an abstract ethical judgment about the colonial project of which Blackader was a part.

Rather than expounding on all ten rulers portrayed in the hall, Blackader discusses only briefly the pillar of Tirumala Nāyaka and two sculptural reliefs from Parañcōti Muṉivar's seventeenth-century *Tiruviḷaiyāṭal Purāṇam*: Sundareśvara as a sow feeding piglets and as a *cittar* ('holy man') feeding sugarcane to an elephant. As examined in chapter 2, Śiva's appearance in Madurai is retold in sixty-four episodes or "games" (*viḷaiyāṭals*). Referring to the pillars he omits, Blackader writes: "The other pillars represent stories of a similar kind, too tedious to be laid before this learned Society; but from all some moral may be drawn."[49] Blackader flattens the whole spiritual geography of the temple in one sentence: "from all some moral may be drawn." The details of the moral parameters and lessons of the Hindu stories, and thus the complexity of Hindu ethics and spirituality, are completely absent.

Upon returning to London after several years in Madurai, Blackader sent the ink sketches and bronze replicas, along with his written observations about Indian history and Hindu mythology, to Joseph Banks (1743–1820) for appraisal and submission to the Society of Antiquaries, should they find the materials "sufficiently curious" to deserve notice.[50] The Society of Antiquaries consisted largely of wealthy aficionados of rare artifacts. They are depicted in a satirical cartoon by George Cruikshank (Figure 3.6) as buffoons; distinguished Society fellows, including Banks, sit around a table strewn with various "curious" objects: a pig-feeding trough marked "Sarcophagus," a coal scuttle tagged "an Ancient Shield," and a chamber pot labelled "Roman Vase." Blackader asked whether the Society of Antiquaries considered his submission worthy of greater scrutiny

Figure 3.6 George Cruikshank, *The Antiquarian Society*, hand-colored etching, 20 × 38 centimeters, 1812

Source: 1862, 1217.562 © The Trustees of the British Museum.

and more serious academic inquiry: the Society was engaged in a program that was often self-consciously *scientific* as much as it was aesthetic and historical. Learned societies helped to assemble the intellectual scaffolding for the colonizing enterprise by providing both the *methods* and the *rationalization* for transformative experimentation with government in the subcontinent.

Joseph Banks and William Jones

The writings of the Asiatick Society of Bengal offer a powerful illustration of the *logic* and *aesthetics* of colonial government. In 1785, Sir Charles Wilkins, one of the first European Sanskrit scholars in the East India Company and charter member of the Asiatick Society of Bengal, translated the *Bhagavad Gītā* (Skt, 'Song of the lord') into English for the first time, with strong support from Governor-General Hastings. The *Bhagavad Gītā*, revered as sacred by Hindu traditions and still embedded in contemporary Hindu spiritual practices, did not escape being subsumed under the rhetoric of "antiquity" and "curiosity"—the "Advertisement" of Wilkins' *The Bhăgvăt-Gēētā, or Dialogues of Krēēshnă and Ărjōōn* stated: "The antiquity of the original, and the veneration in which it hath been held for so many ages, by a very considerable portion of the human race, must render it one of the greatest curiosities ever presented to the literary world."[51] Wilkins, as a pioneer scholar of British India, helped make Calcutta and its Asiatick Society the locus of a strain of Orientalism that combined the study of Indian antiquity with service to the East India Company: establishing the dominion of British government in

Bengal required an army of civil servants with a vast scholarly knowledge of Indian languages, law, and literature.[52]

The attention the Asiatick Society of Bengal gave to objects of 'curiosity' differed from the leisurely fixation that the Society of Antiquaries' landowning elite had for curious antiquities. Among the Society of Antiquaries' members, Banks was peculiar in his interests outside Europe. A naturalist and patron of sciences, Banks traveled the world on scientific expeditions as a member of Captain James Cook's first Pacific voyage, studying natural history and learning from indigenous people.[53] He kept journals of his early travels that display a "remarkable eagerness to learn from the native people" and, perhaps, a mitigated sense of superiority and condescension.[54] Banks admired non-European and non-Christian civilizations, and his appreciation reflected the humanistic ideals of British Enlightenment: he recognized civilizations outside Europe not only as fellow members of a shared 'humanity,' but he also believed that these civilizations could *surpass* European civilization in certain aspects.[55] Banks' curiosity for the ancient civilizations of China and India stemmed from the possibility that these civilizations had advanced beyond Europe in some ways, and that Europeans could thus learn from them.

In India, Banks' concerns went further than the economic undertakings that preoccupied much of the East India Company in the subcontinent, indicated by his esteem for the region's literature and culture. When the papers of Nathaniel Brassey Halhed, the East India Company official who wrote extensively on Bengali grammar and Hindu law, became available for sale in 1795, Banks urged the British Museum, London, to purchase the collection.[56] In 1790, Banks encouraged the work of Samuel Davis, a Bengal civil servant and Royal Society fellow who researched Hindu astronomy.[57] Scattered among Banks' papers are notes on Hindu funeral practices, Hindu beliefs about transmigration of souls, Brahmin rites, and Parsi customs.[58] Banks seemed chiefly absorbed in acquiring traditional knowledge that could benefit British civilization. In his 1811 paper "A Project in the Establishment of a Botanic Garden in the Island of Ceylon," Banks presses for a careful study of Ceylonese herbal doctors who are "far more skilful than Europeans are willing to admit."[59] He also appreciated Indian craft skills—in his 1791 letter to East India Company military surgeon in Bombay and Bombay Medical Board president Dr Helenus Scott, Banks wrote:

> Nothing in my opinion is more interesting to the progress of Arts in Europe than Communications from well informd [*sic*] men of minute practise of Indian workmen but nothing I am Confident is more dificult [*sic*] to Obtain, I Look upon the Arts of India as the Ruins of a vast Fabric of Science raisd [*sic*] many ages ago to a hight [*sic*] probably far superior to that on which we Europeans now pride ourselves....[60]

We observe the same type of rhetoric—celebrating the ancient "ruins" of an older civilization that once exceeded European civilization—in Banks' 1792 letter to former governor of Madras Lord George Macartney, who was to lead an embassy in China:

> The Chinese appear to me to posess [*sic*] the Ruin of a State of Civilisation in which when in Perfection the human mind had carried all kinds of Knowledge to a much higher Pitch than the Europeans have ... the great inventions ... Gunpowder[,] Printing[,] the Arabic notation of figures ... [and] Paper making with infinite others upon which the very state of Science & Civilisation absolutely depends were only reinvented if not perhaps Stolen from that Country, their Porcelane [*sic*] is a chef d oeuvre of Chemistry which Europeans have not yet been able to attain & their very Tea depends upon a Chemical Process we are unable to imitate ... to Learn these arts alone would be to /*grant*/ /give/ to Europe an invaluable blessing....[61]

Banks' comments here can help to clarify the function of British scholarly enthusiasm in Indian art and architecture, a reflection of the mission statement of the Society of Antiquaries director who assembled collections in service of an empire "penetrating into the remotest periods of their origin." The 'humanism' that motivated Banks' inquiry into foreign civilizations sprang not only from scientific and academic curiosity, but also from a *civilizational logic* aimed at improving and advancing the British imperial mission by seeking the common origins of scientific knowledge and the technical capabilities it develops. If the Indian and Chinese civilizations once possessed a level of science and art that far surpassed that of contemporary Europe, then the Europeans could potentially recapture those heights by studying the 'ruined' remains of those ancient societies.

Banks was a friend and patron of William Jones, the renowned philologist who founded the Asiatick Society of Bengal. Their connection began early when Jones and Banks attended Harrow, a boarding school for boys in London. Both men studied at Oxford, and both were elected as Fellows of the Royal Society: Banks in 1766 and Jones in 1772. By this time, Jones' reputation in Oriental languages and literature was well established, following the publication of his 1771 *A Grammar of the Persian Language* and 1772 *Poems, Consisting Chiefly of Translations from the Asiatick Languages.* Jones and Banks shared mutual friends in London's social and literary circles: they came in contact during Royal Society meetings and weekly dinners at Samuel Johnson's Literary Club.[62] The Royal Society under Banks' leadership and its periodical *Philosophical Transactions* served as models for Jones' Asiatick Society and journal, *Asiatick Researches: or, Transactions.*[63] Jones entrusted Banks with his Sanskrit and Arabic manuscripts for safekeeping until his return to England, and he asked they be deposited in the Royal Society library should he not survive the journey.[64]

Letters exchanged between Banks and Jones from 1787 to 1792 illustrate the production of 'India' as an object of European scientific inquiry during the late eighteenth century. As European intellectuals came to "know" India more scientifically, "to live in it with greater authority and discipline than ever before,"[65] there was increasing engagement in the curatorial enterprise that described, categorized, and 'discovered' the diversity of India and its culture. Jones contributed to numerous academic endeavors: managing scholarship on India through the Asiatick Society of Bengal, working as a distinguished high court judge at Calcutta, introducing Indian ideas to Europe as a preeminent Orientalist publisher, translating literary and legal texts into English, and formulating Indo-European comparative grammar and modern comparative-historical linguistics (an effort to 'uncover' the affinity between Sanskrit, Greek, and Latin[66]). He perceived his work as a chiefly *scientific* endeavor, and he expressed immense interest in natural sciences, especially botany. Jones employed both Europeans and Indians to search for specific plant specimens requested by Banks, and his letters to Banks provide detailed botanical classifications, descriptions, and samples.[67] For instance, when Banks asked for information about Dacca cotton and seeds, Jones sent along a cotton pincushion.[68] In a letter dated March 16, 1791, Banks comments on Jones' English translation of Kālidāsa's Sanskrit *Abhijñānaśākuntalam* ('The recognition of Śakuntalā'), and he encourages Jones to seek information about the flora and fauna mentioned in the ancient drama.[69] In one of his last letters to Banks, dated October 18, 1791, Jones is delighted that Banks enjoyed Kālidāsa's "poem," and supplies the scientific names for various botanical references in the it.[70] However, Banks' queries to Jones went beyond 'mere' academic matters, and included technical inquiries addressed to problems of government. On behalf of the British government, which depended on alliances with landowning elites, Banks hunted for cotton plants that could flourish in British colonies (for the Privy Council Committee for Trade), and other cash crops to cultivate in a botanic garden in Calcutta (for the East India Company), using the machinery of colonial government to advance research in agronomy and horticulture with political and economic aims.[71]

William Jones' 1789 translation of Kālidāsa's play on Śakuntalā was a significant event that introduced "the literary East to the West."[72] Published the same year as Blackader's letter presentation to the London Society of Antiquaries, the Indian drama generated much awareness and appeal among Western scholars: within seven years, it was reprinted three times in Britain and retranslated into French, German, and Italian. Johann Wolfgang von Goethe modeled the Prologue to *Faust* after its story, and even Thomas Jefferson owned a copy of the play. The late eighteenth to early nineteenth centuries were a period of abundant fascination with India and the Sanskrit language in Europe. The study of Indian antiquities and Sanskrit, according to an idea widely prevalent in Europe, would bring about an "Oriental Renaissance."[73] Like Jones' text, Wilkins' translation of the *Bhagavad Gītā* enjoyed a great response in Europe and America (especially among transcendentalist writers of New England), and was rendered into French and Russian around 1787. Europe looked with admiration towards the civilizations of Asia: both Jones and Wilkins emphasized India's rich linguistic, humanistic, and scientific past contained in the Sanskrit works that they introduced to an unsuspecting Europe. The "Oriental Renaissance," fueled by the popularity and diffusion of Company-sponsored translations and research journals penned by Calcutta-based Orientalists, fortified the idea of a common Indo-European or Indo-Aryan cultural heritage.[74] Jones' identification of a genetic link between Sanskrit and the classical languages of Western Europe (and of a religious link between Hindus, Greeks, and Romans evidenced by their deities[75]) aligned with Banks' philological fascination with the shared origins of languages and peoples. Banks' research in comparative linguistics enabled him, for example, to supply material for William Marsden's 1785 *Archaeologia* paper about the relationship between Roma language and Hindustani.[76] Ancient Indian civilization became—in the words of Romila Thapur—"almost as a lost wing of early European culture."[77] The idea of historical and cultural 'unity' between the colonizer and the colonized became a basic ideological premise of British imperial ambitions in India.

Conclusion

Madurai's religious sites were, to Blackader, "remarkable monuments" that indicated the exceptional level of achievement of 'exotic' Dravidian-style architecture. Banks, the recipient of Blackader's "outbursts of fascinated wonder," was a seasoned world traveler who likewise admired Indian civilizational achievements, as did his colleague Jones.[78] While Jones and Banks both employed a "systematic curiosity" that characterizes the "curatorial" genre of scholarship identified by Amartya Sen,[79] both men were deeply embedded in "magisterial" commitments to the East India Company and British colonial rule.

The scholars of Indian Orientalism often expressed deep fondness and compassion for Indian society and Indians themselves.[80] Their liberal, compassionate attitude was entrenched in a scientific discourse which placed them in authoritative positions both *in* India itself and *about* India as it affected their compatriots in Britain, who 'knew' and understood the colony only through texts produced in India and delivered back to London. Said writes on this period of scholarship on India:

> Their inauguration of Orientalism was a considerable feat. It made possible a scientific terminology; it banished obscurity and instated a special form of illumination for the Orient; it established the figure of the Orientalist as central authority *for* the Orient; it legitimized a special kind of specifically coherent Orientalist work; it put into cultural circulation a form of discursive currency by whose presence the Orient henceforth would be *spoken for*, above all, the work of the inaugurators carved out a field of study and a family of ideas which in turn could form a community of scholars whose lineage, traditions, and ambitions were at once internal to the field and external enough for general prestige.[81]

The three men featured in this chapter each served different roles in the "community of scholars" reported by Said, a complex network that claimed the right to speak *about* and *on behalf of* an imagined Indian civilization. This production of scholarship and scientific authority was internal to the material domination of colonial rule: Blackader penned his letter while his employer was battling south Indian rulers in the Anglo-Mysore Wars; his work involved providing medical services for Company soldiers.[82] Jones became an expert on India not only as an academic scholar, but also as a judge and jurist for the East India Company post in Calcutta. As a patron of science, Banks' intellectual curiosity about India, infused with a romantic empathy towards its subject, fits readily into the policy concerns of an imperial government seeking to maximize its investments in the Indian colony and manage its relations with landholding elites in the colonial metropole. Situated in a broader colonial dynamic, their liberal, empathetic projects sought to 'recreate' and 'restore' India in the image of British civilization; they cultivated a discourse of common ancestry through which Hindu and British culture could be joined, and British civilization could be delivered to its destined apex.

Notes

1. Adam Blackader, "XL. Description of the Great Pagoda of Madura, and the Choultry of Trimul Naik, in a Letter from Mr. Adam Blackader, Surgeon, to Sir Joseph Banks, Bart. P. R. S. F. A. S.," *Archaeologia, or, Miscellaneous Tracts Relating to Antiquity. Published by the Society of Antiquaries of London* 10 (1792): 449–459.
2. Pagoda, a tiered-tower with multiple eaves found in east Asia, is the term the British used to label temples in the Indian subcontinent during their rule. N. E. Kindersley, East India Company civil servant in the Madras Presidency, defines choultry as "a building, generally open ... and is an usual appendage to *Hindoo* temples. Number of them are, however, to be found on the high roads in the Peninsula, totally unconnected with any religious edifices ...

for the general accommodations of travellers...." He also describes the choultry of "Tremul-Naig" and includes drawings by a "Hindoo" in the style of Blackader's images. See N. E. Kindersley, *Specimens of Hindoo Literature: Consisting of Translations, from the Tamoul Language, of Some Hindoo Works of Morality and Imagination, with Explanatory Notes: To Which Are Prefixed Introductory Remarks on the Mythology, Literature, &c. of the Hindoos* (London: W. Bulmer and Co., 1794), 329–334.

3. This chapter problematizes a prevalent contention that William Hodges as well as Thomas and William Daniell (subjects of chapter 4) were "the first to supply first-hand information about Indian architecture." See Mildred Archer, *Indian Architecture and the British 1780–1830* (Feltham, Middlesex: Country Life Books, 1968), 25. This assertion does not hold true for south Indian architecture. The outbreak of the Second Anglo-Mysore War (1780–1784) prevented Hodges from exploring south of the country, including its Bṛhadīśvara temple in Tanjavur. For his *Choix de vues de l'Inde, dessinées sur les lieux, pendant les années 1780, 1781, 1782, et 1783, et executées en aqua tinta, par W. Hodges.... Select Views in India, Drawn on the Spot, in the Years 1780, 1781, 1782, and 1783, and Executed in Aqua Tinta, by William Hodges, R.A.* (London: Printed [by Joseph Cooper] for the author; and sold by J. Edwards, 1786–1788), Hodges composed his only image of south India—plate 23: *A View of the Great Pagoda at Tanjore*—using a sketch made by Mr Topping, his friend and an East India Company surveyor. Hodges acknowledges Topping in his 1793 *Travels in India*, in which he also mentions briefly a Hindu temple in Madras. See William Hodges, *Travels in India, During the Years 1780, 1781, 1782, & 1783* (London: Printed for the author, and sold by J. Edwards, 1793), 10–11. The Daniells, who had direct experience of south India, did not publish their images of the region until their second *Oriental Scenery* in 1798.
4. Amartya Sen, "Indian Traditions & the Western Imagination," *Dædalus* 134, no. 4 (Fall 2005): 168–185.
5. See Philip J. Stern, *The Company-State: Corporate Sovereignty and the Early Modern Foundations of the British Empire in India* (Oxford and New York: Oxford University Press, 2011).
6. "Indian Capital and the Emergence of Colonial Society," in C. A. Bayly, *Indian Society and the Making of the British Empire*, The New Cambridge History of India II.1 (Cambridge: Cambridge University Press, 1988), 45–78.
7. Founded in 1660 in London, the Royal Society is the oldest scientific academy in continuous existence with eminent scientists as its members.
8. "A very curious Model, & some drawings of the Temples and Choultree at Madura were exhibited to the inspection of the Society by Adam Blackader Esq. thro' the hands of Sir Joseph Banks Bart., accompanied with a description of those extraordinary Buildings, in a letter addressed to him by Mr. Blackader," *Minute Book of the Society of Antiquaries of London*, vol. XXIII: MDCCLXXXIX, from

January 8, 1789, to December 23, 1790 (Thursday, July 2, 1789), 160, Society of Antiquaries Library, London. The Society moved to send a letter to Blackader to acknowledge the model and drawings, to thank him for allowing their exhibition, and to reassure him that they will be cared for while in their custody. *Council of the Society of Antiquaries*, vol. III. MDCCLXXXV, from April 8, 1785, to December 16, 1803 (Friday, July 3, 1789, 1 o'clock p.m.), unpaginated.

9. Joan Evans, *A History of The Society of Antiquaries* (Oxford: Oxford University Press, 1956), 36.
10. Evans, *A History of The Society of Antiquaries*, 40.
11. Evans, *A History of The Society of Antiquaries*, 58.
12. Lucy Peltz, "Aestheticizing the Ancestral City: antiquarianism, topography and the representation of London in the long eighteenth century," *Art History* 22, no. 4 (November 1999): 472–494, 479–485. Peltz writes that the Society of Antiquaries' collecting of metropolitan antiquities prints was a "passive mode of antiquarian inquiry" (479), seen as "an acceptable alternative to action" (483). Beginning in 1786, Richard Gough, director of the London Society of Antiquaries, tried to expand the Society's activities to include the protection and preservation of ancient buildings. See John M. Frew, "Richard Gough, James Wyatt, and Late 18th-Century Preservation," *Journal of the Society of Architectural Historians* 38, no. 4 (December 1979): 366–374, 366.
13. *A Copy of the Royal Charter and Statutes of the Society of Antiquaries of London and of Orders and Regulations Established by the Council of the Society* (London: J. B. Nichols, 1837), 1–2.
14. "Introduction: Containing an Historical Account of the Origin and Establishment of the Society of Antiquaries," *Archaeologia, or, Miscellaneous Tracts Relating to Antiquity. Published by the Society of Antiquaries of London* 1 (1770): ii. Gough authored the introduction. See "Memoirs and Remains of Eminent Persons. Memoir of Richard Gough, Esq. of Enfield," *Monthly Magazine; or, British Register* 27, part I for 1809, no. 183 (April 1, 1809): 260–263 (London: Printed for Richard Phillips, undated), 261.
15. "XXXII. An Account of Some Artificial Caverns in the Neighbourhood of Bombay. By Mr. William Hunter, Surgeon in the East Indies," "XXXIV. Account of a Curious Pagoda near Bombay, Drawn up by Captain Pyke, Who Was Afterwards Governor of St. Helena. It Is Dated from on Board the Stringer East-Indiaman in Bombay Harbour 1712, and Is Illustrated with Drawings. This Extract Was Made from the Captain's Journal in Possession of the Honourable the East-India Company. By Alexander Dalrymple, Esq. F. R. and A. SS. and Communicated to the Society, Feb. 10, 1780," and "XXXV. Extract by the Late Smart Lethieullier, Esq. from the Papers of the Late Charles Boon, Esq. Governor of Bombay, Giving an Account of the Great Pagoda on the Island of Salset," *Archaeologia, or, Miscellaneous Tracts Relating to Antiquity. Published*

by the Society of Antiquaries of London 7 (1785): 286–302, 323–332, and 333–336. Hunter mentions the Jogheswari Caves by its former name, Ambola.

Gough chose papers for *Archaeologia* by "trawling" through existing meeting minutes and selecting presented papers that combined quality with a wide-ranging mix that would appeal to Society fellows. See Susan Pearce, "Antiquaries and the Interpretation of Ancient Objects, 1770–1820," in *Visions of Antiquity: The Society of Antiquaries of London 1707–2007*, ed. Susan Pearce (London: Society of Antiquaries of London, 2007), 147–171, 151.

16. Richard Gough, *A Comparative View of the Antient Monuments of India, Particularly Those in the Island of Salset near Bombay, as Described by Different Writers, Illustrated with Prints* (London: John Nichols, 1785), iii–iv.

17. William Jones, "A Discourse on the Institution of a Society, for Inquiring into the History, Civil and Natural, the Antiquities, Arts, Sciences, and Literature of Asia. By the President," *Asiatick Researches: or, Transactions of the Society Instituted in Bengal, for Inquiring into the History and Antiquities, the Arts, Sciences, and Literature, of Asia* 1 (Calcutta: Manuel Cantopher and London: P. Elmsly, 1788): xii–xiii, xv.

While the Royal Society focused primarily on natural history (botany, zoology, mineralogy, geography/topography), mathematics, mechanical philosophy (astronomy, optics, navigation, and so on), and chemistry, especially after Sir Isaac Newton's 1703 election as president (see Thomas Thomson, *History of The Royal Society, From Its Institution to the End of the Eighteenth Century* [London: Robert Baldwin, 1812], vii–viii), it did engage in antiquarian research, however, in a more structured and systematic way than the London Society of Antiquaries (see M. C. W. Hunter, "The Royal Society and the Origins of British Archaeology: I," *Antiquity* 45, no. 178 [June 1971]: 113–121 and "The Royal Society and the Origins of British Archaeology: II," *Antiquity* 45, no. 179 [September 1971]: 187–192). Like the Royal Society, the Asiatick Society actively retrieved, restored, preserved, and studied South Asia's ancient remains in an organized fashion.

18. India-related subjects published in *Archaeologia* after 1792 to 1992 include maces found at a fort in Agra, north India (1812), coins located in ancient mounds in south India (1827), a dish featuring Dionysos from the Hindu Kush, Punjab (1897), and a Sassanian bowl discovered in the Northwestern Province of India (1912).

19. Blackader, in "Description of the Great Pagoda of Madura," 454–456, discusses the reasons for the choultry's existence (the Nāyaka ruler's desire for fame and for ritual observance) and provides an explanation of its construction. He lists the step-by-step process that includes the hollowed-out sand cavities for installing the stone columns, the new stone pillars' figural carvings, the capital's structural placement, and the roof's elaborate composition. Stone slabs forming the Pudu

Maṇḍapam's roof were rolled to the top on an earthen ramp surrounding the pillars. The earth was removed when finished. After its completion, priests consecrated the pillared hall through special prayers and offerings, as dancing girls performed and the temple deities' festival images witnessed.

20. Blackader, "Description of the Great Pagoda of Madura," 449.
21. Stephen Greenblatt, *Marvelous Possessions: The Wonder of the New World* (Chicago: The University of Chicago Press, 1991).
22. Greenblatt, *Marvelous Possessions*, 135.
23. Gough, *A Comparative View of the Ancient Monuments of India*, vii–x. Gough cites from Pierre d'Hancarville's *Recherches sur l'origine, l'esprit et les progrès des arts de la Grèce; sur leurs connections avec les arts et la religion des plus anciens peuples connus; sur les monumens antiques de l'Inde, de la Perse, du reste de l'Asie, de l'Europe et de l'Égypte* (Londres: Chez B. Appleyard, 1785).
24. Greenblatt, *Marvelous Possessions*, 135.
25. Blackader, "Description of the Great Pagoda of Madura," 450.
26. John Guy, "Tirumala Nāyak's Choultry: An Eighteenth Century Model," in *Makaranda: Essays in Honour of Dr. James C. Harle*, ed. Claudine Bautze-Picron (Delhi: Sri Satguru Publications, 1990), 207–213. The Victoria and Albert Museum collection is entitled "Trimul Naik's Choultry (Indian Antiquities) (Architectural Details) Drawings."
27. Mildred Archer, *Company Paintings: Indian Paintings of the British Period* (London: Victoria and Albert Museum; Ahmedabad: Mapin Publishing Pvt. Ltd., 1992), 41. These drawings are labeled with the collection number "7766" and followed by the image number.
28. Blackader, "Description of the Great Pagoda of Madura," 456.
29. Blackader, "Description of the Great Pagoda of Madura," 456.
30. Edward W. Said, *Orientalism* (London: Penguin Books, 2003 [1978]), 231.
31. The Victoria and Albert Museum has the largest section of the model: its art inventory documents that J. Heywood Hawkins gifted five piers (three with corbels) and two sections of the architrave in 1870, and another pier arrived in 1875 from the Gutherie Collection. Two additional piers entered the Ashmolean Museum in 1894 through another branch of the Hawkins family (see Guy, "Tirumala Nāyak's Choultry," 208).
32. Archer, *Company Paintings*, 43.
33. Matthew H. Edney, *Mapping an Empire: The Geographical Construction of British India, 1765–1843* (Chicago and London: The University of Chicago Press, 1997 [1990]), 167.
34. For a description of parallel techniques employed by the British in Egypt, see Timothy Mitchell, *Colonising Egypt* (Berkeley and Los Angeles: University of California Press, 1991 [1988]).
35. Blackader, "Description of the Great Pagoda of Madura," 451–452.

36. Blackader, "Description of the Great Pagoda of Madura," 452.
37. Blackader, "Description of the Great Pagoda of Madura," 450.
38. "ART. XI. Archaelogia, or, Miscellaneous Tracts relating to Antiquity. Vol. X," *Monthly Review; or, Literary Journal* 10 (January–April 1793 [February 1793]): 169–175, 174–175 (London: Printed for R. Griffiths, 1793).
39. C. J. Fuller, "The Divine Couple's Relationship in a South Indian Temple: Mīnākṣī and Sundareśvara at Madurai," *History of Religions* 19, no. 4 (May 1980): 321–348, 322.
40. Philippa Levine, introduction to *Gender and Empire*, ed. Philippa Levine (Oxford and New York: Oxford University Press, 2007 [2004]), 1–13, 1, 7.
41. Catherine Hall, "Of Gender and Empire: Reflections on the Nineteenth Century," in *Gender and Empire*, ed. Philippa Levine (Oxford and New York: Oxford University Press, 2007 [2004]), 46–76, 53.
42. Ronald Inden, *Imagining India* (Bloomington: Indiana University Press, 2000 [1990]), 4, 86–87.
43. Blackader, "Description of the Great Pagoda of Madura," 456.
44. Barbara M. Benedict, *Curiosity: A Cultural History of Early Modern Inquiry* (Chicago and London: The University of Chicago Press, 2001), 160.
45. Benedict, *Curiosity: A Cultural History of Early Modern Inquiry*, 160.
46. Michel Foucault, *Ethics: Subjectivity and Truth*, vol. I, ed. Paul Rabinow (New York: The New Press, 1997 [1994]), xxx.
47. Benedict, *Curiosity: A Cultural History of Early Modern Inquiry*, 116.
48. Vijay Mishra, *Devotional Poetics and the Indian Sublime* (Albany: State University of New York, 1998), 7.
49. Blackader, "Description of the Great Pagoda of Madura," 458.
50. Blackader, "Description of the Great Pagoda of Madura," 450.
51. Charles Wilkins, *The Bhăgvăt-Gēētā, or Dialogues of Krēēshnă and Ărjōōn; In Eighteen Lectures; with Notes. Translated from the Original, in the Sănkrēēt, or Ancient Language of the Brāhmăns* (London: Nourse, 1785). Wilkins relied on the assistance of an Indian Brahmin scholar in Benares to help him translate the *Bhagavad Gītā*. See Richard H. Davis, "Wilkins, Hastings, and the First English '*Bhagavad Gītā*,'" *International Journal of Hindu Studies* 19, no. 1/2 (April–August 2015): 39–57.
52. Jenny Sharpe, "The Violence of Light in the Land of Desire; or, How William Jones Discovered India," *Boundary 2* 20, no. 1 (Spring 1993): 26–46. Richard H. Davis notes that earlier East India Company–sponsored publications on Hindu law and Bengali language had a more direct application to the needs of colonial administration than *The Bhăgvăt-Gēētā*, a principal text of Hindu devotionalism. See Davis, "Wilkins, Hastings, and the First English '*Bhagavad Gītā*,'" 48.

53. Joseph Banks was a famous English naturalist who took part in Captain James Cook's first great voyage (1768–1771), a scientific expedition aboard the *HM Bark Endeavour* to the south Pacific. His name is found in the regions of his travels: Banks Peninsula on South Island, New Zealand; Banks Islands in modern-day Vanuatu; Banks Island in the Northwest Territories, Canada; Canberra suburb of Banks, Australia; and the Sydney suburb of Bankstown, Australia. Banks' image even appeared on the five-dollar note in Australia. Around eighty species of plants bear his name and he is credited with introducing eucalyptus, acacia, and mimosa to the West. The genus *Banksia* is also named after him. See Patrick O'Brian, *Joseph Banks: A Life* (London: Collins Harvill, 1987).
54. John Gascoigne, *Joseph Banks and the English Enlightenment: Useful Knowledge and Polite Culture* (Cambridge: Cambridge University Press, 1994), 16.
55. Gascoigne, *Joseph Banks and the English Enlightenment,* 178–179. For example, the Tahitians' ability to forecast weather, the effectiveness of their fishhooks, their procedure for dyeing clothes, and the scarless aftermath of their surgical practice.
56. Neil Chambers, *Joseph Banks and the British Museum: The World of Collecting, 1770–1830* (London: Pickering & Chatto, 2007), 94. Nathaniel Brassey Halhed's publications include *A Code of Gentoo Laws, or, Ordinations of the Pundits, from a Persian Translation, Made from the Original, Written in the Shanscrit Language* (London, 1776) and *A Grammar of the Bengal Language* (Printed at Hooghly in Bengal, 1778).
57. Joseph Banks to Samuel Davis, Soho Square, March 18, 1790, from "Letters from Sir William Jones to the late Samuel Davis, Esq., F. R. S., &c. from 1785 to 1794, chiefly relating to the Literature and Science of India, and elucidatory of the early History of the Asiatic Society of Bengal; with a Plate. Communicated by John Francis Davis, Esq., F. R. S., M. R. A. S., &c." in *Transactions of the Royal Asiatic Society of Great Britain and Ireland* 3, no. 1 (1831): 1–31 (London: Parbury, Allen, & Co., 1831), 29–30. Davis (1760–1819) later became accountant general in Bengal (1804) and an East India Company director in London (1810).
58. Gascoigne, *Joseph Banks and the English Enlightenment*, 180. A Parsi settlement began in India (primarily Bombay) when Zoroastrian refugees migrated from their original homeland in medieval Islamic Persia beginning in the eighth century CE.
59. Joseph Banks, "A Project in the Establishment of a Botanic Garden in the Island of Ceylon with a View to an Increase of the Resources of That Colony & an Improvement of the Science of Botany in Europe," BO 1:39, 1811, Sutro Library, California State Library, San Francisco.
60. Joseph Banks to Helenus Scott, Soho Square, March 17, 1791, in Neil Chambers, ed., *The Indian and Pacific Correspondence of Sir Joseph Banks, 1768–1820*, vol. III: *Letters 1789–1792* (London: Pickering & Chatto, 2010), 213.

61. Joseph Banks to George Macartney, Soho Square, January 22, 1792, in Chambers, *Letters 1789–1792*, 330.
62. Garland Cannon, "Sir William Jones, Sir Joseph Banks, and the Royal Society," *Notes and Records of the Royal Society of London* 29, no. 2 (March 1975): 205–230, 206–207; William Jones, *A Grammar of the Persian Language* (London: W. and J. Richardson, 1771) and *Poems, Consisting Chiefly of Translations from the Asiatick Languages* (Oxford: Clarendon Press, 1772).
63. "The Introduction," *Asiatick Researches 1* (1788): iii–viii, v; Jones, "A Discourse on the Institution of a Society," *Asiatick Researches* 1 (1788): x–xi.
64. William Jones to Joseph Banks, Krishnanagar, October 18, 1791, in Chambers, *Letters 1789–1792*, 288; William Jones to Sir Joseph Banks, Calcutta, January 29, 1792, MM.3.45, Royal Society Archives, London. Jones died in 1794 in Calcutta and the Royal Society donated the documents to the British Library, London.
65. Said, *Orientalism*, 22.
66. William Jones, "XXV. The Third Anniversary Discourse, Delivered 2 February, 1786. By the President," *Asiatick Researches* 1 (1788): 415–431, 421–423. Although Jones was not the first to notice the relationship, he is often credited with establishing the Indo-European family of languages and founding comparative linguistics. See Lyle Campbell, "Why Sir William Jones Got It All Wrong, or Jones' Role in How to Establish Language Families," *Anuario del Seminario de Filología Vasca "Julio de Urquijo"* (International Journal of Basque Linguistics and Philology) 40, nos. 1–2 (2006): 245–264.
67. Garland Cannon, ed., *The Letters of Sir William Jones*, vol. II (Oxford: At Clarendon Press, 1970), 786, 790, 814–815, 842–844, 854, 891–896, 903–904, and 906. See also Cannon, "Sir William Jones, Sir Joseph Banks, and the Royal Society," 208–217.
68. Williams Jones to Joseph Banks, Krishnanagar, September 24, 1788, in Neil Chambers, *The Indian and Pacific Correspondence of Sir Joseph Banks, 1768–1820*, vol. II: *Letters 1783–1789* (London: Pickering & Chatto, 2009), 336–337.
69. Cannon, "Sir William Jones, Sir Joseph Banks, and the Royal Society," 217. Banks' letter is missing. William Jones, *Sacontalá, or The Fatal Ring; An Indian Drama by Cálidás: Translated from the Original Sanscrit and Prácrit* (Calcutta: Printed and sold by Joseph Cooper, 1789).
70. William Jones to Joseph Banks, Krishnanagar, October 18, 1791, in Chambers, *Letters 1789–1792*, 286–288.
71. John Gascoigne, *Science in the Service of Empire: Joseph Banks, the British State and the Uses of Science in the Age of Revolution* (Cambridge: Cambridge University Press, 1998), 111–146; Adrian P. Thomas, "The Establishment of Calcutta Botanic Garden: Plant Transfer, Science, and the East India Company, 1786–1806," *Journal of the Royal Asiatic Society* 16, no. 2 (July 2006): 165–177.

72. Garland Cannon and Siddheswar Pandey, "Sir William Jones Revisited: On His Translation of the Śakuntalā," *Journal of the American Oriental Society* 96, no. 4 (October–December 1976): 528–535, 528.
73. Raymond Schwab, *The Oriental Renaissance: Europe's Rediscovery of India and the East, 1680–1880* (New York: Columbia University Press, 1984), 33–47.
74. First used by Europeans in the late eighteenth century to propose kinship ties, the concept of Aryan would be redefined in "white" racial terms during the nineteenth century. See Thomas R. Trautmann, *Aryans and British India* (Berkeley: University of California Press, 1997). About the popularity of Orientalists' publications beyond India, see Trautmann, *Aryans and British India*, 29–30.
75. William Jones, "On the Gods of Greece, Italy, and India, Written in 1784, and Since Revised, By the President," in *The Works of Sir William Jones. In Six Volumes*, vol. I (London: G. G. and J. Robinson, and R. H. Evans, 1799), 229–280.
76. Marsden's paper, in the form of a letter to Banks, appeared in volume 7 of *Archaeologia* (1785), which also contains the Bombay cave articles mentioned earlier in the chapter. See William Marsden, "XLIII. Observations on the Language of the People Commonly Called Gypsies. In a Letter to Sir Joseph Banks, Bart. P. R. S. From Mr. Marsden, F. S. A.," *Archaeologia, or, Miscellaneous Tracts Relating to Antiquity. Published by the Society of Antiquaries of London* 7 (1785): 382–385. Marden credits Banks for supplying much of the material (383).
77. Romila Thapur, "Interpretations of Ancient Indian History," *History and Theory* 7, no. 3 (1968): 318–335, 319.
78. Sen, "Indian Traditions and the Western Imagination," 180.
79. Sen, "Indian Traditions and the Western Imagination," 171.
80. In his professional and personal associations with Indians, Jones treated them as "fellow human beings." He requested that a cure for *elephantiasis* be tested in London so that the disease might be eradicated in India. He introduced to Bengal a tree bearing farinaceous fruit that could end famines. He encouraged his Asiatick Society colleagues to accept Indian members. And he contributed to charitable causes and discouraged slavery in India. See Garland Cannon, "Sir William Jones and the Association between East and West," *Proceedings of the American Philosophical Society* 121, no. 2 (April 29, 1977): 183–187, 185.
81. Said, *Orientalism*, 122.
82. Donald McDonald, "The Indian Medical Service. A Short Account of Its Achievements 1600–1947," *Proceedings of the Royal Society of Medicine* 49, no. 1 (January 1965): 13–17, 16. The four Anglo-Mysore Wars, or battles with the rulers of Mysore, Haider 'Alī Khān and Tipū Sulṭān, took place in 1767–1769, 1780–1784, 1790–1792, and 1799.

4

Tracing the Vernacular

Drawing Madura into Debates over Language in British India

Introduction

Thomas Daniell and his nephew William journeyed from England to India in 1786, hoping to profit from a British market hungry for depictions of life in the British colony. They traveled as itinerant artists and earned their living by rendering original, first-hand impressions of India. The Daniells published six volumes of aquatints for *Oriental Scenery*, presenting India pictorially to elite British residents and newly moneyed East India Company servants returning to London. Later, William Daniell took advantage of the booming nineteenth-century literary marketplace by converting the aquatints from *Oriental Scenery* into engravings for the *Oriental Annual.* The *Oriental Annual* was a mass-produced, moderately priced drawing-room annual, part of an early Victorian print culture that married part-fictional, part-historical travel narrative with exotic pictures, aimed at the literate middle class that emerged during Britain's industrial revolution. Volume II (1798) of *Oriental Scenery* and volume III (1836) of the *Oriental Annual* feature images and commentary about Madurai (which the British called "Madura") and the Pudu Maṇḍapam (described as "choultry").

Through the genre of British literary annuals, the small southern temple town of Madurai became entangled in imperial debates over the government of the British colony as a whole. William Daniell's engravings in the *Oriental Annual* featured the commentary of Hobart Caunter, a British cleric who claimed to have traveled with the Daniells; Caunter's notes accompanied images of Madurai and the Pudu Maṇḍapam, but they were addressed to a brewing debate over the medium of instruction in government-sponsored schools in British India, deliberated in Bengal, the seat of East India Company operations. Influenced by the same debates, Letitia Elizabeth Landon's poem about the Madurai temple in another literary annual published the same year, *Fisher's Drawing Room Scrap-Book* III (1836), relayed the problem of colonial education within a nascent discourse of bourgeois feminist morality. These texts illustrate how Indian architecture was transported and transposed by professional artists to accommodate the aesthetic tastes of an emerging British consumer class. In the early nineteenth century, as the fates of British subjects in the colony and the metropole were more intimately intertwined, the Madurai temple became a prop for deliberating a central problem of colonial rule: the official language and methods of education in British India.

Artists seeking adventure

Thomas Daniell (1749–1840) was an accomplished artist who traveled to India to make his fortune as a painter and engraver. Daniell was inspired by William Hodges (1744–1797), whose popular collection *Select Views in India in the Years 1780–1783* featured aquatints adapted from sketches of Indian architecture "drawn on the spot."[1] Like Hodges, Daniell wanted to tap into the thriving market for consumption of a distant Orient—when the East India Company granted him official authorization to travel to India on their ship, he set sail in 1785, joined by his sixteen-year-old nephew William (1769–1837) as assistant and apprentice.

The Daniells journeyed for nine months via China before landing in Calcutta, where they captured the city's skyline, government buildings, river *ghats*, churches, and temples in twelve colored aquatints, *Views in Calcutta* (1786–1788).[2] They sold their prints to wealthy British residents of Calcutta in the Bengal Presidency and generated enough income to finance their travels on the Indian subcontinent. For two years, the Daniells visited north and eastern India and drew field sketches of monuments, hill forts, mosques, temples, and landscape views. The tours of India were arduous, and they endured rugged terrain, hot climate, lost baggage, and bandits. Thomas and William traveled with a few servants, including a house steward, table servant, watchman, and tent-pitchers. Upon their 1791 return to Calcutta and after collecting more funds from their art sales, the Daniells embarked on the second phase of their tour: a journey through south India. They sailed to Madras in March 1792, this time with much greater manpower, as they took advantage of the East India Company's defeat of Tipū Sulṭān in the Third Anglo-Mysore War (1790–1792), which brought once inaccessible land under British control.[3]

Back in England, the Daniells selected from their large inventory of on-site pencil sketches and quick watercolors, which they transformed into oil paintings and finished aquatints. The aquatint method was a tedious and time-consuming printmaking process that involved etching a copperplate with nitric acid and producing a print resembling a watercolor: the Daniells spent the next thirteen years (1795–1808) making 144 aquatints published in six folio volumes called *Oriental Scenery*.[4] The first volume's images of Mughal architecture catered to a British fascination with the waning Mughal empire; the East India Company's

Figure 4.1 Thomas and William Daniell, *The Council House, Calcutta*, hand-colored aquatint, 54 × 73.7 centimeters, 1797

Source: Thomas and William Daniell, *Oriental Scenery: Twenty-Four Views in Hindoostan, Taken in the Year 1792; Drawn by Thomas Daniell, and Engraved by Himself and William Daniell; and, with Permission, Respectfully Dedicated to the Right Honourable Henry Dundas, One of His Majesty's Principal Secretaries Of State, President of the Board Of Commissioners for the Affairs of India, Treasurer of the Navy, &c. &c. &c.* (London: Thomas Daniell, August 1797), plate 3. Yale Center for British Art, Paul Mellon Collection.

London-based Court of Directors considered the prints a valuable source of information, and purchased thirty copies.[5] The second volume begun in 1797 (*Oriental Scenery: Twenty-Four Views in Hindoostan, Taken in the Year 1792*) features pictures of the two East India Company coastal footholds of Calcutta and Madras (Figures 4.1 and 4.2), and of the Hindu peninsular south of Madurai, Tiruchirappalli, and Tanjavur (called Madura, Trichinopoly, and Tanjore). The Daniells included six aquatints and captions of Madurai's fort, palace, temple, and the Pudu Maṇḍapam (Figures 4.3 and 4.4).

The final image of Madurai is plate 18, entitled *Tremal Naig's Choultry, Madura*, with the following descriptive note, documenting the hall's measurements, important iconography, and function for its British readers:

> The Choultry of Rajah Tremal Naig is considered as one of the finest works of its kind in the south of Hindoostan. Its general form is that of a parallelogram, three hundred and twelve feet in length, by one hundred and twenty-five feet in width; and

Figure 4.2 Thomas and William Daniell, *Western Entrance of Fort St George*, hand-colored aquatint, 54 × 73.7 centimeters, 1798

Source: Thomas and William Daniell, *Oriental Scenery: Twenty-Four Views in Hindoostan, Taken in the Year 1792*, plate 12. Yale Center for British Art, Paul Mellon Collection.

Figure 4.3 Thomas and William Daniell, *Ruins of the Palace, Madura*, hand-colored aquatint, 54.6 × 74.7 centimeters, 1798

Source: Thomas and William Daniell, *Oriental Scenery: Twenty-Four Views in Hindoostan, Taken in the Year 1792*, plate 17. Yale Center for British Art, Paul Mellon Collection.

Figure 4.4 Thomas and William Daniell, *An Hindoo Temple, at Madura*, hand-colored aquatint, 54.6 × 74.7 centimeters, 1798

Source: Thomas and William Daniell, *Oriental Scenery: Twenty-Four Views in Hindoostan, Taken in the Year 1792*, plate 16. Yale Center for British Art, Paul Mellon Collection.

> consists of one large hall, the ceiling of which is supported by six ranges of columns, about twenty-five feet in height, many of them formed of single stones, and the whole composed of grey granite. This view contains half the centre ile [*sic*]. On the second pillar to the right hand is the effigy of the Rajah with three of his wives, to whom, for his munificence, the Hindoos still continue to pay divine honours. Beyond the Rajah, and on the pillars opposite to him are other statues representing his family. In the ceiling are the twelve signs of the zodiac; and a number of mythological figures carved in basso relievo, are interspersed through the building, which, together with a profusion of other decorations, are executed with an uncommon degree of skill and attention.
>
> The Choultry is an edifice which in the Deccan is always found attached to Hindoo temples, and appropriated to the use of the religious; they are likewise erected on the public roads for the accommodation of travellers.[6]

The Daniells' view of the *maṇḍapam* looks inward from the east towards the temple (Figure 4.5). The temple's east side is at the opposite end of the hall, but the artists exaggerated the hall's length by including a dark cavernous space where a street and a temple façade are located. The hall basks in the morning sun's rays that

Figure 4.5 Thomas and William Daniell, *Tremal Naig's Choultry, Madura*, hand-colored aquatint, 54.6 × 74.7 centimeters, 1798

Source: Thomas and William Daniell, *Oriental Scenery: Twenty-Four Views in Hindoostan, Taken in the Year 1792,* plate 18. Yale Center for British Art, Paul Mellon Collection.

filter from the left between the pillars to spotlight the sculpted columns. On the right, the illuminated Tirumala Nāyaka stone statue stands directly opposite the shadowed Viśvanātha Nāyaka, the founder of the Madurai Nāyaka dynasty. A few people gather near the pillar of Tirumala Nāyaka: one woman raises her clasped palms and another holds a brass pot at her waist, while one man gestures towards the ruler's portrait and another prostates before the king, paying "divine honours." A clay pot and fruit basket rest on the warm sepia-colored floor that gradates to a pale blue in the back, where other individuals stand, sit, or engage in conversation.

No other plate in *Oriental Scenery* II contains such visibly etched outlines as the Pudu Maṇḍapam one. These lines highlight and emphasize the profusion of sculptural details, embellishments, and figures on the pillars. Plate 18 appears as both an engraved and painted image, where stark etched lines contrast with broad watercolor-like effects. However, a 'true' aquatint consists "not of lines of varying depth or thickness, as in an etching or a copper-plate engraving, but of tones, approximating to the washes of a water-colour drawing."[7] The Pudu Maṇḍapam plate contains mostly engraved, linear elements: it is not a genuine aquatint, and is the only such image in the entire *Oriental Scenery* collection.[8] William Daniell may have played a significant role in producing this illustration, as he is listed in *Oriental Scenery* II for the first time as engraver; this unique engraving would become important as a reincarnation in the *Oriental Annual* nearly forty years later.

Oriental consumption and the emerging middle class

The nineteenth-century industrial revolution created new forms of class stratification in Britain.[9] From the boom in manufacturing appeared both the working class of factory laborers and a new middle class comprised of factory owners, merchants, and businessmen. Situated loosely below the aristocracy and above the workers, the emerging middle class pursued reforms in education and social policy that prioritized merit and achievement rather than one's birth or aristocratic privilege.[10] With the explosive economic expansion and urban growth of the late eighteenth and early nineteenth centuries, the reading public swelled, stimulated by rising incomes, greater leisure, and improved literacy. By 1830, the new middle class was consuming large quantities of books, magazines, and newspapers, which supported many professional writers.[11] Drawing-room annuals, or "gift-books," were an important feature of print culture and dominated the literary market from 1822 to 1857; the typical annual was an elaborately bound book that combined poetry or prose with engravings of people or places.[12] Intended for middle-class readers (because of their relative affordability), the annuals were especially popular among women.[13]

In 1833, observing the emergence of this new reading public and the business potential in marketing literary annuals, Rev. Hobart Caunter (1794–1851) collaborated on a series of oriental 'views' with William Daniell. Caunter had worked as a cadet in India until around 1810, when he decided there was "nothing on the continent of Asia to interest him."[14] However, India remained on his mind: he wrote about his impressions in an 1814 poem, "The Cadet," and an 1836 book, *The Romance of History. India.*[15] *The Oriental Annual, or Scenes in India* capitalized on Daniell's name, artistic talent, and expertise on India. Owing to the commercial success of *Oriental Scenery*, Daniell had earned a reputation as a talented artist and a prolific printmaker in England: he exhibited numerous views of India, Scotland, and Britain at London's Royal Academy, and completed series such as *A Brief History of Ancient and Modern India* (1802–1805) and *View of London* (1812). Unlike his uncle, William began focusing on representations of Indian figures and waterside scenes, concentrating less on topography and more on oriental fantasy.

The leather-like cover of *Oriental Annual* evokes the oriental scenery of India: embossed with intertwined serpents and gilded with a figure of a *mahārāja* (Indian king) on an elephant howdah with an attendant and mahout (Figure 4.6).

Figure 4.6 Cover, *Oriental Annual*, 20.2 × 12.7 centimeters, 1834

Source: William Daniell and Rev. Hobart Caunter, *The Oriental Annual, or Scenes in India; Comprising Twenty-Five Engravings from Original Drawings by William Daniell, R.A. and a Descriptive Account by the Rev. Hobart Caunter, B.D.* (London: Edward Bull, 1834). Image courtesy of Murphy Library Special Collections/ARC, University of Wisconsin-La Crosse.

The annual consists of gilt-edged pages of commentary and engravings based on drawings given to Caunter by William Daniell. Nearly all of the forty-eight Indian 'views' Daniell contributed to the Royal Academy from 1826 to 1837 are engraved in the *Oriental Annual*.[16] The *Oriental Annual* was celebrated by contemporary magazines and newspapers upon its release: it was called "the Aurora of the Annuals" by the *Literary Gazette*, "one of the most animate pictures that has ever been issued from the press" by *The Atlas*,[17] and "unrivalled in its class for the permanent interest and instructive character of its matter ... for the clearness and strength of its composition ... for the splendor of its illustrations and of its more mechanical adornments" by *The Spectator*.[18] William Daniell's obituary in the 1837 issue of the *Gentleman's Magazine* contained these words of praise:

> "Oriental Annual" ... is a work deservedly ranking high among that class of periodicals to which it belongs, whether we consider the beauty and fidelity of the drawings, the interesting variety of the subjects, the admirable manner in which the plates are engraved, or the valuable information conveyed in the text.[19]

Joseph Wilson Lowry (1803–1879), an accomplished engraver, contributed two prints to accompany information about Madurai and the Pudu Maṇḍapam in chapters III and IV of the third volume of the *Oriental Annual* (1836).[20] Lowry's images were characteristic of monochrome, steel-engraved illustrations in mass-produced books for middle-class consumers, marketed at cheaper prices than the expensive, limited-quantity, large-format volumes of hand-colored aquatints like the Daniells'.[21] The rapid expansion of the book market increased the demand for engravers experienced in steel-plate engravings, since the hardness of steel created more durable plates than copper, and were needed for continuous reprint production. The texture of steel also allowed for cutting clean edges in the engraved plate that imparted distinct lines and finer detail.[22]

Despite the intricate process involved in producing each image, engravers were often considered "mere transcribers of other men's work, not original artists."[23] For *Oriental Annual* III's illustrative engraving of the Pudu Maṇḍapam, Lowry copied the Daniells' plate 18 from the 1798 *Oriental Scenery* II with some minor alterations. The black-and-white tones and the profusion of fine dark lines render the steel engraving "The Choultry of Tremal Naig at Madura" (in chapter IV: "The Nayaca Dynasty") harsher than the original aquatint (Figure 4.7). In the foreground, two pillars sheltered from the bright light herald the hall's central portion: the granite pillars of Tirumala Nāyaka and his ancestors. The sun-drenched royal portraits on one side contrast significantly with the shaded portrayals across the hall. Light thrust onto the sculptures accentuates the contours of the Nāyakas' corpulent bodies. The shadows cast menacing marks on the bright stone floor while the monochromatic scheme gives the engraving an ominous tone absent from the original, colored aquatint. The lack of color in the *Oriental Annual* led one *Spectator* reviewer to describe the engravings as "cold and tame."[24]

The image of the interior view of the long hall and its stone pillars is accompanied by several pages of information about the Madurai Nāyakas. Caunter wrote about the foundational history of the dynasty from Viśvanātha Nāyaka, before describing Tirumala Nāyaka ("Trimalla Nayaca" or "Trimal Naig") and the Pudu Maṇḍapam at the temple. Caunter identifies the Pudu Maṇḍapam as a chronicle of the deeds of Tirumala Nāyaka and his ancestors "in a material more durable than marble."[25] In describing the particulars of the pillared hall, Caunter lifted almost verbatim from the notes to *Oriental Scenery* II's plate 18; but he also added his own impressions, speculating on Tirumala Nāyaka's motives for commissioning the immense granite pillars. Caunter believed that Tirumala's decision to install stone depictions of himself and his relatives near the statuary of significant deities indicated a selfish desire for personal fame under the guise of religious philanthropy.[26]

Figure 4.7 W. Daniell R. A. (artist) and J. Lowry (engraver), *The Choultry of Tremal Naig at Madura*, engraving, 9.8 × 14.9 centimeters, 1836

Source: William Daniell and Rev. Hobart Caunter, *The Oriental Annual, or Scenes in India; Comprising Twenty-Two Engravings from Original Drawings by William Daniell, R.A. and a Descriptive Account by the Rev. Hobart Caunter, B.D.* (London: Edward Churton, 1836), between pages 50 and 51.

In the first volume of *Oriental Annual* (1834), Caunter made a point of reminding readers of his own authoritative knowledge as a traveler of India, and of William Daniell's proficiency in illustrating Indian scenes—but Caunter's account was fabricated.[27] Although Daniell supplied Caunter with information for the text, Caunter's narrative gives the impression that he had personally accompanied the peripatetic artists on their journey. He wrote, for example: "We spent several days at Mahabalipuram, examining all the extraordinary monuments of art in its neighborhood.... Mr. William Daniell took the opportunity, during our stay, of making several very accurate and finished drawings; and here he found subjects in every respect worthy of his pencil."[28] In actuality, Caunter was born the year the Daniells left India; he arrived in the subcontinent about sixteen years after their departure.

Caunter attached his narrative to the Daniells' to furnish it with the authenticity of a travel narrative, to give himself credibility in the eyes of the British reading public, and to add to the 'mystique' of his account of the Orient. He supplemented his own observations and imaginations of India with facts obtained from various other sources.[29] Caunter appears to have effectively fooled his readers: *The Spectator* described the narrative form of the text as "a tour, intermingled with individual portraiture and historical episodes" and praised the book's ability to convey "the spirit of fiction without its untruth."[30] In fact, Caunter did not particularly like India at all. Caunter's writing lamented Madura's narrow, dirty streets, filthy huts, cattle herds, obstructed drains, and stagnant water that "is not attractive to the traveler."[31] In Caunter's opinion, only Madurai's *antiquity*—its reputation as a seat of learning (with a college and preeminent scholars) and its extraordinary edifices erected by Tirumala Nāyaka—was worthy of recognition. Caunter's writing was typical of Orientalist tropes about British India that celebrated its 'glorious' ancient past, while mourning the degraded present.

British paternalism and the evangelical mission

Although much of Caunter's writing in the *Oriental Annual* is drawn from supplementary sources, one passage stands out as unusual in his narrative about Madurai. Caunter makes a sudden detour from his description of Madurai as a "now miserable and dilapidated city," and discusses how the city fell from its previous apex as a "celebrated seat of learning" where "it was as rare to find a poor villager who could not read as it is now to find one who can."[32] Caunter believed that English people were under the "erroneous impression" that Indians were "semi-barbarians" due to the relative inferiority of Indian scholarly achievements at that moment. To make the point, the *Oriental Annual* quotes from an 1835 letter sent by Sir Alexander Johnston (1775–1849), a colonial judge in Ceylon and a Royal Asiatic Society member, to British politician Charles Grant (1778–1866):

> Education has always, from the earliest period of their history, been an object of public care and of public interest to the Hindoo governments on the peninsula of India. Every well-regulated village under those governments had a public school and a public schoolmaster. The system of instruction in them was that which, in consequence of its efficiency, simplicity, and cheapness, was a few years ago introduced from Madras into England, and from England into the rest of Europe. Every Hindoo parent looked upon the education of his child as a solemn duty, which he owed to his God and to his country, and placed him under the schoolmaster of his village as soon as he had attained his fifth year....[33]

This passage refers to the "Madras System of Education," an invention of Rev. Andrew Bell (1753–1832), a Church of England clergyman and educationist, who observed Malabar schoolchildren teaching each other to write letters of the alphabet in the sand. Bell employed the idea of "mutual tuition"—older students teaching younger ones—as superintendent of the East India Company's Military Male Orphan Asylum in Madras by developing a hierarchy of monitors, grouping children by ability, and prohibiting learning by rote memorization or copying abstract lectures.[34] After a ten-year stay in India, Bell adapted the methods he studied in India into the system of national education in England; Caunter sought to demonstrate how Britain had benefited from the Indian traditions imported by Bell, "for which his name will be immortalized in its annals."[35] Over several pages, Caunter lauds the "literary Hindoos" of the distant past and diagnoses the beginning of the decline in "Hindoo learning" to the "Mahomedan [Muslim] conquest."[36] Caunter believed that the Indian intellect could be restored: "The more … the treasures of their forefathers' wisdom is brought into view, the more certainly shall we find that in the mental resources they were not at all behind the ancient Egyptians."[37]

The discourse of 'restoration,' a central premise of Caunter's narrative in the *Oriental Annual*, was integral to the logic of colonization: British tutelage was understood as a means of restoring the lost glory of a decaying Indian civilization. Caunter described the celebrated poet Tiruvaḷḷuvar ("Tiru Valuvir"), who authored *Tirukkuṟaḷ*, a compilation of Tamil sayings on a moral, ethical life that is a staple of Indian education in the Tamil areas; he also discussed Tiruvaḷḷuvar's sister, Auvaiyār ("Avyar"), a poet who penned simple didactic Tamil poems found in school textbooks. Tiruvaḷḷuvar and Auvaiyār were accomplished *paṟaiyar*s, or 'untouchables,' who lived sometime during the third century BCE to the first century CE in the Madurai area.[38] In the late eighteenth century, *Tirukkuṟaḷ* caught the attention of European missionaries and British civil servants, who were drawn to the text's non-sectarian, non-idolatrous teachings. By 1831, *Tirukkuṟaḷ* was one of the first books published in translation from the College of Fort St George in the East India Company's Madras Presidency.[39] Many nineteenth-century European writers concentrated on Tiruvaḷḷuvar's mixed-caste parentage (half-Brahmin, half-Paṟaiyar) and his defeat of the Saṅgam poets in the ancient literary academy of Madurai, which Caunter recounted briefly in his *Oriental Annual*.[40]

Caunter's writing on the Tamil poets was not only a commentary on Indian history, but also a critique of the mechanisms of colonial administration. Caunter perceived the accomplishments of Tiruvaḷḷuvar and Auvaiyār as evidence of the "liberal spirit" of the ancient Hindu society, as a "Pariah and his sister" obtained admission to the highest seat of learning in Madurai, and Auvaiyār's writing was still highly esteemed "among the gems of Hindoo literature."[41] Caunter suggested that the high regard for the brother and sister's works indicated a tolerance for the poets' pariah status that was absent in India in his own time:

> … their numerous works have been adopted as class-books for the higher orders of scholars in all the Hindoo seminaries of learning throughout India. This is sufficient proof that the modern prejudices, which are the bitter fruits of caste, did not exist, or but in a very limited degree, while literature flourished in Hindostan.[42]

The Hindu caste system (which Caunter called an "odius system"[43]) was commonly denounced by British missionaries, while at the same time it was exploited by colonial administrators who constructed the emerging bureaucratic state around caste classifications, and used ethnographic and demographic techniques to segregate the Indian population.[44] Caunter's writing was part of a body of discourse within British imperial thought about the history of Hindu society, the caste system, and the proper methods of reshaping it.

A critical debate in Caunter's time—and the point of intersection of the politicians, administrators, poets, and scholars named in the third chapter of *Oriental Annual* III—was the question of the *language* in government-sponsored education in British India. The debate over designing a system of public education for the British colony began with Governor-General Warren Hastings' decision in 1781 to establish a *madrasā* (Muslim educational institution) in Calcutta, and his encouragement of Oriental languages and literature in the Bengal Presidency. Hastings felt that it had been the "Wisdom of every well regulated Government, both in India and in Persia to promote by such Instructions the Growth and Extension of liberal Knowledge," and that this high scholarly achievement had disappeared in the time of the Mughals.[45] Hastings explained the political utility of reviving Indian culture and learning in a 1784 letter: "Every accumulation of knowledge ... obtained by social communication with people over whom we exercise a dominion founded on the right of conquest, is useful to the state."[46] To Hastings, effective governance depended on "acculturated" British officials who could administer policy according to traditional Indian rules, through a sophisticated understanding of indigenous institutions, laws, customs, and languages.[47] Hastings wrote in his introduction to Charles Wilkins' translation of the Hindu holy book, *Bhagavad Gītā*:

> Every instance which brings their [Indian] real character home to observation will impress us with a more generous sense of feeling for their natural rights, and teach us to estimate them by the measure of our own. But such instances can only be obtained in their writings: and these will survive when the British dominion in India shall have long ceased to exist, and when the sources which it once yielded of wealth and power are lost to remembrance.[48]

What may appear at first in Hastings' writing as sympathy for Indians' "natural rights" is in fact thinly veiled cultural imperialism: Hastings believed that Indians in the present could only be respected in terms of the achievements of their distinguished forefathers, the authors of ancient religious texts such as the *Gītā*. The Hindu scriptures, in Hastings' view, comprise "a single exception, among all the known religions of mankind, of a theology accurately corresponding with that of Christian dispensation, and most powerfully illustrating its fundamental doctrines."[49] For Hastings, the most valuable aspects of the *Gītā* were those that confirmed and "corresponded" with Christianity.[50]

East India Company director Charles Grant (1746–1823) made great efforts during this period to more effectively incorporate Christian education into colonial government. In 1792, Grant wrote his pamphlet *Observations on the State of Society among the Asiatic Subjects of Great Britain*, an influential missionary apologia for importing British Christianity and British schooling norms in colonial education. In his *Observations*, Grant argued for evangelical reform and conversion, believing in the transformative benefits of Christian light and truth to a degenerate Indian society:

> The true cure of darkness, is the introduction of light. The Hindoos err, because they are ignorant; and their errors have never fairly been laid before them. The communication of our light and knowledge to them, would prove to be the best remedy for their disorders....[51]

The pamphlet was circulated to the East India Company's Court of Directors, Board of Control, and Parliament, and, thanks to Grant's persistent lobbying, Parliament lifted the ban on European evangelical missions in India in 1813. Grant's proposal sowed the seeds for an ardent campaign to 'enlighten' Indian education and society, in which evangelical attitudes would play a crucial role.[52]

Charles Grant's son, also named Charles, was the recipient of Johnston's 1835 letter on the question of language quoted in Caunter's *Oriental Annual* III. As president of the Board of Control, the younger Grant retained his father's religious zeal, and he pressed for the renewal of the 1833 Charter Act, which extended the scope of the East India Company's mission to include "the commerce of this country, and of securing the good government, and promoting the religious and moral improvements of the people of India."[53] The Charter created a new supreme council for India with a post for a law member, a position offered to Thomas Babington Macaulay (1800–1859), who served under Governor-General Lord William Bentinck and joined his brother-in-law Charles E. Trevelyan, a Company administrator, in advancing an Anglicist policy of cultural reform that sought to cultivate Christian values through English-language education.

Bourgeois feminist reflections on imperial ethics

In 1834, a controversy arose concerning the allotment of Company money for native students in higher education in the British colony.[54] The Orientalist faction, led by Indian education department secretary H. T. Prinsep, was deeply respectful of Indian classical education (Sanskrit, Persian, and Arabic) and sought to "engraft" Western knowledge and innovations onto Indian cultural traditions.[55] The Anglicist faction, on the other hand, perceived little value in traditional Indian education and imagined a 'modern' India realized through English-language education.[56] Thomas Macaulay, president of the Committee of Public Education, argued vehemently for teaching European literature and science in India, in English only. His program, outlined in his 1835 *Minute on Indian Education*, required that the British "do our best to form a class who may be interpreters between us and the millions whom we govern; a class of persons Indian in blood and colour, but English in tastes, in opinions, in morals and in intellect."[57] Acting under Macaulay's influence, Bentinck established the 1835 English Education Act, which was "of opinion that the great object of the British Government ought to be the promotion of European literature and science amongst the natives of India, and that all the funds appropriated for the purpose of education should be best employed on English education alone."[58]

Although the education debate centered primarily in the administrative capital in Bengal, the Madurai temple became a prop in this conflict thanks to the writings of Alexander Johnston, a British judge who spent his youth in Madurai, where his father worked as a paymaster under governor of Madras Lord George Macartney. Trained by Christian Friedrich Schwartz, a German missionary with the Society for Promoting Christian Knowledge, and Thomas Munro, an East India Company army officer, Johnston learned local vernaculars such as Tamil, Telugu, and Hindustani, and studied Hindu, Muslim, and Buddhist customs, cultivating a "lifelong sympathy with Indians." As a judge, Johnston promoted a system of universal education, opened employment for the Ceylonese, and emancipated slaves.[59] Upon his return to England, Johnston helped found the Royal Asiatic Society of Great Britain and Ireland in 1823, and presided as vice-president of this society devoted to the history, languages, cultures, and religions of Asia.

When Johnston was eleven years old, an East India Company colonel named Colin Mackenzie stayed with his family in Madurai. Mackenzie and Johnston's father formed a plan to revive the Tamil Saṅgam, the ancient college, in an abandoned ruin built by the Nāyakas and gifted by the Nawāb of Arcot: they obtained an account of this college and copies of the plans from Madurai-based missionaries Robert de Nobili and Constantine Beschi.[60] Although the project was never finished during the elder Johnston and Mackenzie's lifetimes, Johnston wanted to see his father's idea to conclusion,[61] an endeavor described in Caunter's narrative in the *Oriental Annual*.[62] According to Caunter's account, Johnston shared his father's interest in recovering a traditional system of education in India by resuscitating Madurai as "a seat of learning" as it had once been. In his 1835 letter to Grant, Johnston described reverently, according to Rama Mantena, "the ancient traditions of education and literary creativity in South India" and argued for continuing historical research with governmental encouragement to further intellectual exchange between Britain and its colony.[63] Johnston may have served as an informant for some of Caunter's stories in the *Oriental Annual*—Caunter donated a copy of the annual at the January 18, 1834, Royal Asiatic Society meeting that Johnston chaired; impressed by the presentation, the Society decided to subscribe to the series.[64]

In the same year that the *Oriental Annual* was published with a narrative of Madurai's decline and quotes from Johnston's letter on colonial education, another popular British drawing-room annual printed a poem addressed to the same topic: Letitia Elizabeth Landon's "Hindoo Temples and Palace at Madura" in *Fisher's Drawing Room Scrap-Book* (1836). Landon wrote poetry both as a passion and as a means of supporting her family after the death of her father. She submitted her poems to journals under the pen name L. E. L., and she authored and edited several drawing-room annuals during the 1820s and 1830s. She was zealous in pursuing prominent editors and an expert at tailoring her writing to the tastes of literary consumers; she became a prominent figure—"an important cultural icon"—in the London literary scene and her work was widely circulated and read throughout the world.[65] The new middle-class consumerism driving the nineteenth-century literary marketplace created novel professional opportunities for women like Landon. Usually published in November and December, annuals were designed for gift-giving and were especially marketed towards women, who took special interest in the publications.[66] From 1832 to 1852, the London-based *Fisher's Drawing Room Scrap-Book* featured 36 engravings, each accompanied by a poem (sometimes about a foreign and 'exotic' destination) in large-format books to be displayed on a drawing room table. Landon served as its first editor for eight volumes, and she composed poems based on steel-plate engravings supplied by the publisher. In the introduction of the 1832 volume, Landon explained that the prints were "selected rather for their pictorial excellence than their poetic capabilities."[67] In a letter to *Literary Gazette* editor William Jerdan, she indicated that the *Drawing Room Scrap-Book* (as the title suggests) was primarily a means of selling extra prints left over from other publications:

> Every great print seller has I believe on hand—a number of engravings more than the actual demand. What I propose is to make a selection from the prettiest of these and form then into an Annual.... How well the collection of prints previously published has answered in the case of the Drawingroom Scrap Book ... people like pretty pictures.[68]

Landon lacked first-hand knowledge of India.[69] Yet many of her poems pursued an Indian theme, where she often reproduced romantic fantasies of India tailored to curious consumers interested in "Indian views;"[70] examples include "The Nizam's Daughter," "Hindoo and Mahomedan Buildings," "The Hindoo Girl's Song," and "Ruins about the Taj Mahal."[71] Landon wrote "Hindoo Temples and Palace at Madura" to accompany W. Floyd's engraving of W. Purser's drawing (Figure 4.8).[72] In the image, two trees form a leafy canopy over a long-distance view (from the north) of the temple's towering gateways, the palace's lofty structures, and a meandering path traveled by villagers. Its aesthetic quality is unlike the Daniells' scenes, more closely resembling William Hodges' landscapes where natural elements and living creatures dominate the foreground and frame distant architectural subjects (Figure 4.9). Landon's poem reads:

HINDOO TEMPLES AND PALACE AT MADURA[73]

LITTLE the present careth for the past,
Too little,—'tis not well!
For careless ones we dwell
Beneath the mighty shadow it has cast.

Its blessings are around our daily path,
We share its mighty spoil,
We live on its great toil,
And yet how little gratitude it hath.

Look on these temples, they were as a shrine
From whence to the far north
The human mind went forth,
The moral sunshine of a world divine—

That inward world which maketh of our clay
Its temporary home;
From when those lightnings come,
That kindle from a far and better day.

The light that is of heaven shone there the first,
The elements of art,
Mankind's diviner part;
There was young science in its cradle nurst.

Mighty the legacies by mind bequeathed,
For glories were its pains
Amid those giant fanes,
And mighty were the triumphs it achieved.

A woman's triumph* mid them is imprest,
One who upon the scroll
Flung the creative soul,
Disdainful of life's flowers and of its rest.

Vast was the labour, vast the enterprise,
For she was of a race
Born to the lowest place,
Earth insects, lacking wings whereon to rise.

How must that youthful cheek have lost its bloom,
How many a dream above
Of early hope and love
Must that young heart have closed on like a tomb.

Such throw life's flowers behind them, and aspire
To ask the stars their lore,
And from each ancient store
Seek food to stay the mind's consuming fire.

Her triumph was complete and long, the chords
She struck are yet alive;
Not vainly did she strive
To leave her soul immortal on her words.

A great example she has left behind,
A lesson we should take,
Whose first task is to wake
The general wish to benefit our kind.

Our sword has swept o'er India; there remains
A nobler conquest far,
The mind's ethereal war,
That but subdues to civilize its plains.

Let us pay back the past the debt we owe,
Let us around dispense
Light, hope, intelligence,
Till blessings track our steps where'er we go.

O England, thine be the deliverer's meed,
Be thy great empire known
By hearts made all thine own,
By thy free laws and thy immortal creed.

Landon was most likely inspired to write about Madurai and its temple by Alexander Johnston, and he supplied the poet with the cultural and historical references for her composition.[74] Mirroring Caunter's narrative in the *Oriental Annual*, Landon included some explanatory notes lauding Madurai's former "might, majesty, and dominion," and described various historical achievements attributed to the city: the embassy sent to Augustus Caesar in the second century,

Figure 4.8 W. Purser (artist), Captain Chapman, Royal Engineers (sketcher), and W. Floyd (engraver), *The Celebrated Hindoo Temples, & Palace, at Madura*, engraving, 11.7 × 18.7 centimeters, 1836

Source: Letitia Elizabeth Landon, *Fisher's Drawing Room Scrap-Book, 1836. With Poetical Illustrations by L. E. L.* (London and Paris: Fisher, Son, & Co., Berlin: Asher, New York: Jackson, 1836), between pages 50 and 51.

the origin of measurements of Hindu astronomers, the invention of numerals, the Tamil Saṅgam—the legendary college that fascinated Johnston and his father—and the "fine pagoda and choultry in its neighborhood."[75]

The poem's title refers to Madurai's temple and palace, like the illustrations in *Oriental Scenery* and the *Oriental Annual*, but the poem makes no mention whatsoever of the palace, and offers only a few words about the temple.[76] Many stanzas in the poem could have been written about any number of "Hindoo temples," and are not necessarily particular to the one in Madurai. The singular south Indian temple in the accompanying image seems to stand in for Indian civilization as a whole. The poem begins with a bold exclamation about a "mighty shadow," the immensity of India's exalted past, in which those in the present dwell "carelessly"—she suggests that the British have reaped the rewards of the great civilization ("share its mighty spoil"), but show little gratitude for it. In stanza three, Landon criticizes the conceit of European moral superiority by appealing to the spiritual and intellectual dimensions of the temples, "from whence ... the human mind went forth." In the fourth stanza, Landon uses Christian concepts to indicate the moral qualities of Hindu worship, and she describes the "inward world," an allusion to soul or spirit, which resides within the temple, "maketh of our clay." Extending this analogy, she writes in stanza five that the "light ... of heaven shone there [the temple] first," indicating a belief that Hindu ancients were the spiritual predecessors to Christianity. The divine "light" of knowledge and reason shone on India *before* Europe, and thus early scientific discoveries were "nurst" there.[77]

Landon acknowledges the poet Auvaiyār, Tiruvaḷḷuvar's sister, in a footnote to stanza seven, with the annotation: "I allude to the celebrated Avyia. She was a Pariah of the lowest class, but obtained such literary distinction, that her works are to this day the class-books of the scholars of the highest rank and caste in all the Hindoo schools of the peninsula of India."[78] In subsequent stanzas, Landon narrates the story of Auvaiyār, focusing on her supposed low-caste origins and advanced age. The Tamil root of Auvaiyār is *avvai*, meaning mother, old woman, or female ascetic: according to legend, Auvaiyār prayed to have her youth taken away. Auvaiyār, now old, was no longer sought after by youthful lovers, so she could "stay the mind's consuming fire" and focus on her philosophical and devotional pursuits. In stanzas eleven and twelve, Landon describes Auvaiyār's "triumph," her literary didactic works—*Ātticūṭi* ('Śiva who wears the *ātti* flower,' an alphabetical list of pithy quotations), *Koṉṟaivēyntaṉ* ('King/Lord who wears the *koṉṟai* flower,' a short moral code), *Mūturai* ('Ancient wise sayings'), and *Nalvaḻi* ('Good path')—whose aphorisms survived

Figure 4.9 William Hodges, *A View of Part of the Fort of Lutteefpoor* [*Latifpur*], gray wash and graphite on paper, laid down on 19th century wash mount, 48.7 × 66.7 centimeters, c. 1781

Source: William Hodges, *Choix de vues de l'Inde, dessinées sur les lieux, pendant les années 1780, 1781, 1782, et 1783, et executées en aqua tinta, par W. Hodges.... Select Views in India, Drawn on the Spot, in the Years 1780, 1781, 1782, and 1783, and Executed in Aqua Tinta, by William Hodges, R.A.*, vol. I (London: Printed [by Joseph Cooper] for the author; and sold by J. Edwards, 1786–1788), no. 9. Yale Center for British Art, Paul Mellon Collection.

several centuries up to British rule. Sayings from *Ātticūṭi*, such as "Avoid anger," "Help others as much as possible," and "Never stop learning," are still prescribed in Tamil elementary education curriculum, and in stanza twelve, Landon's poem celebrates the eternal lessons imparted by Auvaiyār's poetry: "the chords/She struck are yet alive."

Landon's poem is a form of critique, and thus a method of correction and refinement: the writing is not explicitly *opposed* to empire, but rather seems concerned with altering the ethical parameters of colonial rule. In stanza thirteen, Landon speaks with the voice of empire, in unison with the colonizing power and its moral and civilizational imperatives: she refers to "our sword" which has swept across India as a noble conquest; but a nobler conquest, she writes, is "the mind's ethereal war," the spiritual conflict entailed in efforts to "civilize its plains." In the final stanzas, she addresses the empire directly: "O England, thine be the deliverer's meed." Here, the "deliverer" may refer to the Christian prophet or to the Hindu ancients, on whom "the light of heaven shone" first—in either case, the British empire is the deliverer's "meed" (reward), and its "immortal creed" eternally destined. These stanzas contain an ambivalent ethical prescription for empire: to repay its debts, the empire must make the hearts of its subjects "all thine own." Landon suggests that India must enjoy the "free laws" of the British, and Indian subjects must identify themselves with the imperial project and recognize it as benevolent; if the British empire carries the immortal destiny of Christianity, it must "dispense light, hope, intelligence, till blessings track our steps where'er we go."

The figure of Auvaiyār appears in the text as a vehicle for proto-feminist commentary on imperial ethics. Landon twice refers to Auvaiyār's renunciation of "life's flowers," a polysemic allusion to a conventional symbol of femininity and domestication, and to the worldly and embodied pursuits Auvaiyār declined in favor of the "immortal" and spiritual aims of intellectual, scholarly, and creative endeavors. Auvaiyār's story is framed as "a woman's triumph," and Auvaiyār's exalted status within the Indian tradition can be read as a veiled criticism of the status of female poets in Landon's own time and place.[79] Landon describes herself as following the "great example" she imagines in Auvaiyār's story, and her first task is "to wake/The general wish to benefit our kind." Whatever animated Landon's ethical ambivalence towards the mechanisms of colonial rule, her writing unambiguously endorsed the empire's evangelical mission, and it was interpreted as such: the final stanza of the poem was printed as an anonymous epigraph by the Christian Literature Society for India, in a book celebrating the "the happiness, the prosperity, and the welfare" brought to India by Pax Britannica.[80]

Landon was a strong supporter of efforts to expand female education in India, a movement mobilized by Christian missionaries and a major subject of debates about colonial education in the early nineteenth century.[81] When Scottish missionary Alexander Duff arrived in Calcutta in 1830, one of the first topics he heard discussed by Hindu College students was "whether females ought to be educated."[82] Operating within evangelical motifs of moral rescue and emancipation, Duff raised concerns in Britain about the abject conditions of Indian women:

> In defining the position of woman in society—her duties and obligations—the first principle and essence of Hindu legislation is, that, in a peculiar sense, she is *subject to man from the cradle to the grave* ... from her birth to her death woman must never in any thing have a will of her own—must never dare to aspire to independence. Instead of being a help meet [*sic*] for man, she must for ever and ever be satisfied with being his humble slave—his crouching and submissive drudge.[83]

As a prolific writer of pamphlets and letters to the government, Duff was an ardent advocate of English-language education, and he aligned with the Anglicists in debates over the medium of education in the British empire. With the help of Raja Ram Mohan Roy (1772–1859), a Bengali intellectual and leading Indian social reformer, Duff opened an English-medium curriculum school for the sons of the Bengali elite, where they studied Christianity and liberal arts. When Duff returned to Scotland to raise money for Calcutta's Church of Scotland Mission, he lectured to the Scottish Ladies' Association about female education in India.[84] This discourse was also targeted to the indigenous leaders in the British colony: in notes to her poem on Madurai, Landon acknowledges the efforts of Anne Seymour Damer, an accomplished sculptor and relative of Alexander Johnston, whom Johnston asked to send a gift to the Tanjavur king—a bust of a British war hero—to impress upon the king the virtues of female education.

Jean Fernandez described Landon's poem as a meta-text in which the poet could "contemplate the Imperial character of patriarchal aesthetics and ... situate her resistance to it in the figure of the Indian woman."[85] In this way, Landon performs a 'doubling' that imagines the bourgeois metropolitan woman in the subject position of a subaltern poet. Gayatri Chakravorty Spivak articulated the stakes of this genre of feminist individualism, a product of the age of imperialism in which women were interpellated as subjects along the twin axes of "child-bearing" and "soul-making": "The first is domestic-society-through-sexual-reproduction cathected as 'companionate love'; the second is the imperialist project cathected as civil-society-through-social-mission."[86] Indeed, the character of Auvaiyār in Landon's poem explicitly rejects the first axis of subjectivation in favor of the second—she renounces her beauty and rejects her suitors, and pursues an "immortal" and "ethereal" battle of souls, in which the triumph of the British empire is the ordained, eternal conclusion. In celebrating her imagined Auvaiyār, who exemplified the possibility of rupture within the dominant registers of gender subjectivation, Landon recruited the ancient poet to a bourgeois feminist morality that saw, in its reflection, colonization as a prerequisite for the uplift of Hindu women.[87]

Conclusion

The influence of Alexander Johnston is apparent in both Letitia Elizabeth Landon's poem and Hobart Caunter's fictitious travel narrative, which appeared in popular literary annuals in 1836. As a prominent member of London's Royal Asiatic Society and a respected authority on India, Johnston was concerned with countering the Anglicist position in debates over the medium of instruction in British India. Johnston recognized the cultural, linguistic, and religious heterogeneity of India because of his lived experiences in Madurai. He made considerable efforts to promote indigenous languages, in part through his sponsorship of Colin Mackenzie, the Surveyor-General of India, whom Johnston had met in Madurai during his youth and remained in contact when an adult.[88] As surveyor-general, Mackenzie and his native assistants collected an impressive archive (the subject of chapter 5) containing literature, local tracts, inscriptions, translations, plans, drawings, coins, images, and antiquities throughout the Deccan, including significant materials written in south Indian languages and Sanskrit.[89] After Mackenzie's death, Johnson spoke before the Select Committee of the House of Commons on the Affairs of the East India Company in 1832, in which he claimed "the most valuable collection of historical documents relative to India" would help the British gain concrete knowledge to rule India with specificity and sensitivity.[90] He insisted that learned natives complete the collection "to show the people of India ... that those who compose the Parliament have ... the means of ... adapting any measures which they may introduce into India to the peculiar circumstances of the country, and to the manners and feelings of the people."[91]

Despite the efforts of Johnston and his cohort, the Anglicists prevailed, and in 1835 it was determined that government education funds would be used exclusively for English-language education. Nevertheless, in the face of Thomas Macaulay's racist and vociferous assault on non-English languages, Orientalist advocates of classical Indian languages continued their campaign.[92] Simultaneously, a third, "Vernacularist" faction emerged, championed by Brian Houghton Hodgson, the British scholar of Nepal. From 1835 to 1839, the Vernacularists unsuccessfully pushed for mass education through indigenous languages, in hopes of reversing the program of English supremacy.[93] The Vernacularists, who supported the everyday spoken languages of the masses, at first seemed diametrically opposed to the Orientalists, who favored the "high-culture" of the elite. The General Committee of Public Instruction in Bengal resolved this schism by promoting the pairing of vernacular and classical education.[94] Hodgson wrote a series of letters from 1835 to 1848 reiterating the importance of indigenous language education and his critique of Macaulay: "it is infinitely more practicable to make Europeans familiar with the words and things of India, than to make Indians familiar with the words and things of Europe."[95] Although Hodgson was critical of the classical languages ("Sanskrit, Arabic, Persian have proved the curse of this land"[96]), he confessed an "unlimited preference" for the Orientalist position.[97] Both factions believed that Britain's mission in India was to revive rather than replace Indian civilization.

With high stakes, influential figures like Alexander Johnston seized upon the changing dynamics in the British metropole to influence the outcome of these disputes in their favor. Novel technologies and an emerging consumer market in Britain altered both the *appearance* and the *function* of visual representations of India in the early nineteenth century. Whereas the Daniells' printed intricate, limited-edition volumes for elite consumption, Caunter and Landon mass-produced engraved, relatively affordable books for a much wider readership. These writers transformed a small temple town into a potent symbol in debates over the ethics of empire and the methods of colonial rule. Johnston encouraged professional writers to use the specific history of Madurai and its temple to shape public discourse about the ethical stakes of empire. However, although they disagreed on their preferred pedagogy, all three factions in the language debate assumed a common method of governance in India: "an influential class was to be coopted as the conduit of Western thought and ideas."[98] Despite the intricacies and internal antagonisms of the various positions on education reform, they nevertheless converged at the same point—the requirement of British paternalism and the responsibility to revive Indian civilization from a state of decay.

Notes

1. William Hodges, *Choix de vues de l'Inde, dessinées sur les lieux, pendant les années 1780, 1781, 1782, et 1783, et executées en aqua tinta, par W. Hodges.... Select Views in India, Drawn on the Spot, in the Years 1780, 1781, 1782, and 1783, and Executed in Aqua Tinta, by William Hodges, R.A.* (London: Printed [by Joseph Cooper] for the author; and sold by J. Edwards, 1786–1788).
2. See Thomas Daniell, *Views in Calcutta* (Calcutta, 1786–1788), and Thomas Daniell and William Daniell, *A Picturesque Voyage to India; by the Way of China. By Thomas Daniell, R.A. and William Daniell, A.R.A.* (London: Longman, Hurst, Rees & Orme, 1810).
3. Mildred Archer, *Early Views of India: The Picturesque Journeys of Thomas and William Daniell 1786–1794* (London: Thames and Hudson Ltd., 1980), 141.
4. Thomas and William Daniell published six volumes of engravings of Indian views, known collectively as *Oriental Scenery*: I. *Oriental Scenery: Twenty-Four Views in Hindoostan, Taken in the Years 1789 and 1790; Drawn and Engraved by Thomas Daniell, and, with Permission, Respectfully Dedicated to the Honourable Court of Directors of the East India Company* (London: Robert Bowyer, March 1, 1795); II. *Oriental Scenery: Twenty-Four Views in Hindoostan, Taken in the Year 1792; Drawn by Thomas Daniell, and Engraved by Himself and William Daniell; and, with Permission, Respectfully Dedicated*

to the Right Honourable Henry Dundas, One of His Majesty's Principal Secretaries of State, President of the Board of Commissioners for the Affairs of India, Treasurer of the Navy, &c. &c. &c. (London: Thomas Daniell, August 1797); III. *Oriental Scenery: Twenty-Four Views in Hindoostan, Drawn and Engraved by Thomas & William Daniell, and, with Permission, Respectfully Dedicated to the Right Honourable George Viscount Lewisham, President of the Board of Commissioners for the Affairs of India* (London: Thomas Daniell, June 1801); IV. *Twenty-Four Landscapes, the Fourth Series: Views in Hindoostan; Drawn and Engraved by Thomas and William Daniell, with Permission Respectfully Dedicated to the Right Honourable George O'Brien, Earl of Egremont* (London: Thomas Daniell, May 1807); V. *Antiquities of India: Twelve Views from the Drawings of Thomas Daniell R.A. & F.S.A.; Engraved by Himself, and William Daniell; Taken in the Years 1790 and 1793; Dedicated Respectfully to the Society of Antiquaries of London* (London: Thomas Daniell, 1800); and VI. *Hindoo Excavations: In the Mountain of Ellora, near Aurungabad in the Decan, in Twenty-Four Views; Respectfully Dedicated to Sir Charles Warre Malet, Bart. Late the British Resident at Poonah; Engraved from the Drawings of James Wales, by and under the Direction of Thomas Daniell* (London: Thomas Daniell, June 1, 1804).

5. Joseph Farington, entry for Thursday, June 4, 1795, in *The Diary of Joseph Farington*, vol. II: January 1795–August 1796, ed. Kenneth Garlick and Angus Macintyre (New Haven: Yale University Press for the Paul Mellon Centre for Studies in British Art, 1978), 349.
6. Thomas and William Daniell, *Oriental Scenery. One Hundred and Fifty Views of the Architecture, Antiquities, and Landscape Scenery of Hindoostan. Drawn and Engraved by Thomas and William Daniell*, vol. I (London: [G. Norman for] the Authors, 1816), 2nd series, 10.
7. Thomas Sutton, *The Daniells: Artists and Travellers* (London: The Bodley Head, 1954), 88.
8. Sutton, *The Daniells*, 91.
9. E. P. Thompson, *The Making of the English Working Class* (New York: Vintage Books, 1963).
10. Simon Gunn and Rachel Bell, introduction to *Middle Classes: Their Rise and Sprawl* (London: Phoenix, 2003), 11–23; Simon Gunn, *The Public Culture of the Victorian Middle Class: Ritual and Authority in the English Industrial City 1840–1914* (Manchester: Manchester University Press, 2000).
11. T. W. Heyck, *The Transformation of Intellectual Life in Victorian England* (New York: St Martin's Press, 1982), 25.
12. Margaret Linley, "The Early Victorian Annual (1822–1857)," *Victorian Review* 35, no. 1 (Spring 2009), 13–19.

13. Katherine D. Harris, "Feminizing the Textual Body: Female Readers Consuming the Literary Annual," *The Papers of the Bibliographical Society of America* 99, no. 4 (December 2005): 573–622.
14. H. C. G. Matthew, "Caunter, John Hobart (1792–1851)," *Oxford Dictionary of National Biography*, vol. X (Oxford: Oxford University Press, 2004), 579–580, 579.
15. Hobart Caunter, *The Cadet; A Poem, in Six Parts: Containing Remarks on British India. To Which Is Added, Egbert and Amelia; In Four Parts: with Other Poems*, 2 vols. (London: Printed for Robert Jennings, by J. Moyes, 1814); Rev. Hobart Caunter, *The Romance of History. India*, 3 vols. (London: Edward Churton, 1836).
16. Sutton, *The Daniells*, 140–141.
17. Advertisement for publisher Edward Churton's "New Illustrated Works" at the end of Victor Jacquemont, *Letters from India; Describing a Journey in British Dominions of India, Tibet, Lahore, and Cashmere during the Years 1828, 1829, 1830, 1831*, vol. I (London: Edward Churton, 1834).
18. Hobart Caunter and William Daniell, *Oriental Annual. Lives of the Moghul Emperors. By the Rev. Hobart Caunter, B.D. With Twenty-Two Engravings from Drawings by William Daniell R.A.* (London: Charles Tilt, 1837), after page 240, citing *The Spectator*, October 17, 1835.
19. "Obituary.—William Daniell, Esq. R. A.," *Gentleman's Magazine* 8, New Series (July–December 1837 [October 1837]): 429–430, 429 (London: William Pickering; John Bowyer Nichols and Son, 1837).
20. William Daniell and Hobart Caunter, *The Oriental Annual, or Scenes in India; Comprising Twenty-Two Engravings from Original Drawings by William Daniell, R.A. and a Descriptive Account by the Rev. Hobart Caunter, B.D.* (London: Edward Churton, 1836), 29–58.
21. Basil Hunnisett, *Steel-Engraved Book Illustration in England* (Boston: David R. Godine, 1980), 3.
22. Hunnisett, *Steel-Engraved Book Illustration in England*, 6.
23. Hunnisett, *Steel-Engraved Book Illustration in England*, 56; about the process, see pages 42–52.
24. "From *The Spectator*: Embellishments of the Annuals," *Museum of Foreign Literature, Science, and Art* 23 (July–December 1833 [December 1833]): 713–714, 714 (Philadelphia: E. Littell & T. Holden, New York: G. & C. & H. Carvill, Boston: Kane & Co., 1833). "The plates are engraved with extreme care and neatness; but as works of art they are cold and tame. This fault does not lie with the engravers: Mr. Daniell's style is more remarkable for accuracy and smoothness than force.... It would have been a great improvement had the plates

been engraved in aquatint, and coloured afterwards, as Mr. Daniell's other works are. In another volume, perhaps this will be done."

25. Daniell and Caunter, *Oriental Annual* 3 (1836), 51.
26. Daniell and Caunter, *Oriental Annual* 3 (1836), 52:

> Trimal Naig was determined to erect an edifice that should be worthy of such a sacred concourse; and sensible, moreover, of the extreme veneration paid to any sculptured representation of their favourite deities, by placing them in connexion with the effigies of his own ancestors before the eyes of the devotees, whose minds, when about to visit their grand shrine, were always excited to a high degree of devotional enthusiasm, he was fully aware that he should divide their reverence, and attain for his progenitors, and for himself eventually, a sort of popular canonization. Thus, his ambition, though disguised under the plausible mask of public spirit and veneration for the sanctity of religion, was the mainspring of those splendid erections which have immortalized his name in the native chronicles of the southern peninsula of India.

Adam Blackader (the subject of chapter 3) expressed similar sentiments.

27. William Daniell and Hobart Caunter, "Address," in *Oriental Annual, or Scenes in India; Comprising Twenty-Five Engravings from Original Drawings by William Daniell, R.A. and a Descriptive Account by the Rev. Hobart Caunter, B.D.* (London: Edward Bull, 1834), before the list of engravings at the book's beginning.
28. Daniell and Caunter, *Oriental Annual* 1 (1834), 34–35.
29. For example, a fantastical description and image of a tiger hunt in chapter III entitled "Madura—Caste—Hindoo Literature."
30. Daniell and Caunter, *Oriental Annual* 4 (1837), after page 240, citing *The Spectator,* October 17, 1835.
31. Daniell and Caunter, *Oriental Annual* 3 (1836), 37–38.
32. Daniell and Caunter, *Oriental Annual* 3 (1836), 29.
33. Daniell and Caunter, *Oriental Annual* 3 (1836), 31–32.
34. Andrew Bell, *The Madras School, or Elements of Tuition: Comprising the Analysis of an Experiment in Education, Made at the Male Asylum, Madras; With Its Facts, Proofs, and Illustrations....* (London: T. Bensley, 1808).
35. Daniell and Caunter, *Oriental Annual* 3 (1836), 32.
36. Daniell and Caunter, *Oriental Annual* 3 (1836), 33, 36.
37. Daniell and Caunter, *Oriental Annual* 3 (1836), 32.
38. According to *Periya Purāṇam* (the poetic account of the canonical poets of Tamil Śaivism), *paṟaiyar*s were agricultural laborers and leather traders, considered outcastes, and forbidden to enter temples. R. Nagaswamy, *Studies*

in Ancient Tamil Law and Society (Madras: Tamil Nadu State Department of Archaeology, 1978), 100.

39. Stuart Blackburn, "Corruption and Redemption: The Legend of Valluvar and Tamil Literary History," *Modern Asian Studies* 34, no. 2 (May 2000): 449–482, 452, 459.
40. Daniell and Caunter, *Oriental Annual* 3 (1836), 32–34.
41. Daniell and Caunter, *Oriental Annual* 3 (1836), 33.
42. Daniell and Caunter, *Oriental Annual* 3 (1836), 35.
43. Daniell and Caunter, *Oriental Annual* 3 (1836), 30.
44. Nicholas B. Dirks, *Castes of Mind: Colonialism and the Making of Modern India* (Princeton: Princeton University Press, 2001), 27–28, 49, 79–80.
45. Lynn Zastoupil and Martin Moir, eds., *The Great Indian Education Debate: Documents Relating to the Orientalist-Anglicist Controversy, 1781–1843* (Richmond, Surrey: Curzon Press, 1999), 74, citing the minute by Warren Hastings, Governor-General of Fort William in (Calcutta) Bengal, April 18, 1781.
46. Warren Hastings to Nathaniel Smith, Esquire, Banaris, October 4, 1784, in Charles Wilkins, *The Bhăgvăt-Gēētā, or Dialogues of Krēēshnă and Ărjŏŏn; In Eighteen Lectures; with Notes. Translated from the Original, in the Sănkrēēt, or Ancient Language of the Brāhmăns* (London: C. Nourse, 1785), 13.
47. David Kopf, *British Orientalism and the Bengal Renaissance: The Dynamics of Indian Modernization 1773–1835* (Berkeley and Los Angeles: University of California Press, 1969), 17–18.
48. Warren Hastings to Nathaniel Smith, in Wilkins, *The Bhăgvăt-Gēētā*, 13.
49. Warren Hastings to Nathaniel Smith, in Wilkins, *The Bhăgvăt-Gēētā,* 10.
50. For further discussion, see Tristanne J. Connolly, "'The Authority of the Ancients': Blake and Wilkins' Translation of the *Bhagvat-Geeta*," in *The Reception of Blake in the Orient*, ed. Steve Clark and Masashi Suzuki (London: Continuum, 2006), 145–158, 153.
51. Charles Grant, *Observations on the State of Society among the Asiatic Subjects of Great Britain, Particularly with Respect to Morals; and on the Means of Improving It—Written Chiefly in the Year 1792* (Ordered, by the House of Commons to be printed, June 15, 1813), 76.
52. Rowan Strong, *Anglicanism and the British Empire c. 1700–1850* (Oxford and New York: Oxford University Press, 2007), 156.
53. Henry Beveridge, *A Comprehensive History of India, Civil, Military and Social from First Landing of the English to the Suppression of the Sepoy Revolt Including an Outline of the Early History of Hindoostan,* vol. III (London: Blackie and Son, 1862), 234, citing Charles Grant's speech to the House of Commons, June 13, 1833.

54. G. O. Trevelyan, *The Competition Wallah* (London and Cambridge: Macmillan and Co., 1864), 409–410.
55. John Leonard Clive, *Macaulay: The Shaping of the Historian* (New York: Alfred A. Knopf, 1973), 330, 346–347.
56. A group of influential Indians under Raja Ram Mohan Roy's leadership also argued for teaching the English language and a modern European education to improve Indian society. See Raja Ram Mohan Roy to Lord William Amherst, Governor-General in Council, Calcutta, December 11, 1823, in Charles E. Trevelyan, *On the Education of the People of India* (London: Longman, Orme, Brown, Green, & Longmans, 1838), 65–71, and Nancy L. Adams and Dennis M. Adams, "An Examination of Some Forces Affecting English Educational Policies in India: 1780–1850," *History of Education Quarterly* 11, no. 2 (Summer 1971): 157–173, 166–167.
57. Charles Hay Cameron, *An Address to Parliament on the Duties of Great Britain to India in Respect of the Education of the Natives, and Their Official Employment* (London: Longman, Brown, Green, and Longmans, 1853), 78, citing Thomas B. Macaulay's *Minute on Education*, February 2, 1835.
58. Zastoupil and Moir, *The Great Indian Education Debate*, 195, citing "Resolution of the Governor-General of India in Council in the General Department," March 7, 1835.
59. H. G. Keene, "Johnston, Sir Alexander (1775–1849)," rev. Roger T. Stearn, in *Oxford Dictionary of National Biography*, vol. XXX (Oxford: Oxford University Press, 2004), 334–335.
60. "Proceedings of the Anniversary Meeting of the Royal Asiatic Society, Held on the 6th of May, 1837," *Journal of the Royal Asiatic Society of Great Britain and Ireland* 4, no. 2 (London: John W. Parker, 1837): xvii–xlvi, xxxiii, fn. 10.

    Colonel Colin Mackenzie helped Johnston's maternal grandfather, Lord Francis Napier, to research the life and work of John Napier, the inventor of the English logarithms, before coming to India. When he stayed with the Johnston family in Madurai, Mackenzie tutored the young Johnston in mathematics. See James T. Rutnam, *The Early Life of Sir Alexander Johnston (1775–1849) Third Chief Justice of Ceylon* (Colombo: Law & Society Trust, 1988), 5–6.
61. Rutnam, *Early Life of Sir Alexander Johnston*, 8.
62. Daniell and Caunter, *The Oriental Annual* 3 (1836), 39–41.
63. Rama Mantena, "The Question of History in Precolonial India," *History and Theory* 46, no. 3 (October 2007): 396–408, 400, fn. 11, referring to Alexander Johnston to Charles Grant, President of the Board of Control, March 10, 1835.
64. "Proceedings of the Royal Asiatic Society, Saturday, January 18th, 1834," *Journal of the Royal Asiatic Society of Great Britain and Ireland*, 1, no. 1 (London: John W. Parker, 1834): 149–150, 149. "Annual Report of the Royal

Asiatic Society of Great Britain and Ireland, 10th May, 1834," *Journal of the Royal Asiatic Society of Great Britain and Ireland* 1, no. 2 (1834): iii–xv, ix.

65. Virginia Blain, "Letitia Elizabeth Landon, Eliza Mary Hamilton, and the Genealogy of the Victorian Poetess," *Victorian Poetry* 33, no. 1 (Spring 1995): 31–51, 38, 45, 47; Glennis Byron, "Landon, Letitia Elizabeth (1802–1838)," in *Oxford Dictionary of National Biography*, vol. XXXII (Oxford: Oxford University Press, 2004), 391–394, 392–393. Places include New York, Paris, Berlin, and St Petersburg. See "Fisher's Drawing Room Scrapbook," The Victorian Web, 2020, http://victorianweb.org/periodicals/scrapbook/index.html, accessed December 14, 2021.
66. Jennifer Wallace, "Classics as Souvenir: L.E.L. and the Annuals," *Classical Receptions Journal* 3, no. 1 (2011): 109–128.
67. Letitia Elizabeth Landon, introduction to *Fisher's Drawing Room Scrap-Book; With Poetical Illustrations by L. E. L.* (London: Fisher, Son, and Jackson, 1832), unpaginated.
68. Letitia Elizabeth Landon to William Jerdan, circa 1834, in *Letters by Letitia Elizabeth Landon,* ed. F. J. Sypher (Ann Arbor, MI: Scholars' Facsimiles & Reprints, 2001), 100.
69. However, Landon did educate herself about India. For example, for her poem "Skeleton Group in Rameswur, Caves of Ellora," in *Fisher's Drawing Room Scrap-Book; With Poetical Illustrations by L. E. L.* (London: Fisher, Son, and Jackson, 1832), she acknowledges *Asiatic Researches*, the journal of the Asiatic Society of Bengal (discussed in chapter 3) as the source of her information (32). The Society changed the spelling to "Asiatic" beginning in 1825.
70. Letitia Elizabeth Landon to William Jerdan, *Letters by Letitia Elizabeth Landon*, 100.
71. Originally published in *Fisher's Drawing Room Scrap-Book*, these poems were later republished in Letitia Elizabeth Landon, *The Poetical Works of Miss Landon* (Philadelphia: E. L. Carey and A. Hart, 1839).
72. The image entitled *The Celebrated Temples, & Palace, at Madura* and based on Captain Chapman of the Royal Engineers' sketch typifies how publisher Fisher, Son & Co. drew from their stockpile of engravings depicting India that were originally drawn by amateur artists in the British military and later recycled in other publications. See James M'Kenzie-Hall, "Illustrated Travel: Steel Engravings and Their Use in Early Nineteenth-Century Topographical Books, with Special Reference to Henry Fisher & Co." (PhD diss., Nottingham Trent University and Southampton Solent University, 2011), 92–106. The same engraving precedes explanations of Madura's "celebrated" college, temple, pillared hall, and Nāyaka ruler in Lieut. George Francis White, *Views in India, Chiefly among the Himalaya Mountains* (London: Fisher, Son, and Co., 1838), 91–92.

73. Letitia Elizabeth Landon, "Hindoo Temples and Palace at Madura," in *Fisher's Drawing Room Scrap-Book; With Poetical Illustrations by L. E. L.* (London and Paris: Fisher, Son, & Co.; Berlin: Asher; New York: Jackson, 1836), 50–51. The poem was republished without the engraving in Landon, *The Poetical Works of Miss Landon*, 313–314, and Emma Roberts, *The Zenana and Minor Poems by L. E. L. with a Memoir by Emma Roberts* (London: Fisher, Son, & Co., 1839), 207–211 (as "On An Engraving of Hindoo Temples").
74. Explanatory note after Landon, "Hindoo Temples and Palace at Madura," 51. In an undated letter to Mrs. S. C. Hall, Landon discusses completing some Indian-themed poems for *Fisher's Drawing Room Scrap-Book* (that appeared in 1834) and meeting "Sir — —," who shared information about Indians. This "Sir" could be Sir Alexander Johnston. See Laman Blanchard, *Life and Literary Remains of L. E. L.*, vol. I (London: Henry Colburn, 1841), 100–102.
75. Landon, *Fisher's Drawing Room Scrap-Book* (1836), 51.
76. As Jerome McGann observes in his *The Poetics of Sensibility: A Revolution in Literary Style* (Oxford: Clarendon Press, 1996), there exists in Landon's poems an "odd and disturbing disjunction between the events elaborated in the poem and the scene rendered in the picture" (167).
77. For a discussion of this light versus dark motif in evangelical missionary thought, see Strong, *Anglicanism and the British Empire*, 49, 129.
78. Landon, *Fisher's Drawing Room Scrap-Book* (1836), 51. Avyia or Auvaiyār also appears in Caunter's text, where she is described as Tiruvaḷḷuvar's sister. In Landon's poem, there is no mention of her brother. According to Kamil V. Zvelebil, "There are in Tamil literature at least three, if not more well-known poetesses by the name Auvaiyār (the name itself means 'venerable old lady')." See Kamil V. Zvelebil, *Companion Studies to the History of Tamil Literature* (Leiden and New York: E. J. Brill, 1992), 54, fn. 64. Zvelebil also states that Auvaiyār is one of the "least tangible figures in Tamil literature," although she is perhaps the first Tamil author to be translated into a European language given the popularity of her didactic verses. See Kamal Veith Zvelebil, *Tamil Literature* (Wiesbaden, Germany: Otto Harrasowitz, 1974), 125. In 1708, German Protestant missionary Bartholomaeus Ziegenbalg (1683–1719) translated Auvaiyār's *Koṉṟaivēntaṉ*. An early nineteenth-century example is Robert Fellowes' chapter LIV, "Short Lessons and Moral Maxims of the Singhalese and Malabars, Taken from the Malabar Book and Connevendam," and chapter LV, "Sayings of a Female Sage," in his *History of Ceylon, from the Earliest Period to the Year MDCCCXV; with Characteristic Details of the Religion, Laws, & Manners of the People and a Collection of Their Moral Maxims & Ancient Proverbs. By Philalethes, A.M. Oxon. To Which Is Subjoined, Robert Knox's Historical Relation of the Island, with an Account of His Captivity during a Period of Near Twenty Years* (London: Joseph Mawman, 1817), 315–322.

79. Glennis Stephenson, "Letitia Landon and the Victorian Improvisatrice: The Construction of L.E.L.," *Victorian Poetry* 30, no. 1 (Spring 1992): 1–17.
80. *The Beautiful Garden of Ind: A Dream and Its Interpretation. By A Friend of India* (London and Madras: The Christian Literature Society for India, 1897), 37–38.
81. Baptist missionaries founded the Calcutta Female Juvenile Society for the Education of Native Females in 1819. The first boarding school for girls began in Tirunelveli in 1821. The growing interest in female educational reform is marked by the formation of such organizations as the Ladies' Society for Native Education in Calcutta and the Vicinity (1824), the Society for the Promotion of Female Education in the East (1834), the Church of Scotland Women's Association (1837), and the Indian Female Normal School and Instruction Society (1852). See James S. Dennis, *Christian Missions and Social Progress: A Sociological Study of Foreign Missions*, vol. III (New York: Fleming H. Revell Company, 1906), 10–12. Indian social reformers also pushed for female education and opened schools for girls. See Geraldine Forbes, *Women in Modern India*, The New Cambridge History of India IV.2 (Cambridge: Cambridge University Press, 1996), 32–63.
82. George Smith, *The Life of Alexander Duff, D.D., LL.D.*, vol. I (London: Hodder and Stoughton, 1879), 150.
83. Alexander Duff, "Female Education in India: Being the Substance of an Address Delivered at the First Annual Meeting of the Scottish Ladies' Association for the Promotion of Female Education in India, in 1839," in *Missionary Addresses Delivered before the General Assembly of the Church of Scotland, in the Years 1835, 1837, 1839. With Additional Papers on Female Education, and the Danish, or Earliest Protestant Mission to India* (Edinburgh: Johnstone & Hunter, 1850), 217–273, 222–223 (emphasis in the original).
84. Smith, *The Life of Alexander Duff*, 104–136, 373–374.
85. Jean Fernandez, "Graven Images: The Woman Writer, the Indian Poetess, and Imperial Aesthetics in L. E. L.'s 'Hindoo Temples and Palaces at Madura,'" *Victorian Poetry* 43, no. 1 (Spring 2005): 36.
86. Gayatri Chakravorty Spivak, "Three Women's Text and a Critic of Imperialism," *Critical Inquiry* 12, no. 1 (Autumn, 1985): 243–261, 244.
87. Spivak, "Three Women's Text and a Critic of Imperialism," 244–245.
88. "ART. XXIX. Biographical Sketch of the Literary Career of the Late Colonel Colin Mackenzie, Surveyor-General of India; Comprising Some Particulars of His Collection of Manuscripts, Plans, Coins, Drawings, Sculptures, &c. Illustrative of the Antiquities, History, Geography, Laws, Institutions, and Manners, of the Ancient Hindús; Contained in a Letter Addressed by Him to the Right Hon. Sir Alexander Johnston, V.P.R.A.S. &c. &c.," *Journal of the Royal Asiatic Society of Great Britain and Ireland* 1, no. 2 (1834): 333–364, 333–334.

89. H. H. Wilson, "List of the Collections Made by the Late Colonel Mackenzie," in *The Mackenzie Collection. A Descriptive Catalogue of the Oriental Manuscripts, and Other Articles Illustrative of the Literature, History, Statistics and Antiquities of the South of India; Collected by the Late Lieut. Col. Colin Mackenzie, Surveyor General of India*, 2nd ed. (Madras: Higginbotham and Co., 1882 [1828]), 14–15.
90. "Sir Alexander Johnston, Called in, and Examined," July 19, 1832, *Minutes of Evidence Taken before the Select Committee of the House of Commons on the Affairs of the East India Company*, I. Public (London: Ordered, by the House of Commons, August 16, 1832), 254–257, 254, para. 1930, and 255–256, para. 1932.
91. "Sir Alexander Johnston, Called In, and Examined," 256, para. 1937.
92. In a letter to Bengali intellectual Ram Camul Sen, Sanskritist Horace Hayman Wilson wrote: "It is a visionary absurdity to think of making English the language of India." H. H. Wilson to Ram Camul Sen, Oxford, August 20, 1834, in Peary Chand Mittra, *Life of Dewan Ramcomul Sen* (Calcutta: I. C. Bose & Co., 1880), 17.
93. John D. Windhausen, "The Vernaculars, 1835–1839: A Third Medium for Indian Education," *Sociology of Education* 47, no. 3 (Spring 1964): 254–270.
94. Clive, *Macaulay: The Shaping of the Historian*, 359.
95. Brian Houghton Hodgson, preface to "Section XIV: Pre-eminence of the Vernaculars; or, the Anglicists Answered: Being Four Letters on the Education of the People of India," in *Miscellaneous Essays Relating to Indian Subjects*, vol. II (London: Trübner & Co., 1880), 255–348, 256.
96. Hodgson, "Pre-eminence of the Vernaculars," 257.
97. Hodgson, "Pre-eminence of the Vernaculars," 256. Although Hodgson reverses his earlier attacks against English in his fourth letter dated 1843, in outlining his proposed educational college, he offers that enlightenment rationality and the values and principles of modernity would be codified in the indigenous languages themselves ("indigenate a sound literature in India") so as to produce "a perpetual fount for the supply of good books and good teachers." He is basically saying that in the interest of effectiveness, in terms of ensuring the durability of the colonial governing project (that is, the durability of the values that colonial rule will impart upon the native people), it is better to use both indigenous languages and English. The point is that the enlightenment knowledge is "INDISPUTABLE" (caps in the original)—this is a universal reason that is not constrained to any particular language; so in order to make this knowledge "attractive" and to "produce the essence," it must be "spread ... with systematic skill"—in other words, a hybrid form of education is best. See Hodgson, "Pre-eminence of the Vernaculars," 321–322.
98. Gauri Viswanathan, *Masks of Conquest: Literary Study and British Rule in India* (New York: Columbia University Press, 1989), 34.

5

Illustrating Madura

Art as 'History' and State-Building

Introduction

On January 16, 1845, Captain John Lock donated a volume of miscellaneous drawings he had commissioned to the East India Company Library in London.[1] The first five drawings, dated 1841, depict occupations and festivals in Madras. One painting shows a row of dark-complexioned Hindu pilgrims and ascetics, and another displays musicians, Brahmins, and dancing girls participating in a raft festival (Figure 5.1). In both images, figures appear extracted from a larger scene, detached from their original environs, and plunked horizontally onto the open space. Inscribed at the bottom of each painting is "Just Gantz. Popham's Broadway. No. 35. Madras 1841," the inscription of artist and architect Justinian Gantz (1802–1862) who operated a lithographic press with his father, John Gantz (1772–1853), an East India Company draughtsman of Austrian origin.[2] Their press, Gantz & Sons (rival to the famous bookseller Higginbotham), was in George Town's main commercial street in Fort St George, the headquarters of the East India Company's Madras Presidency.

Lock's book, called *Hindoo & Architectural Drawings in Southern India*, contained three illustrations of Madurai and Rameswaram, two major pilgrimage sites in peninsular India. These mainly sepia wash watercolors were produced by W. G. P. Jenkins, William Walter Whelpdale, and Ravant Naik: Jenkins and Whelpdale served in the Madras Army in the 1830s, and Naik was likely a Madurai artist working as an East India Company draughtsman.[3] Two paintings portray Tirumala Nāyaka's palace courtyard and his Pudu Maṇḍapam at the Mīnākṣī-Sundareśvara temple (Figure 5.2). In each image, the edifice encompasses the entire page in a beige, brown, and blue tricolor scheme. The commanding frontal view of these buildings draws the viewer inward into its dark interior depths, as the use of shadow obscures and conceals the interior of buildings and produces a sense of mystery.

Figure 5.1 Justinian Gantz, *Pilgrims and Hindu Ascetics*, Madras, watercolor, 29.3 × 49.1 centimeters, 1841

Source: Inscribed in ink, "Pilgrims, Sainashees, Bairaghees, Pandarams, Just Gantz. Popham's Broadway. No. 35. Madras 1841." © The British Library Board, WD553.

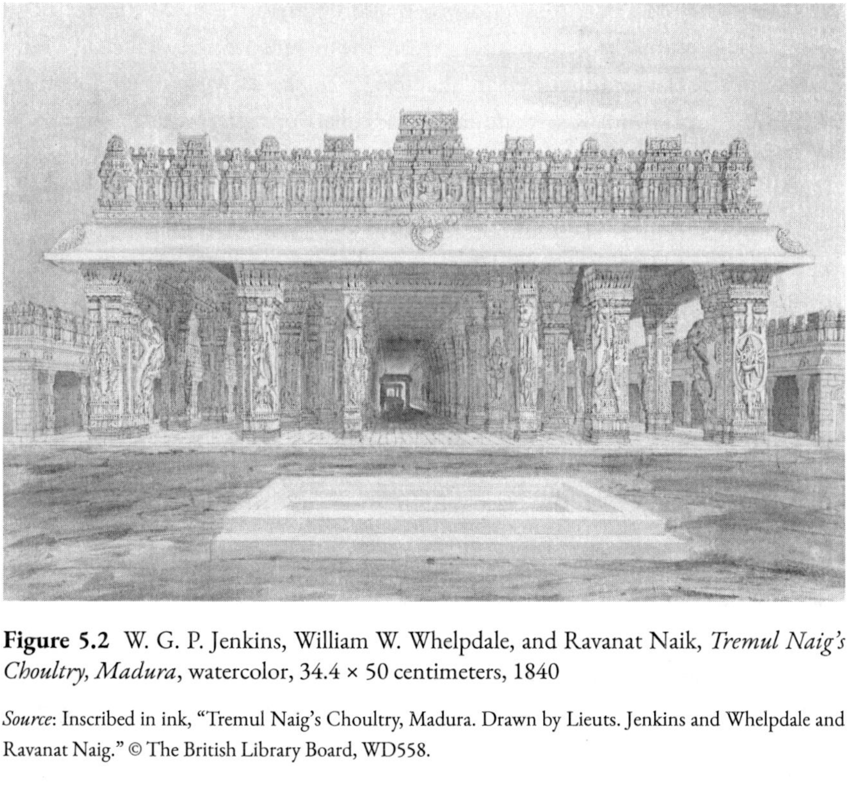

Figure 5.2 W. G. P. Jenkins, William W. Whelpdale, and Ravanat Naik, *Tremul Naig's Choultry, Madura*, watercolor, 34.4 × 50 centimeters, 1840

Source: Inscribed in ink, "Tremul Naig's Choultry, Madura. Drawn by Lieuts. Jenkins and Whelpdale and Ravanat Naig." © The British Library Board, WD558.

Hindoo & Architectural Drawings captures various aspects of south Indian life: people of diverse castes and occupations—often dressed in colorful costumes and reveling in religious festivals—flank static depictions of a temple, palace, and pillared hall. This juxtaposition of bodies and buildings illuminated two interconnected fascinations for the British in India: ethnicity and architecture. As a collector, Lock patronized many artists and purchased their paintings of India; *Tremul Naig's Choultry* is one souvenir that Lock brought back to England to exhibit a flavor of the British colony. Private wonder cabinets were a common feature of the late Renaissance, collections of curios that "celebrated nothing but itself as rare, sensational, and unusual," without much concern for 'historical' value.[4] The collections of colonial officials, like Captain Lock, were novel in that they had a *public* agenda: to create "an illusion of cognitive control over their experience in India" and to produce a "sense of knowledge and control to be repatriated to the metropolis."[5]

Colin Mackenzie, an East India Company employee, and Ram Raz, a Royal Asiatic Society member, were two prolific collectors who worked in India in the decades before Lock; their efforts can also be classified under the rubric of "colonial collections," but they differed from the private projects of men like Lock and Adam Blackader (discussed in chapter 3). In the early nineteenth century, Mackenzie and Ram Raz commissioned collections to produce 'historical' knowledge of India that would advance both *science* and *state-building* in the colony. Colonial administrators and metropolitan scholars revisited Mackenzie and Ram Raz's materials posthumously, as they searched for information about the colony's local history, laws, manners, and religion.

Both Mackenzie and Ram Raz solicited architectural drawings of Tirumala Nāyaka's Pudu Maṇḍapam ("choultry"); their work was privately financed, but sponsored by the colonial state and scholarly societies in Britain, respectively. These pictures, though incredibly detailed, are isolated fragments and incomplete renderings of the temple architecture: the fragmentary nature of the images shaped colonial imaginations of the monument, and informed the mechanisms of government of the colony. Through these illustrations we see how artistic interpretations of Indian civilization, heritage, and material culture were incorporated into governing projects through *native informants* who actively participated in the production of useful knowledge about architecture, space, and place: natives took part in producing 'south India' as a category that could be analyzed as a rational problem of government during the colonial period and has had lasting ramifications through independence to the contemporary.

Colin Mackenzie as soldier and surveyor

Colin Mackenzie was born in 1753 to a merchant and postmaster from Stornoway, Isle of Lewis in the Hebrides. Not much is known about Mackenzie's life before he left his job as local customs officer for Stornoway to serve in the East India Company's Madras Army in 1783. Mackenzie's decision to seek a career in India was influenced by Sir Alexander Johnston's maternal grandfather, Lord Francis Napier. Mackenzie, recognized for his mathematical abilities, was hired by Lord Napier to locate information about Indian mathematics and the Hindu system of logarithms for the biography of John Napier, who discovered logarithms in the early seventeenth century.[6] The Earl of Seaforth arranged Mackenzie's appointment to the Madras Establishment Engineers. Shortly after his arrival, Mackenzie visited Lord Napier's daughter, Hester Johnston, who was living in Madurai (referred to as "Madura") with her husband, an East India Company employee. Interested in continuing her late father's project, Mrs Johnston had employed "the most distinguished Brahmins in the neighbourhood." Mackenzie's encounter with the Brahmins in Madurai convinced him that the most important materials for documenting Indian history would be found in different parts of the peninsula, and he conceived a plan to make an expansive collection, to which he dedicated the next nearly forty years of his life.[7]

It took Mackenzie some time to realize his ultimate ambition, because of his commitments to the East India Company and the enormous technical challenges of governing the colony. In a letter dated February 1, 1817, to his friend Alexander Johnston, Mackenzie described his early years in India from 1783 to 1796: "For these thirteen years ... there is little to shew [*sic*] beyond the journals and notes of an officer employed in all the campaigns of the time...." Mackenzie's extensive involvement in the military conquest of India informed a belief in the intimate attachments of war and science—he wrote:

> That science may derive assistance, and knowledge be diffused, in the leisure moments of camps and voyages, is no new discovery; but, ... I am also desirous of proving that, in the vacant moments of an Indian ... campaign ..., such collected observations may be found useful ... to record facts of importance to philosophy and science.[8]

During his military career, Mackenzie developed the survey as an essential institution of colonial government, through which he mapped territories and reported on land conditions in British India. Mackenzie's surveys not only functioned as a method of obtaining knowledge of the colonial 'other' to be governed, but they also helped to provide technical assistance for significant military conquests.[9] From 1784, Mackenzie carried out surveys in Dindigul and Nellore and conducted road surveys in Northern Circars. He reduced forts during the Third Anglo-Mysore War (1790–1792) against British foe Tipū Sulṭān, became engineer and surveyor in Hyderabad for the Nizām, and mapped the Deccan in 1793; Mackenzie's knowledge of the country, his surveying abilities, his detailed plans and sketches, and his engineering duties played an important role in Tipū Sulṭān's downfall in the 1799 siege of Seringapatam, a decisive British victory in the last Anglo-Mysore war.[10] Mackenzie convinced the British authorities that a "more complete knowledge" of India was fundamentally necessary for effective government of the colony.[11] He was appointed surveyor of Mysore and conducted a topographical survey of the region from 1799 to 1808. He created the position of Madras surveyor-general in 1810, which he occupied before completing geographical and statistical reports from 1811 to 1813.[12] In 1815, he was appointed the first surveyor-general of India and promoted to colonel in 1819.[13] He died in Calcutta two years later.

By the time of Mackenzie's 1817 letter to Johnston, the East India Company was the *de facto* ruler of India, with Calcutta as the seat of the governor-general and the Government of India, which reported to the Court of Directors in London. Mackenzie's scientific inquiries into religious texts, architecture, and material culture in the southern peninsula were made possible by the British defeat of Tipū Sulṭān, the Muslim ruler of Mysore, in 1799. After the war, the only rival powers remaining in the south were the Marāṭhās and the Nizām of Hyderabad; to ensure that neither rival could regain independent status, the British set about restructuring and reforming the political institutions of the conquered territory—an important component of this program was a survey, led by Mackenzie, to establish the contents of the territory and its boundaries.[14] Mackenzie considered the survey a diagnostic tool for improving society; his concerns ranged from weather, climate, and topography to architecture, literature, and class structure. Peter Robb termed Mackenzie's method as "analytical geography"—attempting to define a rational or scientific basis for natural and social phenomena by identifying general rules or patterns, "to understand how the region and people had come to be as they were."[15] Mackenzie applied the same exhaustive, scientific rigor to the study of 'history' as he did to topography; in his own words:

> The elucidation of the History of the several Governments that have rapidly succeeded in this Stage will I conceived be very interesting, as by the Inscriptions, Grants & other Documents that came into my hands, a regular Progress is traced up to the first Mahomedan invasion in the 13th Century ... & in several instances still further, these consist not merely of a dry Chain of uninteresting facts but are

> connected by various illustrations of the genious [*sic*] & manner of the People, their Several Systems of Government & of Religion, & of the predominant causes that influence their Sentiments & opinions to this day; lights are derived on the Tenures of lands, the origin & variety of the several classes, and the genius and Spirit of the Government prevalent generally in the South for centuries from Several Documents illustrating claims & pretention not foreign to modern discussions; ... confirming the utility of this undertaking to the existing Government from a knowledge of Institutions that influence so considerable a part of the Population of Empire.[16]

Here Mackenzie conveys his interest in the "Progress" that pervaded Hindu society before the arrival of Islam (he was especially interested in Mysore and the south, which had many monuments that escaped the "Fanatic depredations" of Islamic invasions).[17] The "History" he documented was not merely an effort to define the 'other' to be governed, but also an attempt to write the history of "Empire" as a universal *whole*.[18]

Colin Mackenzie as national collector

Mackenzie's chief contribution and lasting legacy is the colossal compilation and preservation of archival materials gathered during his tours of south India, of which the architectural drawings of Tirumala Nāyaka's Pudu Maṇḍapam comprise a small portion. Mackenzie understood the utility of historical records to the British government: in 1804, Mackenzie wrote to George Buchan, the chief secretary to the Madras Presidency in Fort St George, that the collection he was accumulating would be helpful in

> illustrating the General History of this part of the Peninsula, & which I conceived might be useful to the Interests of my Employers; as tending to the acquisition of authentic information of the Revolutions & Institutions of a Country whose Internal Government may be assisted by this species of knowledge.[19]

Mackenzie made his case for the study of Hindu history in his "Introductory Memoir: Of the Use and Advantage of Inscriptions & Sculpted Monuments in Illustrating Hindoo History":

> The Advantages of collating and comparing Ancient Inscriptions & thence deriving illustrations & credible evidence of remarkable events; of explaining doubtful dates & facts, elucidating what is obscure or uncertain & rejecting what is fabulous or absurd in the more Ancient History of Countries, of Institutions, & of Science is so well known, and deemed so useful in developing the Earlier State of the Nations of Europe, that their application in that of India might be deemed equally desirable.

> This indeed appears to have been always sufficiently understood; & the opportunity of collecting a sufficient body of authentic Documents of this Nature, has been wanting rather than a just estimation of their value & utility, or a laudable & zealous Spirit of liberal research.[20]

Mackenzie's agenda was *civilizational*—the "Spirit of liberal research" that guided the emergence of modern science in Europe, and thus shaped the development of *nations* in Europe, could in turn foster the development of institutions of government and science in India. The colonial state government in Madras agreed to support Mackenzie's efforts to amass 'historical materials' relating to the ancient history and institutions of south India and instructed its officers in the judicial, revenue, and medical departments to assist him.[21]

Mackenzie lamented his inability to study the indigenous languages of India, because of his extensive commitments to the British military campaigns; consequently, he required native assistants to arrange and translate the documents for his collection. In his 1817 letter to Johnston, Mackenzie expressed his opinion on the problem of studying native languages:

> A knowledge of the native languages in particular, which is so essentially requisite, could never be assiduously cultivated, in consequence of the frequent changes and removals from province to province, from garrison to camp, and from one desultory duty to another. Official encouragements to study the languages of the vast countries that have come under our domination since my arrival in India, were reserved for happy times, and for those who are more fortunate in having leisure for the purpose. From the evils of famine, penury, and war, the land was then slowly emerging; and it struggled long under the miseries of bad management, before the immediate administration of the south came under the benign influence of the British government.[22]

Shortly after his return from Ceylon, he hired a team of highly educated native assistants at his own expense. He wrote: "Accident ... threw in my way those means that I have since unceasingly employed ... of penetrating beyond the common surface of the antiquities, the history, and the institutions, of the south of India.... The connexion I then formed with one person, a native and a Bráhman, was the first step...."[23] The native in question, Cavelly Venkata Boriah, a young Telugu Niyōgi Brahmin scholar, became Mackenzie's close confidant and, along with his brother Lakshmayya, was chiefly responsible for researching and translating ancient manuscripts and other textual artifacts.[24]

From a military perspective, native informants were regarded as tools or instruments for acquiring 'intelligence' necessary for administering the vast territories newly under British control. Colonel Mark Wilks, acting Resident of Mysore and author of 1810 *Historical Sketches of the South of India*, wrote of Boriah and his brother after Boriah's death: "Major Mackenzie has been particularly fortunate in the choice of his instruments, one of these ingenious natives ... had the merit of first tracing the outline of the plan which has been so successfully pursued, and his surviving brother is a man of singular literary zeal and scrupulous research." Wilks commented on the exceptional difficulty of Mackenzie's task, which could not be achieved without significant cooperation from the native assistants:

> The facility which Major Mackenzie has acquired in directing the operations of a large establishment maintained by him for this express purpose and in seizing at once what is useful in the materials which they collect is the result of a long experience: the path is untrodden and it has too few attractions and too many discouragements ever to be trodden by another.[25]

In addition to native informants with the requisite linguistic and cultural expertise, Mackenzie's undertaking required the massive labor force of the East India Company civil and military administration, including the services of the Company's surveyors and sepoy guards.[26] Sanskrit scholar and Orientalist Horace Hayman Wilson, who catalogued Mackenzie's manuscripts and artifacts after his death, recounted how Mackenzie's gathering methods were intertwined with his official work as surveyor-general:

> The collection of books, papers, and inscriptions went hand in hand with the survey ... being accompanied in his journies by his native assistants, who were employed to take copies of all inscriptions, and obtain from the Brahmans of the temples, or learned men in the towns or villages, copies of all records in their possession, or original statements of local traditions....[27]

The enormous technical challenges of assembling Mackenzie's collection required a combination of the precise knowledge of native informants, the coercive influence of the East India Company's military apparatus, and the administrative resources of the colonial authority's civil bureaucracy.

Although Mackenzie's project was the most immense and valuable collection of historical documents on India ever brought together, he had little direct East India Company monetary support for his antiquarian activities. He used his personal military salary to finance his research into Indian and Javanese history, religion, philosophy, art, ethnology, folklore, and mathematics. He relied overwhelmingly on Indian assistants, who were at first reticent to help—to induce their support, he offered (in addition to salaries and traveling expenses) "presents, gratuities and hopes of future reward" to gain their confidence and "to excite the ardour and abstract their attention from every other object, but that upon which they were employed...."[28] Upon his death, Mackenzie's widow, aided by attorneys Palmer & Co., appealed to the East India Company for compensation, even though it was impossible to determine Mackenzie's actual expenditure given his haphazardly kept accounts.[29]

Mackenzie's choultry drawings

Mackenzie understood the indigenous institutions he encountered in India as antagonistic to his inherited conception of 'history' and its attendant forms of 'truth.' He commented that "regular historical narrations and tracts are seldom found among the Natives, and such notices as exist, are generally preserved in the form of religious legends and popular poems and stories."[30] The "regular" forms of 'history' to which Mackenzie was accustomed—records and narratives conveying 'correct' and 'chronological' information—were in India dominated by prophecies and folk tales more or less divorced from obvious "historical" references. Mackenzie puzzled over the Hindus' "indifference" to the "important events" of the past:

> The contentions of their Philosophic & Religious Sects all equally hostile to the Monuments & writings of their opponents; the Despotic Nature of their System of Government, unfriendly to the just development of Historic truth; & concurring with these, to the mode of education & to Superstition may be attributed, as much perhaps as to Climate, that peculiar Apathy & indifference to the passing occurrences of the day, as well as to the more important events of former times, that so remarkably distinguish the present race of Hindoos in regard to Ancient History while so much of their Serious attention is occupied by Legendary Tales or Romantic Stories.[31]

In the face of these myriad causes of Hindu apathy towards historical "truth" (as Mackenzie understood it), Mackenzie sought the exhaustive accumulation of evidence containing any clues to historical knowledge of India; he felt that "every 'traditionary account' contained some potentially useful historical information and wished to leave nothing uncollected or unexplored."[32]

Mackenzie's work exposes the emergence of "history" and the "archive" as technologies of government in the British colony. As Rama Mantena observes, "Preserving Indian pasts came with a price—the price of an emerging positivist history that judged according to its rather narrow principles that Indian records of the past were merely accidentally historical and not self-consciously so." The view of history as a "rational science" was a new development in Britain at that time, emerging alongside the professionalization of "history" as an academic discipline and the refinement of methods of analysis that could make a unique claim to the production of "true memory."[33] Pierre Nora detailed how the "archive" became a chief instrument of the new science of history:

> Modern memory ... relies entirely on the specificity of the trace, the materiality of the vestige, the concreteness of the recording, the visibility of the image.... The less memory is experienced from within, the greater its need for external props and tangible reminders of that which no longer exists except *qua* memory—hence the obsession with the archive that marks an age and in which we attempt to preserve not only all of the past but all of the present as well.[34]

Guided by this "obsession" with assembling a systematic, chronological record, Mackenzie amassed a colossal archive: 1,568 literary manuscripts, 2,070 local tracts, 8,076 inscriptions, 2,159 translations, 79 plans, 2,630 drawings, 6218 coins, 106 images, and 40 antiquities, which would later be housed in the British Library, London, the Government Oriental Manuscripts Library, Madras, and museums in both England and India.[35]

In the context of positivist historical science, Mackenzie believed architectural monuments were essential to compensating legends and folk stories in producing the true 'history' of India. He wrote on the "Use and Advantage of Inscriptions & Sculptured Monuments in Illustrating Hindoo History":

> In such circumstances when more authentic authorities are wanting recurrence for information could be only made to
>
> 1. Such Monuments of Antiquity as have survived the wrack of ages, of the numerous changes of Government & of Religion consisting of Inscriptions, Sculptures, Coins &c and the remains of Ancient Cities, Temples & other Edifices.
> 2. To the Literary Records of Hindoo Science, Philosophy, & Religion still preserved in their Books & Writings; or in the Records of their Temples; which tho' generally defective in Chronological arrangement were yet presumed to contain some notices of remarkable events, celebrated personages, & changes of Dynasties that by the aid of existing Ancient Monuments might elucidate the History & Institutions of this Country.[36]

Mackenzie hoped that material artifacts—such as temple architecture, sculptures, and inscriptions—could overcome the dearth of written documents for constructing histories of local rulers and the changing of dynasties.[37] During his surveys in south India, Mackenzie collected and chronicled innumerable details that resulted in a large portfolio of drawings. Mackenzie's assemblage of drawings came from four sources: (*a*) Mackenzie himself, who sketched while in the field; (*b*) Mackenzie's friends and colleagues, who sent him illustrations; (*c*) Mackenzie's civil servants, which included Anglo-Indian surveyors educated at the Madras Military Male Orphan Asylum and the East India Company's Surveying School in Madras between 1794 and 1810 and worked on Mackenzie's survey; and (*d*) Mackenzie's draughtsmen.[38] Mackenzie, his artists, and draughtsmen drew or painted narrative sculpture, landscape scenes, and local architecture during their geographical surveys.[39] The collection, relative to its vast scope, contains very little annotation. According to nineteenth-century architectural historian James Fergusson, Mackenzie "was the most industrious and successful collector of drawings and manuscripts that India has ever known; but he could not write. The few essays he attempted are meager in the extreme, and nine-tenths of his knowledge perished with him."[40] Since Mackenzie did not contextualize his extensive collection with explanatory essays or notes, by more closely scrutinizing his *drawings* we may find Mackenzie's "voice."[41]

Mackenzie directed his native assistants to keep journals and extensive explanations of "the Country, the Buildings, Temples, Sculptures, & every remarkable object" they spotted in their travels.[42] Mackenzie specifically "deputed" Boriah, his extraordinarily gifted interpreter, to "collect information useful for the office ... such as materially to promote the interest of the Honorable Company"—in this way, Boriah himself became the most important instrument for assembling the 'history' of south India and defining its 'culture.'[43] More than merely an informant with impressive linguistic abilities, Boriah was described by Mackenzie as the "first step of my introduction into the portal of Indian knowledge."[44] Boriah accompanied Mackenzie during the 1798 campaign against Mysore's Tipū Sulṭān and the 1799 siege of Seringapatam that led to the ruler's demise.[45] He reassured Indians who were "surprised and alarmed" by European presence,[46] and collected and translated many oral accounts in the course of their travels.[47] Boriah also recruited a team of Indian researchers for Mackenzie and trained them to gather historical, literary, and cultural data.[48] Boriah, as Mackenzie's head interpreter and translator until his untimely death in 1803, exemplified an important kind of knowledge production that emerged during British rule: the native informant proficient in the languages of traditional texts, knowledgeable of local customs, competent in the English language and Western norms of scholarship, and serviceable to the agenda of the colonial governing project.[49]

In 1802, Boriah compiled for Mackenzie a list of thirty-five items of interest necessary for constructing a history of south India. The two sections most relevant to our analysis of the Madurai temple are 20, "Particular Account of the most Ancient & Modern Buildings, most Remarkable Pagodas, Temples, Palaces & their origin & other Ancient Monuments," and 24, "History of the Carnatic Hindoo Kings from Ancient to Modern time ... [of] the Kings of Madura...."[50] Of the 1,700 drawings at the British Library, there are several hundred illustrations of temples, mostly line drawings of architecture and sculpture, some produced by Indian artists.[51] A collection of fifty-one drawings contains systematic sketches of sculptures and architectural details of Tirumala Nāyaka's Pudu Maṇḍapam.[52] The drawings in *Sculptures at Madura. Pagoda & Choultry of Trimul Naig* are executed in black ink with red touches on figures' lips and gray smudges to illustrate depth and shadow on the figures' bodies. The Madurai temple images intermix with the Pudu Maṇḍapam pictures with no organization or order—at times, it is difficult to determine a particular sculpture's location. For instance, the scene of Mīnākṣī and Sundareśvara's marriage presided by Viṣṇu (*Kalyāṇasundaram* discussed in Chapter 2) (Figure 5.3) appears as a sculpture both near the god's shrine and in the pillared hall's west entrance, but it is unclear which sculpture was the reference for the artist.

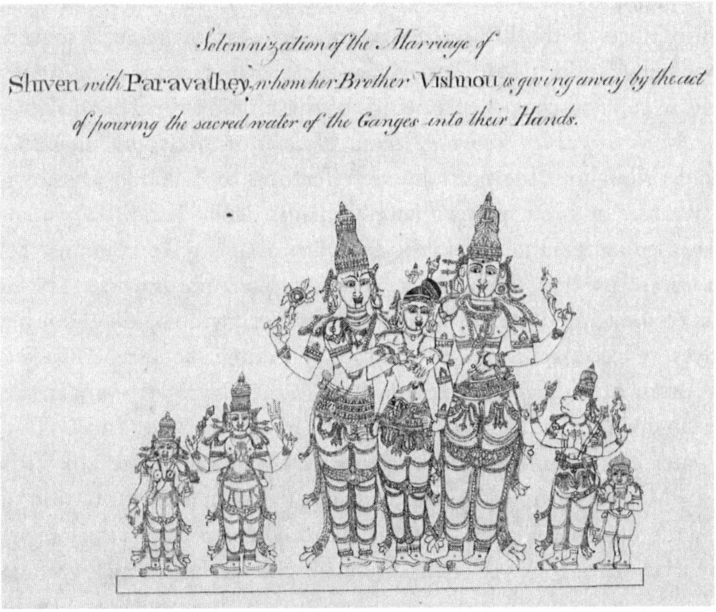

Figure 5.3 Anonymous, Mīnākṣī Kalyāṇam, pencil and ink on paper, 37.1 × 24.8 centimeters, c. 1801–1805

Source: *Sculptures at Madura. Pagoda & Choultry of Trimul Naig. 51 Drawings*. Caption: "Solemnization of the Marriage of Shiven with Paravathey, whom her Brother Vishnou is giving away by the act of pouring the sacred water of the Ganges into their Hands." © The British Library Board, Mackenzie Collection WD1063 (f. 12).

The drawings of the Pudu Maṇḍapam housed in the British Library indicate Mackenzie's dual focus on Hindu architectural monuments and the genealogy of royal families; the ritual geography of the temple is absent, replaced by abstract images of deities and kings.[53] Paired figural groups like Tripurasaṁhāramūrti (Śiva as vanquisher of the three demon cities) and Rāvaṇānugṛhamūrti (Śiva as benevolent one when demon king Rāvaṇa shakes his mountain abode), Taṭātakai (Mīnākṣī) and Īśāna (Śiva), and Ekapādamūrti (one-legged form of Śiva with Brahmā and Viṣṇu) and Gajasaṁhāramūrti (Śiva as destroyer of the elephant demon) are linked by their placement in the Pudu Maṇḍapam—though there is no reference to the temple's physical layout, nor the rituals that determined its configuration (Figures 5.4 to 5.6). Some pairs are rendered as full pillars, other pairs are shown on bases only, and a few pairs are reproduced without any column support. Overall, the individuated figures are considered important, not their placement within the temple complex, or their architectural embellishments and supports. The composite column of Tirumala Nāyaka and his consorts is the only figure drawn with two views: side and frontal (Figure 5.7), signaling the importance of the hall's royal patron. In the architectural drawings and accompanying captions, Mackenzie's native informants convey some interest in the religious stories and characters; one title of this album is *Sculptured Figures of the Hindoo Mythology taken from the Pagoda & Choultry of Trimul Naig at Madura*. Scattered throughout the portfolio are references to "Hindoo Mythology" and short synopses of a few myths.[54] Several images depict Hindu *purāṇa*s (ancient texts that eulogize Hindu deities); the Tirumala Nāyaka columns, Mīnākṣī's *vimāṉam*, and the Rāya Gōpuram are purely architectural drawings. These images, extracts of the temple site in the form of abstract mythological and genealogical narratives, reflect Mackenzie's program of collecting a comprehensive archive of diverse, often 'quasi-historical' records that could, in aggregate, compensate for the absence in literary documents informing the 'history' of south India.

A watercolor painting of Fort Defiance near Madurai (Figure 5.8), credited to a sketch by Mackenzie in 1784, shows turbaned natives manually operating a water-drawing mechanism for irrigation near a palace-like structure in the foreground, as Āṉaimalai (a sacred rock mass called Elephant Hill) and the Mīnākṣī-Sundareśvara temple's tall gateways or *gōpuram*s loom in the distance. Fort Defiance was called "Tamakam" (Tamil, Tamukkaṁ, 'summer house') and refers to the domed building in the lower right-hand corner of the watercolor, possibly built by the Madurai Nāyaka rulers Tirumala or Rāṇi Maṅgammāḷ (r. 1689–1706 CE). In an 1826 letter to the East India Company's Court of Directors, Alexander Johnston narrates how Tamakam was given to his father by the Nawāb of Arcot, and calls the building "the choultry called Fort Defiance," referring to its use as an outpost

Figure 5.4 Anonymous, Tripurasaṁhāramūrti and Rāvaṇānugṛhamūrti, pencil and ink on paper, 37.1 × 24.8 centimeters, c. 1801–1805

Source: Sculptures at Madura. Pagoda & Choultry of Trimul Naig. 51 Drawings. Caption: "Eswaren or Shiven in the act of setting out to war with the Trepuram Three formidable Damons" and "Ravenan lifting Kylassum or the Paradise of Shiven." © The British Library Board, Mackenzie Collection WD1063 (f. 14).

in the siege of Madurai.[55] Mackenzie was in Dindigul Valley near Madurai while he served with a corps of Indian troops and conducted his first surveys; he may have commissioned the drawings of the Madurai temple and pillared hall from J. Newman or C. Ignatio, his draughtsmen at that time.

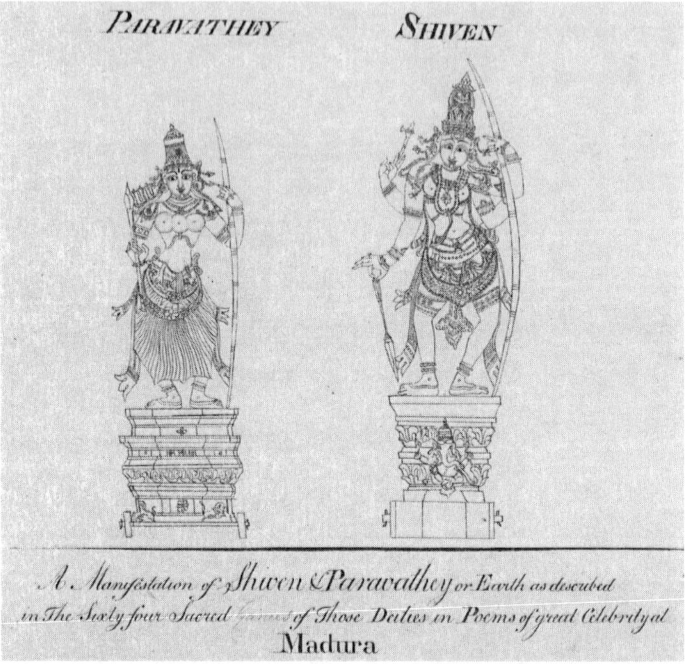

Figure 5.5 Anonymous, Taṭātakai and Īśāna, pencil and ink on paper, 37.1 × 24.8 centimeters, c. 1801–1805

Source: *Sculptures at Madura. Pagoda & Choultry of Trimul Naig. 51 Drawings*. Caption: "A Manifestation of Shiven & Paravathey on Earth as described in the Sixty-four Sacred Games of Those Deities in Poems of great Celebrity at Madura." © The British Library Board, Mackenzie Collection WD1063 (f. 8).

The watercolor of Fort Defiance conveys a common motif of the views in Mackenzie's archive: the conspicuous absence of anything British, and the dominating presence of Indian workers in a landscape dotted with Hindu monuments. Mackenzie depended on, and had utmost respect for, native informants who could mediate the Hindu 'past' through ethnographic, epigraphic, and architectural evidence. Although colonization was the very condition of possibility of producing the visual representations, the colonizer is largely 'absent' from the images. We can draw a conceptual link between the painting of Fort Defiance and another view of Dindigul from Mackenzie's collection, a portrayal of a British man, maybe Mackenzie himself, sitting on the ground beside a turbaned and bearded Indian (Figure 5.9). Nicholas Dirks describes this watercolor painting:

> The picture presents Mackenzie listening intently to his Indian guide, who is speaking and gesturing towards an architectural site that is mostly hidden behind

Figure 5.6 Anonymous, Ekapādamūrti and Gajasaṁhāramūrti, pen and ink on paper, 37.1 × 24.8 centimeters, c. 1801–1805

Source: *Sculptures at Madura. Pagoda & Choultry of Trimul Naig. 51 Drawings.* Caption: "The Hindoo Triad of Deity or Trimoortee" and "Describing the Tremendous Elephant raised by the Incantations of the Reshess of Daracavanum for the destruction of Shiven & Shiven tearing it open, & making Garments of it. The Sacrifices of these Reshees on this occasion produced the Institution of the Liṅgam Worship." © The British Library Board, Mackenzie Collection WD1063 (f. 6).

shrubs and palm trees on the left side of the picture. The gnarled hill that makes the centerpiece for the picture has a crenolated fort wall halfway up and a South Indian style temple on its top. With the object of Mackenzie's quest thus exalted and displayed above, below we see utter equality between the figures; in this picture

Figure 5.7 Anonymous, Tirumala Nāyaka and his consorts, pen and ink on paper, 37.1 × 24.8 centimeters, c. 1801–1805

Source: *Sculptures at Madura. Pagoda & Choultry of Trimul Naig. 51 Drawings.* Caption: "Front and Side Views of Trimul Naig & his Wives forming the most conspicuous Pillar in the Choultry bearing his name at Madura." © The British Library Board, Mackenzie Collection WD1063 (f. 52).

we can see the extraordinary quality of a man who had as much respect for his native informants as any other colonial personage of his time, if not more. Only Mackenzie's red coat signals his difference. Only our sense of Mackenzie's colonial project permits a reading of this picture as a sign of Mackenzie's self-depicted authority and authenticity.[56]

Figure 5.8 Colin Mackenzie, *General View of Fort Defiance, near Madura*, watercolor, 30.1 × 46.6 centimeters, 1784

Source: Inscribed in ink, "Fort Defiance and the Landscape near it, near Madura, in 1784. Originally sketched by C McK." © The British Library Board, Mackenzie Collection WD633.

Figure 5.9 Anonymous, *View of Dindigul with an English Officer and an Indian in the Foreground*, watercolor, 20 × 23.8 centimeters, 1790

Source: Inscribed in ink, "View of Dindigul (?) 1790." © The British Library Board, Mackenzie Collection WD640.

Mackenzie's "voice" in his collection is harmonized with the 'voice' of his native informants, demonstrating what C. A. Bayly characterizes as "the ideal of informed British rule."[57] Mackenzie, like many of his contemporaries in British India, aspired to ameliorate and restore an Indian civilization that had fallen into ruin. Mackenzie's positivist historical project was not merely a matter of scientific curiosity; it was embedded in a broader program of the British military to better 'know' India such that the colonial state could be more effectively governed: "the individualist myth that sustained colonial rule: the ideal of the lone colonial officer and sage, standing at the centre of a web of untainted knowledge, the man who 'knows the country'. British rule might be saved from damnation if liberal judgment were based on pure information."[58] Of course, this "pure information" was fragmentary, and its "web" was hardly untainted; through the co-optation of native intellectuals, the 'material culture' manufactured by the colonial gaze ultimately subsumed the *lived* culture of the temple, successfully transforming it into an object of 'heritage' and 'historical' curiosity.

Ram Raz as interpreter and informant

Ram Raz (1790–1833) exemplifies a similar form of native informant that emerged in nineteenth-century British India: proficient in the classical and vernacular languages of traditional texts, competent in English and Western scholastic methods, and well versed in Hindu customs.[59] Like Boriah, he was an essential conduit for the production of knowledge about Hindu architectural monuments for Europeans newly connected to the Indian colony. Like Mackenzie, he directed his energies towards constructing a history of a pre-Islamic and unsullied Hindu architecture.[60] Born in Tanjavur to apparent descendants of the last Vijayanagara king, Ram Raz worked as a lawyer in the 16th Regiment of the Madras Native Infantry, where he refined his knowledge of English and several south Indian languages. While employed as a clerk in the Military Auditor General Office, he impressed civil administrators with his 1815 translation of Tipū Sulṭān's code of revenue regulations.[61] At the East India Company's College of Fort St George in the Madras Presidency, he was appointed head of the College Office and later head English master.[62] During his time there, Ram Raz studied Sanskrit, mathematics, geography, and astronomy. He met Captain Henry Harkness, who recommended him to the commissioner of Mysore; Harkness later wrote the preface to Ram Raz's 1834 *Essay on the Architecture of the Hindús*. Ram Raz was appointed judge in Bangalore and in 1828, elected a corresponding member of the Royal Asiatic Society of Great Britain and Ireland.[63]

Established in 1823 in London, the Royal Asiatic Society was intended to be the British counterpart to the Asiatick Society of Bengal founded in 1784.

Ram Raz was commissioned by the Society to "impart to the European world ... information not yet before them"—he began collecting information for a translation of the *śilpaśāstras*, traditional texts that delineate the standards for religious Hindu iconography, focusing primarily on architecture.[64] Concurrently, draughtsmen working for the Madras Survey Department produced many detailed drawings of south Indian temples in Tanjavur, Tiruvalur, Kancipuram, Tiruvannamalai, Srirangam, and, of course, Madurai. By the end of 1831, the drawings and Ram Raz's translation were completed and presented to the Royal Asiatic Society. A committee comprising Alexander Johnston, Colonel Charles Joseph Doyle, and Graves Haughton discussed the publication of the materials, while other fellows including artist William Daniell and architects William Wilkins and Charles R. Cockerell appraised the work.[65] *Essay on the Architecture of the Hindús* was published posthumously in 1834, financed by the Oriental Translation Fund of the Royal Asiatic Society.

Essay on the Architecture of the Hindús is the earliest written analysis in English of the traditional south Indian temple architectural canons, originally composed in Sanskrit. Ram Raz's *Essay* provides technical information compiled from various fragmented sources, concentrating on the aesthetic treatise *Mānasāra*, the most complete of the documents he acquired. His translation introduced *Mānasāra* to a European audience for the first time. The *Mānasāra* is a sprawling text that encompasses the politics of man-made things, and the social stratifications that determine access to those things; however, Ram Raz focused only on the part of the *śilpaśāstras* pertaining to temple planning and construction, and prescriptions for the proportions of architectural elements. The essay concentrates on the conventions and measurements of six principal parts of a south Indian Hindu temple: pedestal (*upapīṭha*), base (*adhiṣṭhāna*), pillar (*stambha*), entablature (*prastāra*), tower (*vimāṉam*), and gateway (*gōpuram*).[66] Because Ram Raz's work remains the authoritative translation of this text, Jennifer Howes argues that his narrow view of the *śilpaśāstras* has persisted as the dominant interpretation of art historians and architects to this day.[67]

The architectural forms expounded in Ram Raz's book are strictly theoretical, and almost entirely separated from their context as living temples. For example, plate II labeled as *Athisthánas or Bases* displays various types of bases, subcomponents, and measurements, presumably copied from temples Ram Raz visited for his research (Figure 5.10). These forms are extracted from existing south Indian temples and drawn with precision; however, we do not know from which temples the components originated, or their locations *within* those temples, with a few exceptions annotated with brief contextual descriptions. The drawings emphasize mainly the 'pure' architectural elements, often erasing

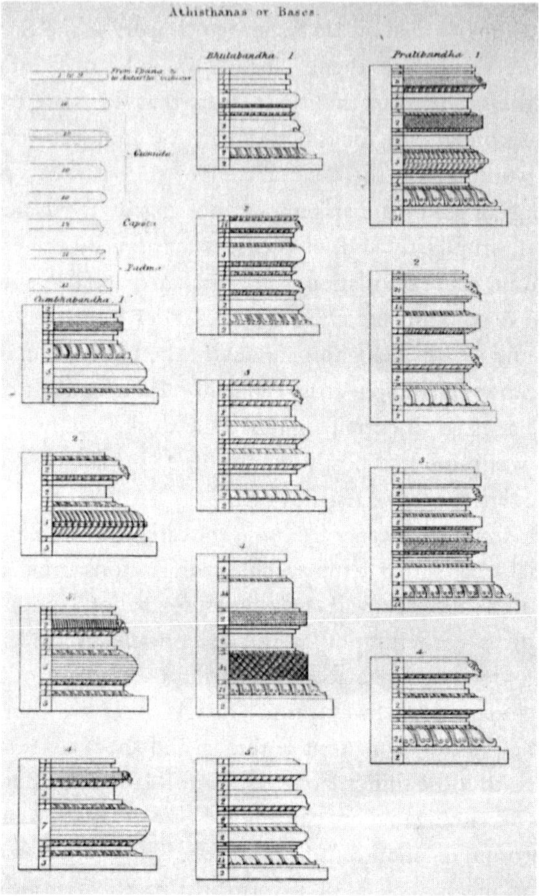

Figure 5.10 Day & Hagle, *Athisthánas or Bases*, lithograph, 26.5 × 18 centimeters, 1834

Source: Rám Ráz, *Essay on the Architecture of the Hindús* (London: Published for the Oriental Translation Fund of Great Britain and Ireland; by John William Parker, 1834), plate II.

the figural reliefs that appear on the surface of those elements. For instance, plate XXIII, *The Vimána of Sri Rangam*, depicts some sculptural detail and ornamentation of the *vimāṉam* but leaves the walls blank between the thin black lines, and plate XXX, *The Vimána of Vaycunthanatha at Conjeveram*, provides a side view with no figural sculptural detail (Figures 5.11 and 5.12). This method drew heavily from European conventions used to denote neoclassical buildings, to make 'Hindu architecture' more accessible for Western consumption—the result is the erasure of overwhelming sculptural detail that fills the temple towers and walls.

Figure 5.11 Day & Hagle, *The Vimána of Sri Rangam* (front elevation), lithograph, 27.5 × 19 centimeters, 1834

Source: Rám Ráz, *Essay on the Architecture of the Hindús*, plate XXIII.

Ram Raz's translation was lauded in the first volume of the Royal Asiatic Society's journal for proving the benefits of "promoting the cultivation of their mental powers among the natives, and diffusing a general taste for the English language in India."[68] The essay was described as the

> first attempt to convey in a systematic form, any idea of the principles by which the artists of India were guided in their construction of those elaborate and massive structures, which, erected while their country was under the dominion of its native

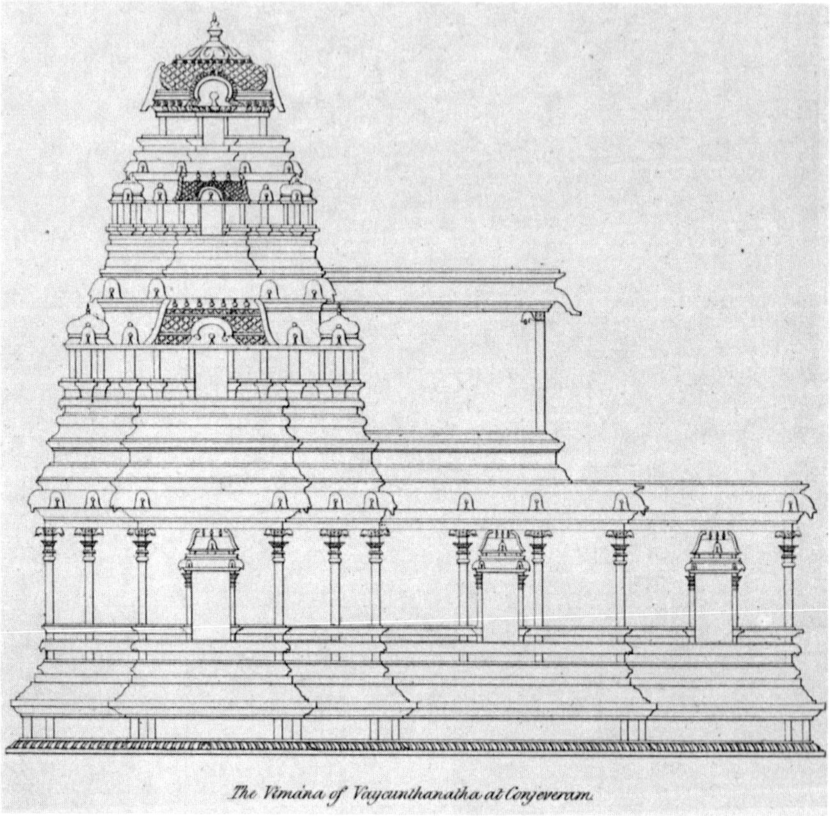

Figure 5.12 Day & Hagle, *The Vimána of Vaycunthanatha at Conjeveram*, lithograph, 23.5 × 20 centimeters, 1834

Source: Rám Ráz, *Essay on the Architecture of the Hindús*, plate XXX.

sovereigns, and in the zenith of its power and glory, still, in many instances survive the devastating inroads of invading races more or less ruthless and unsparing, to excite the wonder and admiration of the strangers who now direct the destinies of that ancient land; and in this view alone it would be highly valuable; but when it is remembered, that this first attempt proceeds from a highly-informed and intelligent native of India,—one, who, while well versed in the learning of his country, was also instructed in the literature of the Western world, and was thus enabled to compare, contrast, and judge for himself, the value of such a work must be considered much enhanced. That it will lead to other and more extended efforts of a different kind there can be little doubt, by which, what may be wanting in the present, will be supplied, and what is erroneous, will be corrected....[69]

Echoing Mackenzie's statements on the deleterious influence of Islamic incursions into India, the commentary in the Royal Asiatic Society journal celebrates Ram Raz's contributions to the understanding of Hindu architecture that survived "the devastating inroads of invading races." Only by virtue of his Western education is Ram Raz capable of effectively "comparing, contrasting, and judging" Hindu architecture. In this way, he represented to his sponsors the civilizational benefits of colonization, which would especially serve the advancement of *European* knowledge: the commentator remarked that, without further education of Indian natives,

> [i]t would ... otherwise be impossible to carry on researches into the history, manners, antiquities, &c., of India, to the extent that is desirable.... We [Europeans] shall not ... be in possession of all the knowledge on these subjects we require, until the natives are enabled and persuaded to join in the search, and communicate the results themselves.[70]

Although Ram Raz's translation of the *śilpaśāstra*s was well received by its European audience, Samuel Parker observes that many of the concepts it contains are un-translatable within the natural metaphors of the English language; thus, the text must resort to "a hybridized stew of vernacular, Sanskrit, and Sanskrit-derived technical terms integrated into sentences composed with English grammar and parts of speech." The result is "neither English nor Sanskrit, but a newly emergent, cross-cultural, technical dialect more or less intelligible only to a subculture of academic specialists."[71] Ram Raz inhabits the space between two traditions, as he cannot occupy either position fully or coherently. The same ambivalence characterizes the templates that accompany his *Essay*: temple components are illustrated by way of Western line drawing techniques, and their details and context are entirely lost in the 'translation' to these conventions.

As a native informant, Ram Raz mediated between an Indian ethnicity, of which he was representative, and the European scholarly world that supported him. His extensive knowledge of languages enabled him to gather his literary sources and data that were largely inaccessible to European scholars: interviews with Brahmin pundits, Sanskrit scholars, architects, temple builders, and sculptors. As a translator, he could reconcile the ancient technical knowledge of upper-caste Brahmins who authored and transmitted the treatises with the everyday practical knowledge of the 'humble' artisans who utilized their skills.[72] At times, there was no mutual dependence between the abstract theory and the actual process:[73] when Ram Raz could not decipher some abstruse architectural vocabulary in the text, he sought help from a practicing sculptor of the "*Cammata* tribe" in Tanjavur who was versed in the architecture's applied side.[74] Tapati Guha-Thakurta confirms Ram Raz's exceptional position in the world of European scholarship: "It was left to the new native expert to bypass this deadlock and perform a new act of mediation: between norms and practices, the texts and the temples, and, most important, between a uniquely Indian theme and its Western connoisseurs."[75]

Ram Raz as nationalist scholar

Although Ram Raz adopted a reverential attitude towards his patrons and audience in his writing, *Essay on the Architecture of the Hindús* provided critical counter-narratives to the dominant scholarly accounts on 'Hindu architecture' of his European contemporaries.[76] He targeted European scholars' prevailing assumption that Hindu architecture was indebted to 'Western' inspiration, specifically the assumed affinity between Indian architecture and classical Egyptian, Greek, and Roman forms.[77] On the first page of the *Essay*, Ram Raz disputes a number of assumptions about the *śilpaśāstras* made by William Jones, the prominent Orientalist (discussed in chapter 3). Jones shared Mackenzie's sentiment that, because the Hindus' "history" was lost in a "cloud of fables," visual record and material culture were crucial to understanding India's past;[78] he drew a connection between Indian and Egyptian ancient architecture supported by the writings of classical Greco-Roman authors.[79] In an 1828 letter to Richard Clarke of the Madras Civil Service that forms the *Essay*'s preface, Ram Raz directly challenges Jones:

> A correct account and accurate elucidation of the art of building practised by the *Hindús*, must throw considerable light on the early progress of architecture in general. Some of the western authors have traced a certain resemblance in the leading features of the buildings in Egypt and India, and have thence concluded that there has very early been a communication of architectural knowledge between the two countries. But it is not altogether improbable that this resemblance may be merely owing to accident; inasmuch as in architecture as well as in any other art, indispensably necessary to the comfort of mankind, two or more nations may possess something in common, without having any intercourse with each other, for the wants felt by man begin the same, it is not surprising that the remedies resorted to for supplying them should be also similar or nearly so. If, on the other hand, however, both these countries had actually any communication in early ages, it is hard to determine which of them may have been indebted to the other. The western writers on antiquities have not placed this matter beyond a doubt.[80]

In Ram Raz's 'humanist' narrative, there is no necessary Western origin for Hindu temple architecture. If the 'wants' of human beings are universal, then the remedies for those wants should bear some resemblance for all human beings; indeed, one of the principal objects of his concern is "architecture *in general*" (emphasis mine), as a human phenomenon. Further, if there was some contact or influence between countries in ancient times, then it is just as readily possible that the Egyptians were influenced by the Indians, rather than the reverse. Through his translation of the *śilpaśāstras*, Ram Raz strove to convince a skeptical West that Indian art, like ancient classical art of Europe, was based on a systematic theory or science of artistic representation—and to convince European scholars that elements of Indian architecture may, in many ways, be superior to Western classical conventions.[81]

In the broader context of British colonial politics, Upinder Singh argues that Ram Raz may be considered "India's first architectural nationalist."[82] Although he culled from documents written primarily in south India and provided drawings of mostly Dravidian temple structures, his essay helped to define a unified 'Indian architecture' that 'stood in' for the whole of the subcontinent: the Royal Asiatic Society judged his translation of a treatise on south Indian temples as 'pan-Hindu' and 'pan-Indian.'[83] Ram Raz's essay sought to establish through archival research an independent national history for India. However, he did not construct a chronological history of various artistic styles, nor did he produce a historical typology of architectural techniques. Instead, he attempted only to undermine the overwhelming certainty of Western writers as to the 'foreign' origins of Indian architectural knowledge: he wrote,

> I will not venture ... to form an opinion as to this alleged affinity in the architecture of Egypt and India. I humbly presume, therefore, that until the *Silpa Sástra* of the *Hindús* is correctly illustrated and laid before the public, the question as to whether the Hindu art owes its origin to the one or the other of the two countries must remain problematical.[84]

The narrative of civilizational history to which Ram Raz contributed was reproduced by subsequent intellectuals who studied the same texts. Writing on a twentieth-century translation of the *Mānasāra* by Prasanna Kumar Acharya, Indian painter Abanindranath Tagore commented that acquainting oneself with the ancient text was necessary for a "thorough knowledge of Indian Art," and that Acharya's writings "are fit to give a correct account of Indian Art to the world at large."[85] In this way, the translation of the *Mānasāra* was linked to the nationalist imagination of India as a unified civilization.[86]

Ram Raz's *Essay* received a warm reception in Europe. In an 1834 review in the *Architectural Magazine*, Scottish architect John Claudius Loudon called the *Essay* "eminently useful" to painters, scene decorators, architects, cabinet makers, and ornament designers.[87] Indeed, it influenced German art historian Franz Kugler, who drew from *Essay* for the section on "India" in his 1842 *Handbuch der Kunstgeschichte* ('Handbook of art history').[88] It also inspired English designer Owen Jones' thinking about Hindu architectural ornament for his 1856 *The Grammar of Ornament*, a popular source book for ornamentation and patterns that encouraged experimental techniques at many design schools.[89]

Ram Raz's choultry drawings

After Ram Raz's death, the Royal Asiatic Society posthumously published his treatise on Hindu architecture, as an expression of gratitude by those who pursued "authentic information respecting the arts and sciences of India."[90] The Society's high regard for Ram Raz was informed not only by his pathbreaking *Essay on the Architecture of the Hindús*, but also by his contribution to the reporting of material culture: the January 5, 1833, minutes of the Council for the Royal Asiatic Society offer "special thanks" to him for both his *Essay* and the "fifty-two sheets of drawings of the columns in the celebrated temple at Madura" that he gave to the Council.[91] These sheets, depicting fifty-two columns of Tirumala Nāyaka's Pudu Maṇḍapam and palace in Madurai, elicited great interest among Royal Asiatic Society Council members, who resolved that

> means be adopted to procure accounts of all the different histories, mythological and otherwise which are represented in different parts of India either modern or ancient by sculpture or by painting; and especially the Naigs of Madura as represented in the sculptures of the pillars of Trimul Naig's Choultry at Madura.[92]

Perhaps animated by these drawings, the only ones of the Madurai temple in their collection, the Committee of Correspondence decided on March 21, 1834, that "endeavours be made to obtain accounts of all the buildings erected by Trimul Naig."[93]

Included with Ram Raz's illustrations of the "Poothoo Mundabom of Tirmul Naick at Madura" is a list in Tamil and English of all the columns sketched. He painstakingly identified the subjects and gods of each pillar numbered according to a ground plan of the Pudu Maṇḍapam labeled as 50, but now missing; it was reprinted in James Fergusson's 1876 *History of Indian and Eastern Architecture* (Figure 5.13).[94] The style of the Pudu Maṇḍapam drawings differs

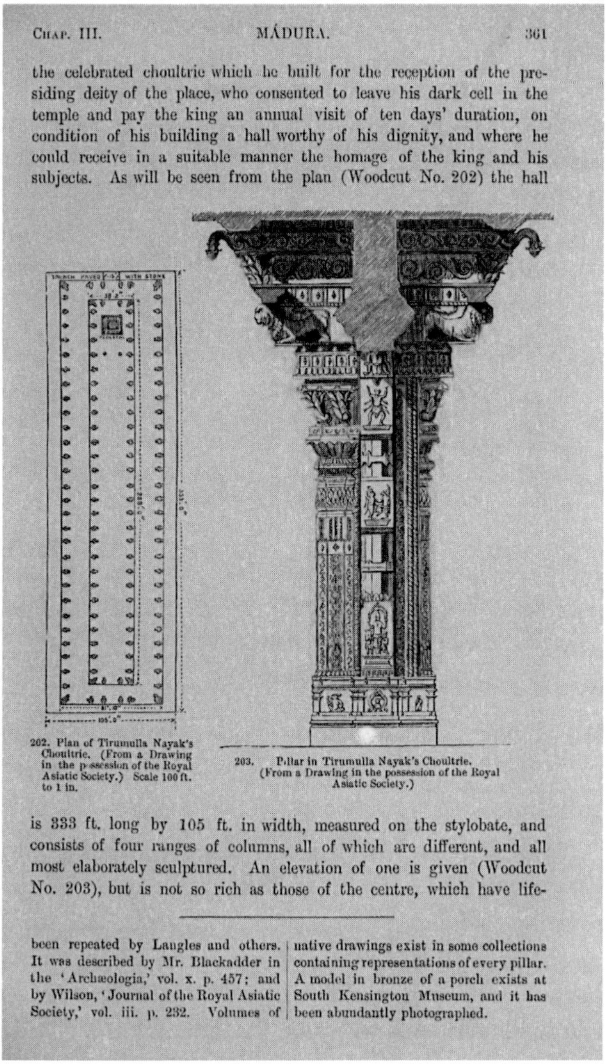

CHAP. III. MÁDURA. 361

the celebrated choultrie which he built for the reception of the presiding deity of the place, who consented to leave his dark cell in the temple and pay the king an annual visit of ten days' duration, on condition of his building a hall worthy of his dignity, and where he could receive in a suitable manner the homage of the king and his subjects. As will be seen from the plan (Woodcut No. 202) the hall

202. Plan of Tirumulla Nayak's Choultrie. (From a Drawing in the possession of the Royal Asiatic Society.) Scale 100 ft. to 1 in.

203. Pillar in Tirumulla Nayak's Choultrie. (From a Drawing in the possession of the Royal Asiatic Society.)

is 333 ft. long by 105 ft. in width, measured on the stylobate, and consists of four ranges of columns, all of which are different, and all most elaborately sculptured. An elevation of one is given (Woodcut No. 203), but is not so rich as those of the centre, which have life-

been repeated by Langles and others. It was described by Mr. Blackadder in the 'Archæologia,' vol. x. p. 457; and by Wilson, 'Journal of the Royal Asiatic Society,' vol. iii. p. 232. Volumes of native drawings exist in some collections containing representations of every pillar. A model in bronze of a porch exists at South Kensington Museum, and it has been abundantly photographed.

Figure 5.13 "Plan of Tirumulla Nayak's Choultrie" and "Pillar in Tirumulla Nayak's Choultrie" (from drawings in the possession of the Royal Asiatic Society)

Source: James Fergusson, *History of Indian and Eastern Architecture* (London: John Murray, 1876), 361.

vastly from the artwork in Ram Raz's *Essay*. In *Essay on the Architecture of the Hindús*, the linear configurations and thick black outlines in the accompanying plates emphasize the temple's bare architectural components. For instance, *vimāṉams*, typically profuse with ornamentation, are totally stripped of detail.

Figure 5.14 Unknown, Eastern entrance (*right*) with entablature, equestrian figure, *yāḷi*, and Gajasaṁhāramūrti, pen and ink with wash, 64 × 90.3 centimeters, 1826

Source: Inscribed in ink, "No 3, No 2, No 1." 034.057: Royal Asiatic Society of Great Britain and Ireland, London.

By contrast, the set of Pudu Maṇḍapam pen, ink, and wash drawings abound with sculptural forms and color to underscore the columns' diverse subject matter: they exhibit red and pink touches on garments, lips, hands, ears, and nostrils, green traces on the Nāyaka consorts' skirts, and black coloring in the beards, hair, eyes, and ornamental features. Ram Raz's architectural drawings present primarily frontal views, and some illustrations include the elaborate roof structure to give a sense of the sculptural layout of the place. There is a definite order to his pictures: they begin with two images of the eastern entrance and proceed with interior views and sculptural portrayals of the monument before ending with two renditions of the western entrance (Figures 5.14 to 5.17).

Ram Raz's drawings of the Pudu Maṇḍapam can be interpreted as continuous with Mackenzie's project of producing a 'historical record' of ancient India through the meticulous documentation of material culture. Like the commentary and engravings in his *Essay on the Architecture of the Hindús,* the aim of the Pudu Maṇḍapam depictions was to present fundamental principles of Indian design and to provide "a correct and accurate elucidation of the art of building practiced

Figure 5.15 Unknown, Candra ('Moon' god) and Sundareśvara as a sow feeding piglets, pen and ink with wash, 62.4 × 33.5 centimeters, 1826

Source: Inscribed in ink, "No 7, No 8." 034.059: Royal Asiatic Society of Great Britain and Ireland, London.

by the *Hindús*."[95] However, the two projects differ in significant ways. Whereas the *Essay*'s lithographs show generic temple types, the Pudu Maṇḍapam drawings point to a specific temple site. While Ram Raz's *Essay* deals primarily with building

Figure 5.16 Unknown, Kālī, marriage of Mīnākṣī and Sundareśvara, and Brahmā, pen and ink with wash, 55.3 × 49.6 centimeters, 1826

Source: Inscribed in ink, "No 37, No 38, No 43, No 42." 034.073: Royal Asiatic Society of Great Britain and Ireland, London.

components such as pedestals, bases, columns, *vimāṉams*, and *gōpurams*, and the relative proportions of the various elements that comprise those parts, the Pudu Maṇḍapam illustrations focus on the pillars' design and appearance. And although his first work does not discuss artists, patrons, or historical events in particular detail, his Pudu Maṇḍapam sculptural images offer very specific indication of the location (Madurai), patron (Tirumala Nāyaka), possible motives for construction (the Nāyaka king's desire for perpetuity), and historical context (Nāyaka era) (Figure 5.18).

Figure 5.17 Unknown, Western entrance (*right*) with entablature, equestrian figures, and Rāvaṇānugr̥hamūrti, pen and ink with wash, 64.5 × 83.8 centimeters, 1826

Source: Inscribed in ink, "No 47, No 48, No 49." 034.077: Royal Asiatic Society of Great Britain and Ireland, London.

Figure 5.18 Étienne Alexander Rodrigues, Nāyaka royal portraits—north side, pen and ink with wash, 63.7 × 94.6 centimeters, 1826

Source: Inscribed in ink, "No 23, No 24, No 25, No 26, No 27, No 28." 034.068: Royal Asiatic Society of Great Britain and Ireland, London.

Conclusion

The figure of the native informant produces sites of colonial hybridity, occupying a space separate from hegemonic discourses rooted in either Western or Sanskritic ideals. In the Pudu Maṇḍapam drawings discussed in this chapter, Colin Mackenzie's draughtsmen concentrated on south Indian Hindu mythological histories, while Ram Raz's draughtsmen boldly detailed south Indian Hindu iconography. Both Mackenzie and Ram Raz were driven by their individual passions and personal ambitions; however, their scholarly endeavors are situated within the broader trajectory of novel modes of knowledge production, systematic methods of writing 'history' that had complex attachments to the rationalizations for colonial rule in the late eighteenth to early nineteenth centuries. Dirks described Mackenzie's scientific and artistic activities as "caught between the Enlightenment assurance that the knowledge of the East would fill in the total picture of world history and the colonial one that knowledge of the East would simply confirm the triumph of the West."[96] Ram Raz's work conveys a similar sort of 'trap': his articulation of a unique Indian national history also produced a coherent and unified 'nation,' which was the rational object of colonial government. Mackenzie and Ram Raz's contributions to the collection of material culture in the form of temple architecture participated actively in the construction of 'India' as a whole, and 'south India' in particular.

The Pudu Maṇḍapam drawings helped to manufacture a 'history' of south Indian society. They provide, as Thomas Trautmann writes, "a view *from* the South, of India as a whole."[97] These drawings are fragments that build a speculative whole—speculative, because the spectator never 'sees' the entire architectural monument, only *fragments*, which are curated for the purpose of conveying a specific conceptual framework for imagining 'Indian architecture.' In an analogous way, through the curation of material culture from south India, the consumer of this new academic knowledge could understand the 'whole' of 'India.' Images of Mīnākṣī and Sundareśvara from *Tiruviḷaiyāṭal Purāṇam*, the sacred history of Madurai, a particular place from southern peninsula, come to stand for the entire subcontinent and its political, social, and religious histories.

These ways of rendering 'architecture' and 'history' were first tested and refined in the context of a colonial government: native informants like Cavelly Venkata Boriah and Ram Raz were necessary instruments of government, and their essential role in the mechanisms of knowledge production was informed by the *strategies* of governing. Boriah, as Mackenzie's trusted assistant, helped produce an imagined 'India' that could be analyzed within a rational framework of government; Ram Raz similarly contributed to this imagination of 'India,' in a form that anticipated later nationalist narratives about a unified, exceptional Indian civilization. The installation of regimes of knowledge in the colonial period had profound reverberations: parallel techniques of government, refined and reformed in various ways but nonetheless traceable to this earlier moment in the recent colonial past, followed into the government of the postcolonial Indian state.

As the East India Company developed the administrative apparatuses of the modern state in India from 1770 to 1840, there was an important period of "colonial transition" marked by greater involvement in south Indian society and politics.[98] This period came after British territorial gains during the Third and Fourth Anglo-Mysore Wars, and saw the emergence of dedicated civil servants such as Mackenzie and Ram Raz, who each had a profound influence in shaping certain areas of administration.[99] Their collections, although effectively administered 'outside' the ordinary mechanisms of state institutions, cannot be divorced from their participation in the British colonial enterprise in India. Mackenzie's surveys not only concerned military, fiscal, and territorial interests, but also allowed for the interpretation of British India in terms of concepts of 'society,' 'culture,' and 'history,' emerging from novel frameworks of social science; in the same way, Ram Raz's examinations of Indian architecture produced for an English audience an imagination of the 'true' and 'scientific' nature of the Indian subcontinent. These men not only created knowledge for the radically interventionist British colonial government—they "established that knowledge production itself as a task for the state."[100] The methods and institutions they assembled would have lasting significance for both the colonial government and the subsequent postcolonial government.

Notes

1. Inscribed on the inside cover of *Hindoo & Architectural Drawings in Southern India*: "Given to the Library of the East India Company by John Lock, 16th Jany 1845." See Mildred Archer, *British Drawings in India Office Library,* vol. II: Official and Professional Artists (London: H. M. Stationery Office, 1969), 607. Other illustrations include dancing girls with musicians, stick bearers, and a procession scene. WD552–556: British Library Asia, Pacific, and Africa Collections, London. The book, which is no longer bound, is listed in *A Catalogue of the Library of The Hon. East-India Company* (London: J. & H. Cox, 1845), 69.
2. The *East-India Register* describes Justinian as a "miniature painter" of primarily colonial residences, although he practiced as an architect in Madras. He ventured into newspaper publishing with the 1859 purchase of the Madras

Presidency leading daily, the *Madras Times*. See S. Muthiah, "Printer, Painter, and Much Else," *The Hindu*, December 25, 2006, http://www.thehindu.com/todays-paper/tp-features/tp-metroplus/printer-painter-and-much-else/article3205151.ece, accessed December 14, 2021.

3. Mildred Archer, *Company Paintings: Indian Paintings of the British Period* (London: Victoria and Albert Museum, 1992), 40. See also Mildred Archer, *British Drawings in the India Office Library,* vol. I: Amateur Artists (London: Her Majesty's Stationery Office, 1969), 233. These drawings are catalogued as WD557-559 in the British Library, London.
4. Carol A. Breckenridge, "The Aesthetics and Politics of Colonial Collecting: India at World Fairs," *Comparative Studies in Society and History* 13, no. 2 (April 1989): 195–216, 200.
5. Breckenridge, "The Aesthetics and Politics of Colonial Collecting," 211. A knowledge and control only heightened by Lock's book donation to the East India Company Library in London.
6. "Sir Alexander Johnston, Called in, and Examined," July 19, 1832, *Minutes of Evidence Taken before the Select Committee on the Affairs of the East India Company* I. Public (London: Ordered, by the House of Commons, August 16, 1832), 254–257, 254, para. 1930.
7. The 1828 catalogue of Mackenzie's collection describes it as "the most expensive and most valuable collection of historical documents relative to India that ever was made by any one individual in Europe or in Asia." See H. H. Wilson, "Lt.-Col. Colin Mackenzie, C.B., and the 'Mackenzie Collection,'" in *The Mackenzie Collection. A Descriptive Catalogue of the Oriental Manuscripts, and Other Articles Illustrative of the Literature, History, Statistics and Antiquities of the South of India; Collected by the Late Lieut. Col. Colin Mackenzie, Surveyor General of India,* 2nd ed. (Madras: Higginbotham and Co., 1882 [1828]), vii–xviii, viii.
8. Colin Mackenzie to Alexander Johnston, Madras, February 1, 1817, in "ART. XXIX. Biographical Sketch of the Literary Career of the Late Colonel Colin Mackenzie, Surveyor-General of India; Comprising Some Particulars of His Collection of Manuscripts, Plans, Coins, Drawings, Sculptures, &c. Illustrative of the Antiquities, History, Geography, Laws, Institutions, and Manners, of the Ancient Hindús; Contained in a Letter Addressed by Him to the Right Hon. Sir Alexander Johnston, V.P.R.A.S. &c. &c.," *Journal of the Royal Asiatic Society of Great Britain and Ireland* 1, no. 2 (London: John W. Parker, 1834), 333–364, 334, 336.
9. Nicholas B. Dirks, "Guiltless Spoilations: Picturesque Beauty, Colonial Knowledge, and Colin Mackenzie's Survey of India," in *Perceptions of South Asia's Visual Past*, ed. Catherine B. Asher and Thomas R. Metcalf (New Delhi:

American Institute of Indian Studies; Madras: Swadharma Swarajya Sangha; New Delhi: Oxford & IBH Publishing Co., 1994), 211–232, 216. For a discussion of maps as "weapons of imperialism," see J. B. Harley, "Maps, Knowledge, and Power," in *The Iconography of Landscape: Essays on the Symbolic Representation, Design and Use of Past Environments*, ed. Denis Cosgrove and Stephen Daniels (Cambridge: Cambridge University Press, 1988), 277–312, 282–283.

10. R. H. Phillimore, *Historical Records of the Survey of India (Published by the Order of the Surveyor General of India)*, vol. I: 18th Century (Dehra Dun, UP: Survey of India, 1945), 349–352; W. C. Mackenzie, *Colonel Colin Mackenzie: First Surveyor-General of India* (Edinburgh and London: W. & R. Chambers, Ltd., 1952), 26–76; Roderick Mackenzie, *A Sketch of the War with Tippoo Sultaun; or, a Detail of Military Operations, from the Commencement of Hostilities at the Lines of Travancore in December 1789, until the Peace Concluded before Seringapatam in February 1792, in Two Volumes* (Calcutta: J. Sewell, 1799), vol. I: 82, 82 (fn.), vol. II: 144 (fn.), 145, 149 (fn.).
11. Colin Mackenzie to Alexander Johnston, "Biographical Sketch of the Literary Career of the Late Colonel Colin Mackenzie," 338.
12. R. H. Phillimore, *Historical Records of the Survey of India (Published by the Order of the Surveyor General of India)*, vol. II: 1800 to 1815 (Dehra Dun, UP: Survey of India, 1950), 419–428.
13. Prior to his promotion, Mackenzie was Lieutenant (1789), Captain (1793), Major (1806), Brevet Lieutenant-Colonel (1809), and Regimental Lieutenant (1810). See Mackenzie, *Colonel Colin Mackenzie, First Surveyor-General of India*, 26.
14. Tobias Wolffhardt, *Unearthing the Past to Forge the Future: Colin Mackenzie, the Early Colonial State and the Comprehensive Survey of India*, trans. Jane Rafferty (New York and Oxford: Berghahn Books, 2018), 117–118.
15. Peter Robb, "Completing 'Our Stock of Geography', or an Object 'Still More Sublime': Colin Mackenzie's Survey of Mysore, 1799–1810," *Journal of the Royal Asiatic Society* 8, no. 2 (1998): 181–206, 199.
16. Colin Mackenzie quoted in Robb, "Completing 'Our Stock of Geography,'" 199.
17. Colin Mackenzie, "Introductory Memoir: Of the Use and Advantage of Inscriptions & Sculptured Monuments in Illustrating Hindoo History," undated, Mss Eur/Mackenzie General 18, F109/72, f. 2, BL APAC.
18. Robb, "Completing 'Our Stock of Geography,'" 184–185.
19. Colin Mackenzie to George Buchan Esq., Chief Secretary to Government, Fort Saint George, February 28, 1804, Papers relating to the Mysore Survey, including reports and letters on its progress from Capt. Colin Mackenzie to

H. Traill and other supporters of the project (1802–1807), Mss Eur F228/39, no. 20, f. 27, BL APAC.

20. Mackenzie, "Introductory Memoir: Of the Use and Advantage of Inscriptions & Sculptured Monuments in Illustrating Hindoo History," f. 1.
21. "Memorandum," Madras, February 14, 1808, Madras Public Consultations, volume 341A, ff. 2907–2917, Tamil Nadu State Archives and Historical Research, Chennai.
22. Colin Mackenzie to Alexander Johnston, "Biographical Sketch of the Literary Career of the Late Colonel Colin Mackenzie," 335.
23. Colin Mackenzie to Alexander Johnston, "Biographical Sketch of the Literary Career of the Late Colonel Colin Mackenzie," 335.
24. Niyōgis are "a class of secular (*laukika*) brahmins who typically supported themselves by accepting appointments (*niyōgamu*) to political and administrative service" in the Andhra region. See Phillip B. Wagoner, "Precolonial Intellectuals and the Production of Colonial Knowledge," *Comparative Studies in Society and History* 45, no. 4 (October 2003): 783–814, 795. This ascendant class of Telugu writing scribes changed the intellectual landscape of south India through their *karaṇam* (record-keeper, accountant) traditions. See Velcheru Narayana Rao, David Shulman, and Sanjay Subrahmanyam, *Textures of Time: Writing History in South India 1600–1800* (Delhi: Permanent Black, 2001), 19–21, 93–139, 190–191.
25. Major Mark Wilks, Acting Resident of Mysore, to George Buchan Esq., Chief Secretary to Government, Mysoor, March 4, 1807, Board's Collections 6426 to 6428 (1809–1810), vol. 280, IOR/F/4/280, ff. 94–95, BL APAC. Wilks authored: *Historical Sketches of the South of India, in an Attempt to Trace the History of Mysoor; From the Origin of the Hindoo Government of That State, to the Extinction of the Mohammedan Dynasty in 1799*, vol. I (London: Longman, Hurst, Rees, Orme, and Brown, 1810).
26. Robb, "Completing 'Our Stock of Geography,'" 188.
27. Wilson, *The Mackenzie Collection. A Descriptive Catalogue of the Oriental Manuscripts*, 9–10. Ironically, these native scholars were not allowed to finish or catalogue Mackenzie's project after his death, although Wilson mentions the necessity of having native translators to ensure accuracy. See "Report of Proceedings Connected with Collections Made by the Late Colonel Mackenzie in Illustration of Oriental Literature and History": Extract Bengal Public Consultations, January 18, 1822, H. H. Wilson to C. Lushington, Secretary to Government in the General Department, Board's Collections 22906–22929 (1826–1827), vol. 867, IOR/F/4/867, f. 59, BL APAC.
28. "Report of Proceedings Connected with Collections Made by the Late Colonel Mackenzie in Illustration of Oriental Literature and History": Palmer & Co. to

Charles Lushington, Secretary to Government, General Department, October 19, 1822—Monies to the Executrix to the Late Colonel Mackenzie, ff. 164–165.

29. "Report of Proceedings Connected with Collections Made by the Late Colonel Mackenzie in Illustration of Oriental Literature and History": Extract Public Letter from Bengal to Messrs Palmer & Co., Attornies to the Executix to the Late Colonel Mackenzie Surveyor General of India, January 1, 1823, ff. 16–17.
30. Nicholas B. Dirks, "Colonial Histories and Native Informants: Biography of an Archive," in *Orientalism and the Postcolonial Predicament: Perspectives on South Asia*, ed. Carol A. Breckenridge and Peter van der Veer (Philadelphia: University of Pennsylvania Press, 1993), 279–313, 291, citing Colin Mackenzie, "Memorandum of the Means of Procuring Historical Materials regarding the South of India," document no. 65 in Box 3 from uncatalogued miscellaneous papers in the Mackenzie Collection (1802–1814), BL APAC.
31. Mackenzie, "Introductory Memoir: Of the Use and Advantage of Inscriptions & Sculptured Monuments in Illustrating Hindoo History," f. 1.
32. Dirks, "Colonial Histories and Native Informants," 290.
33. Rama Mantena, "The Question of History in Precolonial India," *History and Theory* 46, no. 3 (October 2007): 396–408, 399.
34. Pierre Nora, "General Introduction: Between Memory and History," in *Realms of Memory: The Construction of the French Past, volume I: Conflicts and Divisions*, ed. Pierre Nora (New York: Columbia University Press, 1996), 1–20, 8.
35. Wilson, *The Mackenzie Collection. A Descriptive Catalogue of the Oriental Manuscripts*, 14–15. See also "Report of Proceedings Connected with Collections Made by the Late Colonel Mackenzie in Illustration of Oriental Literature and History": Extract Bengal Public Consultations, August 22, 1822, H. H. Wilson to C. Lushington Esq., Acting Chief Secretary to Government, Fort William, ff. 116–118. Museums include the British Museum, London; Government Museum, Chennai; Indian Museum, Kolkata; National Museum, New Delhi; and Victoria & Albert Museum, London.
36. Mackenzie, "Introductory Memoir: Of the Use and Advantage of Inscriptions & Sculptured Monuments in Illustrating Hindoo History," ff. 1–2.
37. Rama Sundari Mantena, *The Origins of Modern Historiography in India: Antiquarianism and Philology, 1780–1880* (New York: Palgrave Macmillan, 2012), 65.
38. See Dirks, "Guiltless Spoilations," 218, and Jennifer Howes, *Illustrating India: The Early Colonial Investigations of Colin Mackenzie (1784–1821)* (Oxford: Oxford University Press, 2010), 12–13. The Military Male Orphan Asylum in Madras was founded in 1789 to provide a "practical Education" in reading, spelling, writing, arithmetic, morality, and Christianity to the illegitimate sons ("half-cast" children) of British fathers and Indian mothers. See Andrew

Bell, *The Madras School, or Elements of Tuition: Comprising the Analysis of an Experiment in Education, Made at the Male Asylum, Madras; with Its Facts, Proofs, and Illustrations....* (London: T. Bensley, 1808), xii, 1–2, 151–152.

39. Among his list of collected materials, Mackenzie outlined these drawings:

> II. Drawings.
>
> Views and sketches of remarkable places.
>
> Plans of Cities, Fortresses, Battles, Sieges, &c.
>
> Ditto of Ancient Cities and Temples, &c. as Beejanagur, Halla, Bede, and other ancient capitals.
>
> Elevations and Sections of Ditto.
>
> Collection of Drawings illustrative of the state and Progress of the arts of design, of sculpture, &c. &c. among the Hindoos, 2 Volumes large Folio.
>
> Ditto of ditto of Various Plants, Trees, Flowers, executed during the Surveys 4 vols. Folio.
>
> Ditto of ditto of the Costume of the various classes of Inhabitants of India, the different sects of religion &c. &c. 3 Volumes Folio.

"Report of Proceedings Connected with Collections Made by the Late Colonel Mackenzie in Illustration of Oriental Literature and History": Brief view of the Collection of notes, observations and journals of 34 years and of Collections of manuscripts, Inscriptions, drawings &c. for the last 19 years made by Colonel Mackenzie in India, exclusive of a considerable collection of Native manuscripts in all languages of India, ff. 80–82. See also "Biographical Sketch of the Literary Career of the late Colonel Colin Mackenzie," 348.

40. James Fergusson, *History of Indian and Eastern Architecture* (London: John Murray, 1876), 638.
41. Dirks, "Guiltless Spoilations," 214.
42. Colin Mackenzie to Lakshman Boria, Madras, May 12, 1803, Mss Eur/ Mackenzie General 21, section 56, f. 287, BL APAC.
43. Cavelly Venkata Ramaswamie, *Biographical Sketches of Dekkan Poets, Being Memoirs of the Lives of Several Eminent Bards, Both Ancient and Modern, Who Have Flourished in Different Provinces of the Indian Peninsula, Compiled from Authentic Documents* (Calcutta: 1829), 157.
44. Colin Mackenzie to Alexander Johnston, "Biographical Sketch of the Literary Career of the Late Colonel Colin Mackenzie," 335.
45. T. V. Mahalingam, "Colonel Colin Mackenzie," in *Mackenzie Manuscripts: Summaries of the Historical Manuscripts in the Mackenzie Collection*, vol. 1 (Tamil and Malayalam), ed. T. V. Mahalingam (Madras: University of Madras, 1972), i–xxii, viii–ix; Ramaswamie, *Biographical Sketches of Dekkan Poets,*

158–159; N. Venkata Rao, "Pioneers of English Writing in India: The Cavally Telugu Family," *Annuals of Oriental Research* 18, no. 2 (1963): 1–33, 5–6.

46. Colin Mackenzie, "Account of Extracts of a Journal by Major C. Mackenzie," *Asiatic Researches: or, Transactions of the Society Instituted in Bengal, for Inquiring into the History and Antiquities, the Arts, Sciences, and Literature, of Asia* 9 (London: Vernor, Hood, and Sharpe, etc., 1809), 272–278, 273–274.
47. For example: Cavelly Boria, "IV. Account of the Jains, Collected from a Priest of This Sect, At Mudgeri: Translated by Cavelly Boria, Bráhmen, for Major C. Mackenzie," *Asiatic Researches: or, Transactions of the Society Instituted in Bengal, for Inquiring into the History and Antiquities, the Arts, Sciences, and Literature, of Asia* 9 (London: Vernor, Hood, and Sharpe, etc., 1809): 244–271.
48. David M. Blake, "Colin Mackenzie: Collector Extraordinary," *British Library Journal* 17, no. 2 (Autumn 1991): 128–150, 131–132.
49. Upinder Singh, *The Discovery of Ancient India: Early Archaeologists and the Beginnings of Archaeology* (Delhi: Permanent Black, 2004), 307.
50. Colin Mackenzie, "Paper Submitted to Me by C. Boria Bramin. Heads under Which a History of the Carnatic May Be Composed viz: October 30th 1802," Mss Eur/Mackenzie General 9, f. 2, BL APAC.
51. Howes, *Illustrating India,* 153, 119.
52. Inscribed on the original cover is "Sculptures at Madura" and in red ink: "Pagoda & Choultry of Trimul Naig. 51 Drawings." "Book 11" is an "Album of 51 drawings (57 folios) of buildings, sculpture and paintings in the temple and choultry of Tirumala Nayyak at Madura. c. 1801–05." Mackenzie's drawings were purchased in 1823 and most drawings arrived at the British Library in July 1823, after Wilson catalogued them using Mackenzie's notes and work. Wilson mentions them briefly ("Antiquities of *Madura* ... 51") in his *The Mackenzie Collection. A Descriptive Catalogue of the Oriental Manuscripts*, 581. According to art historian and archivist Mildred Archer, who organized the British Library's India Office Collections of Prints and Drawings, the library recorded the drawings in a handlist entitled "Mackenzie Collection: Drawings," now preserved as Mss Eur D562/3. Each book or portfolio of drawings was assigned a 'book' number and an additional number in red ink was put on each separate drawing following Mackenzie's own arrangement. Apart from these two lists (Wilson's and the British Library's), "the drawings have never been fully described, and, as a result, little notice has been taken of a large collection of visual materials which not only illustrates many of Mackenzie's own manuscripts but also documents his career" (Mildred Archer, *British Drawings in the India Office Library*, vol. II: Official and Professional Artists (London: Her Majesty's Stationery Office, 1969) 473–474). Jennifer Howes' *Illustrating India: The Early Colonial Investigations of Colin Mackenzie (1784–1821)* is an attempt to make sense of the drawings Mackenzie collected during his

four-decade career in India. The British Library lists twenty-three books of drawings: eight portfolios of loose drawings and fifteen bound volumes. Over the course of time, the volumes have been rebound and the loose drawings mounted. The British Library has: 384 separate drawings (WD569–952) originally contained in portfolios numbered by the Library as "Portfolios 1–5 and 7"; 14 miscellaneous drawings (WD538, 539, 1328–1330, 1475, 2618–2652), which were among Mackenzie's papers; 107 miscellaneous maps and plans (WD2626–2732); 914 drawings (WD953–955, 1061–1069, 2880) bound in thirteen volumes originally numbered by the Library as "Books 9–21." See Archer, *British Drawings in the India Office Library* II, 474. Archer catalogued all Mackenzie drawings with the "WD" (Western Drawings) prefix, even though she knew that Indian artists drew some images. See Howes, *Illustrating India,* 236.

53. These drawings are undated; however, Mackenzie's informants were collecting material in Madurai around 1801–1805 during Mackenzie's 1799–1810 Mysore Survey, which became the assigned British Library date.
54. For example, the captions for the sculptural details of the *yāḷi* and other mythical creatures for f. 50 of WD1063 include: "The Yalu-a Fabulous creature of the Hindoo Mythology" and "Fabulous Creatures of the Hindoo Mythology."
55. On June 2, 1826, Alexander Johnston wrote a letter to the East India Company's Court of Directors, stating that his father and Madura paymaster, Samuel Johnston, was given Tamakam as his residence by the Nawāb of Arcot in 1782, when he found his house in Madura fort ill-suited. Johnston's father renovated the ruined and abandoned building. See W. Francis, *Madras District Gazetteers: Madura*, vol. I (Madras: Printed by the Superintendent, Government Press, 1906), 262–264.
56. Dirks, "Guiltless Spoilations," 223.
57. C. A. Bayly, "Knowing the Country: Empire and Information in India," *Modern Asian Studies* 27, no. 1 (February 1993): 3–43, 34.
58. Bayly, "Knowing the Country: Empire and Information in India," 3.
59. Singh, *The Discovery of Ancient India*, 307.
60. Madhuri Desai, "Interpreting an Architectural Past: Ram Raz and the Treatise in South Asia," *Journal of the Society of Architectural Historians* 71, no. 4 (December 2012): 462–487, 464, 467.
61. N. S. Ramaswami, *Madras Literary Society: A History, 1812–1984* (Madras: Madras Literary Society, 1985), 65.
62. In his capacity as College of Fort St George head English master and Madras School Book Society secretary, Ram Raz wrote a critique of elementary education in Karnataka, south India. See Ram Raz, "State of Education in Southern India," *Asiatic Journal and Monthly Register for British India and Its*

Dependencies 24 (July–December 1827 [November 1827]): 584–586 (London: Parbury, Allen, & Co., 1827).

63. London, May 24, 1828, Minutes of Council, vol. 2 (March 1827 to December 1829), 85, Royal Asiatic Society of Great Britain and Ireland Library, London.
64. Henry Harkness, preface to Rám Ráz, *Essay on the Architecture of the Hindús* (London: Published for the Oriental Translation Fund of Great Britain and Ireland; By John Walker Parker, 1834), iii–xiv, iii–iv (fn.). The preface ends with letters from or about Ram Raz.
65. Raymond Head, *Catalogue of Paintings, Drawings, Engravings and Busts in the Collection of the Royal Asiatic Society* (London: The Royal Asiatic Society, 1991), 101; May 11, 1833, Minutes of General Meetings, vol. 4 (January 1833 to July 1835), 64, RAS.
66. Forty-eight plates of lithographed line drawings accompany descriptions of each form. Plates are labeled as "Lithographed for the Royal Asiatic Society by Day & Haghe, Lithographers to the King, Gate St. Lincoln Inn Fields." Mr Haghe was a well-known lithographic artist. "Annual Report of the Royal Asiatic Society of Great Britain and Ireland, 10th May, 1834," *Journal of the Royal Asiatic Society of Great Britain and Ireland* 1, no. 2 (London: John W. Parker, 1834): iii–xv, xiii. The first four architectural terms are in Sanskrit while the last two are in Tamil.
67. Jennifer Howes, *The Courts of Pre-Colonial South India: Material Culture and Kingship* (London and New York: RoutledgeCurzon, 2003), 9.
68. "Proceedings of the Anniversary Meeting of the Royal Asiatic Society, Held on Saturday, the 10th of May, 1834," *Journal of the Royal Asiatic Society of Great Britain and Ireland* 1, no. 1 (London: John W. Parker, 1834): 157–170, 166.
69. "Annual Report of the Royal Asiatic Society of Great Britain and Ireland, 10th May, 1834," xiii–xiv.
70. "Proceedings of the Anniversary Meeting of the Royal Asiatic Society, Held on Saturday, the 10th of May, 1834," 166.
71. Samuel K. Parker, "Text and Practice in South Asian Art: An Ethnographic Perspective," *Artibus Asiae* 63, no. 1 (2003): 5–34, 6.
72. Harkness, preface to Rám Ráz, *Essay on the Architecture of the Hindús*, iv, and Ram Raz to Richard Clarke, Esq., Madras, January 13, 1828, in Rám Ráz, *Essay on the Architecture of the Hindús*, xii.
73. G. H. R. Tillotson, "Farangi and Babu: Two Early Theories of Indian Architecture," *India International Centre Quarterly* 20, no. 1/2, Perceiving India: Insight and Inquiry (Spring–Summer 1993): 209–224, 221.
74. Ram Raz to Richard Clarke, Esq., Madras, October 13, 1827, in Rám Ráz, *Essay on the Architecture of the Hindús*, x. "Cammata" tribe may refer to the Kammāḷaṉ or Viśvakarma castes.

75. Tapati Guha-Thakurta, *Monuments, Objects, and Histories: Institutions of Art in Colonial and Postcolonial India* (New York: Columbia University Press, 2004), 94.
76. For example, the first page of the *Essay* disputes Orientalist William Jones' estimate of the number of subjects in the *śilpaśāstra*s. See Rám Ráz, *Essay on the Architecture of the Hindús*, 1. Later, the text refutes Sanskritist H. H. Wilson's assigned dates for south Indian dynasties. See Rám Ráz, *Essay on the Architecture of the Hindús*, 10.
77. Even eighteenth-century British landscape artist William Hodges (discussed briefly in chapter 4) refuted the idea that Indian art and architecture should be understood through Greek or Roman norms: in his 1793 *Travels in India*, although Hodges at times expresses himself through Greek references (the buildings in Madras' Fort St George offered him "an appearance similar of a Grecian city in the age of Alexander"), he argues that architecture varied according to region, climate, and material, and that Egyptian, Hindu, Moorish, and Gothic architecture were "spontaneous produce of genius in different countries." William Hodges, *Travels in India, During the Years 1780, 1781, 1782, & 1783* (London: Printed for the author, and sold by J. Edwards, 1793), 2, 64, 75. For a discussion of Hodges and Ram Raz, see Phiroze Vasunia, *The Classics and Colonial India* (Oxford: Oxford University Press, 2013), 176–184.
78. These comprised four general media: language and letters, philosophy and religion, sculptural and architectural remains, and written records of their sciences and arts.
79. William Jones, "XXV. The Third Anniversary Discourse, Delivered 2 February, 1786, By the President," *Asiatick Researches: or, Transactions of the Society Instituted in Bengal for Inquiring into the History and Antiquities, the Arts, Sciences, and Literature, of Asia* 1 (Calcutta: Manuel Cantopher and London: P. Elmsly, 1788): 415–431, 421, 427–428.
80. Ram Raz to Richard Clarke, January 13, 1828, in Rám Ráz, *Essay on the Architecture of the Hindús*, xiii.
81. For example, on pedestals made by Hindu artisans, Ram Raz writes, "most finished specimens ... may be justly said to surpass any thing of the kind in Grecian or Roman orders, both in the beauty of their proportions and richness of their ornaments." Rám Ráz, *Essay on the Architecture of the Hindús*, 23.
82. Singh, *The Discovery of Ancient India*, 312.
83. Harkness, preface to Rám Ráz, *Essay on the Architecture of the Hindús*, iii–v. See also the announcement of Ram Raz's *Essay on the Architecture of the Hindús* in "New Publications: *Essay on the Architecture of the Hindús*. By Rám Ráz, Native Judge and Magistrate at Bangalore, Corresponding Member of the Royal Asiatic Society of Great Britain and Ireland. With Forty-eight Plates.

4to. London. Published for the Royal Asiatic Society, by J. W. Parker. 1834," *Journal of the Royal Asiatic Society of Great Britain and Ireland* 1, no. 1 (1834): 145–146. Although the May 11, 1833 meeting minutes acknowledge that Ram Raz's essay expounds on the architectural system of Hindus as practiced in the southern peninsula, the Society's choice of title, *Essay on the Architecture of the Hindús*, masks the actual geographical focus. May 11, 1833, Minutes of General Meetings, vol. 4 (January 1833 to July 1835), 62, RAS.

84. Ram Raz to Richard Clarke, January 13, 1828, in Rám Ráz, *Essay on the Architecture of the Hindús*, xiii.
85. Prasanna Kumar Acharya, *Architecture of Mānasāra* (London: Oxford University Press, 1933), 1A (as part of the reviews of Acharya's translations at the book's end).
86. Howes, *The Courts of Pre-Colonial South India*, 9.
87. J. C. Loudon,"Reviews. ART. I. *Essay on the Architecture of the Hindús*. By Rám Ráz, Native Judge and Magistrate at Bangalore, Corresponding Member of the Royal Asiatic Society of Great Britain and Ireland. 4to, pp. 64. 48 plates. London, 1834," *Architectural Magazine, and Journal of Improvement in Architecture, Building, and Furnishing, and in the Various Arts and Trades Connected Therewith* 1, no. 1 (London: Longman, Rees, Orme, Brown, Green, & Longman, 1834): 267–273, 273.
88. Franz Kugler, *Handbuch der Kunstgeschichte* (Stutgart: Verlag von Ebner & Seubert, 1842), 114, fn. 2. See also Partha Mitter, *Much Maligned Monsters: A History of European Reactions to Indian Art* (Chicago and London: The University of Chicago Press, 1992 [1977]), 184, 219–220.
89. Owen Jones, *The Grammar of Ornament. Illustrated by Examples from Various Styles of Ornament* (London: Day and Son, Lithographers to the Queen, 1856), 2 in chapter XIII: "Hindoo Ornament." Along with Loudon and Kugler, Jones was one of the first writers outside the Indological tradition to give "serious consideration" to Ram Raz's work, all the more extraordinary since Jones himself was not primarily interested in architecture or sculpture. See Mitter, *Much Maligned Monsters*, 233.
90. February 26, 1834, Minutes of the Committee of Correspondence (May 1831 to July 1842), 137, RAS.
91. London, January 5, 1833, Asiatic Society of Great Britain and Ireland Minutes of Council, vol. 3 (February 1830 to March 1833), 151, RAS. There were actually 23 sheets depicting the 52 columns in the pillared hall and palace.
92. February 5, 1834, Minutes of the Committee of Correspondence (May 1831 to July 1842), 131, RAS.
93. Proceedings of the Committee of Correspondence, March 21, 1834, Minutes of the Committee of Correspondence (May 1831 to July 1842), 139, RAS.

94. James Fergusson, *History of Indian and Eastern Architecture* (London: John Murray, 1876), 361. The three artists, Etienne Rodriguez, J. Clamp, and W. MacViccars, were draughtsmen for the Survey Department in Madras. See Head, *Catalogue of Paintings, Drawings, Engravings and Busts in the Collection of the Royal Asiatic Society*, 104.
95. Ram Raz to Richard Clarke, January 13, 1828, in Rám Ráz, *Essay on the Architecture of the Hindús*, xiii.
96. Dirks, "Guiltless Spoilations," 230.
97. Thomas R. Trautmann, *The Madras School of Orientalism: Producing Knowledge in Colonial South India* (New Delhi: Oxford University Press, 2009), 3 (emphasis in the original).
98. David Washbrook, "South India 1770–1840: The Colonial Transition," *Modern Asian Studies* 38, no. 3 (July 2004): 479–516.
99. Wolffhardt, *Unearthing the Past to Forge the Future*, 100.
100. Wolffhardt, *Unearthing the Past to Forge the Future*, 12, 288.

6

Photographing Madura

The Living Temple as a Site of Ruin

Introduction

In 1933, Edith Storrs offered a large donation of photographs from her family collection to the Victoria and Albert Museum, London: "I do not want them," she wrote in her letter, "as this house is not v[ery] big, but if you think that any of them are of interest now, & would care to look through them, I will gladly send them...."[1] Captain Linnaeus Tripe, Storrs' grand-uncle, was a photographer working for the East India Company's Madras Presidency in the mid-nineteenth century, and he produced many prints of the Tamil country in south India. With the arrival of photography in India during the 1840s, the expeditions of British soldiers and civil servants were recorded in extravagant albums with extensive annotations, which gave credibility to the imperial project and catered to the British public's craving for oriental travel narratives.

Some scholars have argued for an analytical separation between these photographs and the texts which accompany them. John Falconer, British Library's former curator of visual arts from the Indian subcontinent, believed that only the photographs' written explanations convey a clear political agenda, whereas the images in themselves were "politically neutral interpretations of architecture and topography."[2] For instance, J. A. C. Boswell of the Madras Civil Service expressed in his commentary of Tripe's 1858 *Views of Ryakotta and Other Places in the Salem District*: "Every thing speaks in language that cannot be mistaken, that a brighter day has already dawned in India." In Boswell's writing, the ruins of a dilapidated fort were a solemn and picturesque reminder of "the anarchy which generally prevailed" in earlier periods of history, contrary to "Christian European Civilization" that would make the "influences of her Government manifest in their social, moral, and political advancement." The extraordinary images represented the 'reward' of civilizational conquest: "There is a magnificent view from the top of Ryakotta hill that will well repay the difficulty of ascent."[3]

Falconer's assessment of 'neutrality' in Tripe's photographs is premised on the problematic notion that the camera captures images detached from the subjectivity of the photographer. As John Berger reminds us,

> a photograph bears witness to a human choice being exercised.... A photograph, whilst recording what has been seen, always and by its nature refers to what is not seen. It isolates, preserves and presents a moment taken from a continuum.... All its references are external to itself ... *what it shows invokes what is not shown.*[4]

Tripe understood his commission from the Madras Presidency as an undertaking to collect a visual record of the material culture of south India, in topographic, architectural, and ethnographic terms. Though he photographed various forts and palaces of antiquarian and architectural importance, he focused his lens primarily

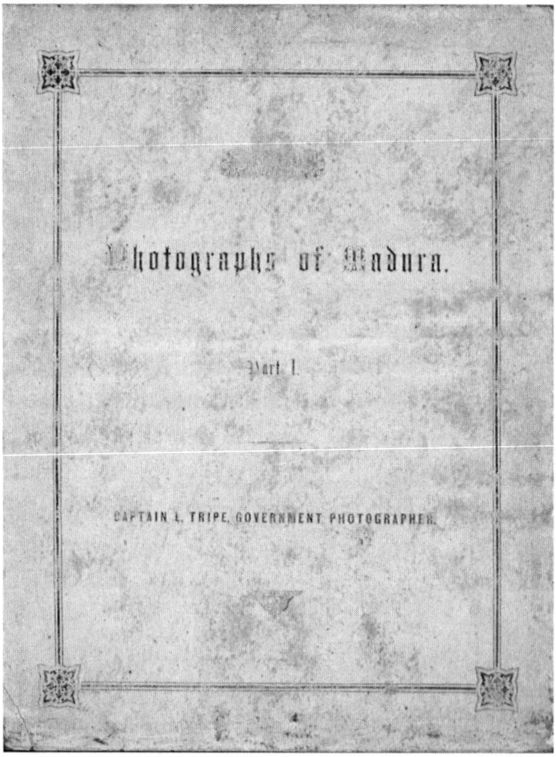

Figure 6.1 Cover, *Photographic Views in Madura, Part I*, 57.3 × 45.3 centimeters, 1860

Source: Linnaeus Tripe, *Photographic Views in Madura. By Captain L. Tripe, Government Photographer, Madras Presidency. Part I. With Descriptive Notes, by Martin Norman, Esq. M. C. S. 1858* (Madras: Madras Presidency, 1860). The Metropolitan Museum of Art, New York, 2005.100.381.1, www.metmuseum.org.

on religious structures. The photographs circulated in four 1860 government-mandated, documentary albums called *Photographic Views in Madura* (Figure 6.1), specifically those of columned spaces at the Mīnākṣī-Sundareśvara temple, problematize the notion that "honest, scientifically sanctioned pictures ... were supposed to escape artifice, personal interest, and subjective response."[5] The photograph is bound up in a certain discursive context and ideological agenda that are visible not only in the political and economic context in which the photographs are generated, but also in the actual methods and techniques of the photographers 'in the field.' The documentary mission in India relied upon a particular understanding of what constitutes 'history' that served to rationalize British paternalism in India. The photographs of the living Madurai temple constitute an essential mechanism of the colonial apparatus' governing strategy: constructing an archaeological vision of India as a dying civilization.

The emergence of photography as an art of the state

The complex history of photography in India is bound up in the broader history of photography as a "technical practice."[6] Photography arrived in India shortly after its emergence in Europe, when William Henry Fox Talbot and Louis Jacques Mandé Daguerre introduced the public to their photographic methods in 1839. Although Talbot's process of negative–positive photography on paper eventually furnished the basis for contemporary photography, Daguerre's invention dominated early photography in India. The daguerreotype was initially valued for its accurate and minutely detailed (but reversed) image produced on a silver-surfaced metal plate; however, its popularity was short-lived due to its time-consuming process, difficulty of operation, and high cost, as well as its cumbersome method of duplication. By the mid-1850s, Talbot's calotype process and Frederick Scott Archer's wet collodion process had largely replaced the daguerreotype.

The shift in photographic techniques, and the development of cheaper ways of printing, coincided with the colonial government's official sponsorship of photography. Recognizing the enormous potential of emergent photographic technologies, the East India Company's Court of Directors in London issued a directive in 1855 urging the Bengal Presidency to replace costly draughtsmen (the subject of chapter 5) with photographers to provide a visual record of India. They described photography as

> the means by which representations may be obtained of scenes and buildings, with the advantages of perfect accuracy, small expenditure of time and moderate cost. We have recently desired the Government of Bombay to discontinue the employment of draughtsmen in the delineation of antiquities of Western India, and to employ

> photography instead, and it is our desire that this method be generally substituted throughout India, in cases where it may be considered desirable by the Government to obtain representation of objects of interest.[7]

Photography was a technologically promising new science, providing a less expensive, quicker, and more 'accurate' method of rendering "objects of interest" to the Company. In addition to producing a more 'correct' visual record of India, photography helped to transform and reshape British imaginations of the colony. Early British photography of India's architectural heritage served to preserve a 'disappearing' past, while providing new points of reference for growing academic and popular knowledge of the subcontinent. A 'precise' representation of historical monuments, geological features, botanical elements, and indigenous inhabitants could give the English public a concrete image of the land and the people being governed. Following the initiative of Governor-General Lord Charles John Canning (1812–1862), an official photographer was appointed in each presidency; Linnaeus Tripe was selected as government photographer for the East India Company's Madras Presidency in 1856.

Tripe (1822–1902) was an Indian Army officer for the 12th Madras Native Infantry, photographing Burmese architecture after the 1852 Second Anglo-Burmese War and Britain's annexation of parts of Burma. He earned a reputation as a talented photographer when jurors at the 1855 Madras Exhibition of Raw Products, Arts, and Manufactures of South India declared his photographs of the Hoysala temples in the Carnatic area "the best series of photographic views on paper."[8] Tripe's photographs soon appeared in the Madras Photographic Society meetings published in the *Madras Journal of Literature and Science.*[9] When Tripe became the official photographer for the Madras Presidency, he was selected as an "Officer who could be deputed to various parts of the south of India for the purpose of taking Photographic representations of the many interesting objects there ... edifices, sculptures and inscriptions of much beauty or interest both historical and artistic."[10] Tripe lived in Bangalore where the mild climate was more conducive for printing, but traveled to Madras for two months of every year to teach photography at the Government School of Industrial Arts.

Tripe received a budget of 28,368 rupees for a period of twenty-six months, and he traveled nearly 700 miles from December 1857 to April 1858 taking photos (mostly calotypes), eventually published in eleven large albums.[11] These prints, created from 275 large paper negatives, 16 large glass negatives, and 160 stereographs on glass, span Tripe's journey across south India, the first-ever photographic record of this region: photographs of Madura (Madurai), Poodoocottah (Pudukkottai), Salem District, Seringham (Srirangam), Tanjore

(Tanjavur), and Trichinopoly (Tiruchirappalli), and stereographs of Madura, Trichinopoly, Tanjore, and their surrounding areas.[12] After his journey, the Photographic Society of Madras awarded Tripe a silver medal for his large views taken in Madura, Trichinopoly, and Tanjore.[13]

Tripe traveled by horseback with his Indian assistant C. Iyahswamy Pillay, a Government School of Industrial Arts instructor of photography in Madras. Traveling in hot and humid weather with limited water supply, they pitched tents and hauled heavy equipment in four bullock carts: several weighty cameras, sturdy tripods, washing tables, canvas tents, negative paper reams, necessary chemicals like nitrate silver, and deep glass dishes. Pillay was responsible for the lengthy printing process, which involved the use of highly toxic and often dangerous substances.[14] Little else is known about Pillay and his influence on the photographic expedition, except that he took many of his own photographs during his travels with Tripe that were exhibited at the Madras Photographic Society show.[15]

Prior to his travels, Tripe outlined the primary responsibilities of a government photographer in an 1856 mandate letter to the governor-general's private secretary:

> 1st and chiefly to secure before they disappear the objects in the Presidency that are interesting to the Antiquary, Architect, Sculptor, Mythologist and Historian.
>
> 2nd Simultaneously to obtain Illustrations of the Races under this Government, of their customs [,] dress, occupations. I would include arms, implements, musical instruments &c.
>
> There may be features of the Country, characteristic of peculiar Geological facts; that may be deemed worthy of being represented. Also Forest Trees, in short, I would select any object with which, people, at a distance, can only become acquainted, by means of representation. The Picturesque may be allowed perhaps, supplementally.
>
> 3rd The instruction of Subordinates.
>
> To gain information on all these points should be my first and most important preparation. To arrange the information so as to go on through Districts working right and left without omitting any valuable subject, will require a very methodic mapping of the Country....[16]

Despite the initially ambitious scope of Tripe's commission, he eventually narrowed his focus to primarily architectural sites, especially Hindu temples still in worship use. Tripe's letter is striking when compared to the mandate issued by the photographer for the Bombay Presidency, the only other official photographer working in India at that time, who was tasked with merely "taking copies by Photographic process, of the ancient sculptures and Inscriptions in this Presidency."[17] Tripe had a more detailed agenda: he imagined both specialized and general audiences and listed specific anthropological and archaeological facets to be explored. In particular, his concern for securing images of things "before they disappear" indicates an understanding of his subjects as impermanent artifacts, which would inevitably vanish under the neglectful stewardship of a ruined civilization.

Following the 1857 military mutiny and civilian revolt,[18] the British Crown replaced the East India Company in 1858; after spending nearly 50 million pounds (or 500 million rupees) to quell the uprisings, the new administration needed to reconsider its financial commitments.[19] Madras Presidency governor Charles E. Trevelyan reacted with disgust upon reading Tripe's financial report and the high expenditures spent for photographic material in early 1859: "This bill must, I presume, be paid—but I submit for the consideration of my Colleagues whether the Government Photographic Establishment is not an article of high luxury which is unsuited to the present state of our finances."[20] In 1859, the Court of Directors determined that maintaining a government-employed photographer was too costly, and it suspended Tripe's post. When Tripe fought to keep the Madras photographic establishment from closing, the government asked him to make a list of "such ancient buildings or inscriptions, as are rapidly falling to decay, and require being recorded photographically at an early date, 'ere they pass away altogether."[21] Tripe listed sixteen locations in need of urgent photography, and argued that it was vital for him to record less attractive buildings that would be overlooked by commercial or artistic photographers—but Tripe was unable to convince his government sponsors of the necessity of his job.

The British Crown finally determined that private photographers could more effectively achieve the task of visually documenting the colony. In mid-June 1959, the government informed Tripe of the establishment's "*immediate*" closure: the work of private photographers was not only "financially right," but also "conducive to the object of having the monuments of the country pictured and explained in an able and intelligent manner."[22] The technology previously considered a more cost-effective alternative to draughtsmen was too expensive for government subsidy; now, photography of monuments and antiquities once restricted to government employees was opened to any photographer.[23] Tripe's assignment ended in 1860; he continued his photography as a part-time hobby while serving in the regiment.

Photographic erasure of everyday life

Tripe's photos illustrate a common theme of early British photography in India: the production of narratives of archaeological ruin in a living society. Photographs of the roofed ambulatory passageways at the Mīnākṣī-Sundareśvara temple from his *Photographic Views in Madura* best demonstrate Tripe's attempt to transform a living temple into an archaeological remain: this section concentrates on images of the corridor along the tank that leads to Mīnākṣī's shrine (Figure 6.2); a corridor leading to Sundareśvara's shrine (Figure 6.3); the aisle on the south side of the Pudu Maṇḍapam ("Trimul Naik's choultry") (Figure 6.4); and the Pudu Maṇḍapam's central nave (Figure 6.5).

A 'living temple' is a sacred site that is a space of active worship: the enshrined deity attracts pilgrims and devotees offering prayers and seeking blessings. A temple is no longer 'living' if it has been abandoned, or its consecrated deity has been removed or is no longer venerated. A 'living temple' stands in obvious contrast to a 'ruin,' a concept that played an important role in European visual art and architecture in the eighteenth century.[24] In his 1903 study on the "cult of monuments," Aloïs Riegl distinguishes between the "historical value" and "age value" of an architectural monument: the historical value of a building is

Figure 6.2 Linnaeus Tripe, *View of the Sacred Tank in the Great Pagoda*, albumen print from waxed paper (calotype) negative, 29.1 × 37.5 centimeters, 1858

Source: Linnaeus Tripe, *Photographic Views in Madura. By Captain L. Tripe, Government Photographer, Madras Presidency. Part III. With Descriptive Notes, by Martin Norman, Esq. M. C. S. 1858* (Madras: Madras Presidency, 1860), plate 14. Metropolitan Museum of Art 2005.100.381.2.14, www.metmuseum.org.

Figure 6.3 Linnaeus Tripe, *The Viravasuntarayan Mundapam*, albumen print from waxed paper (calotype) negative, 29.5 × 37 centimeters, 1858

Source: Linnaeus Tripe, *Photographic Views in Madura. By Captain L. Tripe, Government Photographer, Madras Presidency. Part III*, plate 2. Metropolitan Museum of Art 2005.100.381.2.2, www.metmuseum.org.

determined by its function as a *document*, a 'correct' and available record of the past that can be interpreted for the purposes of writing history; the age value of a building refers to its function as an indicator of passing time and the forces of nature, a sign of the passage of time and the impermanence of human creations.[25] The concept of historical value emerged during the European Renaissance in the fifteenth century as early methods of preservation of ancient monuments were developed; "the more faithfully a monument's original state is preserved, the greater its historical value: disfiguration and decay detract from it."[26] Whereas historical value attempts to fix or prevent the damage and erosion of time's passage, age value celebrates it:

> It is probably fair to say that ruins appear more picturesque the more advanced their state of decay: as decay progresses, age-value becomes less extensive, that is to say, evoked less and less by fewer and fewer remains, but is therefore all the more intensive in its impact on the beholder.... From the standpoint of age-value[,] one

Figure 6.4 Linnaeus Tripe, *Aisle on the South Side of the Puthu Mundapam, from the Western Portico*, albumen print from waxed paper (calotype) negative, 34.3 × 28.8 centimeters, 1858

Source: Linnaeus Tripe, *Photographic Views in Madura. By Captain L. Tripe, Government Photographer, Madras Presidency. Part II. With Descriptive Notes, 1858* (Madras: Madras Presidency, 1860), plate 2. J. Paul Getty Museum 84.XO.1363.2.2; Digital image courtesy of the Getty's Open Content Program.

> need not worry about the eternal preservation of monuments.... Age-value manifests itself immediately through visual perception and appeals directly to our emotions.[27]

Age value, although it draws on the motive of historical value to preserve a record of the past, is a phenomenon distinctive of modernity: it depends on the ability to produce accurate *dating* of an object based on traces of decay, and it is formed around a nostalgic regret for a romantic past that can no longer be retrieved.[28] We can see both forms of value in Tripe's photographs: Tripe was motivated by a desire to assemble accurate records of monuments of historical value *and* by a desire to convey the ruinous state of Indian civilization. Entirely missing from Tripe's photographic narrative, however, is the *use value* of the buildings: their existence as active places of religious worship is excised completely.

A distinguishing attribute of a 'ruin' is the condition of being arrested or frozen in time and space. In the common usage of the word, 'ruins' are "enchanted,

Figure 6.5 Linnaeus Tripe, *View of the Nave from the Simhasanum at the Westend*, albumenized salted paper print, 27.5 × 36.3 centimeters, 1858

Source: Linnaeus Tripe, *Photographic Views in Madura. By Captain L. Tripe, Government Photographer, Madras Presidency. Part II*, plate 3. Wilson Centre for Photography.

desolated spaces, large-scale monumental structures abandoned and grown over. Ruins provide a quintessential image of what has vanished from the past and has long decayed."[29] Tripe's photographs do not show the monumental temples in the state of architectural deterioration typical of "ruins": there are no leaning walls, toppled pillars, crumbling stones, or overgrown vegetation. Nevertheless, his photographs give the impression of an ancient civilization in *stasis*, abandoned to decay; abstracted from their life and ongoing activity, the temples appear empty, engendering a suspended and silent stillness. In Christopher Woodward's formulation, "a ruin is a dialogue between an incomplete reality and the imagination of the spectator"—the "incomplete" reality rendered by Tripe's photograph is the 'empty' temple captured at a time when its devotees are absent; Tripe's "imagination" depicts an old civilization which has almost disappeared, leaving only its trace behind.[30]

Tripe's photographs distort the geography of the temple to advance a narrative of ruin and abandonment. For example, Tripe characterizes the temple's aisled areas as severed from their purpose as essential pathways of movement throughout the building. The interior corridors are the major routes for devotees roaming the temple and for deities traveling in procession. The Nāyaka portrait sculptures in the Pudu Maṇḍapam stand with palms pressed together in *añjalimudrā*, a gesture of reverence, devotion, and greeting, as they face towards the center of the aisle (rather than in the direction of the enshrined gods). This position indicates the importance of acknowledging worshippers and divine images during their journeys through these spaces. Hindu temples are not only congregative spaces for visitors and ambulatory spaces for devotees entering or exiting the temple, but also places that facilitate the movement of deities' metal embodiments going out of the shrine, through the temple precincts, and beyond. In Tripe's photographs, the role of these columned spaces as conduits for ritual circumambulations or as passageways to ritual destinations is completely absent: there are no *people* in the hallways at all.

In the Madura collection, only one photograph and three stereographs include human figures—of these, only a small number of them are selected to represent

Figure 6.6 Linnaeus Tripe, *Outer Prakarum (or Corridor) on the North Side of the Temple of the God Sundareshwara*, albumen print from dry collodion-on-glass negative, 25.9 × 34.3 centimeters, 1858

Source: Linnaeus Tripe, *Photographic Views in Madura, By Captain L. Tripe, Government Photographer, Madras Presidency. Part III*, plate 12. IS.40:13-1889 © Victoria and Albert Museum, London.

certain 'ethnic types' in posed stances.[31] The primary foci of Tripe's compositions are buildings' contours, architectural features, and pathways. For instance, the photograph of a choultry corridor emphasizes the dramatic, slanted shadows that the columns cast on the stone floor (Figure 6.4). The shadows suggest he may have chosen late mornings for his shots, a time when worshippers would have ordinarily populated the temple.[32] Furthermore, only one photograph reveals the display of processional mounts at a corridor's end; yet in this photo the vehicles appear more like stage props or children's toys than ceremonial instruments (Figure 6.6).[33] Tripe's photographs omit all explicit signs of Hindu spirituality: there are no seated vendors hunched over baskets of flowered garlands, no temple paraphernalia used during daily worship (such as platters lined with coconuts and betel leaves), no sculptures of Hindu deities, and no temple priests dressed in white loincloths with foreheads smeared with sacred ash. Tripe's deliberate censorship of any trace of lived human experience transforms the living temple into 'mere' architecture—an empty monument, a relic of an ancient and celebrated past.[34]

Composition, commodification, and consumption

Tripe used the calotype process to impart a 'romantic' quality to his architectural subject: the use of waxed paper negative (rather than the traditional glass plate) allowed fibers from the negative to transfer onto the paper print, giving the images a soft focus. Tripe was known to manipulate his photographs through experimentation: in the October–December 1856 issue of the *Madras Journal of Literature and Science*, Jesse Mitchell, an adjutant in the Indian Army's 1st Native Veteran Battalion, gave high praise to Tripe's techniques and recommended their study to his colleagues.[35] Maia-Mari Sutnik, assistant curator of the Art Gallery of Ontario's 2003 Linnaeus Tripe exhibition in Toronto, observed that Tripe waxed his negatives, applied paper coatings, retouched negatives to enhance skies and foliage, and used dry collodion and wet-plate. Tripe's experimentation can be seen in the variation from "mat and grainy and dusty textured surfaces ... to rich and deep tonal gradations and delineations of detail" and in images "characterized by broad areas of light and dark" in which the material contrast directs the viewer's attention to certain elements of the composition.[36]

Tripe's photograph of the Pudu Maṇḍapam's south side aisle exemplifies this interplay of light and dark: to Woodward, the use of "sudden contrasts created by shadows, concealments and surprise" was constitutive of the nineteenth-century convention of picturesque depictions of landscapes (Figure 6.4).[37] The term 'picturesque' was applied to eighteenth-century English landscape paintings,

Figure 6.7 Linnaeus Tripe, *The Causeway across the Vaigai River*, albumen print from waxed paper (calotype) negative, 26.9 × 36.1 centimeters, 1858

Source: Linnaeus Tripe, *Photographic Views in Madura. By Captain L. Tripe, Government Photographer, Madras Presidency. Part I*, plate 6. J. Paul Getty Museum 84.XO.698.5.1.6; Digital image courtesy of the Getty's Open Content Program.

as it was the highest compliment for a scene that it "looked like a painting."[38] The aesthetics of the picturesque informed British artists' illustrations of the Indian landscape. Sutnik writes of Tripe, "His pictorial resolutions ... resided in picturesque notions that promoted enhancement of skies with fabricated clouds and retouching leaves and vegetation on his negatives."[39] Tripe's landscape images reflect a picturesque contemplation of nature: the photograph of the causeway over the Vaigai river shows the Mīnākṣī-Sundareśvara temple hovering softly in the distance, enveloped by a sky retouched to add clouds (Figure 6.7).[40] Here (and in figure 6.4), alterations in color, lighting, and texture set him apart from his contemporaries photographing British India during the same period.[41]

Many of Tripe's compositions reflect the aesthetic qualities of European picturesque landscape paintings in communicating ownership, accessibility, and familiarity. Tripe converted foreign and alienating landscapes by rendering them according to aesthetic conventions familiar to his audience: and, in this way, produced a controlled and manageable portrayal of the colony. In Sutnik's words,

Tripe's "approach may well have been [more] a requirement of the taste of the broader market to which he had an obligation than of his own sensibilities."[42] Tripe's techniques were commonplace in the images that filled the colonial tour books of the time, as described by Ann Bermingham:

> The picturesque landscape, as popularized in guidebooks, and the practice of painting and sketching out of doors represented a "democratic" landscape. The topographical landscape developed out of the mapping of country estates and hence was tied to aristocratic patterns of ownership. The landscapes of the great seventeenth-century masters depicted exotic Italian scenery with mythological overtones. The picturesque, by restricting itself to humble English rural scenery, represented a landscape both familiar and accessible. It thus could be widely *consumed*, and with all the more enthusiasm in that the landscape it celebrated was beginning to vanish.[43]

Tripe's travel volumes constructed an imagined India for the British public that systematically erased the indigenous colonial subjects, both by excising human figures and by removing traces of their ritual practices. In commodifying certain Indian cultural sites for Western consumption, these photographs made the colonial occupation of India more palatable—and rational—to British audiences: this new land was cold and empty, but it was pleasing.

Tripe operated, to some extent, within a Christian framework in which *light* suggests a celestial access. In the photograph of the Pudu Maṇḍapam, the *kuḷam* ('tank') wall and Tirumala Nāyaka's unfinished *gōpuram* ('gateway') of the Mīnākṣī temple are situated at the corridor's eastern end (Figure 6.5). Tirumala began but never completed the construction of this huge Rāya ('king') Gōpuram on what is today East Avani Mula Street. In Tripe's photograph, it is almost impossible to discern the wall or the *gōpuram*, significant symbols of Nāyaka temple patronage. The space is recast as an ideal architectural artifact, with a blinding bright light at the horizon, as if at the end of a tunnel. Only the slightest hint of temple walls is visible, like the remains of a ruin. The light conveys the temple architecture's sacred status; yet there are no overt signs of Hindu spirituality to be found.

British photographers like Tripe were informed by Protestant narratives about Hinduism, in particular a Christian disdain for what was perceived as 'immoral' sculpture in Hindu temples. The general goal of British photography was to produce an "objective documentary record" of architectural sites; but, as Falconer observes, these 'objective' records were inevitably distorted by the photographers' positions as "representatives of a foreign ruling class whose Judeo-Christian values were inherently antagonistic to the subject of much of their work."[44] For example,

Thomas Biggs, a photographer of the Bombay Presidency, wrote about 'indecent' Hindu sculptures:

> ... the early date at which the morals of India assumed such a headlong and downward tendency, and anyone who has the opportunity of comparing the ancient and modern sculptures cannot fail to see the gradual but remarkable flight of steps down from artistic beauty and chaste tendency to the greatest deformity and disgusting immortality which the sculptures betray.[45]

Biggs' comment reflects many British observers' concerns about the "downward tendency" of Indian morality and the 'fall' of Indian civilization. Architecture was a common point of reference for moral critiques of India: nineteenth-century British scholars like Henry H. Cole, director of the South Kensington Museum, and architectural historian James Fergusson were fiercely critical of the lavish decoration and ornamentation of south Indian temples. Western scholars' condemnation of ornate facades and complicated temple layout stemmed from an inability to see 'outside' the classical aesthetics found in European art.[46] Temples' decorative motifs and iconographic program serve specific religious and symbolic functions that British scholars could not comprehend. They lauded the relative simplicity of Buddhist monuments over later Hindu ones: Cole wrote that the Buddhist art at Sanchi "testify to the superior skill then possessed by native sculptors as compared with the native productions of modern times" and that the "power of delineating human and other forms was *formerly* greater than is now evinced by the modern Hindu sculptures...."[47] Tripe effaced all traces of idolatry in his photographs of Madurai; his long-distance views of the *gōpurams* at the Mīnākṣī temple avoid close depiction of the profuse Hindu iconography blanketing these gateways (Figure 6.8). The massive architectural structure dominates the page from afar, filling the space and obscuring the rich sculptural detail on the surface.

The removal of human activity and Hindu spirituality from the temple images, combined with the picturesque composition of the photographs, helped to fashion an imagined colonial subject for which foreign rule was morally justified. Mary Louise Pratt noted the tendency of European travel narratives about Africa during the nineteenth century to downplay the "confrontations with the natives" and to concentrate on the "considerably less exciting presentation of landscape."[48] Pratt observes that the discursive configuration "which centers on landscape, separates people from place, and effaces the speaking self"[49] works to present the author of the travel journal a kind of "collective moving eye" that registers its subject with passive receptivity and overt mastery.[50] She writes: "The eye 'commands' what falls within its gaze; the mountains 'show themselves' or 'present themselves'; the

Figure 6.8 Linnaeus Tripe, *The Western Gopuram*, albumen print from waxed paper (calotype) negative, 36.1 × 28.5 centimeters, 1858

Source: Linnaeus Tripe, *Photographic Views in Madura. By Captain L. Tripe, Government Photographer, Madras Presidency. Part III*, plate 9. Metropolitan Museum of Art 2005.100.381.2.9, www.metmuseum.org.

country 'opens up' before the European newcomer."[51] There is no resistance to foreign rule in the images received by the European observer; the land is simply available for consumption, both in the form of material exploitation of the land through colonization and in the form of the photographs themselves. In the conspicuous absence of the agency and lived experience of the colonized subject, one narrative resonates above all others: the moral obligation to colonize, civilize, and restore the fallen civilization.

Architectural history as historical critique

Nineteenth-century architectural historian James Fergusson (1808–1886) reproduced Tripe's photographic images as wood engravings in his 1876 *History of Indian and Eastern Architecture*, the first comprehensive historical account of Indian architecture. Originally from Scotland, Fergusson was an indigo merchant who traveled around India from 1835 to 1842 to survey and document architectural sites. Pramod Chandra describes Fergusson as a "veritable one-man architectural survey, sketching, drawing, making plans, taking careful notes, and above all, doing some very hard thinking."[52] Fergusson mapped his travels according to architectural relics of historical import, as Tripe did, and he sketched and logged these buildings in his diaries. When Fergusson returned to England in the 1840s, he worked as a self-taught architectural historian, transforming his notes into numerous volumes of architectural analysis: *Picturesque Illustrations of Ancient Architecture in Hindostan* (1848), *Illustrations of Various Styles of Indian Architecture. A Series of Fifteen Photographs of Some of the Most Important Buildings in India Erected between B.C. 250 and A.D. 1830* (1869), and his magnum opus, *History of Indian and Eastern Architecture* (1876)[53] that classified ancient Indian architectural sites according to a regional, chronological, and religious taxonomy.

Fergusson participated in the popular colonial narrative that India lacked 'history,' because there were few available written forms that conformed to the conventions of 'historical' knowledge familiar to Europe. For Fergusson, architecture was the only constant and dependable record from which to construct India's 'lost' history. He undertook close, direct observation of monuments,[54] driven by a belief that through careful visual examination one could pick "its whole history out of its stones."[55] Fergusson pored over each stone edifice, attempting to scrutinize its form, style, and artistic motive: "I could read in the chisel marks on the stone the ideas that guided the artist in his design, till I could put myself by his side, and identify myself with him through his work."[56] In his 1866 presentation on Indian architecture before the Society of Arts in London, he asserted the scholarly significance of his research: "It seems almost impossible to over-estimate the value of these stone landmarks in a country where so few books exist, and so little history, and where what does exist is so very untrustworthy."[57]

Fergusson's work depicted an Indian society stuck in perpetual stasis with little or no 'progress' according to the parameters of modernity; since India has no documents, annals, chronicles, records, or any other datable textual artifacts deemed useful for extracting history, British scholars must therefore *create* this history.[58] Fergusson's attitude was typical of nineteenth-century European intellectuals who perceived India largely in terms of chaos and contradiction. German philosopher Georg Hegel argued in his *Philosophy of History* that Indians are "incapable of writing History" because of the "contradictory processes" of the Hindu mind that inevitably cultivate a pure "Ideality" in which rational and definite concepts disintegrate; "it is evident that nothing but abstract thought and imagination can be developed."[59] Nevertheless, Fergusson maintained that Indian architecture could be useful because of the subcontinent's Aryan pedigree, and the pure and rational aspects in its Aryan architecture.[60] Fergusson believed that the Buddha was "undoubtedly of purely Aryan race,"[61] a reading that shaped Fergusson's narrative of an architectural decline from a past golden age:

> [T]he architecture of India is not only the best means of elucidating the manners and customs of the country, but of checking their fables, and is frequently the only means that remain to us; and, if this be so, is it possible to over-estimate its value to those who wish to know who and what the people are or were, whom we have undertaken to guide and govern?[62]

Fergusson considered the Hindu works of art to be "monstrosities," and in comparison to Buddhist monuments, they are "the most barbarous, it may be said the most vulgar, to be found in India, and do more to shake one's faith in the civilization of the people who produced them than anything they did in any other department of art."[63] Whereas the history of European sculpture from the medieval period indicated a "distinct illustration of the progress of the human mind ... [and] of steady forward progress towards higher aims and better execution," the Indian sculptural tradition denoted to Fergusson a clear state of "backward decline."[64]

The civilizational narratives of architectural historians were inevitably imbricated in broader questions of sovereignty with regard to colonial rule: an important premise of Fergusson's 1866 lecture is how the study of architecture could inform the practices of government both in Britain and in India. He wrote that studying India's diverse architectural styles could aid in determining "the ethnological relations of the different races inhabiting India," and help settle debates about "the greatness or decay of the dynasties that ruled that country in ancient times." This knowledge could have important bearing not only on "Indian questions," that is, government of the British Raj, but also for "extending our views"—Indian architectural techniques, as a "living art," could contribute to contemporary British architecture, and even shed light on Britain's "archaeological problems."[65]

Fergusson was concerned about what he perceived as a dangerous trend in European architecture: the rote copying of classical styles. In the eighteenth and early nineteenth centuries, artists were trained in the classics and practiced predominantly Roman and Greek architecture; but, Fergusson observed, the architects merely copied the predecessor styles "without having any real sympathy with it"—furthermore, interest in these arts was confined to the elite classes alone, as "the middle and lower orders of our countrymen had no sympathy with Doric or Corinthian orders, they were content to go without architecture altogether."[66] Fergusson celebrated the reemergence of medieval Gothic styles in his time, but he was wary of his contemporaries returning to unimaginative 'copying.' Gothic revival architecture was part of a broader phenomenon of Gothic nostalgia and resurgence of artisan crafts during the nineteenth century amidst radical economic transformations caused by colonization and industrialization. The study of 'medievalism' was a reaction to the emergence of factory labor and mass production, a manifestation of melancholic nostalgia for craft work and artisanship (the work of carpenters, masons, tailors, dyers, drapers, weavers, basket-makers, and so on) rapidly disappearing in industrializing Britain. Gothic styles offered a moral and spiritual vocabulary in a time of moral and spiritual crisis: rather than join factory workers in their strikes, Victorian intellectuals practiced a "melancholy for work"—"they concentrated, not on the disturbing lost objects, all those disembodied industrial workers whose disembodiment threatened their own imagined integrity, but on a *sense of loss* that they articulated as the 'hand' of an imagined Gothic handicraft."[67]

The revival of Gothic architecture was initially associated with the picturesque ideal that regarded the romantic, nostalgic, and aesthetic qualities of architecture more highly than its structural and functional aspects.[68] By the mid-nineteenth century, many major public buildings in Britain were designed in the Gothic mode, including the Houses of Parliament and the Big Ben. Fergusson encouraged his contemporaries to study Indian architecture to break from the "narrow school of Classical or Gothic art" and perceive how "wide the field [of architecture] is."[69] He embraced the Gothic style because he believed it carried greater emotional resonance with 'lower' classes, but he hoped the study of Indian architecture could invigorate and elevate this movement:

> [The Gothic revival] was an enormous gain, not only because it enlisted a much wider class in the art, but more—because it taught the architects how much wider the field of architectural design was, than had been originally supposed. Unfortunately, we took to copying Gothic art, as we then copied Classical, and so far retarded progress. At last we begin to be tired of reproducing old things, and are beginning to think, instead of copying. The first symptom of this is, that classical designs are not so rigidly classical as they were, but a certain amount of Gothic feeling is instilled into them; and Gothic designs are sometimes not so ludicrously mediæval as they used to be, but a certain amount of refinement and of modern feeling and adaptation is thought expedient.... The two are approaching one another. When they are fused, we shall have an architecture of our own; and I know nothing so likely to lead to such a result, as the study of an entirely foreign style like that of India.[70]

Fergusson warned against mere copying of the narrow conventions of ancient styles, while ignoring the utilitarian intent of architecture:

> [T]here is no form into which stone can be carved which is not beautiful, if it is appropriate to the purpose for which it is employed; and ... no one form is preferable in architecture to any other form, except in so far as it is better adapted constructively ... or ... more aptly expresses the purpose of the building of which it forms a part.[71]

He encapsulated his architectural philosophy in an elegant phrase: "I defy any one to give a good logical reason why the form of a man's nose, or ear, or head, is beautiful." From Indian monuments, architects could learn architectural principles of "common sense"—not only because of the enormous diversity of architectural styles, but also because in India, one may see "those who can neither read, nor write, nor draw, building temples and palaces as beautiful in form and detail as those of their forefathers, and which are not copies, but elaborated on the same principles as resulted in the productions of our great mediæval cathedrals."[72]

Fergusson's work was hugely influential upon British archaeologists in India such as Colonel Alexander Cunningham (1814–1893), who considered Fergusson "amongst the foremost and most successful of the later archaeologists" studying India's past.[73] Cunningham was appointed as an archaeological surveyor in 1861, in a time of increasing British interest in Indian antiquities and monuments and decreasing interest in indigenous philology.[74] Earlier, government-employed artists and photographers documented ancient remains with the East India Company; however, these efforts were sporadic and inconsistent, given the Company's preoccupation with territorial conquest and the overriding concerns of administering the colony. As a self-taught archaeologist, Cunningham undertook a series of tours that marked the beginning of an organized and formal archaeological enterprise in India.[75]

Cunningham initiated the first comprehensive archaeological program in India, after his early involvement in numismatics with Indologist James Prinsep (1799–1840). He argued urgently in his November 1861 letter to Governor-General Canning that

> [d]uring the one hundred years of British domination in India, the Government had done little or nothing towards the preservation of its ancient monuments, which, in the almost total absence of any written history, form the only reliable source of information as to the early condition of the country.... [T]here are many ... which must soon disappear altogether, unless preserved by the accurate drawings and faithful descriptions of the archaeologist.[76]

Cunningham introduced the process of protecting and preserving Indian antiquities through a formal archaeological method, at a time when the government's finances were less hindered and its energies less drawn. Cunningham proposed a plan for documenting northern India:

> I would attach to the description of each place a general survey of the site, showing clearly the positions of all the existing remains, with a ground plan of every building or ruin of special note, accompanied by drawings and sections of all objects of interest. It would be desirable also to have photographic views of many of the remains, both of architecture and sculpture; but to obtain these it would be necessary to have the services of a photographer. Careful fac-similes of all inscriptions would of course be made, ancient coins would also be collected on each site, and all the local traditions would be noted down and compared. The description of each place with all its accompanying drawings and illustrations would be complete in itself, and the whole, when finished, would furnish a detailed and accurate account of the archaeological remains of Upper India.[77]

Cunningham focused on the classification of archaeological remains in India; he gave high value to epigraphy for dating artifacts, and he divided objects into four main categories: architecture, sculpture, coins, and inscriptions. To Cunningham, 'architecture' meant only monumental structures, not ordinary dwellings—he was not particularly interested in knowing about the colonial subjects themselves, nor the artifacts they used in their daily lives.[78] Canning approved Cunningham's proposal, and Cunningham began India's first government-sponsored archaeological survey, as an opportunity to portray British governance in India as "an enlightened ruling power."[79] In his new position as the appointed archaeological surveyor to the Government of India in 1861, Cunningham executed his proposed archaeological investigation that focused on the documentation of ancient ruins. The results of his four-year fieldwork filled twenty-three volumes of *Archaeological Survey of India Reports*.[80]

Artifice of the photographic record

Tripe and Fergusson operated at the genesis of archaeology in India and helped establish Indian architecture as an object of archaeological inquiry. In so doing, they constructed an archaeological imagination that reconstituted India's living temples as 'ruins' through photography. The photographs of the Mīnākṣī temple resemble two photographs of the Viṭṭala temple (in Hampi, the abandoned capital city of the Vijayanagara empire of the fourteenth to sixteenth centuries) taken by Alexander John Greenlaw, the nineteenth-century assistant to the Madras

Figure 6.9 Alexander J. Greenlaw, South-east *Mandapa*, Viṭṭala temple, Vijayanagara, POP print (1906) from waxed paper negative, 38.5 × 44.5 centimeters, 1856

Source: ACP: 99.02.0045, The Alkazi Collection of Photography.

Presidency's superintending engineer (Figures 6.9 and 6.10). Unlike the Mīnākṣī temple, a space of active worship since the seventh century, the Viṭṭala temple has apparently been in disuse since the 1565 fall of the empire. Yet these photographs are composed in a style similar to Tripe's photos of the Madurai temple: a state of abandonment. It is difficult to discern from the two sets of photos which temple is 'living' and which is in 'ruin.' The colonial apparatus depended on constructing an archaeological vision of India as a dying civilization, a discursive strategy that appears in contemporary forms of archaeology. As Nadia Abu El-Haj writes of Israeli archaeological projects in Jerusalem, "standing and partly destroyed buildings were partially restored and reconstructed *as ruins* in order to memorialize more recent histories of destruction, and older stones were integrated into modern architectural forms in order to embody temporal depth."[81] Just as the buildings in Jerusalem were physically reconstructed in the form of ruins, temples in south India were *virtually* reconstructed as abandoned 'memorials' of histories of destruction and decay: "Ruins were not simply *found* ... they were also *made*."[82]

Figure 6.10 Alexander J. Greenlaw, *Mahamandapa* Interior, Viṭṭala temple, Vijayanagara, modern positive (2006) from waxed paper negative, 40.8 × 44.3 centimeters, 1856

Source: ACP: 99.01.0073, The Alkazi Collection of Photography.

Although he spent most of his time in England, Fergusson acted as a mega-curator from his distant base in London, drawing on a large corpus of images collected by photographers who passed through India after the arrival of photography in the British colony. Fergusson recognized the camera's singular importance for producing a historical record of buildings and architectural styles. He wrote, "Photographs tell their own story far more closely than any form of words that could be devised ... by far the most perfect and satisfactory illustration of the ancient architecture of India which has yet been presented to the public."[83] In his 1876 *History of Indian and Eastern Architecture*, he reiterated the importance of supporting photographic documentation of monuments in India:

> There are now very few buildings in India—of any importance at least—which have not been photographed with more or less completeness; and for the purposes of comparison such collections of photographs ... are simply invaluable. For detecting similarities, or distinguishing differences between specimens situated at distances

> from one another, photographs are almost equal to actual personal inspection, and, when sufficiently numerous, afford a picture of Indian art of the utmost importance to anyone attempting to describe it.[84]

In this passage, Fergusson claims that photographs can take the place of on-site examination: "I have learnt as much, if not more, of Indian Architecture [from photographs] during the last two or three years, than I did during my residence in India, and I now see that the whole subject may be made intelligible, and I see how it can be done."[85] For the purposes of scholarship, the living context of the temples was irrelevant; the agenda of British archaeology in India could be served by studying stones alone.

Fergusson was reputed to be a stickler for 'truth' and 'accuracy'; of the lithographs contained in his 1848 *Picturesque Illustrations of Ancient Architecture in Hindostan*, Fergusson wrote: "Whatever defects my views may have as pictures, I feel perfectly certain that they are the most correct delineations of Indian Architecture that have yet been given to the public."[86] For Fergusson, "the public" was constituted solely by citizens of the British metropole—the indigenous people who reside in the colony were little more than academic specimens (and as objects of rational inquiry, they are of far less interest than their temples). However, the 'factual' accuracy of the photographs comes in question when comparing Tripe's photograph of "Trimul Naik's choultry" (Figure 6.5) with Fergusson's version labeled "Tirumalla Nayak's Choultrie, Mádura" in *History of Indian and Eastern Architecture* (Figure 6.11). Ferguson's woodcut image, in the Madura section of chapter 3, "Dravidian Temples," in Book IV, *Dravidian Style*, is accompanied by notes from Captain Edmund David Lyon, commissioned by the colonial government in 1867 upon resumed archaeological interest in the Madras Presidency; although Fergusson edited Lyon's notes, he did not include Lyon's additional photographs of the Madurai temple or pillared hall, which featured sculptures that were absent from Tripe's work.[87]

Fergusson's reproduction of Tripe's picture highlights the artifice of the photographic record: even the most 'correct' image underwent various distortions shaped by a convergence of aesthetic and political considerations. For the interior shot of the dark choultry, Tripe altered the lighting of the pillar structures in an experiment with "day light reflectors."[88] In the near erasure of the gateway and wall through manipulation with only a small portion visible to look like vestiges of a ruin, Tripe reformulated and redesigned the scene to construct his own version of the temple (Figure 6.5). Having never visited the Madurai temple, Fergusson relied entirely on Tripe's altered photograph, and in place of a bright, white light at the end of the hall, he added a glorious setting sun descending in the western horizon while

Figure 6.11 James Fergusson, *View in Tirumulla Nayak's Choultrie, Mádura* (from a photograph), engraving, 1876

Source: James Fergusson, *History of Indian and Eastern Architecture* (London: John Murray, 1876), 363.

three men stand transfixed, their long and gloomy shadows cast upon the stone floor (Figure 6.11). Tripe illuminated the sculpted dynastic figures on the columns with a bright light; Fergusson left the rulers encased in darkness, as if to signify the end of indigenous monarchy in India—reinforced by the setting sun and by a watchful British presence in the three figures. The epistemic violence of Tripe's elimination of the temple wall was extended by Fergusson's rendering of the Pudu Maṇḍapam; this altered version circulated in the seminal text on Indian architecture.

Tripe converted the fluid reality of temple life and religious practice into fixed volumes, registers and inventories of 'authentic' Indian history stamped with the "insignia of colonial authority."[89] The volumes' impressive size—approximately 57 by 45 centimeters—relayed a persuasive and visual reinforcement of imperialist ideology. More than uncovering the 'true history' of India as was their ostensible aim, these photographs offer significant insight into the colonizers' own self-imagination, defined by the India they 'discovered' in their images:

> The camera recorded India in the nineteenth century, but it also projected upon India an understanding of what the British saw, thought and felt about the land and civilization of which they were masters. The great achievement of the photographs was not that they recorded the "real India," but that they presented with such candor how they, and those for whom they worked, felt about India.[90]

Visual volumes like Tripe's and Fergusson's functioned first by obscuring the violence of colonization by eliminating the indigenous subjects, and then by delivering an imagination of India as an empty ruin that required British paternalism for its restoration—thus, a rational framework for India's subsumption into the imperial networks of global trade and industrialization.

A scene at the middle of the nineteenth century illustrates the intersection between the melancholic nostalgia for pre-industrial Britain and the aesthetic demands of colonization discussed in this chapter. London's 1851 Great Exhibition, organized by Cole and Prince Albert, was the first international exhibition of manufactured goods (including jewelry, instruments, toilets, handicrafts, weapons, and so on), and the Exhibition's Medieval Court exhibited many artifacts of Gothic architecture and ornament, a celebration of Gothic aesthetics and morality. At the same time, the Exhibition displayed manufactured goods from around the world, and demonstrated the superiority of India's artisans and craftsmanship—and the possibility that Indian aesthetics could be utilized to advance English society.[91] The juxtaposition of foreign and domestic artifacts had an economic goal as well: to 'market' obscure products with valuable properties, which could be purchased wholesale at discount prices—"In other words, to discover, develop, and create a demand for new raw materials, thus expanding the entire commercial and manufacturing system."[92] Pratt identified the mechanisms of erasure inherent to colonial aesthetics and the economic networks in which colonial representations were embedded:

> The European improving eye produces subsistence habitats as "empty" landscapes, meaningful only in terms of a capitalist future of their potential for producing a marketable surplus. From the point of view of their inhabitants, of course, these same spaces are lived as intensely humanized, saturated with local history and meaning, where plants, creatures, and geographical formations have names, uses, symbolic functions, histories, places in indigenous knowledge formations.[93]

The Exhibition obscured, or altogether removed, the presence of the colonized subject, whose world is imbued with densely saturated local histories and meaning—and replaced that subject, whose labor was implied, with the 'artifact,' the finished, manufactured good. The displacement of the artifact from the world of the colonized subject was, then, rationalized in terms of supplying 'benefit' to the colonized society by integrating the indigenous people into the globalized network of commerce and industry. The photographs of temple ruins may be interpreted in similar terms: the indigenous subject is divorced from the world of experience, and replaced with the 'pure' artifacts of an ancient architecture. The ancient architecture, thus abstracted and severed from its living context, can serve the aesthetic lack of a British society grappling with the contradictions of industrialization—and fold British India into the same mechanisms of capital and industry.

Conclusion

Tripe's photographic artifice produced an archaeological imagination of the living temple as an abandoned ruin. Fergusson reproduced Tripe's photograph within discourses of professional archaeology and architecture that regarded colonization as a civilizing force that could both restore the remains of a fallen society and enrich the British metropole. Although the fields of 'architecture' and 'archaeology' have parallel histories, they evolved into two distinct disciplines, "each revolving around a different method of attaching histories to monuments."[94] While architectural and archaeological approaches were imagined independently and practiced polemically, the two disciplines informed one another in imperial representations of nineteenth-century India as a site of civilizational decay. Tripe and Ferguson furnished images primarily with an interest in architectural theory; however, the photograph and etching of the Pudu Maṇḍapam are fraught with archaeological motifs. In the transference from stone to paper, both visual documents show their subjects as artifacts of neglect and disuse. The movement from architectural analysis to archaeological narrative served a political agenda, in which an aesthetic criteria and a rational framework for colonial 'improvement' were realized through the erasure of colonized subjects: a "textual apartheid that separates landscape from people, accounts of inhabitants from accounts of their habitats, fulfills its logic."[95] Tripe and Ferguson's images of the Madurai temple supplied visual metaphors of light illuminating the darkness of an empty temple (Tripe's blinding light and Fergusson's bright sun that reveal the crumbling walls of the ruin), and they understood their professional roles in the vocabulary of enlightened despotism.

During the nineteenth century, photographic images were given primacy in the documentation of Indian monuments owing to photography's promise of more cheaply delivering an accurate image, and thus a more comprehensive and accurate record of India's 'history.' The photographs in Tripe's collection have been described by contemporary scholars as "politically neutral interpretations" of architecture and topography or "softly toned studies" of south Indian architecture.[96] Tripe's embellishments of the choultry image, and Fergusson's reproduction of that image for his architectural history, undermine this assumption of 'realism' and 'neutrality.' The reality of the photographs is a colonial interpretation, a figment of British imagination of India. A photograph is never ideologically neutral.

Notes

1. Edith S. Storrs to the Victoria & Albert Museum-London, Teddington, July 13, 1933, MA/1/S3660, nominal file: Storrs, Edith S, RP/1933/2814: Victoria & Albert Archive, London. Linnaeus Tripe's photographs at the Victoria and Albert Museum also came from the School of Design, Department of Science and Art, South Kensington Museum (now the V&A), which Tripe and the Madras Government sent in 1861, and from Caroline Lucy, Lady Denison (wife of Sir William Thomas Denison, Governor of Madras from 1861 to 1866), who donated nine albums in 1889.
2. John Falconer, "A Passion for Documentation: Architecture and Ethnography," in *India through the Lens-Photography from 1840–1911*, ed. Vidya Dehejia (Washington, D.C.: Freer Gallery of Art and Arthur M. Sackler Gallery, Smithsonian Institution; Ahmedabad: Mapin Publishing Pvt. Ltd.; Munich and London: Prestel Verlag, 2000), 69–85, 74.
3. John Falconer, *India: Pioneering Photographers 1850–1900* (London: British Library, 2001), 19. For the complete captions, see Janet Dewan, *The Photographs of Linnaeus Tripe: A Catalogue Raissoné* (Toronto: Art Gallery of Ontario, 2003), 375 and 378. While these examples denote sentiments of condescension, a definitive statement about imperialist overtones in all descriptive texts that accompany Tripe's photographs cannot be made. In a cursory reading of *Stereographs of Madura* written by Rev. W. Tracy and *Photographic Views in Madura Part III* written by M. Norman, Esq., no other condescending note towards the native population and of their customs or cultural artifacts was detected. The volumes' authors provide readers with mythological stories associated with the sites, historical data about the kings, and explanatory details of the architectural elements and celebratory religious events.
4. John Berger, "Understanding a Photograph," in *Classical Essays about Photography*, ed. Alan Trachtenberg (New Haven, CT: Leete's Island Book Inc., 1980), 291–294, 293 (emphasis in the original).
5. Joel Snyder, "Territorial Photography," in *Landscape and Power*, ed. W. J. T. Mitchell (Chicago and London: The University of Chicago Press, 2002 [1994]), 175–201, 185.
6. Christopher Pinney, *The Coming of Photography in India* (London: The British Library, 2008), 3.
7. Despatch No. 22 of 1855, February 7, 1855, Despatches to India and Bengal (January 3 to March 28, 1855), IOR/E/4/829, paragraph 3, ff. 623–625, British Library, Asia, Pacific, and Africa Collections, London.
8. Janet Dewan, "Linnaeus Tripe: Critical Assessments and Other Notes," *Photographic Collector* 5, no. 1 (Fall 1984): 47–65, 49.

9. See “Report of the Committee Appointed to Adjudicate the Photographic Society’s Medals—At a Meeting of the Photographic Society held on the 5th May 1859,” *Madras Journal of Literature and Science* (Edited by the Committee of the Madras Literary Society and Auxiliary Royal Asiatic Society), New Series 5, no. 9 (April–September 1859): 175–202, 177–180 (Madras: Pharoah and Co., 1859).
10. T. Pycroft, Chief Secretary to the Government [Madras], to the Secretary of the Government of India, March 11, 1856, Board’s Collection 198041 to 198116 (1857–1858), vol. 2725, IOR/F/4/2725, no. 297, f. 18, BL APAC. Quoting no. 59 of December 29, 1854 letter.
11. The calotype process, also called the talbotype process after its founder, William Henry Fox Talbot, involved

> developing-out of the latent or invisible image formed in the camera on a sheet of paper coated with light-sensitive silver iodide. This developed negative was then fixed in sodium thiosulphate (‘hypo’) to remove unexposed and undeveloped silver compounds and thus stabilise the image. Talbot then contact-printed his negative images, using the salt process to make any number of duplicate copies. While the chemicals and materials used in photography have been refined over the years, Talbot’s procedures for printing positive images from a negative produced in the camera are essentially the same as those followed to this day. (Michael Gray, “The First Photographic Processes: Some Technical Notes,” in *A Shifting Focus: Photography in India, 1850–1900* [London: The British Library, 1995], 27–31, 28–29)

12. Linnaeus Tripe, *Photographic Views in Madura. By Captain L. Tripe, Government Photographer, Madras Presidency. Part I. With Descriptive Notes, by Martin Norman, Esq. M. C. S. 1858* (Madras: Madras Presidency, 1860); Linnaeus Tripe, *Photographic Views in Madura. By Captain L. Tripe, Government Photographer, Madras Presidency. Part II. With Descriptive Notes, 1858* (Madras: Madras Presidency, 1860); Linnaeus Tripe, *Photographic Views in Madura. By Captain L. Tripe, Government Photographer, Madras Presidency. Part III. With Descriptive Notes, by Martin Norman, Esq. M. C. S. 1858* (Madras: Madras Presidency, 1860); Linnaeus Tripe, *Photographic Views in Madura. By Captain L. Tripe, Government Photographer, Madras Presidency. Part IV. With Descriptive Notes, by Rev. W. Tracy, M. A. 1858* (Madras: Madras Presidency, 1860); Linnaeus Tripe, *Photographic Views in Tanjore and Trivady. By Captain L. Tripe, Government Photographer, Madras Presidency. With Descriptive Notes, by the Rev. G. U. Pope. 1858* (Madras: Madras Presidency, 1860); Linnaeus Tripe, *Photographic Views of Poodoocottah. By Captain L. Tripe, Government Photographer, Madras Presidency. 1858* (Madras: Madras Presidency, 1860);

Linnaeus Tripe, *Photographic Views of Ryakotta and Other Places, in the Salem District. By Captain L. Tripe, Government Photographer, Madras Presidency. With Descriptive Notes, by J. A. C. Boswell, Esq. M. C. S. 1858* (Madras: Madras Presidency, 1860); Linnaeus Tripe, *Photographic Views of Seringham. By Captain L. Tripe, Government Photographer, Madras Presidency. 1858* (Madras: Madras Presidency, 1860); Linnaeus Tripe, *Photographic Views of Trichinopoly. By Captain L. Tripe, Government Photographer, Madras Presidency. 1858* (Madras: Madras Presidency, 1860); Linnaeus Tripe, *Stereographs of Madura, Taken by Captain L. Tripe, Govt. Photographer, Madras Presidency. With Descriptions by the Rev. W. Tracy, M. A. 1858* (Madras: Madras Presidency, 1860); Linnaeus Tripe, *Stereographs of Trichinopoly, Tanjore and Other Places in Their Neighbourhood; Taken by Captain L. Tripe, Govt. Photographer, Madras Presidency. 1858* (Madras: Madras Presidency, 1860).

13. Tripe declined the award, since a government photographer is not an amateur. See L. Tripe to Dr A. J. Scott, Bangalore, August 8, 1859, as part of "Report of the Committee Appointed to Adjudicate the Photographic Society's Medals," 190–191.
14. Government School of Industrial Arts Superintendent Alexander Hunter stated that the images in the Madras Presidency albums were "taken by Captain Tripe the late Government Photographer, and printed by C. Iyahswamy Pillay, who is now employed as Photographer, in the Government School of Industrial Arts at Madras." See Alex. Hunter, to the Secretary of the British Museum-London, Madras, August 26, 1861, British Museum Original Papers, vol. LXXII, P.1435, February 6, 1862, British Museum Archive, London.
15. "Proceedings of the Madras Photographic Society. A Meeting of the Photographic Society was held at the School of Arts on the 5th December 1860," *Madras Journal of Literature and Science* (Edited by the Committee of the Madras Literary Society and Auxiliary Royal Asiatic Society), New Series 6, no. 11 (May 1861): 191–197, 196 (Madras: Pharoah and Co., 1861); G. Thomas, *History of Photography, India, 1840–1980* (Hyderabad: Andhra Pradesh State Akademi of Photography, 1981), 12, 19; G. Thomas, "The Madras Photographic Society 1856–61," *History of Photography* 16, no. 4 (Winter 1992): 299–301, 301.
16. Mandate as Photographer to Madras Government, Captain L. Tripe to F. A. Murray Esq., Private Secretary to the Right Honorable the Governor, July 22, 1856, Extract Public Letter from Fort Saint George, November 24, 1856, Board's Collection, 198041 to 198116 (1857–1858), vol. 2725, IOR/F/4/2725, no. 35 of 1856, ff. 7–9, BL APAC.
17. W. Hart, Secretary to Govt, Memorandum, February 17, 1855, Bombay Proceedings, March 3, 1855, IOR/P/351/42, no. 1264, BL APAC.

18. The Indian Mutiny was a widespread but unsuccessful rebellion against British rule in India from 1857 to 1858. Begun in Meerut by Indian troops (sepoys) in service of the East India Company, it spread to Delhi, Agra, Cawnpore (Kanpur), and Lucknow. The 1857 events did not appear to hinder Tripe's photographic expedition in south India, possibly because the disturbances centered primarily in the Gangetic plains in the north. Only the mutiny's aftermath ended Tripe's work to help cut costs. However, the post-Mutiny period spurred a greater vigor in the use of photography for documentation of ethnic types, a project related to the preservation of British rule in India. After the East India Company control shifted to Crown rule in 1858, the state would collect and systematize new forms of knowledge such as ethnographic photography (as a way of classifying people and their attributes) to help guide and protect this new rule beginning in the 1860s. See Christopher Pinney, *Camera Indica: The Social Life of Indian Photographs* (Chicago and London: The University of Chicago Press, 1997), chs. 1 and 2, and J. Forbes Watson and John William Kaye eds., preface to *The People of India: A Series of Photographic Illustrations, with Descriptive Letterpress, of the Races and Tribes of Hindustan, Originally Prepared under the Authority of the Government of India, and Reproduced by Order of the Secretary of State for India in Council*, vol. I (London: India Museum, 1868), first two pages. Scholarship on British photography in India has focused primarily on this kind of photographic use, which leaves pre-revolt photography rendered as politically benign. The crucial argument of this chapter is to challenge this assertion.
19. Sugata Bose and Ayesha Jalal, *Modern South Asia: History, Culture, Political Economy*, 3rd ed. (London and New York: Routledge, 2004), 76.
20. Charles E. Trevelyan, Minute by the Honorable the President, March 30, 1859, Madras Public Consultations (April 1, 1859–July 29, 1859), IOR/P/249/69, no. 46, p. 103, BL APAC.

    Tripe would submit long lists of materials required for his photographic enterprise along with the expenditure of each item. The multiple types of cameras, several kinds of chemicals and lenses, paper and glass plates, printing and binding charges, travel and boarding costs, allowances, and office rent attest to the expensive nature of the photographic production. See, for example, Captain L. Tripe, Government Photographer, to T. Pycroft, Esq., Chief Secretary to Government, Fort Saint George, July 16, 1859, Madras Public Consultations (July 30, 1859–December 31, 1859), August 2, 1859, IOR/P/249/70, no. 33, BL APAC.
21. T. Pycroft, Chief Secretary, Government Order No. 584, April 15, 1859, Madras Public Consultations (April 1, 1859–July 29, 1859), IOR/P/249/69, no. 47, p. 104, BL APAC.

22. C. E. Trevelyan, Minute by the Honorable the President, June 6, 1859, Madras Public Consultations (April 1, 1859–July 29, 1859), IOR/P/249/69, no. 18, p. 348, BL APAC (emphasis in the original).
23. T. Pycroft, Chief Secretary, Government Order No. 964, June 18, 1859, Madras Public Consultations (April 1, 1859–July 29, 1859), IOR/P/249/69, no. 19, p. 348, BL APAC.
24. Thomas J. McCormick, *Ruins as Architecture, Architecture as Ruins* (Dublin, NH: William L. Bauhan, 1999), 20.
25. Aloïs Riegl, "The Modern Cult of Monuments: Its Character and Its Origin" [1903], trans. Kurt W. Forster and Diane Ghirardo, *Oppositions* 25 (Fall 1982): 21–51.
26. Riegl, "The Modern Cult of Monuments," 34.
27. Riegl, "The Modern Cult of Monuments," 32–33.
28. Riegl, "The Modern Cult of Monuments," 29–31.
29. Ann Laura Stoler, "Imperial Debris: Reflections on Ruins and Ruination," *Cultural Anthropology* 23, no. 2 (May 2008): 191–219, 194.
30. Christopher Woodward, *In Ruins* (New York: Pantheon Books, 2001), 139.
31. See *Front of the Mundapam at Secundermalie,* in Tripe, *Photographic Views in Madura Part IV*, plate 13, and *The Shevangungah and Aycoody Zemindar Minors, The Police Ameen of Madura (Ramasawmy Iyer) and His Children,* and *Some of the Kallar Caste,* in Tripe, *Stereographs of Madura*, plates 67–69. Tripe took a few photographs of people (to depict ethnicity or occupation) for the Madura collection, but did not include them in his albums. Other photographs are two *darbār* (royal court) pictures of the Rāja of Tondaiman in Tripe, *Photographic Views of Poodoocottah*, plates 1 and 3, and two images of musicians in Tripe, *Stereographs of Trichinopoly, Tanjore and Other Places in Their Neighborhood*, plates 6 and 9. While these examples demonstrate that Tripe was not averse to photographing people, especially given the difficulty that his subjects endured in order to stand still to prevent shakiness in the image, my point remains: he photographed mainly emptied and evacuated spaces in architectural sites.
32. S. Theodore Baskaran, "Images from Tripe," *Frontline*, July 21, 2001, https://frontline.thehindu.com/other/article30251322.ece, accessed December 14, 2021.
33. Another photograph shows a display of jewels used to decorate the bronze deities' processional images. See *The Pagoda Jewels*, in Tripe, *Photographic Views in Madura Part III*, plate 11.
34. Despite the long exposure time required, the temple photographs of Vijayanagara, contemporary to Tripe's images, contain human figures.
35. "I have only to add, that the method of manipulating is that followed by Captain Tripe and Dr. Neill, which will recommend it more to your notice than

anything I can say in its favour." Jesse Mitchell, "IV. Description of a Plain or Waxed paper Process in Photography," *Madras Journal of Literature and Science* (Edited by the Committee of the Madras Literary Society and Auxiliary Royal Asiatic Society), New Series 1, no. 1 (October 1856–March 1857 [October–December 1856]): 71–80, 80 (Madras: Pharoah and Co., 1857).

36. Maia-Mari Sutnik, "Picturesque Views: A Rediscovery of Photographs by Linnaeus Tripe," in *Linnaeus Tripe: Photographer of British India, 1854–1870*, ed. Janet Dewan and Maia-Mari Sutnik (Toronto: Art Gallery of Ontario, 1986), 1–12, 6.
37. Woodward, *In Ruins*, 139.
38. Ann Bermingham, *Landscape and Ideology: The English Rustic Tradition, 1740–1860* (Berkeley: University of California Press, 1986), 57, 63–78.
39. Sutnik, "Picturesque Views," 7.
40. By Tripe's own admission in his photographic mandate, he adhered to the conventions of the picturesque.
41. I question whether the picturesque aesthetic informs all his photographs. While he fabricated soft mists and clouds and reworked leafy plants that were crucial to the picturesque aesthetic, he did not include figural or animal groups to establish scale, an important guideline in picturesque production according to artist and author William Gilpin in his popular 1792 *Three Essays: On Picturesque Beauty; On Picturesque Travel; and On Sketching Landscape* (London: R. Blamire). Tripe's strong visual order in the architectural photographs in the Madura collection eschew the picturesque notion altogether. In some photographs, he isolated the monuments by avoiding all possible connection between architecture and its surrounding landscape, a link central to the picturesque aesthetic. In other photographs, he emphasized the symmetry of architecture, an approach antithetical to the picturesque principle, since architectural buildings were to be distorted by perspective or depicted from an oblique angle.
42. Sutnik, "Picturesque Views," 7.
43. Bermingham, *Landscape and Ideology*, 85 (emphasis in the original).
44. Falconer, "A Passion for Documentation," 72.
45. Falconer, "A Passion for Documentation," 72.
46. Partha Mitter, "Western Bias in the Study of South Indian Aesthetics," *South Asian Review* 6, no. 2 (January 1973): 125–136, 126.
47. H. H. Cole, preface to *Catalogue of the Objects of Indian Art Exhibited in the South Kensington Museum* (London: George E. Eyre and William Spottiswoode, 1874), 1–43, 13–15 (emphasis in the original). In 1899, the South Kensington Museum was renamed the Victoria and Albert Museum. James Fergusson also celebrated the classical ideals he identified in early Buddhist monuments, and

wrote that the sculptures in Bodh Gaya and Bharhut are "thoroughly original" and "capable of expressing its ideas, and of telling its story with distinctness that never was surpassed, at least in India.... For an honest purpose-like pre-Raphaelite kind of art, there is probably nothing much better to be found elsewhere." James Fergusson, *History of Indian and Eastern Architecture* (London: John Murray, 1876), 34.

48. Mary Louise Pratt, "Scratches on the Face of the Country; or What Mr. Barrow Saw in the Land of the Bushmen," in *"Race," Writing, and Difference*, ed. Henry Louis Gates (Chicago and London: The University of Chicago Press, 1986), 138–162, 141.
49. Pratt, "Scratches on the Face of the Country," 143.
50. Pratt, "Scratches on the Face of the Country," 142.
51. Pratt, "Scratches on the Face of the Country," 143.
52. Pramod Chandra, *On the Study of Indian Art* (Cambridge, MA: Harvard University Press, 1983), 13.
53. James Fergusson, *Picturesque Illustrations of Ancient Architecture in Hindostan* (London: J. Hogarth, 1848); James Fergusson, *Illustrations of Various Styles of Indian Architecture. A Series of Fifteen Photographs of Some of the Most Important Buildings in India Erected between B.C. 250 and A.D. 1830. With a Lecture on the Study of Indian Architecture, Read at a Meeting of the Society of Arts, on 19th December, 1866* (London: Printed for the use of schools of art in the United Kingdom, 1869); Fergusson, *History of Indian and Eastern Architecture*.
54. Tapati Guha-Thakurta, "The Compulsions of Visual Representation in Colonial India," in *Traces of India: Photography, Architecture, and the Politics of Representation 1850–1900*, ed. Maria Antonella Pellizzari (Montreal: Canadian Centre for Architecture; New Haven: Yale Center for British Art, 2003), 108–139, 119–120; Tapati Guha-Thakurta, *Monuments, Objects, Histories: Institutions of Art in Colonial and Postcolonial India* (New York: Columbia University Press, 2004), 14–15.
55. Fergusson, *Picturesque Illustrations of Ancient Architecture in Hindostan*, 59.
56. James Fergusson, *An Historical Inquiry into the True Principles of Beauty in Art, More Especially with Reference to Architecture* (London: Longman, Brown, Green, and Longmans, 1849), xiv.
57. James Fergusson, *On the Study of Indian Architecture, Read at a Meeting of the Society of Arts on Wednesday, 19th December, 1866* (London: John Murray, 1867), 12.
58. Bernard S. Cohn, "The Transformation of Objects into Artifacts, Antiquities, and Art in Nineteenth-Century India," in *Colonialism and Its Forms of Knowledge: The British in India* (Princeton: Princeton University Press, 1996), 76–105, 93.

59. G. W. F. Hegel, *Lectures on the Philosophy of History*, trans. J. Sibree (London: Henry G. Bohn, 1857), 166, 169–170. Hegel has had a significant influence on conceptions of 'history' in modernity. Hegel and others readily accepted naïve Orientalist narratives from early colonial encounters in India—of course, as Romila Thapar observes, ancient Hindus had textual traditions analogous to the "historical consciousness" of European societies, such as the *itihāsa-purāṇa* (Skt, 'that which was believed to have happened in the past') tradition. See Romila Thapar, "Historical Consciousness in Early India," in *Cultural Pasts: Essays in Early Indian History* (New Delhi: Oxford University Press, 2000), 155–172.

    Vijay Mishra in *Devotional Poetics and the Indian Sublime* (Albany: State University of New York, 1998) believes that in spite of his dismal stance on Hindu culture, Hegel is useful in rethinking the sublime in reference to India: "... if we can set aside Hegel's racism, his reading of Indian culture as an instance of an undertheorized sublime that does violence to history and to the imagination demands serious consideration." Mishra explains that Hegel believes that history for the Hindu is nonexistent because the category of the sublime is missing from the culture (9–16). Ranajit Guha in *History at the Limit of World-History* (New York: Columbia University Press, 2002) utilizes Hegel's conception of "World-history" (*Weltgeschichte*) to demonstrate what history practiced outside world history would look like in what he calls "historicality," or the everyday experiences of ordinary people.
60. Beginning in the mid-nineteenth century, philologist and orientalist Max Müller proposed the notion that Sanskrit-speaking, fair-skinned, civilized Aryans invaded India and pushed the indigenous, darker-skinned Dravidian civilization southwards. The "Aryan concept," which began as a new theory of language (Indo-European/Sanskrit for people like Sir William Jones, the subject of chapter 3), developed into a new theory of race for European intellectuals in the late-nineteenth and early-twentieth centuries. See Thomas R. Trautmann, *Aryans and British India* (Berkeley: University of California Press, 1997). In the twentieth century, this theory was revised to an Indo-Aryan migration one. See Thomas R. Trautmann, ed., *The Aryan Debate* (New Delhi: Oxford University Press, 2005).
61. James Fergusson, *Tree and Serpent Worship: or Illustrations of Mythology and Art in India in the First and Fourth Centuries after Christ. From the Sculptures of the Buddhist Topes at Sanchi and Amravati* (London: India Museum, 1868), 62.
62. Fergusson, *On the Study of Indian Architecture*, 12.
63. Fergusson, *History of Indian and Eastern Architecture*, 362–364. In this quote, Fergusson refers specifically to some sculpture in the Pudu Maṇḍapam.
64. Fergusson, *History of Indian and Eastern Architecture*, 34. Fergusson refers to Charles Coleman, *The Mythology of the Hindus, with Notices of Various*

Mountain and Island Tribes, Inhabiting the Two Peninsulas of India and the Neighbouring Islands, and an Appendix, Comprising the Minor Avatars, and the Mythological and Religious Terms, &c. &c. of the Hindus (London: Parbury, Allen, and Co., 1832).

65. Fergusson, *On the Study of Indian Architecture*, 22–23.
66. Fergusson, *On the Study of Indian Architecture*, 14.
67. Kathleen Biddick, *The Shock of Medievalism* (Durham and London: Duke University Press, 1998), 12–13 (emphasis in the original). See also the chapter entitled "Gothic Ornament and Sartorial Peasants," 19–57.
68. "Gothic Revival," *Encylopædia Britannica*, 2021, https://www.britannica.com/art/Gothic-Revival, accessed December 14, 2021.
69. Fergusson, *On the Study of Indian Architecture*, 16.
70. Fergusson, *On the Study of Indian Architecture*, 15.
71. Fergussion, *On the Study of Indian Architecture*, 15.
72. Fergusson, *On the Study of Indian Architecture*, 16.
73. Alexander Cunningham, introduction to *Archæological Survey of India. Four Reports Made during the Years 1862–63–64–65*, vol. I (Simla: Government Central Press, 1871), I–XLIII, XIX. See also Partha Mitter, *Much Maligned Monsters: A History of European Reactions to Indian Art* (Chicago: The University of Chicago Press, 1992 [1977]), 261, and Upinder Singh, *The Discovery of Ancient India: Early Archaeologists and the Beginnings of Archaeology* (Delhi: Permanent Black, 2004), 60–61. Later in his career, Fergusson wrote *Archæology in India, with Especial Reference to the Works of Babu Rajendralal Mitra* (London: Trübner and Co., 1884) in which he engages in a vitriolic debate with Indian scholar Rajendralal Mitra, author of *The Antiquities of Orissa* (Calcutta: Wyman & Co., 1875) and an Asiatic Society of Bengal member.
74. Singh, *The Discovery of Ancient India*, 58.
75. On his tours, Cunningham followed the travels of fourth-century BCE Greek conqueror Alexander the Great and seventh-century CE Chinese Buddhist pilgrim Huen Tsiang and listed as historically important those sites of antiquity determined by these foreigners. See Thomas R. Metcalf, *Ideologies of the Raj*, The New Cambridge History of India III.4 (Cambridge: Cambridge University Press, 1994), 149.
76. Cunningham, preface to *Four Reports Made during the Years 1862–63–64–65*, i–viii, iii. Cunningham quotes from his "Memorandum of Colonel A. Cunningham, of Engineers, regarding a Proposed Investigation of the Archaeological Remains of Upper India."
77. Cunningham, preface to *Four Reports Made during the Years 1862–63–64–65*, viii.

78. Sourindranath Roy, *The Story of Indian Archaeology 1784–1947* (New Delhi: Archaeological Survey of India, 1961), 47.
79. Cunningham, preface to *Four Reports Made during the Years 1862–63–64–65*, ii. Cunningham quotes from "Minute by the Right Hon'ble the Governor General of India in Council on the Antiquities of Upper India,-dated 22nd January 1862."
80. After Cunningham retired from his post and returned to England, he came back to India in 1871 to serve as Director General of the newly established Archaeological Survey of India devoted to archaeological investigation and conservation.
81. Nadia Abu El-Haj, *Facts on the Ground: Archaeological Practice and Territorial Self-Fashioning in Israeli Society* (Chicago and London: The University of Chicago Press, 2001), 164.
82. Abu El-Haj, *Facts on the Ground*, 163 (emphasis added).
83. James Fergusson, introduction to *One Hundred Stereoscopic Illustrations of Architecture and Natural History in Western India, Photographed by Major Gill and Described by James Fergusson* (London: Cundall, Downes, & Company, 1864), iii–viii, viii.
84. James Fergusson, preface to *History of Indian and Eastern Architecture* (London: John Murray, 1876), v–x, v.
85. Fergusson, *On the Study of Indian Architecture*, 6.
86. Fergusson, preface to *Picturesque Illustrations of Ancient Architecture in Hindostan*, iii–iv, iv.
87. Fergusson, *History of Indian and Eastern Architecture*, 364, fn. 2. Capt. (Edmund David) Lyon, *Notes to Accompany a Series of Photographs Designed to Illustrate the Ancient Architecture of Southern India*, ed. James Fergusson (London: Marion & Co., 1870). For a comparison between Tripe and Lyon, see Stéphanie Roy Bharath, "Recording South Indian Architecture: Linnaeus Tripe and Edmund David Lyon," *South Asian Studies* 26, no. 2 (2010): 97–118. With the 1870 establishment of the Archaeological Survey of India, photographing Indian monuments became part of the duties of archaeologists who combined fieldwork with the production of photography (110).
88. Dewan, *The Photographs of Linnaeus Tripe*, 13. In "Separate List of the several items contained in the Contingent Bill of Captain Tripe, Government Photographer, up to 30th November 1857, arranged under the letters A, B and C respectively," in F. Lushington, Esq., Civil Auditor; to T. Pycroft, Esq., Chief Secretary to Government, Fort Saint George, April 22, 1858, Madras Public Consultations (April 9, 1858–June 22, 1858) IOR/P/249/66, no. 12, pp. 167–169, BL APAC. Item #17 on p. 169 is "Mr. Ross' bill for day light Reflectors and Stereoscopic camera," which cost approximately 302 rupees.

89. Homi K. Bhabha, "Signs Taken for Wonders: Questions of Ambivalence and Authority under a Tree outside Delhi, May 1817," in *The Location of Culture* (London and New York: Routledge, 1994), 102–122, 102.
90. Clark Worwick and Ainslee Embree, *The Last Empire: Photography in British India, 1855–1911* (New York: Aperture, 1976), 135.
91. Michael Mann, "Art, Artefacts and Architecture: Lord Curzon, the Delhi Arts Exhibition of 1902–03 and the Improvement of India's Aesthetics," in *Civilizing Missions in Colonial and Postcolonial South Asia: From Improvement to Development*, ed. Carey A. Watt and Michael Mann (London and New York: Anthem Press, 2011), 65–89, 70.
92. Jeffrey A. Auerbach, *The Great Exhibition of 1851: A Nation on Display* (New Haven: Yale University Press, 1999), 100.
93. Mary Louise Pratt, *Imperial Eyes: Travel Writing and Transculturation*, 2nd ed. (New York: Routledge, 2008 [1992]), 60.
94. Guha-Thakurta, *Monuments, Objects, Histories*, 4–5.
95. Pratt, *Imperial Eyes*, 60.
96. John Falconer, "Photography in Nineteenth-Century India," in *The Raj: India and the British, 1600–1947*, ed. C. A. Bayly (London: National Portrait Gallery Publications, 1990), 264–277, 271.

Part III

Living Gods

7

Producing Heritage

Culture as Commodity in Contemporary Madurai*

Introduction

Most Hindu worshippers visit temples for *darśan*—"to see and be seen" by the enshrined deity.[1] More than merely places to pray, temples can also be communal spaces to celebrate religious festivals, attend musical performances, or sit and socialize informally. As pilgrimage sites, some temples draw devotees and tourists from afar. For this reason, a few major temples in the south Indian state of Tamil Nadu house museums within their complexes, to educate the public and at times generate additional revenue through entry fees. For example, the Raṅganātha Svāmi Temple Museum in Srirangam contains Nāyaka-period ivory sculpture, metal inscriptional plates, and weaponry; the museum at the Bṛhadīśvara temple in Tanjavur, a UNESCO World Heritage Site, publicizes the Archaeological Survey of India's conservation work of Cōḻa-period paintings.

The museumification of living cultural and religious forms has also occurred at the Mīnākṣī-Sundareśvara temple through its Temple Art Museum in the Āyirakkāl Maṇḍapam ('thousand pillar hall'). Plans are underway for a proposed second museum in its other pillared hall, Pudu Maṇḍapam, a project backed by temple administrators, state officials, and local businessmen. Interviews with state and municipal government officials, local entrepreneurs, and temple personnel in Madurai and Chennai between 2009 and 2022 illustrate the complex and conflicting stakes surrounding government and private sector attempts to remove commerce from inside the *maṇḍapam*, a long-standing place of business and craft trade. The efforts to transform the *maṇḍapam* are related to larger endeavors to produce 'heritage' as a commodity that can be marketed in the context of a growing cultural tourism industry. When completed, the finished museum will reconfigure the everyday life of the temple, transforming the ephemeral spiritual affects of the

* An earlier version of this chapter, "Producing Heritage: Culture as Commodity in Madurai," was initially published in *International Journal of Tourism Anthropology* 5, no. 1/2 (June 2016): 47–70. Copyright © 2016 Inderscience Enterprises Ltd. Reprinted with the permission of Inderscience Publishers.

temple into static, ahistorical displays that appeal to foreign tourists, including foreign nationals of Indian ancestry and visitors from other parts of India. By building museums, educated middle- and upper-class residents of Madurai hope to represent a Tamil identity coinciding with the globally determined format of 'heritage.' In their bid to accumulate cultural and social capital, the elites repackage versions of local culture they deem 'traditional'; from a desire to make themselves and Madurai appear less 'backwards' and more 'modern,' they are transforming the temple into a more palatable (and more profitable) form.

From *maṇḍapam* to museum

The Āyirakkāl Maṇḍapam sits past small shops in the Vīravacantarāyar Maṇḍapam, where visitors enter the eastern *gōpuram* of the Madurai temple. The hall is built in the architectural metaphor of a chariot drawn by two elephants and it comprises 985 intricately carved stone pillars; two small shrines were added in lieu of the fifteen remaining pillars. The hall was commissioned by Ariyanātha Mudaliyār, minister and commander for the first Nāyaka king of Madurai, Viśvanātha Nāyaka (r. 1529–1564 CE) (the subject of chapter 1) and completed by three succeeding Nāyaka kings. In one legend, the equestrian figure at the hall entrance on the left facing south is Ariyanātha Mudaliyār himself. Others claim it is the god Sundareśvara, who turned foxes into horses for the medieval poet-saint Māṇikkavācakar. Sculptures on eight pillars at the entrance include Gaṇeśa, Murukaṉ on his peacock, and Saraswatī holding a *vīna*; these and other statues portray bodies with anatomical precision and detail and emotively expressive faces. Pillars at the beginning and end of some rows produce musical notes when tapped.

The Āyirakkāl Maṇḍapam was formerly an assembly hall for the king to meet with his officers and constituents.[2] It was (and remains) the *maṇḍapam* for Tiruvātirai, a festival held in Mārkaḻi month (December/January) for Māṇikkavācakar.[3] At the hall's center, after two rows of *yāḷi* (mythical creature) pillars, stands a Pāṇḍyan-era statue of Naṭarāja (dancing form of Śiva), one of three locations to possess such an immovable image; it is anointed with special oil and serenaded by Ōtuvārs (temple ritual performers) who sing the poet-saint's *Tiruvempāvai* hymns before his bronze statue processes around the temple. Early morning at three o'clock, priests perform a bathing ritual (*abhiṣēkam*) for the temple's moveable Naṭarāja images, which are brought to the hall's interior for *ārttirātaricaṉam* ('auspicious time for seeing Naṭarāja during the *tiruvātirai* star day in Hindu astrology'). In 1972, temple authorities decided to convert the Thousand Pillar Hall into the Temple Art Museum to showcase Cōḻa bronzes, Nāyaka ivories, and other artifacts that convey Madurai's historical and religious significance. The temple museum features a seventeenth-century 365-foot-tall wooden entrance door from the eastern gateway, and nineteenth-century Tanjavur-style framed paintings of Mīnākṣī's *paṭṭābhiṣēkam* ('royal coronation') and *tirukkalyāṇam* ('sacred marriage'). Also displayed in the museum are late-nineteenth-century painted murals depicting Parañcōti Muṉivar's *Tiruviḷaiyāṭal Purāṇam,* an important document about Madurai that narrates Śiva's sixty-four divine sports around the city's environs, as examined in chapter 2. Originally commissioned for the 1876 Kumbābhiṣēkam ('temple consecration ceremony'), the paintings were detached from the northern and eastern corridor walls of the Poṟṟāmaraikkuḷam ('golden lotus tank') during the twentieth century to expose earlier paintings. They were retouched and attached to wooden boards in the museum.[4]

In 2007, the Tamil Nadu Department of Tourism began renovations to upgrade the Temple Art Museum into a "world-class heritage museum" at a cost of 155 *lakh* rupees.[5] The renovation was aimed at making the museum "more visual" to attract tourists (Figure 7.1).[6] B. Raja, the temple's joint commissioner and executive

Figure 7.1 Tourists exit the Temple Art Museum, Mīnākṣī-Sundareśvara temple, Madurai, 2011

Source: Photo by author.

Figure 7.2 Central nave, Temple Art Museum, 2011

Source: Photo by author.

Figure 7.3 Display cases exhibit Cōḻa-period bronzes, Temple Art Museum, 2011

Source: Photo by author.

officer appointed by the state's Hindu Religious and Charitable Endowments (HR & CE) Department,[7] made primary decisions about the repairs and renewal with guidance from a Technical Advisory Committee comprising the superintending archaeologist, Archaeological Survey of India, Chennai Circle; curator, Government Museum, Madurai; and dean, School of Architecture and Planning, Chennai. Madurai's Public Works Department sandblasted and illuminated the stone pillars of Nāyaka-period figural deities and mythical *yāḷis*, laid a new granite floor (45 *lakh* rupees[8]), and installed new display cases (Figures 7.2 and 7.3). As new objects in the museum, large poster-like exhibits, such as photographs of the Madurai temple's 2009 Kumbābhiṣēkam, serve to promote tourism across the Tamil region. Further renovations began in March 2020 to encase the wooden-paneled paintings and provide descriptive signage on works of art.[9]

Shops, sewing machines, and sculptures

Temple administrators, state officials, and local entrepreneurs have been initiating efforts to transform a second Nāyaka-constructed hall into a museum for the Mīnākṣī-Sundareśvara temple: the Pudu Maṇḍapam.[10] According to historian R. Venkatraman, retail commerce began at the Pudu Maṇḍapam with a few small shops that sprang up after the British ousted the Nawāb of Arcot (Figure 7.4).[11]

Figure 7.4 Del Tufo & Co., Madras, *Interior of Puthoo Muntapam, Madura*, c. 1890s

Source: Author's private collection.

Figure 7.5 A shopkeeper sells *kuṅkumam* (vermillion power) and *mañjal* (turmeric rhizomes) to temple worshippers, Pudu Maṇḍapam, Madurai, 2011

Source: Photo by author.

Members of the Nawāb's disbanded military were forced to become merchants, transforming the pillared hall's concentric aisle into a busy commercial complex housing shops and tailoring units. The jobless military sold goods such as *kuṅkumam* (vermillion powder used for religious markings), *mañjaḷ* (turmeric rhizomes), and wedding *sārī*s (Figure 7.5). These former Nāyaka men became rich and auctioned the space to other vendors, who later formed a strong union. "There was monetary value and even more so, spiritual value," explained Venkatraman. "Getting a *sārī* from the Pudu Maṇḍapam was like getting one from Mīnākṣī herself."

Until early 2022, merchants sold colorful fabric and tailors stitched this material into decorative items, garments, or bags along the aisle (Figure 7.6). Other stall keepers vended *bindī*s (adhesive forehead decorations), plastic bracelets, toys, kitchen gadgets, *pūjā* items, and handicrafts (Figures 7.7 and 7.8). The outermost trenches situated at a lower level than the central space and the concentric aisle also accommodated stalls: books were sold on the north side, silver and brass vessels could be purchased on the south side. While all stores were mainstays of the Pudu Maṇḍapam, textile shops in particular were linked to the identity of Madurai and its economy; the Nāyakas introduced cotton cultivation in the dry, black soil zones under a project of "agricultural improvement" during their rule in the Madurai

Figure 7.6 Tailors stitch decorative items, garments, and bags, Pudu Maṇḍapam, 2011

Source: Photo by author.

Figure 7.7 Tourists shop at a stall, Pudu Maṇḍapam, 2011

Source: Photo by author.

Figure 7.8 Shoppers browse in front of Śiva Ūrdhvatāṇḍava, Pudu Maṇḍapam, 2009

Source: Photo by author.

environs.[12] A popular tourist guidebook delineates how the Pudu Maṇḍapam participated in both the textile and tourism industries:

> Madurai, a textile centre from way back, teems with cloth stalls and tailors' shops. A great place for getting cottons and printed fabrics is Puthu Mandapam, the pillared former entrance hall at the eastern side of Sri Meenakshi Temple. Here you'll find rows of tailors, all busily treadling away and capable of whipping up a good replica of whatever you're wearing in an hour or two. Quality, designs and prices vary greatly depending on the material and complexity of the design, but you can have a shirt made up for Rs. 100.[13]

Moreover, commercial activity and religious prayer had existed concomitantly in the Pudu Maṇḍapam: daily worship to sculpted images in the aisle did not interfere with day-to-day business (Figures 7.9 and 7.10). However, when religious festivals took place in the Pudu Maṇḍapam, such as the Eṇṇai Kāppu Utsavam (relayed in chapter 2), merchants who worked in small stalls around the perimeter of the hall's central nave had to close their shops. Every afternoon at half past three, temple workers turned off the electricity as a signal that merchants must begin the process of boarding up (Figure 7.11). Shopkeepers and tailors said that early closures created financial hardships for them; however, temple authorities

Figure 7.9 A devotee prays to Śiva Ūrdhvatāṇḍava, Pudu Maṇḍapam, 2011

Source: Photo by author.

Figure 7.10 An evening *pūjā* to Kālī, Pudu Maṇḍapam, 2009

Source: Photo by author.

Figure 7.11 Merchants board up their shops in preparation for Mīnākṣī's Eṇṇai Kāppu Utsavam, or beautification ceremony, 2009

Source: Photo by author.

Figure 7.12 Cleared space in the Pudu Maṇḍapam for Mīnākṣī's circumambulation ritual, 2009

Source: Photo by author.

required the additional room for the ritual procession that occured inside the hall every evening during Mīnākṣī's beautification ceremony (Figure 7.12). The area had to be cleaned also: temple employees swept away debris from the day's mercantile transactions and sprinkled water on the processional aisle before the divine metal image circumambulated there.

The tense relationship between the Pudu Maṇḍapam merchants and the Mīnākṣī temple authorities heightened when state and municipal authorities began efforts to capitalize on the flow of devotees to the temple. The Tamil Nadu Department of Tourism formulates policies and implements programs for developing the state's tourism sector, and markets Tamil Nadu as a tourist destination in several domestic and international ventures and publications under the "Enchanting Tamil Nadu, Experience Yourself" brand statement.[14] The Tamil Nadu Tourism Development Corporation, or TTDC, is a state-owned, public sector undertaking that operates package tours, hotels, and boat houses, commences novel commercial enterprises, and develops schemes to encourage private sector investment.[15] The Department of Tourism and TTDC, with the Madurai Corporation (a civic body that administers the city of Madurai), decided in 2005 to convert Madurai, its landmarks, and other parts of the state into more prominent tourist destinations.[16] In 2008, District Collector S. S. Jawahar maintained that "developing Madurai as a tourist-friendly place is a priority": grass lawns now spruce up the temple's vicinity and new paver tiles on streets outside the temple walls are for "hygiene-conscious foreign nationals."[17] Now, only foot traffic is allowed on these Cittirai Streets, where previously cars, auto rickshaws, and motorcycles could drive and park (Figure 7.13). To further facilitate tourism in and around the temple, other extensive renovations included laying underground electric cable, improving roads, and creating new parks. Correspondingly, the Tamil Nadu state government in Chennai and the local Madurai boosters have succeeded in evicting merchants from the Pudu Maṇḍapam as part of the endeavor to beautify and sanitize the site for use as a museum. Shops within the Pudu Mandapam were relocated to the nearby, recently constructed Kuṉṉathūr Cattiram from February to May 2022 "to restore the pristine beauty of this hall containing numerous sculptures."[18] These efforts seek to utilize the Pudu Maṇḍapam to bring revenue from a globally burgeoning 'heritage tourism' industry: a "facelift" would help the temple "regain its glory as a major attraction for tourists."[19] The HR & CE Department (which manages the state's temples), the Madurai Corporation, and the Tamil Nadu Electricity Board oversaw the entire temple renovation project.

Sanitary space for tourists

These twenty-first century renovation, maintenance, and restoration tactics have created a moment in the temple's life that is reminiscent of earlier colonial sanitation programs, a crucial aspect of urban planning and reform during the

Figure 7.13 Pedestrians stroll on the paved footpath near the west entrance of the Pudu Maṇḍapam, 2009

Source: Photo by author.

nineteenth century in Britain and its colonies. An early area of unease about hygiene was a response to the dangerous living conditions in Britain's industrial cities: in 1842, the British government commissioned civil servant Edwin Chadwick to investigate urban sanitation and recommend methods for improvement. His self-funded inquiry on Great Britain's sanitary conditions described correlations between poor living standards, disease spread, and high mortality rates. Chadwick argued that unhealthy living situations prevented impoverished laborers from working efficiently, which in turn hampered economic growth; he suggested that the government provide clean water, improve drainage systems, and remove refuse from homes and streets.[20] His sanitary report led to the passage of the 1848 Public Health Act, which created local boards to better the sanitary condition of England's towns and densely populated neighborhoods.

Urban sanitary reform was also a serious imperative in British India, where waste removal in the colony initially rose from fears that communicable diseases could spread to European populations.[21] Motivated by the cholera outbreak in Madurai and a medical report citing lack of hygiene as its principal cause, British Collector John Blackburne reorganized the city's urban layout during a ten-year period beginning in 1837 to help stimulate 'circulation' and clean up the city.[22] The major economic and aesthetic concerns of the Victorian sanitation work, which sought to make the city favorable for colonial occupation, can be traced through to contemporary plans to construct a salubrious, dirt-free environment conducive for foreign tourists. The prosperous, privileged citizens believe that the country's large and growing population is the foremost reason for poverty in India; the desire for a 'sanitary' city is connected with widespread class anxiety, in which middle- and upper-class Indians feel uneasiness about the 'unwashed masses' and the social threat posed by the bad health and immoral behavior of the poor.[23] Postcolonial Tamil Nadu administrators' urban reconstruction efforts reflect an "unbroken chain of command" in the legacy of colonial institutions:[24] where British administrators sanitized the environment to create one suitable for colonial settlement, Tamil Nadu state and temple bureaucrats now invoke parallel discourses of hygiene in the name of tourism revenue which will flow to the state's economic elites.

A form of aesthetic judgment underlies these contemporary sanitation concerns: the creation of the clean and beautiful necessitates eliminating the *un*-clean and the *ugly* that violates the tourist's sense of comfort. These aesthetic considerations find traces in nineteenth-century surveys of British India. Captain Edmund David Lyon (1825–1891), while photographing the Madras Presidency's archaeological and architectural antiquities ten years after Captain Linnaeus Tripe (addressed in chapter 6), saw the shops as hampering the Pudu Maṇḍapam's beauty. His caption for his photograph of the central nave reads (Figure 7.14):

> This view shows the central Nave of this magnificent building. It is taken from the east end. The whole of it is generally appropriated as one immense bazaar, every available spot being occupied by the different objects exhibited for sale. The scene on entering is gay and animated, but the stalls detract much from the beauty of the building, which, to be appreciated as it deserves, should be seen clear of all such encumbrances as it is represented in the Photograph.[25]

In his 1883–1884 report, Henry H. Cole, nineteenth-century Curator of Ancient Monuments in India, documented the Pudu Maṇḍapam's unhygienic and unsightly condition during his Madras Presidency tour:

> The flooring is firm but worn. The columns and ceiling are whitewashed. The lower portions of the columns are very dirty, and most of the sculptured figures painted. The roof is sound, but the parapet walls over the east and west end are in ruins. The side walls to the north and south are bare, no parapets having been erected. A portion of the stone coving at the north-west corner is damaged. The sculptured horses on the west side have been slightly mutilated. The tatties and screens put up to enclose the hall are a disgrace to the place. The pavement and colonnade north and south of the building are extremely neglected and dirty, and used as urinals by

Figure 7.14 Edmund David Lyon, *Trimul Naik's Portico. Interior from East Entrance*, albumen silver print, 23.4 × 29 centimeters, 1868

Source: Photograph from an album of 41 albumen prints by Edmund David Lyon. © The British Library Board, Photo 212/1(25).

> the natives. There are several stones bearing inscriptions, but they do not appear to be in their original positions.[26]

Both commentators imagine the hall to be 'clean' and 'beautiful' when it is devoid of its native merchant occupants. The screens that stall keepers erected as makeshift walls (which Cole called a "disgrace") existed until the shops moved (Figure 7.15). Robert Sewell, a civil servant working for the Archaeological Survey of India, wrote disparagingly about the merchant business that diminished the Pudu Maṇḍapam's visual appeal. In his 1882 *Lists of Antiquarian Remains in the Presidency of Madras,* Sewell commented that "[t]he effect of this fine hall is greatly destroyed by the presence in it of a number of shops and stalls for the sale of cloths, etc."[27] W. Francis of the Indian Civil Service wrote in his 1906 *Madura*: "The whole building is perhaps the most remarkable of its kind in south India, but the effect of it is at present sadly marred by the shops and stalls with which the whole centre aisle is crowded."[28] In 1908, temple committee member M. V. Subramania Iyer petitioned the Archaeological Survey of Southern India superintendent, Alexander Rea, to have the Pudu Maṇḍapam cleared of its shops and enclosed

Figure 7.15 The Pudu Maṇḍapam's main entrance on the east side, 2009

Source: Photo by author.

with a locked iron railing. Rea refused to declare the pillared hall an "ancient or national monument" and Iyer could not get the Pudu Maṇḍapam emptied or locked.[29] A. Ki. Parantāmaṉār in his 1995 *Tirumalai Nāyakkar Varalāṟu* ('The history of Tirumala Nāyaka') said that these shops that have ruined the hall's beauty would dismay architect Cumantira Mūrti Ācāri.[30] Late-nineteenth- and early-twentieth-century attempts to eliminate the unattractive shops from the Pudu Maṇḍapam coincided with the colonial state apparatus' official sponsorship of Indian antiquities and monuments with the development of the Archaeological Survey of India.[31]

Giving a "facelift"

The contemporary sanitization of the hall is aimed at the production of 'heritage' as a *commodity* that can draw tourists—and capital—from afar. The link between sanitation and tourism as governing problems is palpable throughout India: foreign visitors often complain about the litter and garbage found at tourist sites, mediocre standards of hygiene in restaurants, presence of primitive or dirty toilets, and absence of public restroom facilities.[32] A study by the Water and Sanitation Program quantified the total economic losses in India due to poor sanitation to 2.4 trillion rupees, or 54 billion US dollars, annually; analogous to these figures, the Indian economy loses approximately 12 billion rupees, or 264 million

US dollars, in potential tourism revenue alone.[33] Connected to the question of sanitation is the perception of prospective travelers that India is a "developing country" affected by poverty and marked by indigent people with appalling (diseased and dangerous) living conditions—a view reinforced by mainstream cinematic representations like the 1992 *City of Joy* and 2008 Oscar-winning *Slumdog Millionaire.*[34] Western sightseers in India often express feeling "moments of disorientation" when encountering beggars in the streets.[35]

Tourism promoters at the Pudu Maṇḍapam are acutely worried that foreign tourists will not visit a 'dirty' place. Sanitation efforts in the museum renovation project try to conceal abject poverty from visitors: in this context, 'sanitation' is not only a desire to get rid of dirt, but also epitomizes an opportunity to totally reconfigure the economic relations of the city. State officials, temple authorities, and private business interests hope that the flow of foreign tourists (rather than the regular devotees) will generate more revenue than the relatively modest rental fees paid by shopkeepers. However, ticket sales alone cannot sustain the upkeep and conservation work in contemporary museums. Museums produce social and cultural "value" by facilitating visitors' "learning experiences,"[36] and state and private capital strive to create attractive spaces that offer such experiences. In Madurai, removing shopkeepers from the Pudu Maṇḍapam was central to this process because the petty traders violated the aesthetics of 'heritage' learning that the Madurai boosters require. In one stroke, these boosters simultaneously undermine perceptions of India as 'unhygienic' and valorize themselves as cosmopolitan and 'modern.' As Noel Salazar notes, tourism workers find "creative ways" to distance themselves from local people and align themselves with tourists: "they prefer to position themselves as different from the represented locals and more similar to their foreign clients in a bid to enhance their own cosmopolitan status and to gain symbolic capital, using their privileged contact with foreigners to nourish their utopias of escape from the harsh local life."[37] If this is true of workers in the tourism industry in general, it is all the more so for the powerful, educated, and moneyed strata of Madurai.

The proposal to evacuate the Pudu Maṇḍapam of its merchants was a joint initiative between government and private sectors: the Tamil Nadu Department of Tourism, Tamil Nadu State Department of Archaeology, HR & CE Department, and Madurai Corporation along with the Confederation of Indian Industry (CII)–Madurai Zone, Development of Humane Action (DHAN) Foundation, and Indian National Trust for Art and Cultural Heritage (INTACH) met with the then district collector U. Sagayam.[38] This government-led, private-sector driven collaboration is exactly what the Government of India's Planning

Commission prescribed in its Tenth Five Year Plan (2002–2007) when it shifted from earlier approaches to tourism and recommended that state governments engage in higher levels of private-sector investment to entice international and elite segments of the tourist market, by fostering rural/ethnic tourism, health tourism, eco-tourism, sport/adventure tourism, and spiritual tourism.[39] Along these lines, the situation in Madurai gained momentum in early 2010, after the Tamil Nadu Department of Tourism organized a "grass root level" seminar at the Mīnākṣī-Sundareśvara temple on preserving Madurai's ancient monuments. G. Vasudevan, Madurai Fortune Pandiyan Hotel director, former CII Tourism Panel convener, and former Travel Club president, spoke about the importance of popularizing Madurai's ancient monuments for foreign tourists. According to Vasudevan, the Pudu Maṇḍapam has many remarkable structures, which were "getting damaged due to the presence of shops."[40] In June, the commissioner of tourism in Chennai received approval and funds from the Government of India's Ministry of Tourism for its proposal to develop a pilgrimage heritage circuit for Madurai–Rameswaram–Kanyakumari. Tamil Nadu often ranks as the top tourist state:[41] tourism works to be completed in Madurai included a tourist complex comprising parking lots and arrival/reception centers as well as the "refurbishment of shops at Pudumandapam inside the Meenakshi Temple by construction of new tourist amenities complex at Kunnathur Chatram, Opp. to the Temple."[42] In October 2010, Union minister M. K. Alagiri laid the foundation for the construction of a multi-level parking structure near the Mīnākṣī temple. *The Hindu* newspaper article on the parking garage and Alagiri's visit defined the proposed renovation of the Pudu Maṇḍapam as a "facelift" for the sake of "tourists from all over the globe."[43]

State government and private bodies involved in the "facelift" believe that the shops selling cloth, books, and vessels had been "spoiling" the Pudu Maṇḍapam's tourist appeal. After visiting the Pudu Maṇḍapam in June 2011, Collector Sagayam instructed temple officials to take immediate steps to remove the encroaching shops.[44] Over 150 tailors and 140 merchants headed by the Maturai Putumaṇṭapam Viyāpārikaḷ Maṟṟum Taiyaltoḻilāḷarkaḷ Caṅkam (Madurai Pudu Maṇḍapam Merchants and Tailors Association[45]) fought a long and contentious battle with government authorities asserting their ancestral right to occupy a commercial space their families had worked for generations. Whenever temple administrators ordered the shopkeepers to vacate, they refused to leave.[46] In 2010, vendors and tailors finally relented after temple officers promised to relocate them to a new spot a few meters from the pillared hall.[47] They were to be evicted after the Madurai Corporation completed construction of the building.

However, a fire near the east gateway of the Madurai temple in February 2018 forced the departure of the shopkeepers sooner than expected. This fire destroyed intricately carved pillars and several stalls that sold plastic toys and *pūjā* articles in the Vīravacantarāyar Maṇḍapam, close to Āyirakkāl Maṇḍapam's Temple Art Museum; a short circuit from illegal connections in one shop may have caused an electrical overload. The fire generated debate as to whether temple shops should discontinue peddling plastic items or artificial jewelry and sell only flowers, coconuts, and *kuṅkumam* that devotees require for worship—or whether shops should be cleared completely from temple premises, an arrangement supported by some right-wing groups.[48] After the fire, temple authorities immediately closed the Pudu Maṇḍapam, citing the absence of easy emergency exits and fire extinguishers as dangerous to tourists and vendors.[49] When temple authorities later evicted the nearly 300 stall keepers from the hall without any prior notice, G. Muthupandi, president of the Madurai Pudu Maṇḍapam Merchants and Tailors Association, urged the Madurai Bench of the Madras High Court to hold the eviction until an alternative site was provided.[50] The Madurai Bench allowed owners to clear their goods from the hall in mid-March; however, without a location to continue their business, they were unable to sell items that adherents typically purchase for the Cittirai festival (explored in chapter 2), a lucrative time for vendors and tailors.[51] In response, the Madurai Pudu Maṇḍapam Merchants and Tailors Association circulated posters with an image of an empty hall—emphasizing that, for the first time in several hundred years, the pillared hall was closed for business during Cittirai (Figure 7.16).[52] In April 2018, Madurai Corporation commissioner S. Aneesh Sekhar stated that work would begin on Kuṉṉathūr Cattiram through the Government of India's Smart Cities Mission, an urban renewal and retrofitting program to make cities citizen friendly and sustainable.[53] However, construction started in August 2019, and the building was completed in January 2021. From June 2018 until the relocation process began in February 2022, merchants and tailors—under the leadership of a robust union—were allowed to continue their businesses within the Pudu Maṇḍapam.[54]

Prior to the move, merchants expressed mixed reactions over the proposed Pudu Maṇḍapam museum: Pooncholai of Balbina Boutique (Pudu Maṇḍapam stall no. 119) marveled at the prospect of the Pudu Maṇḍapam "becoming nice" as a museum exhibiting metal statues; her family purchased commercial property near the temple's north tower to shift their business.[55] Kannan, then joint secretary of the Madurai Pudu Maṇḍapam Merchants and Tailors Association, remarked on the Temple Art Museum, which once housed scattered, poorly illuminated statues, often uncased and corded off by ropes to keep visitors at bay: "We are ready to move because

Figure 7.16 Poster circulated by the Madurai Pudu Maṇḍapam Merchants and Tailors Association, April 2018: "Without shops in Madurai's Pudu Maṇḍapam, the Cittirai festival loses its luster."

Source: G. Muthupandi, President of the Madurai Pudu Maṇḍapam Merchants and Tailors Association.

they (temple authorities) want building for museum. First, they give concrete building, then we will move. They have enough museums, but want one more, for to make money. Politicians make money without any means or reasons."[56] Some Madurai boosters criticized the work of Tamil Nadu state government's HR & CE Department: the highly polished stone floors make the Temple Art Museum (devoted to celebrating Madurai's past) look too "modern," and the sandblasting to clean the Nāyaka-period granite pillars erased some sculptural detailing. These boosters hoped that the department would not make similar mistakes in the Pudu Maṇḍapam renovation.[57]

The government and private investors' interest in the temple's museumification project expands beyond the temple complex, to transforming the city *itself* into a 'modern,' cosmopolitan destination for both travelers and industrialist investors. Vishaal de Mal, built in April 2012, is a multi-utility luxury shopping mall with department stores, restaurants, coffee shops, and theatres;[58] its website describes the mall as designed to "suit the needs of sophisticated Madurai people," and it promised to "change the way Madurai was being perceived." Although the website did not elaborate upon how the city was formerly perceived, it prescribed the cure: a consumerist fantasy of "luxury and high street shopping ... a bewildering brand-mix, together with destination cafes, bistros, restaurants, and bars," an "addictive" experience that will "take care of all the needs of an entire family making it the perfect destination" for both tourists and residents of the city.[59]

This commercial undertaking is intended to create a commercial destination for Madurai's families, while producing a consumerist middle class in Madurai (that is, the "sophisticated Madurai people" who represent the city's moneyed elite—not its laborers, petty traders, or artisans). Central to the formation of middle-class subjects is the "cultivation of a distinct 'cultural milieu' based on taste, judgment, and the acquisition of cultural capital through consumption practices."[60] Since India is predicted to become the world's second largest middle-class consumer market by 2030, behind China but surpassing the United States,[61] the mall venture is not merely an aesthetic or visual 'facelift,' but also a fundamental economic restructuring.

The Madurai Corporation, along with the Government of Tamil Nadu and the Government of India through the Jawaharlal Nehru National Urban Renewal Mission (JnNURM), has endeavored to "fast track" the development of urban infrastructure in Madurai, categorized by the national government as a "heritage city." Projects included provision of adequate drinking water supply, dam construction, solid waste management, and storm water drainage.[62] The Madurai Corporation is the second largest corporation by area in Tamil Nadu. Madurai was constituted as a municipality in 1866 as per the Town Improvement Act of 1865 and upgraded as a corporation in 1971 when its population increased and its administrative boundaries extended.[63] The corporation comprises an executive body headed by the government-appointed municipal commissioner, who oversees the six departments (general, engineering, revenue, town planning, public health, computer wing), and a legislative body, headed by an elected mayor who supervises its 100 members (one from each ward). Some of its functions include urban planning; regulation of land use and construction of buildings; arranging for economic and social development; domestic, industrial, and commercial water supply; public health, sanitation, and solid waste management; and provision of urban amenities and facilities such as parks.[64] Short- and long-term regional development policies, with local, state, and national financial backing, contribute not only to the economic welfare of the region, but can also help emphasize Madurai as a city with modern infrastructure capable of comfortably accommodating its visitors.[65]

At the same time, the Tamil Nadu state government and the CII's Information Technology (IT) panel are promoting and developing Madurai as an ideal city for investing capital in the IT industry. With India's established urban centers already "saturated" in investment activity, "Tier II" cities (like Madurai)—considered not quite a metropolis or highly developed industrial and cultural hub—are rapidly emerging as investment destinations that were once absent from the corporate radar.[66] The Industries Department of the Government of Tamil Nadu has embarked on a vigorous campaign to advertise the state as a business destination for global commerce, which has included, for example, publishing and disseminating a visually appealing illustrative book entitled *Tamil Nadu: Land of Potential* to prospective investors. This publication not only underscores the state's Dravidian culture, classical literature, ancient temples, traditional arts (such as Carnāṭic music and *bharatanāṭyam* dance), natural scenic beauty, and success stories in industrial development, but also champions the "great potential" of Tier II cities like Madurai for IT growth.[67] The Madurai Zone of the CII is also capitalizing on the trend to attract corporate money to Madurai (despite mass media portrayals of Madurai as a place of violence);[68] CII is a non-government, not-for-profit, industry-led, and industry-managed organization founded in 1895 to strengthen industry through partnerships between business, government, and civil society.[69] These development pursuits demonstrate a desire for economic prosperity and a wish to alter how Madurai (and also Tamil Nadu) are commonly perceived.

Museums, museumification, and heritage

Private entrepreneurs and managers of state enterprises in Tamil Nadu see IT and tourism in Madurai as "growth engines for the city."[70] Madurai's economy is mainly agrarian, in which paddy, millet, pulses, and cotton are staple crops; it also has jasmine flower (Madurai *mallikai*), rubber-based, and textile (like *cuṅkaṭi*, painted handloomed cotton) industries.[71] However, because monsoon rains, international competition, and cheaper imports can disrupt agriculture and textile manufacturing, state and private sector representatives seek to promote Madurai's rich tradition, heritage, and culture, with the intention of building a profitable and durable tourist industry. As hotel director Vasudevan explained: "The importance of Madurai as a trade center has lessened during the last ten years. For Madurai to grow economically, we have to look beyond industries. The best option is tourism. The potential for tourism in the Madurai region is immense."[72] Venkatraman, Madurai Kamaraj University's history emeritus professor and longtime advocate of promoting Madurai's historical sites, said, "The Pudu Maṇḍapam has beautiful sculptures carrying the essential features of the Nāyaka period.... Foreigners will come and see, sit and enjoy the sculptures."[73] Imagining the interior of the Pudu Maṇḍapam as a museum, requiring tickets for entry, situates the temple at a specific point in the broader transformation of the city: tourism needs *destinations*, and museums can be lucrative attractions.[74]

The link between museums and tourism is a recent emergence. In the late eighteenth and early nineteenth century, the public museum in Europe developed as a conversion of royal treasure troves and "cabinets of curiosities"[75] into public exhibits of scientifically curated art and antiquities, ethnographies, and natural history for the purpose of educating the masses.[76] Contemporaneous with the refinement of mechanisms of confinement (in the prison, the factory, the asylum, and so on), there was the "opening up" of culturally meaningful objects for visibility and inspection—no longer for the private pleasure of aristocracy and nobility, but for the "organs of public instruction." Tony Bennett defines this "exhibitionary complex" as an instrument for "moral and cultural regulation" of the working classes that operated in parallel to the carceral institutions: the masses were educated in the conduct appropriate to the space of the museum (dressing properly, remaining orderly) before they were admitted to these spaces. The museums of history and archaeology employed burgeoning systems of classification and display to create spaces "through which the stories of nations could be told and related to the longer story of Western civilization's development"; alongside developments in the fields of geology and biology, museums of science and technology "completed the evolutionary picture in representing the history of industry and manufacture as a series of progressive innovations leading up to the contemporary triumphs of industrial capitalism." Anthropology was a critical "disciplinary" 'pillar' in the exhibitionary complex, which connected the history of 'the West' with the history of the colonial 'other' precisely by *separating* them: characterizing 'primitive' people as instances of arrested development that had fallen short of Western civilizational progress.[77]

The first museum of colonial India was created in 1814 by the Asiatick Society of Bengal in Calcutta, to satisfy a desire to collect rare antiquities (for example, ancient monuments, sculptures, coins, and inscriptions) for the perusal of Western Orientalists.[78] The next government museum, the Madras Central Museum, opened in 1851 and focused on natural history and geology.[79] The Indian Museum in Calcutta, the capital of the British Indian empire, opened in 1878, after the Asiatick Society of Bengal, which lacked adequate room and funds to maintain its growing collection, petitioned the government to build an "Imperial Museum."[80] The museum produced "artifacts" that entered colonial discourse as classified objects, based on the colonizers' desire to act as custodians to 'civilizational' items on behalf of the natives.[81] The National Museum in New Delhi was inaugurated on August 15, 1949, exactly two years after independence from British rule, to centralize the new nation's art and antiquities in a single location.[82]

These early museal initiatives illustrate the mutation of former colonial governing mechanisms into the 'sovereignty' of national independence, and the corresponding emergence of novel techniques of government. We can identify three general 'moments' in the history of the museum in south Asia: (*a*) the museum of private explorers and scholars, driven by Orientalist fascination with the Indian subcontinent during early colonization; (*b*) the museum of the British colonial government, driven by scientific missions to name, document, order, classify, and exhibit Indian cultural artifacts to create an archive of empire[83] for effective colonial rule; and (*c*) the museum of the independent national government, driven by a longing to formulate a national identity and unified culture, and to recover India's indigenous traditions from European influence. The Orientalists who produced the first museums wrote extensively on the concepts of 'civilization,' 'nation,' and 'history,' and these concepts informed the techniques of administering the colonial government. When an Indian state became independent from colonial rule, it inherited these very same concepts and employed them in the practice of government: for example, in the production of a national 'heritage' through a museum exhibiting religious art that was never previously tied to any idea of 'national' identity. The national museum relies upon the same conceptions of "nation" inherited from the "colonial master states";[84] ironically, the program of national 'sovereignty' (which seeks to escape from the attachments of colonization) depends largely on the institutional mechanisms and intellectual concepts of colonial rule.

The proposed project in present-day Madurai is a new juncture in the history of the museum: it is part of a larger national scheme to attract capital investment through the curation of sites of cultural importance. The contemporary moment exemplifies the cooperation of the state government in Tamil Nadu, the national government, local authorities, and private investors to divert the flows of capital through the production of 'heritage' that will attract tourists from afar. Producing 'heritage' requires producing an *affect*—of nostalgia, of reverence for the past, and of a shared history. This question of manufacturing 'affect' was not critical to the Orientalists, the colonial government, or the newly independent nation in the earlier museum endeavors: the modern tourism industry has oriented the museum away from *artifacts* towards visitor *services*, designated by the term "experience," a constructed environment that engages the senses, emotions, and imagination.[85] The Pudu Maṇḍapam proposal includes not only displays of objects but also displays of classical and folk dance performances; museum-makers in Madurai foresee marketing the "culture show" of dancers in colorful costumes for the sensuous consumption of foreign tourists.[86] Although these "experiences" bear little resemblance to the traditional practices of the temple, the performances are packaged as "authentic" depictions of local culture, a prominent theme of tourism marketing.[87] Twentieth-century commentaries on the museum (for example, in the work of Theodor Adorno) often lament the cold imprisonment of cultural objects, and the removal of these objects from their living context[88]—as James Boon wrote, an artifact in a museum is "dead."[89] By contrast, the Pudu Maṇḍapam renovators envisage the 'museum' as a place that is alive, exciting, and unique—words that evoke the 'experience' they presume will appeal to tourists: a colorful space that can be photographed and filmed for brochures and videos, and constructed with the aim of producing certain kinds of economic relations.

The cultural economy of pilgrimage in the Madurai temple complex depends on the Pudu Maṇḍapam, as rituals that occur in the pillared hall connect with significant religious festivals in the main temple (as discussed in chapter 2); for example, Eṇṇai Kāppu Utsavam prefixes Poṉṉūñjal, a yearly harvest festival that transpires near Sundareśvara's temple shrine; and Mīnākṣī and Sundareśvara's Tirukkalyāṇam, or annual marriage reenactment celebration, is followed with the divine couple resting in the Pudu Maṇḍapam a month later during Vasantam Utsavam, or spring festival. HR & CE officials claim that tourism initiatives for the Pudu Maṇḍapam will not displace religious practices: they declare a responsibility to preserve not only the temple and its sculptures, but also the venue's intangible cultural heritage such as its rituals.[90] However, the renovations prioritize the demands of cash-carrying foreign tourists over the traditional needs of religious pilgrims. Despite the HR & CE Department's promises, it is unclear how state and private entrepreneurs can balance their current plans with the 'conservation' of the Pudu Maṇḍapam rituals. Government and private sector representatives conceive of the Pudu Maṇḍapam as a money-generating hall. Venkatraman, history professor, recounted: "I suggested a long time back to have the shops removed. I told the district collector that the Pudu Maṇḍapam would mint more money than the temple."[91] Behind such sentiment is that foreign tourists will generate more revenue than domestic religious tourists. Vasudevan, the hotel director and tourism advocate, outlined a three-fold course of action: take out the vendors, restore the Pudu Maṇḍapam (without sandblasting), and incorporate sign boards to identify sculptures so that the Pudu Maṇḍapam "truly becomes a museum."[92] These renovations are envisioned around an imagined paying public of foreign tourists: the sculptures that line the aisle and central nave will receive plaques that name the deities, royal images, and mythological figures located within the structure. These labels will be written in English, Tamil, and Hindi. This bureaucratic intervention in the religious and commercial space privileges the architected museum 'experience' over the intimate and spontaneous affect of daily worship.[93] The "museumification effected by these labels" shifts the sculptures to an entirely new context: now entangled in a web of meaning and expectations that is "international in scope," the sculptures appeal to the needs of foreign, middle-class heritage 'consumers,' rather than the needs of the devotees and locals who once worshipped at or worked alongside the them.[94]

Madurai (along with Varanasi) is the oldest continuously living city in India; as a "heritage" site, it is categorically distinct from sites like Mohenjo Daro, the oldest river-based civilization in South Asia that was lost and forgotten for centuries until its 1920 discovery. From 1972, the United Nations' World Heritage Committee has identified cultural and natural sites around the world to be protected for the purpose of recording historical and natural heritage for the international community.[95] The United Nations Educational, Scientific and Cultural Organization (UNESCO), as guardian of the world's heritage, plays a monitoring role and offers technical assistance and professional training in preservation. In August 2016, the Madras High Court in Chennai asked UNESCO to participate in the restoration of the state's heritage temples and monuments, and it directed Tamil Nadu's HR & CE Department to follow UNESCO's suggestions for conserving and renovating historic shrines according to international conservation standards and the principles of the Āgamas (ancient Hindu manuals that prescribe rituals, methods of temple construction, creation of idols, and worship of deities).[96] The HR & CE Department originated as a central administrative body responsible for supervising Hindu temples in the Tamil region in 1925, and it has been a regular department of the postcolonial state government, headed by a cabinet minister, since 1951. The department controls the administrative and financial (and by default, religious) affairs of most temples, directly through its own personnel in its Chennai headquarters and indirectly through its appointed temple trustees and executive officers.[97] UNESCO's fact-finding team conducted its own study in several temples including Madurai's Mīnākṣī-Sundareśvara temple and informed the Madras High Court in August 2017 (after a three-month tour) that the HR & CE Department lacks the capacity or quality experts to complete work on its monuments, and the "proper system" of documenting, assessing, reporting, and tendering of heritage works.[98] In this way, "heritage" in Tamil Nadu is being contested and transformed not only by domestic agents, but also by global actors, including representatives of international heritage organizations like UNESCO, who are generating new understandings of culture and built heritage throughout the world.

UNESCO explicitly incorporates "heritage tourism" into its preservation mission through the World Heritage and Sustainable Tourism Programme, which advocates for "sustainable tourism" as "an important vehicle for managing cultural and natural heritage."[99] Tourism promoters recognize that the preservation of

Madurai's historic cultural resources can be integrated into a community economic development strategy centered around attracting visitors to extraordinary cultural sites.[100] Urban heritage and architecture are regarded as economic assets, and utilized in the service of corporate enterprises.[101] Research has shown, however, that this strategy is more likely to succeed if "a number of historic sites are available for tourists to visit in a community, leading to longer visits and/or more tourists."[102] To this end, government and the private sector in Madurai have been integrating the city's multifaceted and multi-sited cultural history into a coherent 'package' for tourist consumption. For example, in 2011, they jointly publicized the temple town's landmarks through the Madurai Heritage Walkway, a proposal to pave a path connecting eleven historically significant locations between the Mīnākṣī-Sundareśvara temple (including the Pudu Maṇḍapam) and the Tirumala Nāyaka Palace, lined with informative wayside markers and potted flowers.[103] In Madurai, tourism and heritage work in concert: by curating and annotating 'heritage' sites—identified by a local government according to the requirements of an international body—the Pudu Maṇḍapam is converted into a 'destination.' Thus, the pillared hall becomes economically viable as an exhibit of itself. The tourism industry produces 'heritage' by changing a lived space (the temple) into a commodity (the museum experience) for the mobilization of other commodities (hotels, restaurants, entertainment venues, and so on). Despite the pervasive language of conservation, preservation, and restoration of the Pudu Maṇḍapam's *past*, the discourse of "heritage" is primarily about producing new forms of cultural and economic production in the present.[104]

Heritage discourse serves a special function in narratives of 'progress' and 'development' in India.[105] 'Heritage' sites are 'signs' of the 'past,' a past from which Madurai's citizens are actively distancing themselves in the course of rapid economic development. 'Heritage' is what we no longer are, what we once were, while we are in the process of becoming something else—constructing a site as 'heritage' is fundamentally bound up in fantasies of 'development,' a process of imagining oneself otherwise, and of envisioning certain kinds of futures. The vendors that traded in the temple hall fit neither in the picture of 'development' nor in the picture of 'heritage.' The state's project—which includes transportation, lodging (hotel industry), and mass consumption (shopping, food, admission fees)—has eliminated the local economy of petty traders, who bartered, haggled, and dealt only in cash. State officials, temple authorities, and private capitalists interpret the merchants' hand-to-hand business as illegitimate and 'anti'-heritage—by contrast, their bourgeois reconstruction of the city, bound up in a national mission of rapid economic growth, is legitimate and heritage-positive.

Conflicting notions of 'authenticity' circulate around the activities to transform Madurai into a destination of heritage tourism. As Salazar writes: "Tourism imaginaries ... resonate most clearly in destinations, the physical and mental landscapes where the imaginaries of local residents, tourism intermediaries and tourists meet, and, occasionally, clash."[106] Historian Venkatraman wanted to preserve Madurai's historic and artistic 'aura' in a form that tourists could appreciate. As director of a major hotel, Vasudevan, along with temple authorities and the state tourism department, wanted to promote Madurai as a tourist destination. Industrialists like former CII chairman Ligi George wanted to launch Madurai as a place for economic investment and future business.[107] Upper- and middle-class imaginations of 'heritage,' based on *mobility* (of people, of capital) perceive the city through the tourists' gaze; thus, the image of the Pudu Maṇḍapam as a tourist destination and place for cultural 'education' is more valid. 'Public' sector support for tourism directly benefits these elite classes—not necessarily the mass public of Madurai.

At the Pudu Maṇḍapam, heritage is created through the process of exhibition that involves sanitizing the temple, removing traditional commerce, and converting it into a museum; defining 'whose' heritage is vital in these renovation plans. In the Madurai case, it is about the middle and upper classes' valorization of a secular museum exposition that is counterposed to *darśan*. In this conversion, there is a paradoxical twist to Bennett's "exhibitionary complex."[108] Rather than transform museum visitors into self-improved, self-regulated citizens (when once-private collections are accessible and visible), efforts to create a museum for foreign tourists are actually transforming Madurai boosters' own identities: they visualize themselves as worldly citizens in a postcolonial, autonomous nation-state intimately bound up in the flows of global capital. As Arjun Appadurai and Carol A. Breckenridge observe, museums are "often associated with self-conscious national approaches to heritage, and are tied up with transnational ideologies of development, citizenship, and cosmopolitanism."[109] Museums constitute a key space for a community's imagination.

Conclusion

As India rises on the global economic stage and as transnational capitalism links with the Indian diaspora and foreign tourists, the new marketing of 'heritage' has reached the small temple town of Madurai. The phenomenon of 'heritage tourism' is advanced by the educated, upper and middle classes with a vision of Tamil culture that appeals to 'global' norms, is concerned predominantly with the movement of capital, and has little consideration for the livelihoods of Madurai's vendors, tailors, and poor. Industrialist Ligi George asks, "When the people of Madurai are hungry, how will they look at their heritage?"[110] K. P. Bharathi, DHAN Foundation Tourism Programme leader in Madurai, clarifies the importance of cultural education:

> Tourists come and go away. What about the social, economic, and environmental development of the host country? Local people need to understand that where they live has value. They live in an important place, but don't know it. After learning about it, they will understand the value of the property.[111]

George, Bharathi, and other Indians who deal with traditions from a postcolonial perspective feel that 'history' is often ignored by the people who inhabit it and exploited by the people who want to profit from it. They want to create an awareness that motivates and encourages the local population to respect, appreciate, protect, and gain knowledge in the areas of history, archaeology, and heritage in Madurai. District Collector Sagayam explained during a July 21, 2011, district collectorate meeting, "Our people don't realize their history. We must preserve it."

Overcoming the perceived 'backwardness' of the general populace has become bound up with more complex governing projects with a broader historical scope. Of chief importance to the Madurai reformers is the problem of 'dirtiness' and the aesthetic criteria of foreign capital investment: the various stakeholders in tourism development hope that their attempts at societal betterment, in terms of both appreciation and sanitation, will help counter the general perception that sophisticated (both Western and domestic) tourists have of India being backwards and unhygienic. They also hope that these foreigners will come to recognize Indians *in general* as no longer 'inferior.' In this way, tourism allows for the re-creation of both people and place[112]—adopting "modern" or Western notions of conservation is a performance of the modern state, for the purpose of attracting new consumers and investors.[113] At stake are not only economic problems that the tourism business may or may not solve; the envisioned transformations also entail internal psychological contradictions for elite Indians, which may or may not be resolved through the renovation and sanitation of traditional spaces and sites.

The Pudu Maṇḍapam is being reconstructed to fit the new paradigm of heritage. This institutionalization of 'culture' at the Pudu Maṇḍapam illustrates the interconnection of politics and place in the postcolonial state, where spiritual, governmental, and commercial interests converge and compete with one another. The *maṇḍapam* is what Henri Lefebvre called a "social space":[114] it is not an inert, neutral, or a pre-existing given, but rather an ongoing production of spatial relations negotiating between early modern conceptions of kingship, day-to-day operations of petty merchants, and the demands of international capital. This space, the domain of the lived experience of ordinary people in Madurai, is being uprooted and converted into a new form of commodity, to be 'experienced' from behind static displays or informational placards. In the name of tourism, the museumizing mentality seeks to flatten a once heterogeneous, complex space (where different people and purposes coexist and intermingle) into a singular, *sanitized* space that perpetually reproduces a common, ahistorical 'experience' that can be inhabited by any person—so long as they pay the entry fee.

Notes

1. Diana L. Eck, *Darśan: Seeing the Divine Image in India* (New York: Columbia University Press, 1998), 3. Tamil: *taricaṉam*.
2. T. G. S. Balaram Iyer, *History & Description of Sri Meenakshi Temple* (Madurai: Sri Karthik Agency, 1988 [1984]), 43.
3. Raju Bhattar (priest, Mīnākṣī-Sundareśvara temple, Madurai), in email correspondence with author, July 22, 2013.
4. A. V. Jeyechandrun, *The Madurai Temple Complex (With Special Reference to Literature and Legends)* (Madurai: Publications Division, Madurai Kamaraj University, 1985), 89.
5. Or roughly 370,000 US dollars. *Lakh* is a unit of measurement prevalent in South Asia and is equal to 100,000. "Panel Inspects Thousand Pillar Hall," *The Hindu*, August 5, 2007, https://www.thehindu.com/todays-paper/tp-national/tp-tamilnadu/Panel-inspects-Thousand-Pillar-Hall/article14809927.ece, accessed December 14, 2021.
6. "Renovation Work Begins at Pillar Hall," *The Hindu,* May 8, 2008, http://www.thehindu.com/todays-paper/tp-national/tp-tamilnadu/Renovation-work-begins-at-temple/article15218335.ece, accessed December 14, 2021.
7. The Tamil Nadu state government's HR & CE Department appoints the temple's executive officer who heads the *dēvastānam* (temple's administration).
8. Or about 110,000 US dollars.
9. Sanjana Ganesh, "Facelift for 1,000-Pillar Hall at Madurai Meenakshi Temple," *The Hindu*, March 12, 2020, https://www.thehindu.com/news/national/tamil-nadu/facelift-for-1000-pillar-hall-at-madurai-meenakshi-temple/article31044370.ece, accessed December 14, 2021.
10. An inscription on a cement block found in the pillared hall's central nave during some renovation work reveals that the Pudu Maṇḍapam served as a museum and library for the British: "This museum and library were opened/by T. Austin, ESG., CIE., I.C.S./Advisor to his Excellency of Madras/on 6th March 1942/A.S.

Nayudu/Barrister-at-Law/Executive Officer/Madura Etc. Devasthanums." I thank T. Vijayaraghunathan, Tamil *pulavar*, Mīnākṣī-Sundareśvara temple's Enquiry/Information Center, for showing me this inscription. The British used the space to hold reference books about Madurai. R. Venkatraman (professor emeritus of history, Madurai Kamaraj University, Madurai), in interview with author, December 5, 2011.

11. Venkatraman, interview, July 23, 2011.
12. Prasannan Parthasarathi, *The Transition to a Colonial Economy: Weavers and Kings in South India, 1720–1800* (Cambridge: Cambridge University Press, 2007), 53.
13. Paul Harding, Janine Eberle, Patrick Horton, Amy Karafin, and Simon Richmond, *South India*, 3rd ed. (Victoria, Australia: Lonely Planet Publications, 2005), 369.
14. Government of Tamil Nadu, Tourism, Culture and Religious Endowments Department, *Tourism Policy Note 2016–2017 Demand No. 29* (Chennai: Government of Tamil Nadu, 2016), http://www.tamilnadutourism.org/pdf/Policynoteenglish2016-17.pdf, accessed December 14, 2021.
15. "Tourism-An Overview," Tamil Nadu Tourism Development Corporation, 2019, http://www.tamilnadutourism.org/TN-Overview.html, accessed December 14, 2021. The central government in Delhi institutionalized its role as a tourism provider in 1966 when it formed the Indian Tourism Development Corporation (ITDC) to stimulate tourist facilities in areas that had tourism potential, and corresponding state-level agencies (TDCs) to manage the "growing network" of tourism offices, hotels, restaurants, and handicrafts shops. Tamil Nadu was an early beneficiary of ITDC's first priority to draw tourists away from the popular "Golden Triangle" of Delhi, Agra, and Jaipur; its Tamil Nadu Tourism Development Corporation (TTDC) was created in 1970. See Mary E. Hancock, *The Politics of Heritage from Madras to Chennai* (Bloomington: Indiana University Press, 2008), 123–124.

    Domestic tourism in India progressed primarily along two lines: an older, traditional pattern (still prevalent today) centered on religious pilgrimages to Buddhist, Jain, Sikh, Muslim, and Hindu sacred sites, and a colonial-era pattern when the British escaped the hot season by traveling to cooler hill stations (such as Shimla and Darjeeling) or cooler inland cities (like Bengaluru). See Linda K. Richter, *The Politics of Tourism in Asia* (Honolulu: University of Hawaii Press, 1989), 105. It is only in the postcolonial period that national and regional goals were established for tourism development along economic reasons: tourism would help developing countries overcome poverty as well as forge a national identity. See Nina Rao and K. T. Suresh, "Domestic Tourism in India," in *The Native Tourist: Mass Tourism within Developing Countries*, ed. Krishna

B. Ghimire (London and Sterling, VA: Earthscan Publications Limited, 2001), 198–228, 199.

16. "Tourism Activities to Receive a Boost with Emphasis on Areas in and around Meenakshi Temple," *The Hindu*, November 4, 2005, https://www.thehindu.com/todays-paper/tp-national/tp-tamilnadu/tourism-activities-to-receive-a-boost-with-emphasis-on-areas-in-and-around-meenakshi-temple/article27503884.ece, accessed December 14, 2021.
17. R. Sairam, "Good Harvest for Tourism Promoters Madurai Matters," *The Hindu*, January 15, 2008, http://www.thehindu.com/todays-paper/tp-national/tp-tamilnadu/Good-harvest-for-tourism-promoters-Madurai-Matters/article15144545.ece, accessed December 14, 2021. In the eighteenth century, the East India Company carved out districts in India and placed them under the administration of British collectors. In 1781, George Proctor became Madurai's first collector.
18. "Tourism Activities to Receive a Boost with Emphasis on Areas in and around Meenakshi Temple." Legal issues between the Madurai Corporation and a project consultant stalled the construction of Kuṉṉathūr Cattiram. See "Who'll Clear This 17th Century Mandapam in Madurai?" *New Indian Express*, October 22, 2012, https://www.newindianexpress.com/states/tamil-nadu/2012/oct/22/wholl-clear-this-17th-century-mandapam-in-madurai--417815.html, accessed December 14, 2021. As a result, shifting the shops was delayed, the reason being the "Indian government." Kannan (former joint secretary of the Madurai Pudu Maṇḍapam Merchants and Tailors Association), in interview with author, June 7, 2017. The construction project and the relocation efforts continued to be "bogged in court cases and politics of corruption." Venkatraman, email correspondence, October 23, 2017. Construction resumed in August 2019, and after its completion in early 2021, the Tamil Nadu chief minister M. K. Stalin inaugurated Kuṉṉathūr Cattiram on August 30, 2021. See "50 Yrs on, Traders All Set to Move out of Pudhu Mandapam," *Times of India*, September 3, 2021, https://timesofindia.indiatimes.com/city/madurai/50-yrs-on-traders-all-set-to-move-out-of-pudhu-mandapam/articleshow/85881442.cms, accessed December 14, 2021.
19. S. Annamalai, "Madurai to Have Yet Another Tourist Attraction," *The Hindu*, September 28, 2006, http://www.thehindu.com/todays-paper/tp-national/tp-tamilnadu/madurai-to-have-yet-another-tourist-attraction/article3082195.ece, accessed December 14, 2021. A similar effort to remove commerce and restore a *maṇḍapam* in the name of heritage and tourism took place in Hampi, the Vijayanagara imperial city and UNESCO World Heritage Site in Karnataka, India. In March 2012, the High Court directed the Archaeological Survey of India to take action under the Ancient Monuments and Archaeological Sites and

Remains Act 1958 to clear encroachments and illegal commercial activity outside the Virūpākṣa temple. People residing and operating in the Virūpākṣa Bazaar, a long street lined with *maṇḍapams*, were removed. "India's Hampi Heritage Site Families Face Eviction from Historic Ruins," *The Guardian*, May 26, 2012, https://www.theguardian.com/world/2012/may/27/hampi-india-heritage-temples-eviction, accessed December 14, 2021; John M. Fritz and George Michell, "Living Heritage at Risk: Searching for a New Approach to Development, Tourism, and Local Needs at the Grand Medieval City of Hampi," *Archaeology*, November/December 2012, https://www.archaeology.org/issues/53-1211/letter-from/247-india-living-heritage-at-risk, accessed December 14, 2021; Sunitha Rao, "Encroachments Gnawing at Hampi's Glorious Heritage," *Times of India*, January 12, 2014, https://timesofindia.indiatimes.com/city/bengaluru/encroachments-gnawing-at-hampis-glorious-heritage/articleshow/28694984.cms, accessed December 14, 2021.

20. Edwin Chadwick, *Report to Her Majesty's Principal Secretary of State for the Home Department, from the Poor Law Commissioners, on an Inquiry into the Sanitary Condition of the Labouring Population of Great Britain; With Appendices. Presented to Both Houses of Parliament, by Command of Her Majesty, July, 1842* (London: W. Clowes and Sons, 1842).
21. See chapter 4, "The City Must Be Clean," in Veena Talwar Oldenburg, *The Making of Colonial Lucknow, 1856–1877* (Princeton: Princeton University Press, 1984), 96–144.
22. Anne Viguier, "An Improbable Reconstruction: The Transformation of Madurai, 1837–47," *Indian Economic and Social History Review* 48, no. 2 (April 2011): 215–239.
23. Niheer Dasandi, "What Do Indian Middle Class Attitudes to Poverty Tell Us about the Politics of Poverty Reduction?" The Developmental Leadership Program Research Paper 33, January 2015, https://www.dlprog.org/publications/research-papers/what-do-indian-middle-class-attitudes-to-poverty-tell-us-about-the-politics-of-poverty-reduction, accessed December 14, 2021.
24. Oldenburg, *The Making of Colonial Lucknow*, 264.
25. Capt. (Edmund David) Lyon, *Notes to Accompany a Series of Photographs Designed to Illustrate the Ancient Architecture of Southern India*, ed. James Fergusson (London: Marion & Co., 1870), 11. The photograph that accompanies the caption shows a canopy over Tirumala Nāyaka's statue indicating that it was taken during a festival time.
26. H. H. Cole, "Appendix U: Great Temple to Siva and His Consort at Madura," in *Preservation of National Monuments. Third Report of the Curator of Ancient Monuments in India, for the Year 1883–84* (Calcutta: Printed by the Superintendent of Government Printing, 1885), cliii–clvii, clvii.

27. Robert Sewell, *Archæological Survey of Southern India, Lists of Antiquarian Remains in the Presidency of Madras. Compiled under the Orders of Government*, vol. I (Madras: E. Keys, at the Government Press, 1882), 292.
28. W. Francis, *Madras District Gazetteers: Madura*, vol. 1 (Madras: Printed by the Superintendent, Government Press, 1906), 271.
29. Carol A. Breckenridge, "The Śrī Mīṉākṣī-Sundareśvara Temple: Worship and Endowments in South India, 1833–1925" (PhD diss., University of Wisconsin-Madison, 1976), 349, citing M. V. Subramania Iyer to A. Rea, September 4, 1908, Mīṉākṣī Temple Record Room, Madurai. The Pudu Maṇḍapam's central nave is kept locked throughout the year and opened only during religious festivals.
30. A. Ki. Parantāmaṉār, *Tirumalai Nāyakkar Varalāṟu* (Tamiḻ) (Ceṉṉai: A. Cō. Cantāṉa Ilakkumi, 1995), 97. In chapter 1, the architect's name appears differently to align with Taylor's spelling.
31. Alexander Cunningham, *Archæological Survey of India: Four Reports Made during the Years 1862-63-64-65*, vol. I (Simla: Government Central Press, 1871), i–viii.
32. David Wilson, "Paradoxes of Tourism in Goa," *Annals of Tourism Research* 24, no. 1 (1997): 52–75.
33. *The Economic Impacts of Inadequate Sanitation in India: Inadequate Sanitation Costs India Rs. 2.4 Trillion (US$53.8 Billion)* (New Delhi: Water and Sanitation Program-World Bank, 2010), http://www.wsp.org/sites/wsp.org/files/publications/wsp-esi-india.pdf, accessed December 14, 2021.
34. Anya Diekmann and Kevin Hannam, "Touristic Mobilities in India's Slum Spaces," *Annals of Tourism Research* 39, no. 3 (July 2012): 1315–1336.
35. Kristin Lozanski, "Encountering Beggars: Disorienting Travelers?" *Annals of Tourism Research* 42 (July 2013): 46–64, 54.
36. See Eilean Hooper-Greenhill, *Museums and Education: Purpose, Pedagogy, Performance* (London and New York: Routledge, 2007).
37. Noel B. Salazar, "Tourism Imaginaries: A Conceptual Approach," *Annals of Tourism Research* 39, no. 2 (April 2012): 863–882, 875.
38. Confederation of Indian Industry (CII) works to create and sustain an environment conducive to the growth of industry in India, partnering industry and government alike. See "About Us," Confederation of Indian Industry, 2021, http://www.cii.in/About_Us.aspx?enc=ns9fJzmNKJnsoQCyKqUmaQ==, accessed December 14, 2021. Development of Humane Action (DHAN) Foundation is a professional development organization initiated in 1997. One of its programs centers on promoting heritage tourism opportunities to alleviate poverty. DHAN Foundation designated 2008–2009 as a 'Year of Heritage': a celebration and conservation of natural and cultural heritages. See DHAN

Foundation, Madurai, "Heritage Matters: Sustaining Development," in *Annual Report 2009*, 3–22, http://www.dhan.org/Downloads/annual_report_2009.pdf, accessed December 14, 2021. Indian National Trust for Art and Cultural Heritage (INTACH) is a non-profit charitable organization, founded in 1984 and dedicated to heritage awareness, conservation, and preservation. See "About INTACH," Indian National Trust for Art and Cultural Heritage, 2016, http://www.intach.org/about.php, accessed December 14, 2021. I attended such a meeting on Thursday, July 21, 2011 when INTACH convener of the Madurai Chapter (Arvind Kumar Sankar), CII Madurai Zone past president (Ligi George), Mīnākṣī-Sundareśvara Temple joint commissioner (P. Jayaraman), an HR & CE engineer, Madurai Corporation commissioner (S. Sebastine), Travel Club president (S. Arumainathan), Tamil Nadu Tourism Department officer, Madurai district (K. Dharmaraj), ATO to Mr Dharmaraj (Umadevi), retired Tamil Nadu State Department of Archaeology officer (Dr V. Vedachalam), Madurai Kamaraj University professor emeritus (Dr R. Venkatraman), CII Tourism Panel convener/Madurai Fortune Pandiyan Hotel director/Travel Club past president (Dr G. Vasudevan), DHAN Foundation Programme leader of Tourism Development (K. P. Bharathi), and others met at the district collectorate to discuss "Madurai Heritage Walk," a dedicated pathway covering twelve historically noteworthy locations between the Mīnākṣī-Sundareśvara temple complex and the Tirumala Nāyaka Palace as an initiative to promote tourism in Madurai.

39. "Tourism," Government of India, Planning Commission, *Tenth Five Year Plan 2002–2007*, vol. II: Sectoral Policies and Programmes (New Delhi: Government of India, 2002), 817–828: chapter 7, section 5, http://niti.gov.in/planningcommission.gov.in/docs/plans/planrel/fiveyr/10th/volume2/10th_vol2.pdf, accessed December 14, 2021. Five Year Plans were centralized economic and social growth programs that India's first prime minister, Jawaharlal Nehru, launched in 1951 inspired by similar plans by USSR's Joseph Stalin. Prime Minister Narendra Modi ended the Plans in 2017. The Government of India announced the first tourism policy in the Sixth Plan period in 1982, specifying developmental objectives and an action plan centered on the travel circuit concept; in the Seventh Plan, tourism was accorded industrial status. See Rao and Suresh, "Domestic Tourism in India," 203.

40. "'Madurai Must Do More to Protect Its Heritage Sites,'" *The Hindu*, February 24, 2010, http://www.thehindu.com/todays-paper/tp-national/tp-tamilnadu/ldquoMadurai-must-do-more-to-protect-its-heritage-sitesrdquo/article15991375.ece, accessed December 14, 2021. Shopkeepers often hammered nails on the pillars, which most likely weakened the structures and destroyed the sculptures. See V. Devanathani, "Pudu Mandapam Battered by Shopkeepers,"

Times of India, August 19, 2013, http://timesofindia.indiatimes.com/city/madurai/Pudu-Mandapam-battered-by-shopkeepers/articleshow/21906234.cms, accessed December 14, 2021.

41. *Tourism Policy Note 2016–2017 Demand No. 29*, 8.
42. Government of Tamil Nadu, Tourism and Culture Department, "Development of Pilgrimage Circuit (Madurai–Rameswaram–Kanniyakumari) in Tamil Nadu under Mega-Tourism Project," G.O. Ms. No. 142, Tourism-Promotion of Tourism-Government of India Assisted Scheme-2010–2011, Issued July 12, 2010, p. 2, http://cms.tn.gov.in/sites/default/files/gos/tour_e_142_2010.pdf, accessed December 14, 2021.
43. "Stone Laid for Multi-Level Parking at Old Central Vegetable Market near Meenakshi Temple," *The Hindu*, October 4, 2010, http://www.thehindu.com/news/cities/Madurai/Stone-laid-for-multi-level-parking/article15768632.ece, accessed December 14, 2021.
44. "17th Century Pudu Mandapam to Be Restored to Its Splendor," *The Hindu*, June 26, 2011, https://www.thehindu.com/news/cities/Madurai/17th-century-pudu-mandapam-to-be-restored-to-its-splendour/article2136754.ece?homepage=true, accessed December 14, 2021.
45. The Madurai Pudu Maṇḍapam Merchants and Tailors Association was formed on December 4, 1974. The union is headed by a president, who keeps all vendors and tailors unified, represents the interests of all vendors and tailors during meetings with temple authorities, and forms a bridge between the Pudu Maṇḍapam employees and the temple officers. G. Muthupandi (president, Madurai Pudu Maṇḍapam Merchants and Tailors Association, and former vendor of stall no. 128, Pudu Maṇḍapam, Madurai), in interview with author, January 6, 2018. There were 154 tailoring shops, 34 utensil shops, 32 bookshops, 32 shops selling *pūjā* articles, 32 selling jewelry and trinkets, and about 15 shops selling tailoring goods.
46. Venkatraman, interview, July 23, 2011.
47. Muthupandi, interview, January 6, 2018. See R. Sairam, "'Lost' Site to Come Alive," *The Hindu*, January 12, 2010, https://www.thehindu.com/news/cities/Madurai/lsquoLostrsquo-site-to-come-alive/article16837153.ece, accessed December 14, 2021.
48. Vinita Govindarajan, "Fire in Madurai's Meenakshi Temple Sparks Demand for Shops to Be Evicted from Complex," *Scroll.in*, February 6, 2018, https://scroll.in/article/867574/fire-in-madurais-meenakshi-temple-sparks-demand-for-shops-to-be-evicted-from-complex, accessed December 14, 2021.
49. "Pudu Mandapam Remains Closed," *The Hindu*, February 5, 2018, http://www.thehindu.com/news/cities/Madurai/pudu-mandapam-remains-closed/article22654739.ece, accessed December 14, 2021.

50. "Plea to Open Shops at Pudu Mandapam," *The Hindu*, March 2, 2018, http://www.thehindu.com/todays-paper/tp-national/tp-tamilnadu/plea-to-open-shops-at-pudu-mandapam/article22901791.ece, accessed December 14, 2021.
51. "Shopkeepers Clear Goods from Pudu Mandapam in Meenakshi Temple," *The Hindu*, March 18, 2018, http://www.thehindu.com/news/cities/Madurai/shopkeepers-clear-goods-from-pudu-mandapam-in-meenakshi-temple/article23284471.ece, accessed December 14, 2021; Muthupandi, email correspondence, April 13, 2018; S. Poorvaja, "'Pudhu Mandapam' Bustling with Devotees," *The Hindu*, May 6, 2014, https://www.thehindu.com/news/cities/Madurai/pudhu-mandapam-bustling-with-devotees/article5981366.ece, accessed December 14, 2021.
52. For Cittirai festival, Pudu Maṇḍapam's tailors made colorful costumes to sell to devotees looking to dress as gods and goddesses. As one tailor shared:

> We do not make too much of a margin selling these clothes but we get a ton of satisfaction. No one cares about religion or caste when they purchase at Pudu Mandapam. After all, I, a Muslim fold my hands and pray to Goddess Meenakshi when I hand over the costume to each customer as part of the tradition.

See "With Chithirai round the Corner, Pudu Mandapam Is on a Roll," *The Hindu*, April 1, 2019, https://www.thehindu.com/news/cities/Madurai/with-chithirai-round-the-corner-pudu-mandapam-is-on-a-roll/article26704415.ece, accessed December 14, 2021.

53. B. Tilak Chandar, "Pudu Mandapam Shopkeepers' Woes to End Soon," *The Hindu*, April 16, 2018, http://www.thehindu.com/news/cities/Madurai/pudu-mandapam-shopkeepers-woes-to-end-soon/article23553548.ece, accessed December 14, 2021.
54. Sanjana Ganesh, "Heritage Bazaar to Come Up at Kunnathur Chathiram Site," *The Hindu*, August 5, 2019, https://www.thehindu.com/news/cities/Madurai/heritage-bazaar-to-come-up-at-kunnathur-chathiram-site/article28817839.ece, accessed December 14, 2021.
55. Pooncholai (former owner of Balbina Boutique, stall no. 119, Pudu Maṇḍapam, Madurai), in interview with author, July 30, 2011 and June 7, 2017.
56. Kannan, interview, July 30, 2011.
57. G. Vasudevan (Madurai Fortune Pandiyan Hotel director, former CII Tourism Panel convener, and past Travel Club president, Madurai), in interview with author, July 21, 2011.
58. A. Shrikumar, "Mall de Madurai," *The Hindu*, March 29, 2012, https://www.thehindu.com/news/cities/Madurai/mall-de-madurai/article3258285.ece, accessed December 14, 2021.

59. "About Us," Vishaal de Mal, April 23, 2013, https://web.archive.org/web/20130423192019/http://www.vishaalmall.com:80/about-us/, accessed December 14, 2021.
60. Li Zhang, "Private Homes, Distinct Lifestyles: Performing a New Middle Class," in *Privatizing China: Socialism from Afar*, ed. Li Zhang and Aihwa Ong (Ithaca and London: Cornell University Press, 2008), 23–40, 25.
61. Homi Kharas, "The Unprecedented Expansion of the Global Middle Class: An Update," Global Economy and Development Working Paper 100, February 2017 (Washington D.C.: The Brookings Institution, 2017), https://www.brookings.edu/wp-content/uploads/2017/02/global_20170228_global-middle-class.pdf, accessed December 14, 2021. See also Homi Kharas and Kristofer Hamel, "A Global Tipping Point: Half of the World Is Now Middle Class or Wealthier," *Brookings*, September 27, 2018, https://www.brookings.edu/blog/future-development/2018/09/27/a-global-tipping-point-half-the-world-is-now-middle-class-or-wealthier/, accessed December 14, 2021.
62. *Jawaharlal Nehru National Urban Renewal Mission: An Update on Projects* (Madurai: Madurai Corporation, 2009), https://fdocuments.us/document/brochures-published-madurai.html, accessed December 14, 2021.
63. "About Madurai." Madurai Corporation, 2021, https://www.maduraicorporation.co.in/aboutus/about-madurai, accessed December 14, 2021.
64. "Institutional Framework," Madurai Corporation, 2021, http://www.maduraicorporation.co.in/aboutus/institutional-framework, accessed December 14, 2021.
65. For information about the link between regional development and cultural/heritage tourism, see Ebru Günlü, İge Pırnar, and Kamil Yağcı, "Preserving Cultural Heritage and Possible Impacts on Regional Developments: Case of İzmir," *International Journal of Emerging and Transition Economies* 2, no. 2 (2009): 213–229.
66. Avantika Chilkoti, "India: Emerging Cities," *Financial Times*, October 19, 2012, https://www.ft.com/content/4fc08f8f-e8a9-3dc5-a7f3-60004804ff5a, accessed December 14, 2021.
67. The Industries Department of Government of Tamil Nadu, *Tamil Nadu: Land of Potential* (Chennai: Global Printing Press, 2010), 59.
68. S. Annamalai, "Chances for Madurai to Be IT Hub," *The Hindu*, September 24, 2012, http://www.thehindu.com/news/cities/Madurai/chances-for-madurai-to-be-it-hub/article3931404.ece, accessed December 14, 2021. See also Pon Vasanth Arunachalam, "IT Sector Growth in Madurai Gaining Momentum," *The Hindu*, December 28, 2015, http://www.thehindu.com/news/cities/Madurai/it-sector-growth-in-madurai-gaining-momentum/article8036576.ece, accessed December 14, 2021.

69. "About Us," Confederation of Indian Industry, 2021.
70. Annamalai, "Chances for Madurai to Be IT Hub."
71. "Agriculture" and "Industries & Commerce," Madurai District Administration, 2021, https://madurai.nic.in/agriculture/, and https://madurai.nic.in/industries-commerce/, accessed December 14, 2021.
72. Vasudevan, interview, July 21, 2011.
73. Venkatraman, interview, July 23, 2011.
74. Barbara Kirshenblatt-Gimblett, *Destination Culture: Tourism, Museums, and Heritage* (Berkeley and Los Angeles: University of California Press, 1998), 132.
75. Cabinets of curiosities, also known as "wonder rooms," were small collections of rare, valuable, historically important, or unusual objects which, like some of today's museums, categorized and told stories about the wonders of the world in Renaissance Europe.
76. See "Formation of the Museum," in Tony Bennett, *The Birth of the Museum: History, Theory, and Politics* (London and New York: Routledge, 1995), 17–58.
77. "The Exhibitionary Complex," in Bennett, *The Birth of the Museum*, 59–88, quoted parts from 68, 73, 77, 83–84.
78. Tapati Guha-Thakurta, *Monuments, Objects, Histories: Institutions of Art in Colonial and Post-Colonial India (Cultures of History)* (New York: Columbia University Press, 2004), 46–47.
79. S. F. Markham and H. Hargreaves, *The Museums of India* (London: The Museums Association, 1936), 176.
80. Indian Museum, Calcutta, *The Indian Museum 1814–1914* (Calcutta: The Indian Museum, 1914), 5–8; Markham and Hargreaves, *The Museums of India*, 123.
81. Gyan Prakash, *Another Reason: Science and the Imagination of Modern India* (Princeton: Princeton University Press, 1999), 23.
82. "About the Museum: History," National Museum, New Delhi, 2019, http://www.nationalmuseumindia.gov.in/en/history, accessed December 14, 2021.
83. Prakash, *Another Reason*, 21–26.
84. Kavita Singh, "The Museum Is National," *India International Centre Quarterly* 29, no. 3/4, India: A National Culture? (Winter 2002–Spring 2003): 176–196, 176.
85. Kirshenblatt-Gimblett, *Destination Culture*, 138.
86. As an example of what is being envisioned, the Tamil Nadu Department of Tourism organized a folk and classical dance performance in January 2018, which "tourists, particularly foreigners, enjoyed." See "Tourists Throng Pudu Mandapam," *The Hindu*, January 14, 2018, https://www.thehindu.com/news/cities/Madurai/tourists-throng-pudu-mandapam/article22440080.ece, accessed December 14, 2021.

87. Deepak Chhabra, Robert Healy, and Erin Sills, "Staged Authenticity and Heritage Tourism," *Annuals of Tourism Research* 30, no. 3 (2003): 702–719.
88. "Valéry Proust Museum," in Theodor W. Adorno, *Prisms*, trans. Samuel and Shierry Weber (Cambridge, MA: MIT Press, 1997 [1981]), 173–185.
89. "Why Museums Make Me Sad (Eccentric Musings)" in James A. Boon, *Verging on Extra-Vagance: Anthropology, History, Religion, Literature, Arts ... Showbiz* (Princeton: Princeton University Press, 1999), 124–142.
90. K. Shaktivel (assistant commissioner-verification officer, Hindu Religious & Charitable Endowments Department, Chennai), in interview with author, August 8, 2011.
91. Venkatraman, interview, July 23, 2011.
92. Vasudevan, interview, July 21, 2011.
93. Michael Herzfeld, A *Place in History: Social and Monumental Time in a Cretan Town* (Princeton: Princeton University Press, 1991), 10–11.
94. Bruce McCoy Owens, "Monumentality, Identity, and the State: Local Practice, World Heritage, and Heterotopia at Swayambhu, Nepal," *Anthropological Quarterly* 75, no. 2 (Spring 2002): 269–316, 301–303.
95. "About World Heritage" and "Archaeological Ruins at Moenjodaro," United Nations Educational, Scientific and Cultural Organization (UNESCO), 2021, http://whc.unesco.org/en/about/ and http://whc.unesco.org/en/list/138, accessed December 14, 2021.
96. "Go by UNESCO Suggestions on Temples, HC Tells State," *The Hindu*, August 25, 2016, http://www.thehindu.com/news/cities/chennai/Go-by-UNESCO-suggestions-on-temples-HC-tells-State/article14588568.ece, accessed December 14, 2021.
97. For HR & CE's history, see Chandra Y. Mudaliar, *The Secular State and Religious Institutions in India: A Study of the Administration of Hindu Public Religious Trusts in Madras* (Wiesbaden: Steiner, 1974). The foundations for the HR & CE's authority were laid in the nineteenth century as British officials pushed for increased government interference in temples. See Franklin A. Presler, "The Legitimation of Religious Policy in Tamil Nādu: A Study of the 1970 Archaka Legislation," in *Religion and the Legitimation of Power in South Asia*, ed. Bardwell L. Smith (Leiden: E. J. Brill, 1978), 106–133, 111.
98. "UNESCO Slams TN Govt for Reckless 'Conservation' Work at Historic Temples, Submits Report to Madras HC," *NEWS Minute*, August 9, 2017, http://www.thenewsminute.com/article/unesco-slams-tn-govt-reckless-conservation-work-historic-temples-submits-report-madras-hc, accessed December 14, 2021.
99. "Sustainable Tourism," United Nations Educational, Scientific and Cultural Organization (UNESCO), 2021, https://whc.unesco.org/en/tourism/, accessed December 14, 2021.

100. Alan Fyall and Brian Garrod, "Heritage Tourism: At What Price?" *Managing Leisure* 3, no. 4 (1998): 213–228, 213.
101. Florian Steinberg, "Conservation and Rehabilitation of Urban Heritage in Developing Countries," *Habitat International* 20, no. 3 (September 1996): 463–475, 464.
102. Vishakha Maskey, Cheryl Brown, and Ge Lin, "Assessing Factors Associated with Listing a Historic Resource in the National Register of Historic Places," *Economic Development Quarterly* 23, no. 4 (August 2009): 342–350, 348.
103. R. Sairam, "Plan to Have 'Heritage Walk' with Dedicated Pathway in Madurai," *The Hindu,* July 22, 2011, http://www.thehindu.com/todays-paper/tp-national/tp-tamilnadu/plan-to-have-heritage-walk-with-dedicated-pathway-in-madurai/article2283944.ece, accessed December 14, 2021. In February 2018, Madurai Corporation sought 50 *crore* (500 million) rupees support from the Government of India's Smart Cities Mission to connect places of historic significance through a chartered route. See Sanjana Ganesh, "Get Ready for a Stride on Madurai's Heritage Walkway," *The Hindu*, February 12, 2018, http://www.thehindu.com/news/cities/Madurai/get-ready-for-a-stride-on-madurais-heritage-walkway/article22727257.ece, accessed December 14, 2021.
104. Dallen J. Timothy and Stephen W. Boyd, "Conserving the Past," in *Heritage Tourism* (Harlow, Essex: Pearson Education Limited, 2003), 87–132.
105. "Heritage" in Tamil Nadu is defined as any building or site that is over a hundred years old. P. Vijaya Kumar (Tamil Nadu Department of Tourism Publication officer, Chennai), in interview with author, August 8, 2011.
106. Salazar, "Tourism Imaginaries," 876.
107. Lugi George (industrialist and former CII chairman, Madurai), in interview with author, July 21, 2011.
108. "The Exhibitionary Complex," in Bennett, *The Birth of the Museum*, 59–88.
109. Arjun Appadurai and Carol A. Breckenridge, "Museums Are Good to Think: Heritage on View in India," in *Museums and Communities: The Politics of Public Culture*, ed. Ivan Karp, Christine Mullen Kreamer, and Steven Lavine, (Washington, D.C. and London: Smithsonian Institution Press, 1992), 34–55, 35.
110. George, interview, July 21, 2011.
111. K. P. Bharathi (Tourism Programme leader, DHAN Foundation, Madurai), in interview with author, July 25, 2011.
112. Michael A. Di Giovine, *The Heritage-scape: UNESCO, World Heritage, and Tourism* (Lanham, MD: Lexington Books, 2009), 208–213.
113. Di Giovine, *The Heritage-scape*, 360–365.
114. Henri Lefebvre, *The Production of Space*, trans. Donald Nicholson-Smith (Cambridge, MA: Blackwell, 1991), 73.

Epilogue

Rejecting the State

Priestly Devotion and Protest in Modern Madurai

The annual Vasantam Utsavam ('spring festival') at the Madurai temple marks the transition to spring in the Tamil month of Vaikāci (May/June). Movable metal embodiments of Mīnākṣī and Sundareśvara (called *utsava mūrti*s) travel from their respective inner sanctums to the Pudu Maṇḍapam, and for ten days, loin-clothed priests perform rituals inside the pillared hall, where water that once filled the channels in the north and south trenches would have cooled the deities. Priests pray for good cultivation, timely rains, generous yield, and general prosperity. Strong men pull the god and goddess in their carts through the hall's inner corridor three times clockwise (*pradakṣiṇa*). When the deities are seated on the polished granite stage within the hall's central nave, the priests offer them (behind a green cloth screen) a covered plate of *puḷiyōtarai* ('tamarind rice'), *nīr mōr* ('spiced buttermilk'), and fruit such as mangos and cucumbers—devotees, priests, and temple officials will later consume the offering.[1] Then, the priests wave hand-held, oil-wicked brass lamps clockwise (*ārati*) in front of the idols (Figure E.1).[2]

Before Mīnākṣī and Sundareśvara depart for their temple shrines, the god and goddess pay tribute to Madurai's famous ruler, Tirumala Nāyaka. After the *ārati*, a priest walks to the stone statuary of the Nāyaka family projecting from columns, and halts at the end of the lineage near the portrayal of Tirumala. The priest conducts rituals on the body of Tirumala's sculpture while the gods watch. The ceremony is the same one done to living people who sponsor the temple: from atop a tall ladder, the priest anoints sandalwood paste on the king's forehead (*cantaṉakkāppu*), ties a silk scarf around his head (*parivaṭṭam*), and places a flower garland around his neck (*mālai mariyātai*) to honor the royal patron (Figure E.2).[3] Acting as a functionary of the god and goddess, the priest presents a plate of coconuts and plantains (*prasādam*) (Figure E.3). Then, Mīnākṣī and Sundareśvara move outward borne in procession. The divine images are held over the shoulders of temple workers, so they are level with the dynastic portraits that display their reverence to the passing gods with pressed palms. When the deities stop at

Figure E.1 Vasantam Utsavam ('spring festival') for Mīnākṣi and Sundareśvara, Pudu Maṇḍapam, 2017

Source: Photo by author.

Figure E.2 From atop a ladder, the priest places a garland (*mālai mariyātai*) on Tirumala Nāyaka's stone image, Pudu Maṇḍapam, 2017

Source: Photo by author.

Figure E.3 The priest presents a plate of coconuts and plantains (*prasādam*), Pudu Maṇḍapam, 2017

Source: Photo by author.

Tirumala Nāyaka's statue (Figure E.4), the priest raises a fire-flamed lamp at them (Figure E.5), and they are finally carried out of the Pudu Maṇḍapam for the return journey to their own *garbhagṛha*.

Temple honors (or *mariyātai*) have long played an important role in the social relations of the temple town. The receipt of temple honors established the king's share (*paṅku*) in the temple, and it was a way of legitimating the social and economic redistribution entailed by the religious ceremony.[4] By worshipping the deity, the ruler asserted his right to render service to the god through ritual, to allocate resources for the ritual, and to administer the complex social apparatus that made the ritual possible (the extraordinary physical and spiritual toil that sustains the temple). The practices of the temple's priests and its devotees can be understood in terms of *bhakti*, or personal devotion to a deity. *Bhakti* is sometimes glossed as "participation," derived from "*bhaj*," meaning "partake, participate"—by saying the divine being's name, by singing of the god, and by undertaking pilgrimage to the holy place, one can participate in divinity.[5] Christian Lee Novetzke explains:

> Just as public sphere requires literacy, the publics of *bhakti* in South Asia require "embodiment," the human as medium. This very useful notion of "embodiment" ... is deeply engaged in the performance of the discourse of *bhakti*. By "discourse"

Figure E.4 A fully venerated Tirumala Nāyaka, Pudu Maṇḍapam, 2017

Source: Photo by author.

> I mean the manifestations of *bhakti* not only in performance through song or literacy, but also through all those actions and bodily displays that make up *bhakti* in the broadest sense, such as ... pilgrimage, *pūjā*, *darśan*, the wearing of signs on the body, and so on. Embodiment, then, is not so much a technique of *bhakti* as its very epicenter: *bhakti* needs bodies.[6]

In the Pudu Maṇḍapam, Mīnākṣī and Sundareśvara are divine bodies, celestial forms embodied in the *mūrti*s ('divine images'). Those who encounter, engage, and experience the deities are devotional bodies, such as the daily worshippers and the priests who execute the ritual worship. The Pudu Maṇḍapam is the sacred place that connects these bodies and defines their relation to one another: it is inscribed sculpturally with scenes and figures from *Tiruviḷaiyāṭal Purāṇam*, the story of the sacred games that situated Madurai as Mīnākṣī and Śiva's domain on earth, and it is decorated with statues of Nāyaka royalty, considered the gods' representatives on earth.[7]

Temple honors cyclically affirm the relationship between the donor, deity, and *maṇṭapappaṭi*, a ceremony within the periodical festival that occurs in a *maṇḍapam*. In the Pudu Mandapam, *bhakti* (as 'devotion' and 'participation') is a regular activity performed and repeated by devotional bodies upon divine bodies, within the sacred space of the pillared hall. The god and goddess's *mūrti*s

Figure E.5 In front of Tirumala Nāyaka's statue, the priest raises a fire-flamed lamp to Mīnākṣi and Sundareśvara before they leave the Pudu Maṇḍapam, 2017

Source: Photo by author.

are brought before the image of Tirumala Nāyaka and priests complete rituals of worship on the monarch's portrait. The priests' bodies are indispensable for the ruler's ritual deification—the priest acts on behalf of the deities, and their spiritual service constitutes the basis of the sovereign's divinity. Priests treat the granite carving of the long-dead king as though it were the auspicious and breathing body of a living donor of the temple; they enact the same rituals to the stone king as they do to the living donor of the temple.

When alive, Tirumala Nāyaka provided resources so that Mīnākṣī and Sundareśvara could be revered in religious festivals that took place in his new hall: Tirumala himself was the locus of these temple functions, which linked the royal body to the bodies of the deities, and authorized the king as the gods' representative. Through acts of charity and gift-giving, Tirumala positioned himself in a direct transactional association with the divine: worship not only involves the donor paying respects to the deity, but also necessitates that the deity gives back to the donor. This reciprocity is represented symbolically by the presentation of a silk scarf to the deity, which is subsequently tied around the donor's head. In another symbolic exchange, after the donor offers to the deity, the deity returns a portion of the offerings (*atikam*) to the donor.[8] Carol A. Breckenridge observes that this cycle of redistribution (*viṉiyōkam*) has a fundamentally *political* function: "The donor ... is confirmed as 'ruler' over his particular domain which is a family, a caste, a monastery, or an estate. By confirming deities and men as rulers, *pūjā* is an exercise of 'politics' clothed in Temple rituals."[9] Through the sacred ceremony,

Figure E.6 Devotees pay reverence to Tirumala Nāyaka, Pudu Maṇḍapam, 2017

Source: Photo by author.

the divine sovereignty of the god and goddess and the political sovereignty of the Nāyakas become fused at the temple site (Figure E.6).

The Nāyakas have not ruled Madurai since the eighteenth century—yet Madurai temple priests (*bhaṭṭārs*) believe that Tirumala Nāyaka and other Hindu kings were the last true protectors of the Madurai temple, based on the rightful Āgamic ordering of society.[10] Āgamas are Sanskrit texts that prescribe the priests' role at Śaiva temples, such as the proper procedures for performing rituals and worshipping of deities, and specify the correct methods of constructing temples and creating idols, and so on. Priests told me throughout my time in Madurai that they did not accept the British colonial government as legitimate successors to the Nāyaka dynasty—nor do they acknowledge the legitimacy of the modern government, that is, the Tamil Nadu state, or its functionaries in the Hindu Religious and Charitable Endowments (HR & CE) Department, which administers the state's temples.[11] Despite the state apparatuses' newfound involvement in the social and economic affairs of the temple (for example, in regulating the flow of bodies through religious tourism, or in regulating state funds endowed to the temple), the state cannot replace the Hindu king in the triangle of interdependencies that joined the south Indian monarch, priests, and deities together at the temple site. As C. J. Fuller writes, today "the link between god and ruler has been broken, and the circle of exchanges between the three parties has been cut."[12]

Priests harbor an extraordinary disdain for the British colonial state and the post-independence state governments that followed it. The Tamil Nadu Hindu Religious and Charitable Endowments Act XXII of 1959 codified the HR & CE Department's financial and managerial control over the state's temples. The priests' antipathy is influenced by the economic status of the temple: unlike in some other Tamil temples, priests at the Mīnākṣī temple do not receive a salary from the HR & CE Department and must rely on *dakṣiṇā* (donation to a priest after a ritual) for their income.[13] An important effect of the 1959 Act was granting the HR & CE Department permission to oversee *iṉāms* (Arabic, 'gift' or 'reward'), or plots of rent-free land that Hindu rulers from the Pāṇḍyas to the Nāyakas gifted to Brahmins, temples, and charities to reward and to publicly recognize them for their religious services. Such grants, which were often engraved on copperplates or stone slabs, were central to the political philosophy of south Indian kingship: they were an essential mechanism of exchange between the kings who sought divine authority and the priests who transmitted divine sovereignty through sacred ritual.[14] As Nicholas Dirks notes:

> One of the fundamental requirements of Indic kingship was that the king be a munificent provider of fertile lands for Brahmans who study and chant the Vedas, perform sacrifices and provide ritual services for the king so as to ensure and protect his prosperity and that of his kingdom; for temples, which were the centers of worship; for festivals ... which renewed the sovereignty of the king and regenerated the kingdom, and which together with temples were central to the constitution and maintenance of the social collectivities of localities, villages, castes, and subcastes; and for *cattirams* (chatrams, also called choultries, which were feeding, sometimes lodging, houses for pilgrims), which provided sustenance and shelter for itinerant Brahmans and pilgrims. The merit (*puṇyam*) of a king who made a grant could be shared by all those who protected the gift, a duty enjoined upon all subsequent kings.[15]

The *iṉām* was a vital means of distributing wealth and administering land—consequently, it was an obvious target of British political interference. The dissolution of privileges given to *iṉāmdārs* ('holders of *iṉāms*') began during nineteenth-century British rule, as the East India Company increased its grip on the Madras Presidency's administrative, economic, judicial, and military powers. British officials moved to invalidate the tax-exempt land grants because they did not generate revenue for the British.[16] In 1824, the London Court of Directors ordered that no new *iṉām* grants be made; in the 1830s and 1840s, the Board of Revenue instructed district collectors to scrutinize every *iṉām* title and to uncover "false" claims; in 1858, an Inam Commission was launched in the Madras Presidency to register all *iṉāms* and issue title deeds with the hope of altering revenue immunities that did not meet British criteria of antiquity, heredity, or conformity into money-generating properties; and during the 1860s, some *iṉām* rights were converted into regular rights (alienable and transferable) in landed property.[17]

In the twentieth century, Indian governments advanced the agenda of the British land reforms, which aimed to break the reciprocal bond between gods, priests, and royal figures. In 1925, the Madras government created an independent Hindu Religious Endowments Board to supervise the financial administration of temple, and in 1951 this Board was replaced with the HR & CE Department. The 1959 Act gave the Tamil Nadu government complete power to sanction the sale or transfer of *iṉām* lands, and eliminated *bhaṭṭa-vṛtti iṉāms* (once comprising more than half of all *iṉāms* in the Madras Presidency[18]) that priests had depended on for subsistence.[19] Section 41 (1) of the Act declared any gift of land exceeding five years "*null and void*."[20] One priest expressed his frustration at the mass confiscation of land swapped for small monetary payments: "The current democratic government after independence has plucked all the land from our hands. They gave compensation, but that one-time settlement will be easily gone away. Land always gives renewable resources, no? This system has come to a failure due to the government's action."[21]

Present-day honors to the Nāyakas establish the Pudu Mandapam as a space to refuse the sovereignty of the modern nation-state. The Nāyaka king's granite portrait serves not only as an icon of his previous reign, but also as a vehicle for priests to conceptualize their own resistance to contemporary political authority. While priests mourn the bodily absence of the patron king, they venerate his bodily presence in the stone image located in the pillared hall. The ritual is a performance of the needful interchange between priests, rulers, and deities in precolonial India that finds no substitute in the present-day democratic nation-state. Nevertheless, the private, embodied claims of a priestly community—in the guise of *bhakti*—illustrate an unconventional form of political agency in Hindu devotion. The reverence of the Nāyaka statue, seen against the backdrop of conflict between temple priests and government officers at the temple site, exposes a deep-rooted antagonism: the priests regard an ancient Hindu king's patronage of the temple more highly than they do the existing political structure.

The priests' ritual is a fundamentally political act, which defies the sovereignty of the modern state by repeatedly conducting the circle of exchange that connects the donor (the Nāyaka king) and the deity (Mīnākṣī) together in the sacred *maṇḍapam* ('pillared hall'), abiding by the seasonal rhythms of the *maṇṭapappaṭi* (the Eṇṇai Kāppu Utsavam and Vasantam Utsavam ceremonies). The adorned figures and the sacred site they inhabit constitute a unique kind of spiritual geography facing extinction, in confrontation with the demands of modern capital in Madurai, which are driving the remaking of the pillared hall into a middle-class tourist destination. Whereas the ornamented god in the temple festival is "conceivable," a colorful, living body in the *bhakti* (devotional and participatory) practices that bind worshippers and deities together, the unornamented god in a museum display case is "naked."[22] As Joanne Waghorne argues, following philosopher Ananda K. Coomaraswamy, the various multicolored accessories on the mobile metal idol are not "ancillary" or subsidiary to the god—these accoutrements are *materially* part of the divine. The ritual celebration of the deity is a basic manifestation of divinity: the Hindu worshipper *experiences* god in partaking of the deity's distinctive representational form, jewels, silks, garlands, and all.

Sundareśvara required a place where he could receive the homage of Tirumala Nāyaka and his subjects—he agreed to leave his "dark cell in the temple and pay the king an annual visit of ten days' duration" on the condition that the monarch construct "a hall worthy of his [Sundareśvara's] dignity."[23] Four centuries after the construction of the Pudu Maṇḍapam, the temple town is a compelling illustration of the internal contradictions of the postcolonial state. Today, there are increasingly aggressive efforts to define a 'Hindu state,' mobilized by a radical, ethnocentric discourse of religious nationalism, while at the same time the basic social and economic relationships that once defined Hindu spirituality are being further eroded and replaced by networks of transnational capital.

Author and activist Arundhati Roy observed that the trickle-down promise of economic liberalization in India was a lie: today, the combined wealth of one hundred of India's richest people comprises one-fourth of the country's gross domestic product (GDP), while 80 percent of the population subsists on less than half a dollar a day, millions suffering from malnutrition and curable disease.[24] For Roy, a useful artifact of Indian capitalism is Antilia, a Mumbai skyscraper belonging to India's richest man, Mukesh Ambani. The "most expensive house" ever built, it boasts twenty-seven floors, three helipads, climate-controlled rooms, hanging gardens, six hundred servants, and six floors of parking for Ambani's fleet of rare automobiles—and, from top to bottom, a "vertical lawn," an external wall of grass attached to a massive metal grid, with dry patches falling off in neat rectangles. "Clearly," Roy wrote, "Trickledown hadn't worked. But Gush-Up certainly has."[25]

We can significantly develop our thinking about the concept of 'sovereignty' by examining its manifestation in architecture, through which mechanisms of power are both articulated in ideal forms and realized through practical use. Far from Mukesh Ambani's palatial home in Mumbai, the reverberations of the postcolonial governing experiment are deeply felt in the temple town in Tamil Nadu. By tracing the transformations of the Nāyaka-era Pudu Maṇḍapam through the centuries, we see how a type of Hindu political spirituality was effectively dismantled, and its institutions progressively reconfigured around the flows of capital interjected by colonization—first by traveling artists and scholars in service of empire, then by indigenous elites educated in the colonial system, and finally by their children who internalized the fantasy of a consumerist middle class elevated by novel configurations of global tourism and trade. In this small temple site, we discover the trace of a political life that has all but disappeared, and the contours of emerging, dangerous political forms that transcend Madurai. The price to be paid for these transformations is still to be determined—but the answer will surely be found between the temple walls.

Notes

1. Such as the *pēṣkār* (heads the temple's internal administration office) and *maṇiyakkāraṉ* (keeps records of the accounts, *vāhanas*, or vehicles for deities' moveable festival images, and assets, as well as the yield from devotee-donated lands to the deity), who attend each day of the festival.
2. I observed the Vasantam Utsavam from May 29 to June 6, 2017.
3. According to a popular temple legend, after the completion of the first Vasantam ('spring') festival that also consecrated the Pudu Maṇḍapam in the seventeenth century, Tirumala Nāyaka received the deity's garland in person as *mariyātai*. For subsequent festivals, he directed that the temple honor be transferred to his life-size portrait within the Pudu Maṇḍapam. See William Taylor, "The Accounts of Tirumali-Naicker, and of His Buildings (As Extracted, for Information, from Written Authorities)," in *Oriental Historical Manuscripts, in the Tamil Language*, vol. II, ed. and trans. William Taylor (Madras: Printed and Published by Charles Josiah Taylor, 1835), 147–155, 155.
4. Arjun Appadurai and Carol Appadurai Breckenridge, "The South Indian Temple: Authority, Honour, and Redistribution," *Contributions to Indian Sociology* 10, no. 2 (July 1976): 187–211, 198.
5. For the idea of *bhakti* (devotion) as participation, see Karen Pechilis Prentiss, *The Embodiment of Bhakti* (New York and Oxford: Oxford University Press, 1999), 24.
6. Christian Lee Novetzke, "*Bhakti* and Its Public," *International Journal of Hindu Studies* 11, no. 3 (2007): 255–272, 261.

7. Barbara A. Holdrege's schema of "divine bodies," "devotional bodies," and "sacred space" provides a useful lens for understanding the function of *bhakti* in the Pudu Maṇḍapam. Focusing on the *Bhāgavata Purāṇa*, the sacred text that conveys an ecstatic form of *bhakti* towards Viṣṇu, and Gauḍīya Vaiṣṇava, a sixteenth-century *bhakti* tradition that promotes a personal relationship with Kṛṣṇa, Holdrege explores how devotees engage their own bodies in Vraja's sacred landscape in north India, where Kṛṣṇa descended to earth as a cowherd boy and engaged in *līlā* (divine play)—this terrain is "sacred" because it contains Kṛṣṇa's bodily presence. See Barbara A. Holdrege, *Bhakti and Embodiment: Fashioning Divine Bodies and Devotional Bodies in Kṛṣṇa Bhakti* (London and New York: Routledge, 2015).
8. "That is to say that he [the donor] is publicly honored in the dramatic context of his own *maṇṭapappaṭi*." Carol Appadurai Breckenridge, "The Śrī Mīṉākṣī-Sundareśvara Temple: Worship and Endowments in South India, 1833-1925" (PhD diss., University of Wisconsin-Madison, 1976), 112–113.
9. Breckenridge, "The Śrī Mīṉākṣī-Sundareśvara Temple," 124.
10. C. J. Fuller, *Servants of the Goddess: The Priests of a South Indian Temple* (Cambridge: Cambridge University Press, 1984), 144.
11. Priests (names withheld to protect their identities) (Mīnākṣī-Sundareśvara temple, Madurai), in interviews with author, December 14, 2011, June 1, 2017, and January 5, 2018. The Tamil Nadu government's HR & CE Department appoints the temple's executive officer, who heads the temple's administration (*dēvastānam*). See S. Rajaraman, *Commentaries on the Tamil Nadu Hindu Religious and Charitable Endowments Act, 1959 (Tamil Nadu Act 22 of 1959)* (Chennai: C. Sitaraman & Co, Pvt. Ltd., 2009), 1–7.
12. Fuller, *Servants of the Goddess*, 109.
13. Priest (name withheld to protect his identity), interview, January 5, 2018.
14. Mohammed Mustafa, "British Policy towards Inam Settlements in Madras Presidency 1801–1871" (PhD diss., University of Hyderabad, 1995), 32–78.
15. Nicholas B. Dirks, *The Hollow Crown: Ethnohistory of an Indian kingdom* (Cambridge: Cambridge University Press, 1987), 121–122.
16. Mohammed Mustafa, "The Shaping of Land Revenue Policy in Madras Presidency: Revenue Experiments—The Case of Chittoor District," *Indian Economic and Social History Review* 44, no. 2 (2007): 213–236, 222. See also David Ludden, *Peasant History in South India* (Princeton: Princeton University Press, 1985), 171. In 1803, the British collector in Madura was instructed to check those *iṉāmdārs* associated with the temple and immune from taxation. See J. H. Nelson, *The Madura Country: A Manual Compiled by Order of the Madras Government* (Madras: Asylum Press by William Thomas, 1868), Part VI: 129–130.

17. C. D. Maclean, *Standing Information Regarding the Official Administration of the Madras Presidency in Each Department, in Illustration of the Yearly Administration Reports* (Madras: E. Keys, at the Government Press, 1877), 163–173; *A Collection of Papers Relating to the Inam Settlement in the Madras Presidency* (Madras: Printed by the Superintendent, Government Press, 1906); David Washbrook, "Economic Depression and the Making of 'Traditional' Society in Colonial India 1820–1855," *Transactions of the Royal Historical Society* 3 (1993): 237–263.
18. Dharma Kumar, "Agrarian Relations: South India," in *The Cambridge Economic History of India Volume 2: c. 1757–c. 1970*, ed. Dharma Kumar (Cambridge: Cambridge University Press, 1989 [1983]), 207–241, 227.
19. Chandra Y. Mudaliar, *State and Religious Endowments in Madras* (Madras: University of Madras, 1976). See also Anthony Good, "'Māmul' and Modernity in a South Indian Temple," *Modern Asian Studies* 35, no. 4 (October 2001): 821–870.
20. Rajaraman, *Commentaries on the Tamil Nadu Hindu Religious and Charitable Endowments Act, 1959*, 83 (italics in original).
21. Priest (name withheld to protect identity) interview, January 5, 2018.
22. Joanne Punzo Waghorne, "Dressing the Body of God: South Indian Bronze Sculpture in Its Temple Setting," *Asian Art* 5, no. 3 (Summer 1992): 9–33, 13–14.
23. James Fergusson, *History of Indian and Eastern Architecture* (London: John Murray, 1876), 361. Fergusson is the subject of chapter 6.
24. "Is India on a Totalitarian Path? Arundhati Roy on Corporatism, Nationalism and World's Largest Vote," *Democracy Now!*, April 9, 2014, https://www.democracy-now.org/2014/4/9/is_india_on_a_totalitarian_path, accessed December 14, 2021.
25. Arundhati Roy, *Capitalism: A Ghost Story* (Chicago: Haymarket, 2014), 7.

Bibliography

Abu El-Haj, Nadia. *Facts on the Ground: Archaeological Practice and Territorial Self-Fashioning in Israeli Society*. Chicago and London: The University of Chicago Press, 2001.

A Catalogue of the Library of The Hon. East-India Company. London: J. & H. Cox, 1845.

A Copy of the Royal Charter and Statutes of the Society of Antiquaries of London and of Orders and Regulations Established by the Council of the Society. London: J. B. Nichols, 1837.

Adams, Nancy L., and Dennis M. Adams. "An Examination of Some Forces Affecting English Educational Policies in India: 1780–1850." *History of Education Quarterly* 11, no. 2 (Summer 1971): 157–173.

Adorno, Theodor W. *Prisms*. Translated by Samuel and Shierry Weber. Cambridge, MA: MIT Press, 1997 [1981].

Agamben, Giorgio. *State of Exception*. Translated by Kevin Attell. Chicago and London: The University of Chicago Press, 2005.

Agnew, John A., and James S. Duncan. "Introduction." In *The Power of Place: Bringing Together Geographical and Sociological Imaginations*, edited by John A. Agnew and James S. Duncan, 1–8. Boston: Unwin Hyman, 1989.

Aruṇakirinātar. *Aruṇakirinātar Aruḷiya Vēl Viruttam, Mayil Viruttam, Cēval Viruttam* (Tamil̲). Commentary by Va. Cu. Ceṅkalvarāya Piḷḷai. Cen̲n̲ai: Tirunelvēlit Ten̲n̲intiya Caivacittānta Nūr̲patippuk Kal̲akam, 1971.

Aiyar, R. Sathyanatha. *History of the Nayaks of Madura*. Introduction by S. Krishnaswami Aiyangar. Madras: Oxford University Press, 1924.

Ali, Daud. *Courtly Culture and Political Life in Early Medieval India*. Cambridge: Cambridge University Press, 2004.

Annamalai, S. "Chances for Madurai to Be IT Hub." *The Hindu*, September 24, 2012. http://www.thehindu.com/news/cities/Madurai/chances-for-madurai-to-be-it-hub/article3931404.ece, accessed December 14, 2021.

———. "Madurai to Have Yet Another Tourist Attraction." *The Hindu*, September 28, 2006. http://www.thehindu.com/todays-paper/tp-national/tp-tamilnadu/madurai-to-have-yet-another-tourist-attraction/article3082195.ece, accessed December 14, 2021.

"Annual Report of the Royal Asiatic Society of Great Britain and Ireland, 10th May, 1834." *Journal of the Royal Asiatic Society of Great Britain and Ireland* 1, no. 2 (1834): iii–xv. London: John W. Parker, 1834.

Annual Report on Epigraphy 1902–1903. Madras: Government of Madras Public Department. G.O., etc., Nos. 655–656, July 24, 1903.

Annual Report on Epigraphy 1908–1909. Madras: Government of Madras Public Department. G.O. No. 538, July 28, 1909.

Annual Report on Epigraphy 1909–1910. Madras: Government of Madras Public Department. G.O. No. 665, July 28, 1910.

Appadurai, Arjun. *Worship and Conflict under Colonial Rule: A South Indian Case*. Cambridge: Cambridge University Press, 1981.

Appadurai, Arjun, and Breckenridge, Carol A. "Museums Are Good to Think: Heritage on View in India." In *Museums and Communities: The Politics of Public Culture*, edited by Ivan Karp, Christine Mullen Kreamer, and Steven Lavine, 34–55. Washington, D.C. and London: Smithsonian Institution Press, 1992.

———. "The South Indian Temple: Authority, Honour, and Redistribution." *Contributions to Indian Sociology* 10, no. 2 (July 1976): 187–211.

Aravamuthan, T. G. *Portrait Sculpture in South India*. Foreword by Ananda K. Coomaraswamy. London: The India Society, 1931.

Archer, Mildred. *British Drawings in the India Office Library*. Vol. I: Amateur Artists. London: Her Majesty's Stationery Office, 1969.

———. *British Drawings in India Office Library*. Vol. II: Official and Professional Artists. London: Her Majesty's Stationery Office, 1969.

———. *Company Paintings: Indian Paintings of the British Period*. London: Victoria and Albert Museum; Ahmedabad: Mapin Publishing Pvt. Ltd., 1992.

———. *Early View of India: The Picturesque Journeys of Thomas and William Daniell 1786–1794*. London: Thames and Hudson Limited, 1980.

———. *Indian Architecture and the British 1780–1830*. Feltham, Middlesex: Country Life Books, 1968.

Armitage, David. "What's the Big Idea? Intellectual History and the Longue Durée." *History of European Ideas* 38, no. 4 (2012): 493–507.

Arokiaswami, M. *The Kongu Country: Being the History of the Modern Districts of Coimbatore and Salem from the Earliest Times to the Coming of the British*. Madras: University of Madras, 1956.

"ART. XI. Archaeologia, or, Miscellaneous Tracts relating to Antiquity. Vol. X." *Monthly Review; or, Literary Journal* 10 (January–April 1793 [February 1793]): 169–175. London: Printed for R. Griffiths, 1793.

"ART. XXIX. Biographical Sketch of the Literary Career of the Late Colonel Colin Mackenzie, Surveyor-General of India; Comprising Some Particulars of His Collection of Manuscripts, Plans, Coins, Drawings, Sculptures, &c. Illustrative of the Antiquities, History, Geography, Laws, Institutions, and Manners, of the Ancient Hindús; Contained in a Letter Addressed by Him to the Right Hon. Sir Alexander Johnston, V.P.R.A.S. &c. &c." *Journal of the Royal Asiatic Society of Great Britain and Ireland* 1, no. 2 (1834): 333–364. London: John W. Parker, 1834.

Arunachalam, Pon Vasanth. "IT Sector Growth in Madurai Gaining Momentum." *The Hindu*, December 28, 2015. http://www.thehindu.com/news/cities/Madurai/it-sector-growth-in-madurai-gaining-momentum/article8036576.ece, accessed December 14, 2021.

Asad, Talad. "The Construction of Religion as an Anthropological Category." In *Genealogies of Religion: Discipline and Reasons of Power in Christianity and Islam*, 27–54. Baltimore: Johns Hopkins University Press, 1993.

Auerbach, Jeffrey A. *The Great Exhibition of 1851: A Nation on Display*. New Haven: Yale University Press, 1999.

Balaram Iyer, T. G. S. *History & Description of Sri Meenakshi Temple*. Madurai: Sri Karthik Agency, 1988 [1984].

Banks, Joseph. "A Project in the Establishment of a Botanic Garden in the Island of Ceylon with a View to an Increase of the Resources of That Colony & an Improvement of the Science of Botany in Europe." BO 1:39, 1811. Sutro Library, California State Library, San Francisco.

Baskaran, S. Theodore. "Images from Tripe." *Frontline*, July 21, 2001. https://frontline.thehindu.com/other/article30251322.ece, accessed December 14, 2021.

Bayly, C. A. *Indian Society and the Making of the British Empire*. The New Cambridge History of India II.1. Cambridge and New York: Cambridge University Press, 1988.

———. "Knowing the Country: Empire and Information in India." *Modern Asian Studies* 27, no. 1 (February 1993): 3–43.

Bayly, Susan. *Saints, Goddesses, and Kings: Muslims and Christians in South Indian Society, 1700–1900*. Cambridge: Cambridge University Press, 1989.

Beck, Brenda E. F. "Colour and Heat in South Indian Ritual." *Man* 4, no. 4 (December 1969): 553–572.

Bell, Andrew. *The Madras School, or Elements of Tuition: Comprising the Analysis of an Experiment in Education, Made at the Male Asylum, Madras; with Its Facts, Proofs, and Illustrations....* London: G. Roake, 1808.

Ben-Dor Benite, Zvi, Stefanos Geroulanos, and Nicole Jerr, eds. *The Scaffolding of Sovereignty: Global and Aesthetic Perspectives on the History of a Concept*. New York: Columbia University Press, 2017.

Benedict, Barbara M. *Curiosity: A Cultural History of Early Modern Inquiry*. Chicago and London: The University of Chicago Press, 2001.

Bennett, Tony. *The Birth of the Museum: History, Theory, and Politics*. London and New York: Routledge, 1995.

Benton, Lauren. *A Search for Sovereignty: Law and Geography in European Empires, 1400–1900*. Cambridge: Cambridge University Press, 2010.

Berger, John. "Understanding a Photograph." In *Classic Essays about Photography*, edited by Alan Trachtenberg, 291–294. New Haven, CT: Leete's Island Book Inc., 1980.

Bermingham, Ann. *Landscape and Ideology: The English Rustic Tradition, 1740–1860*. Berkeley: University of California Press, 1986.

Bes, Lennart. "Sultan among Dutchmen? Royal Dress at Court Audiences in South India, as Portrayed in Local Works of Art and Dutch Embassy Reports, Seventeenth–Eighteenth Centuries." *Modern Asian Studies* 50, no. 6 (2016): 1792–1845.

———. *The Heirs of Vijayanagara: Court Politics in Early Modern South India*. Leiden: Leiden University Press, 2022.

Beveridge, Henry. *A Comprehensive History of India, Civil, Military and Social from First Landing of the English to the Suppression of the Sepoy Revolt Including an Outline of the Early History of Hindoostan*. Vol. III. London: Blackie and Son, Paternoster Row, E. C., 1862.

Bhabha, Homi K. "Signs Taken for Wonders: Questions of Ambivalence and Authority under a Tree outside Delhi, May 1817." In *The Location of Culture*, 102–122. London and New York: Routledge, 1994.

Bharath, Stéphanie Roy. "Recording South Indian Architecture: Linnaeus Tripe and Edmund David Lyon." *South Asian Studies* 26, no. 2 (2010): 97–118.

Biddick, Kathleen. *The Shock of Medievalism*. Durham and London: Duke University Press, 1998.

Blackader, Adam. "XL. Description of the Great Pagoda of Madura, and the Choultry of Trimul Naik, in a Letter from Mr. Adam Blackader, Surgeon, to Sir Joseph Banks, Bart. P. R. S. F. A. S." *Archaeologia, or, Miscellaneous Tracts Relating to Antiquity. Published by the Society of Antiquaries of London* 10 (1792): 449–459.

———. Letter to Sir Joseph Banks. 1789. Item No. 690. Society of Antiquaries Library, London.

Blackburn, Stuart [H.]. "Corruption and Redemption: The Legend of Valluvar and Tamil Literary History." *Modern Asian Studies* 34, no. 2 (May 2000): 449–482.

———. "The Kallars: A Tamil 'Criminal Tribe' Reconsidered." *South Asia: Journal of South Asian Studies* 1, no. 1 (1978): 38–51.

Blain, Virginia. "Letitia Elizabeth Landon, Eliza Mary Hamilton, and the Genealogy of the Victorian Poetess." *Victorian Poetry* 33, no. 1 (Spring 1995): 31–51.

Blake, David M. "Colin Mackenzie: Collector Extraordinary." *British Library Journal* 17, no. 2 (Autumn 1991): 128–150.

Blanchard, Laman. *Life and Literary Remains of L. E. L.* Vol. I. London: Henry Colburn, 1841.

Boon, James A. *Verging on Extra-Vagance: Anthropology, History, Religion, Literature, Arts ... Showbiz*. Princeton: Princeton University Press, 1999.

Boria, Cavelly. "IV. Account of the Jains Collected from a Priest of This Sect at Mudgeri: Translated by Cavelly Boria, Bráhmen, for Major C. Mackenzie." *Asiatic Researches: or, Transactions of the Society Instituted in Bengal, for Inquiring into the History and Antiquities, the Arts, Sciences, and Literature, of Asia* 9 (1809): 244–271. London: Vernor, Hood, and Sharpe, etc., 1809.

Bose, Sugata, and Ayesha Jalal. *Modern South Asia: History, Culture, Political Economy*. 3rd edition. London and New York: Routledge, 2004.

Branfoot, Crispin. "Dynastic Genealogies, Portraiture, and the Place of the Past in Early Modern South India." *Artibus Asiae* 72, no. 2 (2012): 323–376.

———. "'Expanding Form': The Architectural Sculpture of the South Indian Temple ca. 1500–1700." *Artibus Asiae* 62, no. 2 (2002): 189–245.

———. *Gods on the Move: Architecture and Ritual in the South Indian Temple*. London: The Society for South Asian Studies, 2007.

———. "Heroic Rulers and Devoted Servants: Performing Kingship in the Tamil Temple." In *Portraiture in South Asia since the Mughals: Art, Presentation and History*, edited by Crispin Branfoot, 165–197. London and New York: I. B. Tauris & Co., 2018.

———. "Royal Portrait Sculpture in the South Indian Temple." *South Asian Studies* 16, no. 1 (2000): 11–36.

———. "Tirumala Nayaka's 'New Hall' and the European Study of the South Indian Temple." *Journal of the Royal Asiatic Society* 11, no. 2 (2001): 191–217.

Breckenridge, Carol Appadurai. "The Śrī Mīṉākṣī-Sundarēsvarar Temple: Worship and Endowments in South India, 1833 to 1925." PhD diss., University of Wisconsin-Madison, 1976.

———. "The Aesthetics and Politics of Colonial Collecting: India at World Fairs." *Comparative Studies in Society and History* 13, no. 2 (April 1989): 195–216.

Bryce, James. "The Nature of Sovereignty." In *Studies in History and Jurisprudence*. Vol. II, 503–555. New York: Oxford University Press, 1901.

Byron, Glennis. "Landon, Letitia Elizabeth (1802–1838)." In *Oxford Dictionary of National Biography*. Vol. XXXII, 391–394. Oxford: Oxford University Press, 2004.

Campbell, Lyle. "Why Sir William Jones Got It All Wrong, or Jones' Role in How to Establish Language Families." *Anuario del Seminario de Filología Vasca "Julio de Urquijo"* (International Journal of Basque Linguistics and Philology) 40, nos. 1–2 (2006): 245–264.

Cameron, Charles Hay. *An Address to Parliament on the Duties of Great Britain to India in Respect of the Education of the Natives, and Their Official Employment*. London: Longman, Brown, Green, and Longmans, 1853.

Cannon, Garland. "Sir William Jones and the Association between East and West." *Proceedings of the American Philosophical Society* 121, no. 2 (April 29, 1977): 183–187.

———. "Sir William Jones, Sir Joseph Banks, and the Royal Society." *Notes and Records of the Royal Society of London* 29, no. 2 (March 1975): 205–230.

———, ed. *The Letters of Sir William Jones.* Vol. II. Oxford: Clarendon Press, 1970.

Cannon, Garland, and Siddheswar Pandey. "Sir William Jones Revisited: On His Translation of the Śakuntalā." *Journal of the American Oriental Society* 96, no. 4 (October–December 1976): 528–535.

Caunter, Hobart. *The Cadet; A Poem, in Six Parts: Containing Remarks on British India. To Which Is Added, Egbert and Amelia; In Four Parts: with Other Poems.* 2 vols. London: Robert Jennings, 1814.

———. *The Romance of History. India*. 3 vols. London: Edward Churton, 1836.

Caunter, Hobart, and William Daniell. *The Oriental Annual. Lives of the Moghul Emperors. By the Rev. Hobart Caunter, B.D. With Twenty-Two Engravings from Drawings by William Daniell R.A.* London: Charles Tilt, 1837.

Cellinakar Perumpaṟṟapuliyūr Nampi. *Tiruvālavāyuṭaiyār Tiruviḷaiyāṭaṟpurāṇam* (Tamiḻ). Commentary by U. Vē. Cāminātaiyar. Ceṉṉai: Kapīr Accukkūṭattiṟ Patippikkappeṟṟatu, 1972 [1906].

Chadwick, Edwin. *Report to Her Majesty's Principal Secretary of State for the Home Department, from the Poor Law Commissioners, on an Inquiry into the Sanitary Condition of the Labouring Population of Great Britain; With Appendices. Presented to Both Houses of Parliament, by Command of Her Majesty, July, 1842.* London: W. Clowes and Sons, 1842.

Chambers, Neil. *Joseph Banks and the British Museum: The World of Collecting, 1770–1830.* London: Pickering & Chatto, 2007.

———, ed. *The Indian and Pacific Correspondence of Sir Joseph Banks, 1768–1820.* Vol. II: *Letters 1783–1789.* London: Pickering & Chatto, 2009.

———. *The Indian and Pacific Correspondence of Sir Joseph Banks, 1768–1820.* Vol. III: *Letters 1789–1792.* London: Pickering & Chatto, 2010.

Chandar, B. Tilak. "Pudu Mandapam Shopkeepers' Woes to End Soon." *The Hindu*, April 16, 2018. http://www.thehindu.com/news/cities/Madurai/pudu-mandapam-shopkeepers-woes-to-end-soon/article23553548.ece, accessed December 14, 2021.

Chandra, Pramod. *On the Study of Indian Art*. Cambridge, MA: Harvard University Press, 1983.

Chatterjee, Partha. "Colonialism, Nationalism, and Colonized Women: The Contest in India." *American Ethnologist* 16, no. 4 (November 1989): 622–633.

Chekuri, Christopher. "A 'Share' in the 'World Empire': Nayamkara as Sovereignty in Practice at Vijayanagara, 1480–1580." *Social Scientist* 40, no. 1/2 (January–February 2012): 41–67.

Chhabra, Deepak, Robert Healy, and Erin Sills. "Staged Authenticity and Heritage Tourism." *Annuals of Tourism Research* 30, no. 3 (2003): 702–719.

Chilkoti, Avantika. "India: Emerging Cities." *Financial Times*, October 19, 2012. https://www.ft.com/content/4fc08f8f-e8a9-3dc5-a7f3-60004804ff5a, accessed December 14, 2021.

Clive, John Leonard. *Macaulay: The Shaping of the Historian*. New York: Alfred A. Knopf, 1974.

Cohn, Bernard S. *Colonialism and Its Forms of Knowledge: The British in India*. Princeton: Princeton University Press, 1996.

Cole, H. H. *Catalogue of the Objects of Indian Art Exhibited in the South Kensington Museum*. London: George E. Eyre and William Spottiswoode, 1874.

———. *Preservation of National Monuments. Third Report of the Curator of Ancient Monuments in India, for the Year 1883–84*. Calcutta: Printed by the Superintendent of Government Printing, 1885.

Coleman, Charles. *The Mythology of the Hindus, with Notices of Various Mountain and Island Tribes, Inhabiting the Two Peninsulas of India and the Neighbouring Islands, and an Appendix, Comprising the Minor Avatars, and the Mythological and Religious Terms, &c. &c., of the Hindus*. London: Parbury, Allen, and Co., 1832.

Confederation of Indian Industry. "About Us." 2021. http://www.cii.in/About_Us.aspx?enc=ns9fJzmNKJnsoQCyKqUmaQ==, accessed December 14, 2021.

Connolly, Tristanne J. "'The Authority of the Ancients': Blake and Wilkins' Translation of the *Bhagvat-Geeta*." In *The Reception of Blake in the Orient*, edited by Steve Clark and Masashi Suzuki, 145–158. London: Continuum, 2006.

Council of the Society of Antiquaries. Vol. III. MDCCLXXXV. From April 8, 1785, to December 16, 1803. Society of Antiquaries Library, London.

Cunningham, Alexander. *Archæological Survey of India: Four Reports Made during the Years 1862–63–64–65*. Vol. I. Simla: Government Central Press, 1871.

d'Hancarville, Pierre. *Recherches sur l'origine, l'esprit et les progrès des arts de la Grèce; sur leurs connections avec les arts et la religion des plus anciens peuples connus; sur les monumens antiques de l'Inde, de la Perse, du reste de l'Asie, de l'Europe et de l'Égypte*. Londres: Chez B. Appleyard, 1785.

Daniell, Thomas. *Views in Calcutta*. Calcutta: 1786–1788.

Daniell, Thomas, and William Daniell. *A Picturesque Voyage to India; by the Way of China. By Thomas Daniell, R.A. and William Daniell, A.R.A.* London: Longman, Hurst, Rees & Orme, 1810.

———. I. *Oriental Scenery: Twenty-Four Views in Hindoostan, Taken in the Years 1789 and 1790; Drawn and Engraved by Thomas Daniell, and, with Permission, Respectfully Dedicated to the Honourable Court of Directors of the East India Company*. London: Robert Bowyer, March 1, 1795.

———. II. *Oriental Scenery: Twenty-Four Views in Hindoostan, Taken in the Year 1792; Drawn by Thomas Daniell, and Engraved by Himself, and William Daniell; and, with Permission, Respectfully Dedicated to the Right Honourable Henry Dundas, One of His Majesty's Principal Secretaries of State, President of the Board of Commissioners for the Affairs of India, Treasurer of the Navy, &c. &c. &c.* London: Thomas Daniell, August 1797.

———. III. *Oriental Scenery: Twenty-Four Views in Hindoostan, Drawn and Engraved by Thomas & William Daniell, and, with Permission, Respectfully Dedicated to the Right Honourable George Viscount Lewisham, President of the Board of Commissioners for the Affairs of India.* London: Thomas Daniell, June 1801.

———. IV. *Twenty-Four Landscapes, the Fourth Series: Views in Hindoostan; Drawn and Engraved by Thomas and William Daniell, with Permission Respectfully Dedicated to the Right Honourable George O'Brien, Earl of Egremont.* London: Thomas Daniell, May 1807.

———. V. *Antiquities of India: Twelve Views from the Drawings of Thomas Daniell R.A. & F.S.A.; Engraved by Himself, and William Daniell; Taken in the Years 1790 and 1793; Dedicated Respectfully to the Society of Antiquaries of London.* London: Thomas Daniell, 1800.

———. VI. *Hindoo Excavations: In the Mountain of Ellora, near Aurungabad in the Decan, in Twenty-Four Views; Respectfully Dedicated to Sir Charles Warre Malet, Bart. Late the British Resident at Poonah; Engraved from the Drawings of James Wales, by and under the Direction of Thomas Daniell.* London: Thomas Daniell, June 1, 1804.

———. *Oriental Scenery. One Hundred and Fifty Views of the Architecture, Antiquities, and Landscape Scenery of Hindoostan. Drawn and Engraved by Thomas and William Daniell.* Vol. I. London: [G. Norman for] the Authors, 1816.

Daniell, William, and Hobart Caunter. *Oriental Annual, or Scenes in India; Comprising Twenty-Five Engravings from Original Drawings by William Daniell, R.A. and a Descriptive Account by the Rev. Hobart Caunter, B.D.* London: Edward Bull, 1834.

———.*Oriental Annual, or Scenes in India; Comprising Twenty-Two Engravings from Original Drawings by William Daniell, R.A. and a Descriptive Account by the Rev. Hobart Caunter, B.D.* London: Edward Churton, 1836.

Daniels, Stephen. "Arguments for a Humanistic Geography." In *The Future of Geography*, edited by R. J. Johnston, 143–158. London and New York: Methuen, 1985.

Dasandi, Niheer. "What Do Indian Middle Class Attitudes to Poverty Tell Us About the Politics of Poverty Reduction?" The Developmental Leadership Program Research Paper 33, January 2015. https://www.dlprog.org/publications/research-papers/what-do-indian-middle-class-attitudes-to-poverty-tell-us-about-the-politics-of-poverty-reduction, accessed December 14, 2021.

Davis, Richard H. "Wilkins, Hastings, and the First English *Bhagavad Gītā*." *International Journal of Hindu Studies* 19, no. 1/2 (April–August 2015): 39–57.

de Certeau, Michel. *The Practice of Everyday Life.* Translated by Steven F. Rendall. Berkeley and Los Angeles: University of California Press, 1984.

Dehejia, Vidya. "The Very Idea of a Portrait." *ARS Orientalis* 38 (1998): 40–48.

Democracy Now! "Is India on a Totalitarian Path? Arundhati Roy on Corporatism, Nationalism and World's Largest Vote." April 9, 2014. https://www.democracynow.org/2014/4/9/is_india_on_a_totalitarian_path, accessed December 14, 2021.

Dennis, James Shepard. *Christian Missions and Social Progress: A Sociological Study of Foreign Missions.* Vol. III. New York: Fleming H. Revell Company, 1906.

Desai, Madhuri. "Interpreting an Architectural Past: Ram Raz and the Treatise in South Asia." *Journal of the Society of Architectural Historians* 71, no. 4 (December 2012): 462–487.

Despatch No. 22 of 1855, February 7, 1855. Despatches to India and Bengal. January 3 to March 28, 1855. IOR/E/4/829, ff. 623–626. British Library, Asia, Pacific, and Africa Collections, London.

Devakunjari, D. *Madurai through the Ages: From the Earliest Times to 1801 A.D.* Madras: Society for Archaeological, Historical, and Epigraphical Research, 1979.

Devanathani, V. "Pudu Mandapam Battered by Shopkeepers." *Times of India*, August 19, 2013. http://timesofindia.indiatimes.com/city/madurai/Pudu-Mandapam-battered-by-shopkeepers/articleshow/21906234.cms, accessed December 14, 2021.

Dewan, Janet. "Linnaeus Tripe: Critical Assessments and Other Notes." *Photographic Collector* 5, no. 1 (Fall 1984): 47–65.

———. *The Photographs of Linnaeus Tripe: A Catalogue Raissoné.* Toronto: Art Gallery of Ontario, 2003.

DHAN Foundation, Madurai. *Annual Report 2009.* http://www.dhan.org/Downloads/annual_report_2009.pdf, accessed December 14, 2021.

Diekmann, Anya, and Hannam, Kevin. "Touristic Mobilities in India's Slum Spaces." *Annals of Tourism Research* 39, no. 3 (July 2012): 1315–1336.

Di Giovine, Michael A. *The Heritage-scape: UNESCO, World Heritage, and Tourism.* Lanham, MD: Lexington Books, 2009.

Dirks, Nicholas B. *Castes of Mind: Colonialism and the Making of Modern India.* Princeton: Princeton University Press, 2001.

———. "Colonial Histories and Native Informants: Biography of an Archive." In *Orientalism and the Postcolonial Predicament: Perspectives on South Asia*, edited by Carol A. Breckenridge and Peter van der Veer, 279–313. Philadelphia: University of Pennsylvania Press, 1993.

———. "Guiltless Spoilations: Picturesque Beauty, Colonial Knowledge, and Colin Mackenzie's Survey of India." In *Perceptions of South Asia's Visual Past*, edited by Catherine B. Asher and Thomas R. Metcalf, 211–232. New Delhi: American Institute of Indian Studies; Madras: Swadharma Swarajya Sangha; New Delhi: Oxford & IBH Publishing Co., 1994.

———. *The Hollow Crown: Ethnohistory of an Indian Kingdom*. Cambridge: Cambridge University Press, 1987.

Doniger O'Flaherty, Wendy. *The Origins of Evil in Hindu Mythology*. Berkeley and Los Angeles: University of California Press, 1976.

Duff, Alexander. "Female Education in India: Being the Substance of an Address Delivered at the First Annual Meeting of the Scottish Ladies' Association for the Promotion of Female Education in India, in 1839." In *Missionary Addresses Delivered before the General Assembly of the Church of Scotland, in the Years 1835, 1837, 1839. With Additional Papers on Female Education, and the Danish, or Earliest Protestant Mission to India*, 217–273. Edinburgh: Johnstone & Hunter, 1850.

Dumont, Louis. *A South Indian Subcaste: Social Organization and Religion of the Pramalai Kallar*. Translated by M. Moffat, L. Morton, and A. Morton. Oxford and New York: Oxford University Press, 1986.

Eck, Diana L. *Darśan. Seeing the Divine Image in India*. New York: Columbia University Press, 1998.

Edney, Matthew H. *Mapping an Empire: The Geographical Construction of British India, 1765–1843*. Chicago and London: The University of Chicago Press, 1997 [1990].

Entrikin, J.-Nicholas. *The Betweenness of Place: Towards a Geography of Modernity*. Baltimore: Johns Hopkins University Press, 1991.

Evans, Joan. *A History of the Society of Antiquaries*. Oxford: Oxford University Press, 1956.

Falconer, John. "A Passion for Documentation: Architecture and Ethnography." In *India through the Lens: Photography from 1840–1911*, edited by Vidya Dehejia, 69–85. Washington, D.C.: Freer Gallery of Art and Arthur M. Sakler Gallery, Smithsonian Institution; Ahmedabad: Mapin Publishing Pvt. Ltd.; Munich and London: Prestel Verlag, 2000.

———. "Photography in Nineteenth-Century India." In *The Raj: India and the British, 1600–1947*, edited by C. A. Bayly, 264–277. London: National Portrait Gallery Publications, 1990.

———. *India: Pioneering Photographers 1850–1900*. London: British Library, 2001.

Farington, Joseph. *The Diary of Joseph Farington*. Vol. II: January 1795–August 1796, edited by Kenneth Garlick and Angus Macintyre. New Haven: Yale University Press for the Paul Mellon Centre for Studies in British Art, 1978.

Fellowes, Robert. *History of Ceylon, from the Earliest Period to the Year MDCCCXV; with Characteristic Details of the Religion, Laws, & Manners of the People and a*

Collection of Their Moral Maxims & Ancient Proverbs. By Philalethes, A.M. Oxon. To Which Is Subjoined, Robert Knox's Historical Relation of the Island, with an Account of His Captivity during a Period of Near Twenty Years. London: Joseph Mawman, 1817.

Fergusson, James. *An Historical Inquiry into the True Principles of Beauty in Art, More Especially with Reference to Architecture*. London: Longman, Brown, Green, and Longmans, 1849.

———. *Archæology in India, with Especial Reference to the Works of Babu Rajendralal Mitra*. London: Trübner and Co., 1884.

———. *History of Indian and Eastern Architecture*. London: John Murray, 1876.

———. *Illustrations of Various Styles of Indian Architecture. A Series of Fifteen Photographs of Some of the Most Important Buildings in India Erected between B.C. 250 and A.D. 1830. With a Lecture on the Study of Indian Architecture, Read at a Meeting of the Society of Arts, on 19th December, 1866*. London: Printed for the use of schools of art in the United Kingdom, 1869.

———. *On the Study of Indian Architecture, Read at a Meeting of the Society of Arts on Wednesday, 19th December, 1866*. London: John Murray, 1867.

———. *One Hundred Stereoscopic Illustrations of Architecture and Natural History in Western India, Photographed by Major Gill and Described by James Fergusson*. London: Cundall, Downes, & Company, 1864.

———. *Picturesque Illustrations of Ancient Architecture in Hindostan*. London: J. Hogarth, 1848.

———. *Tree and Serpent Worship: or Illustrations of Mythology and Art in India in the First and Fourth Centuries after Christ. From the Sculptures of the Buddhist Topes at Sanchi and Amravati.* London: India Museum, 1868.

Fernandez, Jean. "Graven Images: The Woman Writer, the Indian Poetess, and Imperial Aesthetics in L.E.L.'s 'Hindoo Temples and Palaces at Madura.'" *Victorian Poetry* 43, no. 1 (Spring 2005): 35–52.

Fisher, Elaine M. *Hindu Pluralism: Religion and the Public Sphere in Early Modern South India.* Oakland: University of California Press, 2017.

"Fisher's Drawing Room Scrapbook." *The Victorian Web.* 2020. http://victorianweb.org/periodicals/scrapbook/index.html, accessed December 14, 2021.

Forbes, Geraldine. *Women in Modern India*. The New Cambridge History of India IV.2. Cambridge: Cambridge University Press, 1996.

Foucault, Michel. *Discipline and Punish: The Birth of the Prison.* New York: Vintage, 1995.

———. *Ethics: Subjectivity and Truth*. Vol. I, edited by Paul Rabinow. New York: The New Press, 1997.

———. "Nietzsche, Genealogy, History." In *Language, Counter-Memory, Practice: Selected Essays and Interviews*, edited by D. Bourchard, 139–164. Ithaca: Cornell University Press, 1977.

———. *Power/Knowledge: Selected Interviews and Other Writings 1972–1977*, edited by Colin Gordon. New York: Pantheon Books, 1980.

Francis, W. *Madras District Gazetteers: Madura*. Vol. I. Madras: Printed by the Superintendent, Government Press, 1906.

Freitag, Jason. *Serving Empire, Serving Nation: James Tod and the Rajputs of Rajasthan*. Leiden and Boston: Brill, 2009.

Frew, John M. "Richard Gough, James Wyatt, and Late 18th-Century Preservation." *Journal of the Society of Architectural Historians* 38, no. 4 (December 1979): 366–374.

Fritz, John M., and George Michell. "Living Heritage at Risk: Searching for a New Approach to Development, Tourism, and Local Needs at the Grand Medieval City of Hampi." *Archaeology* (November/December 2012). https://www.archaeology.org/issues/53-1211/letter-from/247-india-living-heritage-at-risk, accessed December 14, 2021.

"From *The Spectator*. Embellishments of the Annuals." *Museum of Foreign Literature, Science, and Art* 23 (July–December 1833 [December 1833]): 713–714. Philadelphia: E. Littell & T. Holden; New York: G. & C. & H. Carvill; Boston: Kane & Co., 1833.

Fuller, C. J. *The Camphor Flame: Popular Hinduism and Society in India*. Princeton: Princeton University Press, 1992.

———. *Servants of the Goddess: The Priests of a South Indian Temple*. Cambridge: Cambridge University Press, 1984.

———. "The Divine Couple's Relationship in a South Indian Temple: Mīnākṣi and Sundareśvara at Madurai." *History of Religions* 19, no. 4 (May 1980): 321–348.

Fyall, Alan, and Brian Garrod. "Heritage Tourism: At What Price?" *Managing Leisure* 3, no. 4 (1998): 213–228.

Ganesh, Sanjana. "Get Ready for a Stride on Madurai's Heritage Walkway." *The Hindu*, February 12, 2018. http://www.thehindu.com/news/cities/Madurai/get-ready-for-a-stride-on-madurais-heritage-walkway/article22727257.ece, accessed December 14, 2021.

———. "Heritage Bazaar to Come Up at Kunnathur Chathiram Site." *The Hindu*, August 5, 2019. https://www.thehindu.com/news/cities/Madurai/heritage-bazaar-to-come-up-at-kunnathur-chathiram-site/article28817839.ece, accessed December 14, 2021.

Gascoigne, John. *Joseph Banks and the English Enlightenment: Useful Knowledge and Polite Culture*. Cambridge: Cambridge University Press, 1994.

———. *Science in the Service of Empire: Joseph Banks, the British State and the Uses of Science in the Age of Revolution*. Cambridge: Cambridge University Press, 1998.

Geertz, Clifford. *Negara: The Theatre State in Nineteenth-Century Bali*. Princeton: Princeton University Press, 1980.

Gilpin, William. *Three Essays: On Picturesque Beauty; On Picturesque Travel; And on Sketching Landscape: To Which Is Added a Poem on Landscape Painting*. London: R. Blamire, 1792.

Goldstone, Brian. "Life after Sovereignty." *History of the Present* 4, no. 1 (Spring 2014): 97–113.

Good, Anthony. "'Māmul' and Modernity in a South Indian Temple." *Modern Asian Studies* 35, no. 4 (October 2001): 821–870.

———. *The Female Bridegroom: A Comparative Study of Life-Crisis Rituals in South India and Sri Lanka*. Oxford: Clarendon Press, 1991.

Goss, Jon. "The Built Environment and Social Theory: Towards an Architectural Geography." *Professional Geographer* 40, no. 4 (November 1988): 392–403.

"Gothic Revival." In *Encylopædia Britannica*. 2021. https://www.britannica.com/art/Gothic-Revival, accessed December 14, 2021.

Gough, Richard. *A Comparative View of the Antient Monuments of India, Particularly Those in the Island of Salset near Bombay, as Described by Different Writers, Illustrated with Prints*. London: John Nichols, 1785.

Government of India, Planning Commission. *Tenth Five Year Plan 2002–2007*. Vol. II: Sectoral Policies and Programmes. New Delhi: Government of India, 2002. http://niti.gov.in/planningcommission.gov.in/docs/plans/planrel/fiveyr/10th/volume2/10th_vol2.pdf, accessed December 14, 2021.

Government of Tamil Nadu, Tourism and Culture Department. "Development of Pilgrimage Circuit (Madurai–Rameswaram–Kanniyakumari) in Tamil Nadu under Mega-Tourism Project." G.O. Ms. No. 142, Tourism-Promotion of Tourism-Government of India Assisted Scheme-2010–2011, Issued July 12, 2010. http://cms.tn.gov.in/sites/default/files/gos/tour_e_142_2010.pdf, accessed December 14, 2021.

Government of Tamil Nadu, Tourism, Culture and Religious Endowments Department. *Tourism Policy Note 2016–2017 Demand No. 29*. Chennai: Government of Tamil Nadu, 2016. http://www.tamilnadutourism.org/pdf/Policynoteenglish2016-17.pdf, accessed December 14, 2021.

Govindarajan, Vinita. "Fire in Madurai's Meenakshi Temple Sparks Demand for Shops to Be Evicted from Complex." *Scroll.in*, February 6, 2018. https://scroll.in/article/867574/fire-in-madurais-meenakshi-temple-sparks-demand-for-shops-to-be-evicted-from-complex, accessed December 14, 2021.

Grant, Charles. *Observations on the State of Society among the Asiatic Subjects of Great Britain, Particularly with Respect to Morals; and on the Means of Improving It.—Written Chiefly in the Year 1792*. Ordered, by the House of Commons to be printed, June 15, 1813.

Gray, Michael. "The First Photographic Processes: Some Technical Notes." *A Shifting Focus: Photography in India 1850–1900*, 27–31. London: The British Library, 1995.

Greenblatt, Stephen. *Marvelous Possessions: The Wonder of the New World*. Chicago: The University of Chicago Press, 1991.

Guha, Ranajit. *History at the Limit of World-History*. New York: Columbia University Press, 2002.

Guha-Thakurta, Tapati. "The Compulsions of Visual Representation in Colonial India." In *Traces of India: Photography, Architecture, and the Politics of Representation 1850–1900*, edited by Maria Antonella Pellizzari, 108–139. Montreal: Canadian Centre for Architecture; New Haven: Yale Center for British Art, 2003.

———. *Monuments, Objects, Histories: Institutions of Art in Colonial and Postcolonial India*. New York: Columbia University Press, 2004.

Günlü, Ebru, İge Pırnar, and Kamil Yağcı. "Preserving Cultural Heritage and Possible Impacts on Regional Developments: Case of İzmir." *International Journal of Emerging and Transition Economies* 2, no. 2 (2009): 213–229.

Gunn, Simon. *The Public Culture of the Victorian Middle Class: Ritual and Authority in the English Industrial City 1840–1914*. Manchester: Manchester University Press, 2000.

Gunn, Simon, and Rachel Bell. *Middle Classes: Their Rise and Sprawl*. London: Phoenix, 2003.

Guy, John. "Tirumala Nāyak's Choultry: An Eighteenth Century Model." In *Makaranda: Essays in Honour of Dr. James C. Harle*, edited by Claudine Bautze-Picron, 207–213. Delhi: Sri Satguru Publications, 1990.

Halhed, Nathaniel Brassey. *A Code of Gentoo Laws, or, Ordinations of the Pundits, from a Persian Translation, Made from the Original, Written in the Shanscrit Language*. London, 1776.

———. *A Grammar of the Bengal Language*. Printed at Hooghly in Bengal, 1778.

Hall, Catherine. "Of Gender and Empire: Reflections on the Nineteenth Century." In *Gender and Empire*, edited by Philippa Levine, 46–76. Oxford and New York: Oxford University Press, 2007 [2004].

Hancock, Mary E. *The Politics of Heritage from Madras to Chennai*. Bloomington: Indiana University Press, 2008.

Harding, Paul, Janine Eberle, Patrick Horton, Amy Karafin, and Simon Richmond. *South India*. 3rd edition. Footscray, Victoria: Lonely Planet Publications, 2005.

Harley, J. B. "Maps, Knowledge, and Power." In *The Iconography of Landscape: Essays on the Symbolic Representation, Design and Use of Past Environments*, edited by Denis Cosgrove and Stephen Daniels, 277–312. Cambridge: Cambridge University Press, 1988.

Harman, William. "How the Fearsome Fish-Eyed Queen Mīṉāṭci Became a Perfectly Ordinary Goddess." In *Goddesses Who Rule*, edited by Elisabeth Benard and Beverly Moon, 33–50. Oxford and New York: Oxford University Press, 2000.

———. *The Sacred Marriage of a Hindu Goddess*. Bloomington: Indiana University Press, 1989.

Harris, Katherine D. "Feminizing the Textual Body: Female Readers Consuming the Literary Annual." *Papers of the Bibliographical Society of America* 99, no. 4 (December 2005): 573–622.

Hart, George L. *The Poems of Ancient Tamil: Their Milieu and Their Sanskrit Counterparts*. New York and New Delhi: Oxford University Press, 1999 [1975].

———. "Women and the Sacred in Ancient Tamilnad." *Journal of Asian Studies* 32, no. 2 (February 1973): 233–250.

Hart, W. W. Hart, Secretary to Govt. Memorandum, February 17, 1855. Bombay Proceedings. March 3, 1855. IOR/P/351/42, No. 1264. British Library, Asia, Pacific, and Africa Collections, London.

Head, Raymond. *Catalogue of Paintings, Drawings, Engravings and Busts in the Collection of the Royal Asiatic Society*. London: The Royal Asiatic Society, 1991.

Hegel, G. W. F. *Lectures on the Philosophy of History*. Translated by J. Sibree. London: Henry G. Bohn, 1857.

Heitzman, James. *Gifts of Power: Lordship in an Early Indian State*. Delhi: Oxford University Press, 2001 [1997].

Heras, Henry. "The Statues of the Nayaks of Madura in the Pudu Mantapam." *Quarterly Journal of the Mythic Society* 15, no. 3 (April 1925): 209–218.

Herzfeld, Michael. *A Place in History: Social and Monumental Time in a Cretan Town*. Princeton: Princeton University Press, 1991.

Heyck, T. W. *The Transformation of Intellectual Life in Victorian England*. New York: St Martin's Press, 1982.

Hinsley, F. H. *Sovereignty*. 2nd edition. Cambridge: Cambridge University Press, 1986.

Hodges, William. *Choix de vues de l'Inde, dessinées sur les lieux, pendant les années 1780, 1781, 1782, et 1783, et executées en aqua tinta, par W. Hodges.... Select Views in India, Drawn on the Spot, in the Years 1780, 1781, 1782, and 1783, and Executed in Aqua Tinta, by William Hodges, R.A.* London: Printed [by Joseph Cooper] for the author; and sold by J. Edwards, 1786–1788.

———. *Travels in India, During the Years 1780, 1781, 1782, & 1783*. London: Printed for the author, and sold by J. Edwards, 1793.

Hodgson, Brian Houghton. *Miscellaneous Essays Relating to Indian Subjects*. Vol. II. London: Trübner & Co., 1880.

Holdrege, Barbara A. *Bhakti and Embodiment: Fashioning Divine Bodies and Devotional Bodies in Kṛṣṇa Bhakti*. London and New York: Routledge, 2015.

Hooper-Greenhill, Eilean. *Museums and Education: Purpose, Pedagogy, Performance*. London and New York: Routledge, 2007.

Hornell, James. *Report to the Government of Madras on the Indian Pearl Fisheries in the Gulf of Mannar*. Madras: Printed by the Superintendent, Government Press, 1905.

Howes, Jennifer. *The Courts of Pre-Colonial South India: Material Culture and Kingship*. London and New York: RoutledgeCurzon, 2003.

———. *Illustrating India: The Early Colonial Investigations of Colin Mackenzie (1784–1821).* New Delhi: Oxford University Press, 2010.

Hudson, [D.] Dennis. "Āṇṭāḷ's Desire." In *Vaiṣṇavī: Women and the Worship of Krishna*, edited by Steven J. Rosen, 171–209. New Delhi: Motilal Banarsidass Publishers, 1996.

———. "Śiva, Mīnākṣi, Viṣṇu—Reflections on a Popular Myth in Madurai." *Indian Economic and Social History Review* 14, no. 1 (January 1977): 107–118.

———. "Two Citrā Festivals in Madurai." In *Religious Festivals in South India and Sri Lanka*, edited by Guy R. Welbon and Glenn E. Yocum, 101–156. New Delhi: Manohar, 1982.

Hultzshe, E., ed. *Epigraphia Indica and Record of the Archæological Survey of India*. Vol. III: 1894–1895. Calcutta: Office of the Superintendent of Government Printing, India, 1894–1895.

Hunnisett, Basil. *Steel-Engraved Book Illustration in England.* Boston: David R. Godine, 1980.

Hunter, Alexander. Alex. Hunter to the Secretary of the British Museum-London, Madras, August 26, 1861. British Museum Original Papers. Vol. LXXII, P.1435, February 6, 1862. British Museum Archive, London.

Hunter, M. C. W. "The Royal Society and the Origins of British Archaeology: I." *Antiquity* 45, no. 178 (June 1971): 113–121.

———. "The Royal Society and the Origins of British Archaeology: II." *Antiquity* 45, no. 179 (September 1971): 187–192.

Hupré, Jean-François. "The Royal Jewels of Tirumala Nayaka of Madurai (1623–1659)." In *The Jewels of India*, edited by Susan Stronge, 63–80. Bombay: Marg Publications, 1995.

Inden, Ronald. *Imagining India.* Bloomington: Indiana University Press, 2000 [1990].

Indian Museum, Calcutta. *The Indian Museum 1814–1914*. Calcutta: The Indian Museum, 1914.

Indian National Trust for Art and Cultural Heritage. "About INTACH." 2016. http://www.intach.org/about.php, accessed December 14, 2021.

"The Introduction." *Asiatick Researches: or, Transactions of the Society Instituted in Bengal, for Inquiring into the History and Antiquities, the Arts, Sciences, and Literature, of Asia* 1 (1788): iii–viii. Calcutta: Manuel Cantopher and London: P. Elmsly, 1788.

"Introduction: Containing an Historical Account of the Origin and Establishment of the Society of Antiquaries." *Archaeologia, or, Miscellaneous Tracts Relating to Antiquity. Published by the Society of Antiquaries of London* 1 (1770): i–xxxix.

Jacquemont, Victor. *Letters from India; Describing a Journey in British Dominions of India, Tibet, Lahore, and Cashmere during the Years 1828, 1829, 1830, 1831.* Vol. I. London: Edward Churton, 1834.

Jeyechandrun, A. V. *The Madurai Temple Complex (With Special Reference to Literature and Legends)*. Madurai: Publications Division, Madurai Kamaraj University, 1985.

Johnson, Nuala. "Cast in Stone: Monuments, Geography, and Nationalism." *Environment and Planning D: Society and Space* 13, no. 1 (1995): 51–65.

Jones, Owen. *The Grammar of Ornament. Illustrated by Examples from Various Styles of Ornament*. London: Day and Son, Lithographers to the Queen, 1856.

Jones, William. "XXV. The Third Anniversary Discourse, Delivered 2 February, 1786. By the President." *Asiatick Researches: or, Transactions of the Society Instituted in Bengal for Inquiring into the History and Antiquities, the Arts, Sciences, and Literature, of Asia* 1 (1788): 415–431. Calcutta: Manuel Cantopher and London: P. Elmsly, 1788.

———. "A Discourse on the Institution of a Society, for Inquiring into the History, Civil and Natural, the Antiquities, Arts, Sciences, and Literature of Asia. By the President." *Asiatick Researches: or, Transactions of the Society Instituted in Bengal, for Inquiring into the History and Antiquities, the Arts, Sciences, and Literature, of Asia* 1 (1788): ix–xvi. Calcutta: Manuel Cantopher and London: P. Elmsly, 1788.

———. *A Grammar of the Persian Language*. London: W. and J. Richardson, 1771.

———. "On the Gods of Greece, Italy, and India, Written in 1784, and Since Revised, By the President." In *The Works of Sir William Jones in Six Volumes*. Vol. I, 229–280. London: G. G. and J. Robinson, and R. H. Evans, 1799.

———. *Poems, Consisting Chiefly of Translations from the Asiatick Languages*. Oxford: Clarendon Press, 1772.

———. *Sacontalá, or The Fatal Ring; An Indian Drama by Cálidás: Translated from the Original Sanscrit and Prácrit*. Calcutta: Printed and sold by Joseph Cooper, 1789.

———. William Jones to Sir Joseph Banks, Calcutta. January 29, 1792. MM.3.45. Royal Society Archives, London.

Jouveau-Dubreuil, G. *Dravidian Architecture*. Edited by S. Krishnaswami Aiyangar. Madras: S.P.C.K. Press, 1917.

Kācinātaṉ, Naṭaṉa, Cu. Irācakōpāl, Ve. Vētācalam, eds. *Tirumalaināyakkar Ceppēṭukaḷ* (Tamiḻ). Ceṉṉai: Tamiḻnāṭu Aracu Tolporuḷ Āyvutturai, 1994.

Kalmo, Hent, and Quentin Skinner, eds. *Sovereignty in Fragments: The Past, Present and Future of a Contested Concept*. Cambridge: Cambridge University Press, 2010.

Kamba Ramayanam: Yuddha Kandam Part 1. Translated by P. S. Sundaram. Tamil Nadu: Department of Tamil Development-Culture, Government of Tamil Nadu, 1994.

Kapadia, Karin. *Siva and Her Sisters: Gender, Caste, and Class in Rural South India*. Boulder, CO: Westview Press, 1995.

Karashima, Noboru. "Nāyakas as Lease-Holders of Temple Lands." *Journal of the Economic and Social History of the Orient* 19, no. 2 (May 1976): 227–232.

Keene, H. G. "Johnston, Sir Alexander (1775–1849)." Revised by Roger T. Stearn. In *Oxford Dictionary of National Biography*. Vol. XXX, 334–335. Oxford: Oxford University Press, 2004.

Kirshenblatt-Gimblett, Barbara. *Destination Culture: Tourism, Museums, and Heritage*. Berkeley and Los Angeles: University of California Press, 1998.

Kharas, Homi. "The Unprecedented Expansion of the Global Middle Class: An Update." Global Economy and Development Working Paper 100, February 2017. Washington, D.C.: The Brookings Institution, 2017. https://www.brookings.edu/wp-content/uploads/2017/02/global_20170228_global-middle-class.pdf, accessed December 14, 2021.

Kharas, Homi, and Kristofer Hamel. "A Global Tipping Point: Half of the World Is Now Middle Class or Wealthier." *Brookings*, September 27, 2018. https://www.brookings.edu/blog/future-development/2018/09/27/a-global-tipping-point-half-the-world-is-now-middle-class-or-wealthier/, accessed December 14, 2021.

Kindersley, N. E. *Specimens of Hindoo Literature: Consisting of Translations, from the Tamoul Language, of Some Hindoo Works of Morality and Imagination, with Explanatory Notes: To Which Are Prefixed Introductory Remarks on the Mythology, Literature, &c. of the Hindoos*. London: W. Bulmer and Co., 1794.

Kopf, David. *British Orientalism and the Bengal Renaissance: The Dynamics of Indian Modernization 1773–1835*. Berkeley and Los Angeles: University of California Press, 1969.

Kugler, Franz. *Handbuch der Kunstgeschichte*. Stutgart: Verlag von Ebner & Seubert, 1842.

Kumar, Dharma. "Agrarian Relations: South India." In *The Cambridge Economic History of India Volume 2: c. 1757–-c. 1970*, edited by Dharma Kumar, 207–241. Cambridge: Cambridge University Press, 1989 [1983].

Kurucāmi, Ta. "Maturai Tirukkōyilil Tirumuṟai Viṇṇappikkum Varalāṟu." In *Maturait Tirukkōyil: Tirukkuṭa Naṉṉīrāṭṭup Peruviḻā Malar* (*The Madurai Temple Complex: Kumbabhisheka Souvenir*) (Tamiḻ and English), edited by A. V. Jeyechandrun, 267–270. Maturai: Aruḷmiku Mīṉāṭci Cuntarēcuvarar Tirukkōyil, 1974.

Landon, Letitia Elizabeth. *Fisher's Drawing Room Scrap-Book; With Poetical Illustrations by L. E. L.* London: Fisher, Son, and Jackson, 1832.

———. *Fisher's Drawing Room Scrap-Book; With Poetical Illustrations by L. E. L.* London and Paris: Fisher, Son, & Co.; Berlin: Asher; New York: Jackson, 1836.

———. *Letters by Letitia Elizabeth Landon*. Edited by F. J. Spher. Ann Arbor, MI: Scholars' Facsimiles & Reprints, 2001.

———. *The Poetical Works of Miss Landon*. Philadelphia: E. L. Carey and A. Hart, 1839.

Lefebvre, Henri. *The Production of Space*. Translated by Donald Nicholson-Smith. Oxford, UK & Cambridge, MA: Blackwell, 1991.

"Letters from Sir William Jones to the late Samuel Davis, Esq., F. R. S., &c. from 1785 to 1794, chiefly relating to the Literature and Science of India, and elucidatory of the early History of the Asiatic Society of Bengal; with a Plate. Communicated by John Francis Davis, Esq., F. R. S., M. R. A. S., &c." In *Transactions of the Royal Asiatic Society of Great Britain and Ireland* 3, no. 1 (1831): 1–31. London: Parbury, Allen, & Co., 1831.

Levine, Philippa. "Introduction." In *Gender and Empire Gender and Empire*, edited by Philippa Levine, 1–13. Oxford and New York: Oxford University Press, 2007 [2004].

Linley, Margaret. "The Early Victorian Annual (1822–1857)." *Victorian Review* 35, no. 1 (Spring 2009): 13–19.

Loudon, J. C. "Reviews. ART. I. *Essay on the Architecture of the Hindús*. By Rám Ráz, Native Judge and Magistrate at Bangalore, Corresponding Member of the Royal Asiatic Society of Great Britain and Ireland. 4to, pp. 64. 48 plates. London, 1834." *Architectural Magazine, and Journal of Improvement in Architecture, Building, and Furnishing, and in the Various Arts and Trades Connected Therewith* 1, no. 1 (1834): 267–273. London: Longman, Rees, Orme, Brown, Green, & Longman, 1834.

Lozanski, Kristin. "Encountering Beggars: Disorienting Travelers?" *Annals of Tourism Research* 42 (July 2013): 46–64.

Ludden, David. *Peasant History in South India*. Princeton: Princeton University Press, 1985.

Lushington, F. F. Lushington, Esq., Civil Auditor; to T. Pycroft, Esq., Chief Secretary to Government, Fort Saint George, April 22, 1858. Madras Public Consultations. April 9, 1858–June 22, 1858. IOR/P/249/66, No. 12, pp. 166–169. British Library, Asia, Pacific, and Africa Collections, London.

Lyon, Capt. (Edmund David). *Notes to Accompany a Series of Photographs Designed to Illustrate the Ancient Architecture of Southern India*. Edited by James Fergusson. London: Marion & Co., 1870.

Mackenzie, Colin. "Account of Extracts of a Journal by Major C. Mackenzie." *Asiatic Researches: or Transactions of the Society Instituted in Bengal, for Inquiring into the History and Antiquities, the Arts, Sciences, and Literature, of Asia* 9 (1809): 272–278. London: Vernor, Hood, and Sharpe, etc., 1809.

———. Colin Mackenzie to George Buchan, Esq., Chief Secretary to Government, Fort Saint George, February 28, 1804. Papers relating to the Mysore Survey, including reports and letters on its progress from Capt. Colin Mackenzie to H. Traill and other supporters of the project. 1802–1807. Mss Eur F228/39, No. 20, ff. 27–28. British Library, Asia, Pacific, and Africa Collections, London.

———. Colin Mackenzie to Lakshman Boria, Madras, May 12, 1803, Mss Eur/Mackenzie General 21, Section 56, ff. 287–288. British Library, Asia, Pacific, and Africa Collections, London.

———. "Introductory Memoir: Of the Use and Advantage of Inscriptions & Sculptured Monuments in Illustrating Hindoo History." Undated. Mss Eur/Mackenzie General 18. F109/72. British Library, Asia, Pacific, and Africa Collections, London.

———."Memorandum." Madras, February 14, 1808. Madras Public Consultations. Volume 341A, ff. 2907–2917. Tamil Nadu State Archives and Historical Research, Chennai.

———. "Paper Submitted to Me by C. Boria Bramin. Heads under Which a History of the Carnatic May Be Composed viz: October 30th 1802." Mss Eur/Mackenzie General 9, ff. 1–3. British Library, Asia, Pacific, and Africa Collections, London.

Mackenzie, Roderick. *A Sketch of the War with Tippoo Sultaun; or, a Detail of Military Operations, from the Commencement of Hostilities at the Lines of Travancore in December 1789, until the Peace Concluded before Seringapatam in February 1792, in Two Volumes*. Calcutta: J. Sewell, 1799.

Mackenzie, W. C. *Colonel Colin Mackenzie, First Surveyor-General of India*. Edinburgh: W. & R. Chambers, 1952.

Maclean, C. D. *Standing Information Regarding the Official Administration of the Madras Presidency in Each Department, in Illustration of the Yearly Administration Reports.* Madras: E. Keys, at the Government Press, 1877.

Madras Department of Epigraphy Annual Report. Madras: Department of Archaeology, 1910.

Madurai Corporation. "About Madurai." 2021. https://www.maduraicorporation.co.in/aboutus/about-madurai, accessed December 14, 2021.

———. "Institutional Framework." 2021. http://www.maduraicorporation.co.in/aboutus/institutional-framework, accessed December 14, 2021.

———. *Jawaharlal Nehru National Urban Renewal Mission: An Update on Projects.* 2009. https://fdocuments.us/document/brochures-published-madurai.html, accessed December 14, 2021.

Madurai District Administration. "Agriculture." 2021. https://madurai.nic.in/agriculture/, accessed December 14, 2021.

———. "Industries & Commerce." 2021. https://madurai.nic.in/industries-commerce/, accessed December 14, 2021.

Mahadevan, Iravatham, ed. and trans. *Early Tamil Epigraphy from the Earliest Times to the Sixth Century A.D.* Cambridge, MA: Harvard University Press, 2003.

Mahalingam, T. V., ed. *Mackenzie Manuscripts: Summaries of the Historical Manuscripts in the Mackenzie Collection.* Vol. I (Tamil and Malayalam). Madras: University of Madras, 1972.

Mahon, Michael. *Foucault's Nietzschean Genealogy: Truth, Power, and the Subject.* Albany: State University of New York Press, 1992.

Mann, Michael. "Art, Artefacts and Architecture: Lord Curzon, the Delhi Arts Exhibition of 1902–03 and the Improvement of India's Aesthetics." In *Civilizing Missions in Colonial and Postcolonial South Asia: From Improvement to Development*, edited by Carey A. Watt and Michael Mann, 65–89. London and New York: Anthem Press, 2011.

Mantena, Rama [Sundari]. *The Origins of Modern Historiography in India: Antiquarianism and Philology, 1780–1880*. New York: Palgrave Macmillan: 2012.

———. "The Question of History in Precolonial India," *History and Theory* 46, no. 3 (October 2007): 396–408.

Markham S. F., and H. Hargreaves. *The Museums of India.* London: The Museums Association, 1936.

Marsden, William. "XLIII. Observations on the Language of the People Commonly Called Gypsies. In a Letter to Sir Joseph Banks, Bart. P.R.S. From Mr. Marsden, F.S.A." *Archaeologia, or, Miscellaneous Tracts Relating to Antiquity. Published by the Society of Antiquaries of London* 7 (1785): 382–385.

Maskey, Vishakha, Cheryl Brown, and Ge Lin. "Assessing Factors Associated with Listing a Historic Resource in the National Register of Historic Places." *Economic Development Quarterly* 23, no. 4 (August 2009): 342–350.

Matthew, H. C. G. "Caunter, John Hobart (1792–1851)." In *Oxford Dictionary of National Biography*. Vol. X, 579–580. Oxford: Oxford University Press, 2004.

Maturai Stāṉikar Varalāṟu (Tamiḻ). *Centamiḻ* 5 (1906–1907): 87–95, 141–148, 220–222, 261–272, 294–300. Maturai: Maturait Tamiḻccaṅka Muttirācālai, 1907.

McCormick, Thomas J. *Ruins as Architecture, Architecture as Ruins.* Dublin, NH: William L. Bauhan, 1999.

McCoy Owens, Bruce. "Monumentality, Identity, and the State: Local Practice, World Heritage, and Heterotopia at Swayambhu, Nepal." *Anthropological Quarterly* 75, no. 2 (Spring 2002): 269–316.

McDonald, Donald. "The Indian Medical Service. A Short Account of Its Achievements 1600–1947." *Proceedings of the Royal Society of Medicine* 49, no. 1 (January 1956): 13–17.

McGann, Jerome. *The Poetics of Sensibility: A Revolution in Literary Style*. Oxford: Clarendon Press, 1996.

McGilvray, Dennis B. *Symbolic Heat: Gender, Health & Worship among the Tamils of South India and Sri Lanka*. Ahmedabad: Mapin Publishing Pvt. Ltd.; Boulder: University of Colorado Museum, 1998.

"Memoirs and Remains of Eminent Persons. Memoir of Richard Gough, Esq. of Enfield." *Monthly Magazine; or, British Register* 27, Part I. For 1809, no. 183 (April 1, 1809): 260–263. London: Printed for Richard Phillips, undated.

Menon, Parvati. "Agrarian Economy of the Carnatic in the 17th and 18th Centuries." PhD diss., Aligarh Muslim University, 1986.

Menon, Ramesh. *Bhagavata Purana*. New Delhi: Rupa & Co., 2007.

Metcalf, Thomas R. *Ideologies of the Raj*. The New Cambridge History of India III.4. Cambridge: Cambridge University Press, 1994.

M'Kenzie-Hall, James. "Illustrated Travel: Steel Engravings and Their Use in Early Nineteenth-Century Topographical Books, with Special Reference to Henry Fisher & Co." PhD diss., Nottingham Trent University and Southampton Solent University, 2011.

Michell, George. *Architecture and Art of Southern India*. The New Cambridge History of India I.6. Cambridge: Cambridge University Press, 1995.

Minute Book Society of Antiquaries of London. Vol. XXIII: MDCCLXXXIX. From January 8, 1789 to December 23, 1790. Society of Antiquaries Library, London.

Minutes of Council. Vol. 2. March 1827–December 1829. Royal Asiatic Society of Great Britain and Ireland Library, London.

Minutes of Council. Vol. 3. February 1830–March 1833. Royal Asiatic Society of Great Britain and Ireland Library, London.

Minutes of General Meetings. Vol. 4. January 1833–July 1835. Royal Asiatic Society of Great Britain and Ireland Library, London.

Minutes of the Committee of Correspondence. May 1831–July 1842. Royal Asiatic Society of Great Britain and Ireland Library, London.

Mishra, Vijay. *Devotional Poetics and the Indian Sublime*. Albany: State University of New York, 1998.

Mitchell, Jesse. "IV. Description of a Plain or Waxed Paper Process in Photography." *Madras Journal of Literature and Science* (Edited by the Committee of the Madras Literary Society and Auxilary Royal Asiatic Society). New Series 1, no. 1 (October 1856–March 1857 [October–December 1856]): 71–80. Madras: Pharoah and Co., 1857.

Mitchell, Timothy. *Colonising Egypt*. Berkeley and Los Angeles: University of California Press, 1991 [1988].

Mitter, Partha. *Much Maligned Monsters: A History of European Reactions to Indian Art*. Chicago and London: The University of Chicago Press, 1992 [1977].

———. "Western Bias in the Study of South Indian Aesthetics." *South Asian Review* 6, no. 2 (January 1973): 125–136.

Mittra, Peary Chand. *Life of Dewan Ramcomul Sen*. Calcutta: I. C. Bose & Co., 1880.

Monier-Williams, Sir Monier. *Brāhmanism and Hindūism; or, Religious Thought and Life in India, as Based on the Veda and Other Sacred Books of the Hindūs*. 4th edition. London: John Murray, 1891.

Mudaliar, Chandra Y. *State and Religious Endowments in Madras*. Madras: University of Madras, 1976.

Mustafa, Mohammed. "British Policy towards Inam Settlements in Madras Presidency 1801–1871." PhD diss., University of Hyderabad, 1995.

———. "The Shaping of Land Revenue Policy in Madras Presidency: Revenue Experiments—The Case of Chittoor District." *Indian Economic and Social History Review* 44, no. 2 (April 2007): 213–236.

Muthiah, S. "Printer, Painter, and Much Else." *The Hindu*, December 25, 2006. http://www.thehindu.com/todays-paper/tp-features/tp-metroplus/printer-painter-and-much-else/article3205151.ece, accessed December 14, 2021.

Nagarajan, Vijaya Rettakudi. "The Earth as Goddess Bhū Devī: Toward a Theory of 'Embedded Ecologies' in Folk Hinduism." In *Purifying the Earthly Body of God: Religion and Ecology in Hindu India,* edited by Lance E. Nelson, 269–295. Albany: State University of New York Press, 1998.

Nagaswamy, R. *Studies in Ancient Tamil Law and Society*. Madras: Tamil Nadu State Department of Archaeology, 1978.

———. *Tantric Cult of South India*. Delhi: Agam Kala Prakashan, 1982.

National Museum, New Delhi. "About the Museum: History." 2019. http://www.nationalmuseumindia.gov.in/en/history, accessed December 14, 2021.

Narayana Rao, Velcheru. "Purāṇa as Brahminic Ideology." In *Purāṇa Perennis: Reciprocity and Transformation in Hindu and Jain Texts*, edited by Wendy Doniger, 85–100. Albany: State University of New York, 1993.

Narayana Rao, Velcheru, David Shulman, and Sanjay Subrahmanyam, *Symbols of Substance: Court and State in Nāyaka Period Tamilnadu*. Delhi and New York: Oxford University Press, 1998.

———. *Textures of Time: Writing History in South India 1600–1800.* Delhi: Permanent Black, 2001.

Narayani, P. A. "King Thirumalai Nayak and the Kallar connection." *The Hindu*, August 24, 2020. https://www.thehindu.com/news/cities/Madurai/king-thirumalai-nayak-and-the-kallar-connection/article32431472.ece, accessed December 14, 2021.

Nelson, J. H. *The Madura Country: A Manual Compiled by Order of the Madras Government*. Madras: Asylum Press by William Thomas, 1868.

New Indian Express. "Who'll Clear This 17th Century Mandapam in Madurai?" October 22, 2012. https://www.newindianexpress.com/states/tamil-nadu/2012/oct/22/wholl-clear-this-17th-century-mandapam-in-madurai--417815.html, accessed December 14, 2021.

"New Publications: Essay on the Architecture of the Hindūs. By Rám Ráz, Native Judge and Magistrate at Bangalore, Corresponding Member of the Royal Asiatic Society of Great Britain and Ireland. With Forty-Eight Plates. 4to. London. Published for the Royal Asiatic Society, by J. W. Parker. 1834." *Journal of the Royal Asiatic Society of Great Britain and Ireland* 1, no. 1 (1834): 145–146. London: John W. Parker, 1834.

NEWS Minute. "UNESCO Slams TN Govt for Reckless 'Conservation' Work at Historic Temples, Submits Report to Madras HC." August 9, 2017. http://www.thenewsminute.com/article/unesco-slams-tn-govt-reckless-conservation-work-historic-temples-submits-report-madras-hc, accessed December 14, 2021.

Nora, Pierre. "General Introduction: Between Memory and History." In *Realms of Memory: The Construction of the French Past, Volume I: Conflicts and Divisions*, edited by Pierre Nora, 1–20. New York: Columbia University Press, 1996.

Novetzke, Christian Lee. "*Bhakti* and Its Public." *International Journal of Hindu Studies* 11, no. 3 (2007): 255–272.

"Obituary—William Daniell, Esq. R. A." *Gentleman's Magazine* 8, New Series (July–December 1837 [October 1837]): 429–430. London: William Pickering; John Bowyer Nichols and Son, 1837.

O'Brian, Patrick. *Joseph Banks: A Life*. London: Collins Harvill, 1987.

Oldenburg, Veena Talwar. *The Making of Colonial Lucknow, 1856–1877*. Princeton: Princeton University Press, 1984.

Pai, Gita V. "Kingship, Images, and Rituals: A Nāyaka Monument in South India, 1635–2009." PhD diss., University of California, Berkeley, 2010.

"Painted Canvas Depicting a Court Scene." Musée National des Arts Asiatiques–Guimet, Paris. https://www.guimet.fr/collections/textiles/toile-peinte-representant-une-scene-de-cour/, accessed December 14, 2021.

Palaniappan, K. *The Great Temple of Madurai*. Madurai: Sri Meenakshisundareswarar Temple Renovation Committee, 1970 [1963].

"Panel From a Box." Virginia Museum of Fine Arts, Richmond. https://www.vmfa.museum/piction/6027262-12968824/, accessed December 14, 2021.

Parañcōti Muṉivar. *Tiruviḷaiyāṭaṟ Purāṇam: Maturaikkāṇṭam* (Tamiḻ). Edited and commentary by Cokkaliṅkam Ceṭṭiyar. Maturai: Mīṉāṭci Cuntarēcuvarar Tirukkōyil, 1973.

———. *Parañcōtimuṉivar Aruḷicceyta Tiruviḷaiyāṭaṟ Purāṇam: Kūṭaṟkāṇṭam* (Tamiḻ). Commentary by Naṭukkāvēri Mu. Vēṅkaṭacāmi Nāṭṭār. Ceṉṉai: Tirunelvēlit Teṉṉintiya Caivacittānta Nūṟpatippuk Kaḻakam, Limiṭeṭ, 1969 [1928].

———. *Parañcōtimuṉivar Aruḷicceyta Tiruviḷaiyāṭaṟ Purāṇam: Tiruvālavāykkāṇṭam* (Tamiḻ). Commentary by Naṭukkāvēri Mu. Vēṅkaṭacāmi Nāṭṭār. Tirunelvēli: Tirunelvēlit Teṉṉintiya Caivacittānta Nūṟpatippuk Kaḻakam, Limiṭeṭ, 1965 [1931].

Parantāmaṉār, A. Ki. *Tirumalai Nāyakkar Varalāṟu* (Tamiḻ). Ceṉṉai: A. Cō. Cantāṉa Ilakkumi, 1995.

Parker, Samuel K. "Text and Practice in South Asian Art: An Ethnographic Perspective." *Artibus Asiae* 63, no. 1 (2003): 5–34.

Parthasarathi, Prasannan. *The Transition to a Colonial Economy: Weavers and Kings in South India, 1720–1800*. Cambridge: Cambridge University Press, 2007.

Pearce, Susan. "Antiquaries and the Interpretation of Ancient Objects, 1770–1820." In *Visions of Antiquity: The Society of Antiquaries of London 1707–2007*, edited by Susan Pearce, 147–171. London: Society of Antiquaries of London, 2007.

Peltz, Lucy. "Aestheticizing the Ancestral City: Antiquarianism, Topography and the Representation of London in the Long Eighteenth Century." *Art History* 22, no. 4 (November 1999): 472–494.

Peterson, Indira V. "Singing of a Place: Pilgrimage as Metaphor and Motif in the Tēvāram Songs of the Tamil Śaivite Saints." *Journal of the American Oriental Society* 102, no. 1 (January–March 1982): 69–90.

Phillimore, R. H. *Historical Records of the Survey of India*. Vol. I: 18th Century. Dehra Dun, UP: Survey of India, 1945.

Phillimore, R. H. *Historical Records of the Survey of India*. Vol. II: 1800 to 1815. Dehra Dun, UP: Survey of India, 1950.

Pinney, Christopher. *Camera Indica: The Social Life of Indian Photographs*. Chicago and London: The University of Chicago Press, 1997.

———. *The Coming of Photography in India*. London: The British Library, 2008.

Poorvaja, S. "'Pudhu Mandapam' Bustling with Devotees." *The Hindu*, May, 6, 2014. https://www.thehindu.com/news/cities/Madurai/pudhu-mandapam-bustling-with-devotees/article5981366.ece, accessed December 14, 2021.

Prabhākaraśāstri, Vēṭūri, ed. *Tañjāvūri Āndhrarājula Caritra* (Telugu). Haidarābādu: Maṇimañjari Pracuraṇa, Vēṭūri Prabhākaraśāstri Memōriyal Ṭrasṭ, 1984.

Prakash, Gyan. *Another Reason: Science and the Imagination of Modern India*. Princeton: Princeton University Press, 1999.

Pratt, Mary Louise. *Imperial Eyes: Travel Writing and Transculturation*. 2nd edition. New York: Routledge, 2008 [1992].

———. "Scratches on the Face of the Country; or What Mr. Barrow Saw in the Land of the Bushmen." In *"Race," Writing, and Difference*, edited by Henry Louis Gates, 138–162. Chicago and London: The University of Chicago Press, 1986.

Prentiss, Karen Pechilis. *The Embodiment of Bhakti*. New York and Oxford: Oxford University Press, 1999.

Presler, Franklin A. "The Legitimation of Religious Policy in Tamil Nādu: A Study of the 1970 Archaka Legislation." In *Religion and the Legitimation of Power in South Asia*, edited by Bardwell L. Smith, 106–133. Leiden: E. J. Brill, 1978.

"Proceedings of the Anniversary Meeting of the Royal Asiatic Society, Held on Saturday, the 10th of May, 1834." *Journal of the Royal Asiatic Society of Great Britain and Ireland* 1, no. 1 (1834): 157–170. London: John W. Parker, 1834.

"Proceedings of the Anniversary Meeting of the Royal Asiatic Society, Held on the 6th of May, 1837." *Journal of the Royal Asiatic Society of Great Britain and Ireland* 4, no. 2 (1837): xvii–xlvi. London: John W. Parker, 1837.

"Proceedings of the Madras Photographic Society. A Meeting of the Photographic Society was held at the School of Arts on the 5th December 1860." *Madras Journal of Literature and Science* (Edited by the Committee of the Madras Literary Society and Auxiliary Royal Asiatic Society), New Series 6, no. 11 (May 1861): 191–197. Madras: Pharoah and Co., 1861.

"Proceedings of the Royal Asiatic Society, Saturday, January 18th, 1834." *Journal of the Royal Asiatic Society of Great Britain and Ireland* 1, no. 1 (1834): 149–150. London: John W. Parker, 1834.

Pycroft, T. T. Pycroft, Chief Secretary to the Government [Madras] to the Secretary of the Government of India, March 11, 1856. Board's Collection. Vol. 2725. 198041 to 198116. 1857–1858. IOR/F/4/2725, No. 297, ff. 17–19. British Library, Asia, Pacific, and Africa Collections, London.

———. Chief Secretary. Government Order No. 584, April 15, 1859. Madras Public Consultations. April 1, 1859–July 29, 1859. IOR/P/249/69, No. 47, pp. 103–104. British Library, Asia, Pacific, and Africa Collections, London.

———. Chief Secretary. Government Order No. 964, June 18, 1859. Madras Public Consultations. April 1, 1859–July 29, 1859. IOR/P/249/69, No. 19, p. 348. British Library, Asia, Pacific, and Africa Collections, London.

Rajarajan, R. K. K., and Jeyapriya Rajarajan. *Mīnākṣī-Sundareśvara: Tiruviḷaiyāṭaṟ Purāṇam in Letters, Design and Art*. Delhi: Sharada Publishing House, 2013.

Rajaram, K. *History of Thirumalai Nayak*. Madurai: Ennes Publications, 1982.

Rajaraman, S. *Commentaries on the Tamil Nadu Hindu Religious and Charitable Endowment Act, 1959 (Tamil Nadu Act 22 of 1959).* Chennai: C. Sitaraman & Co. Pvt. Ltd., 2009.

Ramaswami, N. S. *Madras Literary Society. A History: 1812–1984*. Madras: Madras Literary Society, 1985.

Ramaswamie, Cavelly Venkata. *Biographical Sketches of Dekkan Poets, Being Memoirs of the Lives of Several Eminent Bards, Both Ancient and Modern, Who Have Flourished in Different Provinces of the Indian Peninsula, Compiled from Authentic Documents.* Calcutta: 1829.

Rangachari, V. "The History of the Naik Kingdom of Madura." *Indian Antiquary, A Journal of Oriental Research* 43 (September 1914): 187–192.

———. "The History of the Naik Kingdom of Madura." *Indian Antiquary, A Journal of Oriental Research* 43 (December 1914): 253–262.

———. "The History of the Naik Kingdom of Madura." *Indian Antiquary, A Journal of Oriental Research* 44 (April 1915): 69–73.

———. "The History of the Naik Kingdom of Madura." *Indian Antiquary, A Journal of Oriental Research* 45 (October 1916): 161–171.

———. "The History of the Naik Kingdom of Madura." *Indian Antiquary, A Journal of Oriental Research* 45 (November 1916): 178–188.

———. "The History of the Naik Kingdom of Madura." *Indian Antiquary, A Journal of Oriental Research* 45 (December 1916): 196–204.

Rao, N. Venkata. "Pioneers of English Writing in India: The Cavally Telugu Family." *Annuals of Oriental Research* 18, no. 2 (1963): 1–33.

Rao, Nina, and K. T. Suresh. "Domestic Tourism in India." In *The Native Tourist: Mass Tourism within Developing Countries*, edited by Krishna B. Ghimire, 198–228. London and Sterling, VA: Earthscan Publications Limited, 2001.

Rao, Sunitha. "Encroachments Gnawing at Hampi's Glorious Heritage." *Times of India*, January 12, 2014. https://timesofindia.indiatimes.com/city/bengaluru/encroachments-gnawing-at-hampis-glorious-heritage/articleshow/28694984.cms, accessed December 14, 2021.

Rappaport, Roy A. *Ecology, Meaning, and Religion.* Richmond, CA: North Atlantic Books, 1979.

———. *Ritual and Religion in the Making of Humanity.* Cambridge: Cambridge University Press, 1999.

Ráz, Rám. *Essay on the Architecture of the Hindús.* London: Published for the Oriental Translation Fund of Great Britain and Ireland; By John William Parker, 1834.

———. "State of Education in Southern India." *Asiatic Journal and Monthly Register for British India and Its Dependencies* 24 (July–December 1827 [November 1827]): 584–586. London: Parbury, Allen, & Co., 1827.

"Report of the Committee Appointed to Adjudicate the Photographic Society's Medals—At a Meeting of the Photographic Society held on the 5th May 1859." *Madras Journal of Literature and Science* (Edited by the Committee of the Madras Literary Society and Auxiliary Royal Asiatic Society). New Series 5, no. 9 (April–September 1859): 175–202. Madras: Pharoah and Co., 1859.

"Report of Proceedings Connected with Collections Made by the Late Colonel Mackenzie in Illustration of Oriental Literature and History." Examiners Office, October 1823. Board's Collection. Vol. 867. 22906–22926. 1826–1827. IOR/F/4/867, ff. 1–178. British Library, Asia, Pacific, and Africa Collections, London.

Reynolds, Holly Baker. "Madurai: *Kōyil Nakar.*" In *The City as a Sacred Center: Essays on Six Asian Contexts*, edited by Bardwell Smith and Holly Baker Reynolds, 12–44. Leiden and New York: E. J. Brill, 1987.

Riegl, Aloïs. "The Modern Cult of Monuments: Its Character and Its Origin." [1903] Translated by Kurt W. Forster and Diane Ghirardo. *Oppositions* 25 (Fall 1982): 21–51.

Robb, Peter. "Completing 'Our Stock of Geography', or an Object 'Still More Sublime': Colin Mackenzie's Survey of Mysore, 1799–1810." *Journal of the Royal Asiatic Society* 8, no. 2 (July 1998): 181–206.

Roberts, Emma. *The Zenana and Minor Poems by L. E. L. with a Memoir by Emma Roberts.* London and Paris: Fisher, Son, & Co., 1839.

Roy, Arundhati. *Capitalism: A Ghost Story*. Chicago: Haymarket, 2014.

Roy, Sourindranath. *The Story of Indian Archaeology 1784–1947.* New Delhi: Archaeological Survey of India, 1961.

Richter, Linda K. *The Politics of Tourism in Asia.* Honolulu: University of Hawaii Press, 1989.

Rutnam, James T. *The Early Life of Sir Alexander Johnston (1775–1849), Third Chief Justice of Ceylon*. Colombo: Law & Society Trust, 1988.

Said, Edward W. *Orientalism*. London: Penguin Books, 2003 [1978].

Sairam, R. "Good Harvest for Tourism Promoters Madurai Matters," *The Hindu*, January 15 2008. http://www.thehindu.com/todays-paper/tp-national/tp-tamilnadu/Good-harvest-for-tourism-promoters-Madurai-Matters/article15144545.ece, accessed December 14, 2021.

———. "'Lost' Site to Come Alive." *The Hindu*, January 12, 2010. https://www.thehindu.com/news/cities/Madurai/lsquoLostrsquo-site-to-come-alive/article16837153.ece, accessed December 14, 2021.

———. "Plan to Have 'Heritage Walk' with Dedicated Pathway in Madurai." *The Hindu,* July 22, 2011. http://www.thehindu.com/todays-paper/tp-national/tp-tamilnadu/plan-to-have-heritage-walk-with-dedicated-pathway-in-madurai/article2283944.ece, accessed December 14, 2021.

Salazar, Noel B. "Tourism Imaginaries: A Conceptual Approach." *Annals of Tourism Research* 39, no. 2 (April 2012): 863–882.

Sastri, K. A. Nilakanta. *A History of South India from Prehistoric Times to the Fall of Vijayanagar.* 2nd edition. London: Oxford University Press, 1958 [1955].

———. *The Pāṇḍya Kingdom from the Earliest Times to the Sixteenth Century.* London: Luzac & Co., 1929.

Sathianathaier, R. *Tamilaham in the 17th Century*. Madras: University of Madras, 1956.

Sauliere, A. "The Revolt of the Southern Nayaks." Part 1. *Journal of Indian History* 42, no. 1 (April 1964): 89–105.

———. "The Revolt of the Southern Nayaks." Part 2. *Journal of Indian History* 44, no. 1 (April 1966): 163–180.

Schmitt, Carl. *Political Theology: Four Chapters on the Concept of Sovereignty.* Translated by George Schwab. Chicago and London: The University of Chicago Press, 2005 [1922].

Schwab, Raymond. *The Oriental Renaissance: Europe's Rediscovery of India and the East, 1680–1880.* New York: Columbia University Press, 1984.

Seastrand, Anna Lise. "Praise, Politics, and Language: South Indian Murals, 1500–1800." PhD diss., Columbia University, 2013.

———. "Text, Image, and Portrait in Early Modern South Indian Murals." *Artibus Asiae* 78, no. 1 (2018): 29–60.

Sen, Amartya. "Indian Traditions & the Western Imagination." *Dædalus* 134, no. 4 (Fall 2005): 168–185.

Sewell, Robert. *Archaeological Survey of Southern India, List of Inscriptions, and Sketch of the Dynasties of Southern India. Compiled under the Orders of Government*. Vol. II. Madras: E. Keys, at the Government Press, 1884.

———. *Archaeological Survey of Southern India, Lists of the Antiquarian Remains in the Presidency of Madras. Compiled under the Orders of Government*. Vol. I. Madras: E. Keys, at the Government Press, 1882.

Sharpe, Jenny. "The Violence of Light in the Land of Desire; or, How William Jones Discovered India." *Boundary 2* 20, no. 1 (Spring 1993): 26–46.

Sheehan, James J. "The Problem of Sovereignty in European History." *American Historical Review* 111, no. 1 (February 2006): 1–15

Shenoy, J. P. Lasrado. *Madura: The Temple City*. 2nd edition. Madras: Associated Printers Ltd., 1955 [1937].

Shrikumar, A. "Mall de Madurai." *The Hindu*, March 29, 2012. https://www.thehindu.com/news/cities/Madurai/mall-de-madurai/article3258285.ece, accessed December 14, 2021.

Shulman, David [Dean]. "On South Indian Bandits and Kings." *Indian Economic and Social History Review* 17, no. 3 (July 1980): 283–306.

———. *Tamil Temple Myths: Sacrifice and Divine Marriage in the South Indian Śaiva Tradition*. Princeton: Princeton University Press, 1980.

———. *The King and the Clown in South Indian Myth and Poetry*. Princeton: Princeton University Press, 1985.

———. *The Wisdom of Poets: Studies in Tamil, Telugu, and Sanskrit*. New Delhi: Oxford University Press, 2001.

Simmons, Caleb. *Devotional Sovereignty: Kingship and Religion in India*. New York: Oxford University Press, 2020.

———. "The Goddess on the Hill: The (Re)Invention of a Local Hill Goddess as Chamundeshvari." In *Inventing and Reinventing the Goddess: Contemporary Iterations of Hindu Deities on the Move*, edited by Sree Padma, 217–244. Lanham, MD: Lexington Books, 2014.

Singh, Kavita. "The Museum Is National." *India International Centre Quarterly* 29, no. 3/4, India: A National Culture? (Winter 2002–Spring 2003): 176–196.

Singh, Upinder. *The Discovery of Ancient India: Early Archaeologists and the Beginnings of Archaeology*. Delhi: Permanent Black, 2004.

"Sir Alexander Johnston, Called in, and Examined." July 19, 1832. *Minutes of Evidence Taken before the Select Committee of the House of Commons on the Affairs of the East India Company*, I. Public, 254–257. London: Ordered, by the House of Commons, August 16, 1832.

Smith, George. *The Life of Alexander Duff, D.D., LL.D.* Vol. I. London: Hodder and Stoughton, 1879.

Spivak, Gayatri Chakravorty. "Three Women's Text and a Critic of Imperialism." *Critical Inquiry* 12, no. 1 (Autumn 1985): 243–261.

Spratt, P. *Hindu Culture and Personality: A Psycho-Analytic Study*. Bombay: Manaktalas, 1966.

Stein, Burton. *Peasant State and Society in Medieval South India*. Delhi: Oxford University Press, 1980.

———. *Vijayanagara*. The New Cambridge History of India I.2. Cambridge: Cambridge University Press, 1989.

Steinberg, Florian. "Conservation and Rehabilitation of Urban Heritage in Developing Countries." *Habitat International* 20, no. 3 (September 1996): 463–475.

Stephenson, Glennis. "Letitia Landon and the Victorian Improvisatrice: The Construction of L.E.L." *Victorian Poetry* 30, no. 1 (Spring 1992): 1–17.

Stern, Philip J. *The Company-State: Corporate Sovereignty and the Early Modern Foundations of the British Empire in India*. Oxford and New York: Oxford University Press, 2011.

Stoker, Valerie. *Polemics and Patronage in the City of Victory: Vyāsatīrtha, Hindu Sectarianism, and the Sixteenth-Century Vijayanagara Court*. Oakland: University of California Press, 2016.

Stoler, Ann Laura. "Imperial Debris: Reflections on Ruins and Ruination." *Cultural Anthropology* 23, no. 2 (May 2008): 191–219.

Storrs, Edith S. Edith S. Storrs to the Victoria & Albert Museum-London, Teddington, July 13, 1933. MA/1/S3660, nominal file: Storrs, Edith S, RP/1933/2814. Victoria & Albert Archive, London.

Strong, Rowan. *Anglicanism and the British Empire c. 1700–1850*. Oxford and New York: Oxford University Press, 2007.

Subrahmanyam, Sanjay. *Europe's India: Words, People, Empires 1500–1800*. Cambridge, MA: Harvard University Press, 2017.

Sutnik, Maia-Mari. "Picturesque Views: A Rediscovery of Photographs by Linnaeus Tripe." In *Linnaeus Tripe: Photographer of British India, 1854–1870*, edited by Janet Dewan and Maia-Mari Sutnik, 1–12. Toronto: Art Gallery of Ontario, 1986.

Sutton, Thomas. *The Daniells: Artists and Travellers*. London: The Bodley Head, 1954.

Snyder, Joel. "Territorial Photography." In *Landscape and Power*, edited by W. J. T. Mitchell, 175–201. Chicago and London: The University of Chicago Press, 2002 [1994].

Talbot, Cynthia. *Precolonial Practice: Society, Region, and Identity in Medieval Andhra*. Oxford and New York: Oxford University Press, 2001.

Tamil Nadu Tourism Development Corporation. "Tourism—An Overview." 2019. http://www.tamilnadutourism.org/TN-Overview.html, accessed December 14, 2021.

Taylor, William, ed. and trans. *Oriental Historical Manuscripts, in the Tamil Language*. Vol. II. Madras: Printed and Published by Charles Josiah Taylor, 1835.

Thapar, Romila. "Historical Consciousness in Early India." In *Cultural Pasts: Essays in Early Indian History*, 155–172. New Delhi: Oxford University Press, 2000.

———. "Interpretations of Ancient Indian History." *History and Theory* 7, no. 3 (1968): 318–335.

The Beautiful Garden of Ind: A Dream and Its Interpretation. By a Friend of India. London and Madras: The Christian Literature Society for India, 1897.

The Economic Impacts of Inadequate Sanitation in India: Inadequate Sanitation Costs India Rs. 2.4 Trillion (US$53.8 Billion). New Delhi: Water and Sanitation Program, World Bank, 2010. http://www.wsp.org/sites/wsp.org/files/publications/wsp-esi-india.pdf, accessed December 14, 2021.

The Forest Book of the Rāmāyaṇa of Kampaṉ. Translated by George L. Hart and Hank Heifetz. Berkeley and Los Angeles: University of California Press, 1988.

The Guardian. "India's Hampi Heritage Site Families Face Eviction from Historic Ruins." May 26, 2012. https://www.theguardian.com/world/2012/may/27/hampi-india-heritage-temples-eviction, accessed December 14, 2021.

The Hindu. "17th Century Pudu Mandapam to Be Restored to Its Splendor." June 26, 2011. https://www.thehindu.com/news/cities/Madurai/17th-century-pudu-mandapam-to-be-restored-to-its-splendour/article2136754.ece?homepage=true, accessed December 14, 2021.

———. "Go by UNESCO Suggestions on Temples, HC Tells State." August 25, 2016. http://www.thehindu.com/news/cities/chennai/Go-by-UNESCO-suggestions-on-temples-HC-tells-State/article14588568.ece, accessed December 14, 2021.

———. "Images of Nayak Kings Found in Sri Nellaiyappar Temple." June 6, 2007. https://www.thehindu.com/todays-paper/tp-national/tp-tamilnadu/Images-of-Nayak-kings-found-in-Sri-Nellaiyappar-Temple/article14773856.ece, accessed October 25, 2021.

———. "'Madurai Must Do More to Protect Its Heritage Sites.'" February 24, 2010. http://www.thehindu.com/todays-paper/tp-national/tp-tamilnadu/ldquo Madurai-must-do-more-to-protect-its-heritage-sitesrdquo/article15991375.ece, accessed December 14, 2021.

———. "Panel Inspects Thousand Pillar Hall." *The Hindu,* August 5, 2007. https://www.thehindu.com/todays-paper/tp-national/tp-tamilnadu/Panel-inspects-Thousand-Pillar-Hall/article14809927.ece, accessed December 14, 2021.

———. "Plea to Open Shops at Pudu Mandapam." *The Hindu*, March 2, 2018. http://www.thehindu.com/todays-paper/tp-national/tp-tamilnadu/plea-to-open-shops-at-pudu-mandapam/article22901791.ece, accessed December 14, 2021.

———. "Pudu Mandapam Remains Closed." *The Hindu*, February 5, 2018. http://www.thehindu.com/news/cities/Madurai/pudu-mandapam-remains-closed/article22654739.ece, accessed December 14, 2021.

———. "Renovation Work Begins at Pillar Hall." *The Hindu,* May 8, 2008. https://www.thehindu.com/todays-paper/tp-national/tp-tamilnadu/Renovation-work-begins-at-temple/article15218335.ece, accessed December 14, 2021.

———. "Shopkeepers Clear Goods from Pudu Mandapam in Meenakshi Temple." March 18, 2018. http://www.thehindu.com/news/cities/Madurai/shopkeepers-clear-goods-from-pudu-mandapam-in-meenakshi-temple/article23284471.ece, accessed December 14, 2021.

———. "Stone Laid for Multi-Level Parking at Old Central Vegetable Market near Meenakshi Temple." October 4, 2010. http://www.thehindu.com/news/cities/Madurai/article812701.ece, accessed December 14, 2021.

———. "Tourism Activities to Receive a Boost with Emphasis on Areas in and around Meenakshi Temple." November 4, 2005. https://www.thehindu.com/todays-paper/tp-national/tp-tamilnadu/tourism-activities-to-receive-a-boost-with-emphasis-on-areas-in-and-around-meenakshi-temple/article27503884.ece, accessed December 14, 2021.

———. "Tourists Throng Pudu Mandapam." January 14, 2018. https://www.thehindu.com/news/cities/Madurai/tourists-throng-pudu-mandapam/article22440080.ece, accessed December 14, 2021.

———. "With Chithirai Round the Corner, Pudu Mandapam Is on a Roll." April 1, 2019. https://www.thehindu.com/news/cities/Madurai/with-chithirai-round-the-corner-pudu-mandapam-is-on-a-roll/article26704415.ece, accessed December 14, 2021.

The Industries Department of Government of Tamil Nadu. *Tamil Nadu: Land of Potential*. Chennai: Global Printing Press, 2010.

Thomas, Adrian P. "The Establishment of Calcutta Botanic Garden: Plant Transfer, Science, and the East India Company, 1786–1806." *Journal of the Royal Asiatic Society* 16, no. 2 (July 2006): 165–177.

Thomas, G. *History of Photography, India, 1840–1980*. Hyderabad: Andhra Pradesh State Akademi of Photography, 1981.

———. "The Madras Photographic Society 1856–61." *History of Photography* 16, no. 4 (Winter 1992): 299–301.

Thomson, Thomas. *History of the Royal Society, from Its Institution to the End of the Eighteenth Century*. London: Robert Baldwin, 1812.

Thompson, E. P. *The Making of the English Working Class*. New York: Vintage Books, 1963.

Tillotson, G. H. R. "Farangi and Babu: Two Early Theories of Indian Architecture." *India International Centre Quarterly* 20, no. 1/2 (Spring–Summer 1993): 209–224.

Times of India. "50 Yrs on, Traders All Set to Move out of Pudhu Mandapam." September 3, 2021. https://timesofindia.indiatimes.com/city/madurai/50-yrs-on-traders-all-set-to-move-out-of-pudhu-mandapam/articleshow/85881442.cms, accessed December 14, 2021.

Timothy, Dallen J., and Stephen W. Boyd. *Heritage Tourism*. Harlow, Essex: Pearson Education Limited, 2003.

Tiruvālavāyuṭaiyārkōyil Tiruppaṇimālai (Tamil̲). Edited by Po. Pāṇṭitturaittēvar. Centamil̲p Piracuram-27. Maturai: Maturait Tamil̲ccaṅka Muttirācālai, 1929 [1909]. Includes *Maturaittala Varalāṟu*, pp. 3–13.

Trautmann, Thomas R. *Aryans and British India*. Berkeley and Los Angeles: University of California Press, 1997.

———, ed. *The Aryan Debate*. New Delhi: Oxford University Press, 2005.

———, ed. *The Madras School of Orientalism: Producing Knowledge in Colonial South India*. New Delhi: Oxford University Press, 2009.

Trevelyan, Charles E. Minute by the Honorable the President, March 30, 1859. Madras Public Consultations. April 1, 1859–July 29, 1859. IOR/P/249/69, No. 46, p. 103. British Library, Asia, Pacific, and Africa Collections, London.

———. Minute by the Honorable the President, June 6, 1859. Madras Public Consultations. April 1, 1859–July 29, 1859. IOR/P/249/69, No. 18, p. 348. British Library, Asia, Pacific, and Africa Collections, London.

———. *On the Education of the People of India*. London: Longman, Orme, Brown, Green, & Longmans, 1838.

Trevelyan, G. O. *The Competition Wallah*. London and Cambridge: Macmillan and Co., 1864.

Tripe, Linnaeus. Mandate as Photographer to Madras Government. Captain L. Tripe to F. A. Murray Esq., Private Secretary to the Right Honorable the Governor, July 22, 1856. Extract Public Letter from Fort Saint George, November 24, 1856. Board's Collection. Vol. 2725. 198041–198116. 1857–1858. IOR/F/4/2725, No. 35 of 1856, ff. 3–13. British Library, Asia, Pacific, and Africa Collections, London.

———. Captain L. Tripe, Government Photographer; to T. Pycroft, Esq., Chief Secretary to Government, Fort Saint George, July 16, 1859. Madras Public Consultations. July 30, 1859–December 31, 1859. August 2, 1859. IOR/P/249/70, No. 33. British Library, Asia, Pacific, and Africa Collections, London.

———. *Photographic Views in Madura. By Captain L. Tripe, Government Photographer, Madras Presidency. Part I. With Descriptive Notes, by Martin Norman, Esq. M. C. S. 1858*. [Madras: Madras Presidency], 1860.

———. *Photographic Views in Madura. By Captain L. Tripe, Government Photographer, Madras Presidency. Part II. With Descriptive Notes, 1858*. [Madras: Madras Presidency], 1860.

———. *Photographic Views in Madura. By Captain L. Tripe, Government Photographer, Madras Presidency. Part III. With Descriptive Notes, by Martin Norman, Esq. M. C. S. 1858*. [Madras: Madras Presidency], 1860.

———. *Photographic Views in Madura. By Captain L. Tripe, Government Photographer, Madras Presidency. Part IV. With Descriptive Notes, by Rev. W. Tracy, M. A. 1858*. [Madras: Madras Presidency], 1860.

———. *Photographic Views in Tanjore and Trivady. By Captain L. Tripe, Government Photographer, Madras Presidency. With Descriptive Notes, by the Rev. G. U. Pope. 1858.* [Madras: Madras Presidency], 1860.

———. *Photographic Views of Poodoocottah. By Captain L. Tripe, Government Photographer, Madras Presidency. 1858.* [Madras: Madras Presidency], 1860.

———. *Photographic Views of Ryakotta and Other Places, in the Salem District. By Captain L. Tripe, Government Photographer, Madras Presidency. With Descriptive Notes, by J. A. C. Boswell, Esq. M. C. S. 1858.* [Madras: Madras Presidency], 1860.

———. *Photographic Views of Seringham. By Captain L. Tripe, Government Photographer, Madras Presidency. 1858.* [Madras: Madras Presidency], 1860.

———. *Photographic Views of Trichinopoly. By Captain L. Tripe, Government Photographer, Madras Presidency. 1858.* [Madras: Madras Presidency], 1860.

———. *Stereographs of Madura, Taken by Captain L. Tripe, Govt. Photographer, Madras Presidency. With Descriptions by the Rev. W. Tracy, M. A. 1858.* [Madras: Madras Presidency], 1860.

———. *Stereographs of Trichinopoly, Tanjore and Other Places in Their Neighbourhood; Taken by Captain L. Tripe, Govt. Photographer, Madras Presidency. 1858.* [Madras: Madras Presidency], 1860.

Tuan, Yi-Fu. "Humanistic Geography." *Annals of the Association of American Geographers* 66, no. 2 (June 1976): 266–276.

———. *Space and Place: The Perspective of Experience.* Minneapolis: University of Minnesota, 2014 [1977].

United Nations Educational, Scientific and Cultural Organization. "About World Heritage." 2021. http://whc.unesco.org/en/about/, accessed December 14, 2021.

———. "Archaeological Ruins at Moenjodaro." 2021. http://whc.unesco.org/en/list/138, accessed December 14, 2021.

———. "Sustainable Tourism." 2021. https://whc.unesco.org/en/tourism/, accessed December 14, 2021.

Unni, N. Parameswaran. *Nilakantha Diksita*. Makers of Indian Literature Series. New Delhi: Sahitya Akademi, 1995.

Vasunia, Phiroze. *The Classics and Colonial India*. Oxford: Oxford University Press, 2013.

Viguier Anne. "An Improbable Reconstruction: The Transformation of Madurai, 1837–47." *Indian Economic and Social History Review* 48, no. 2 (April 2011): 215–239.

Vishaal de Mal. "About Us." April 23, 2013. https://web.archive.org/web/20130423192019/http://www.vishaalmall.com:80/about-us/, accessed December 14, 2021.

Viswanathan, Gauri. *Masks of Conquest: Literary Study and British Rule in India*. New York: Columbia University Press, 1989.

Waghorne, Joanne Punzo. "Dressing the Body of God: South Indian Bronze Sculpture in Its Temple Setting." *Asian Art* 5, no. 3 (Summer 1992): 9–33.

Wagoner, Phillip B. "Precolonial Intellectuals and the Production of Colonial Knowledge." *Comparative Studies in Society and History* 45, no. 4 (October 2003): 783–814.

———. "'Sultan among Hindu Kings': Dress, Titles, and the Islamicization of Hindu Culture at Vijayanagara." *Journal of Asian Studies* 55, no. 4 (November 1996): 851–880.

———. *Tidings of the King: A Translation and Ethnohistorical Analysis of the Rāyavācakamu.* Honolulu: University of Hawaii Press, 1995.

Wallace, Jennifer. "Classics as Souvenir: L.E.L. and the Annual." *Classical Receptions Journal* 3, no. 1 (2011): 109–128.

Washbrook, David. "Economic Depression and the Making of 'Traditional' Society in Colonial India 1820–1855." *Transactions of the Royal Historical Society* 3 (1993): 237–263.

———. "South India 1770–1840: The Colonial Transition." *Modern Asian Studies* 38, no. 3 (July 2004): 479–516.

Watson, J. Forbes, and John William Kaye, eds. *The People of India: A Series of Photographic Illustrations, with Descriptive Letterpress, of the Races and Tribes of Hindustan, Originally Prepared under the Authority of the Government of India, and Reproduced by Order of the Secretary of State for India in Council.* Vol. I. London: India Museum, 1868.

White, George Francis. *Views in India, Chiefly among the Himalaya Mountains.* London: Fisher, Son, and Co., 1838.

Wilkins, Charles. *The Bhăgvăt-Gēētā, or Dialogues of Krĕĕshnă and Ărjŏŏn; In Eighteen Lectures; with Notes. Translated from the Original, in the Sănkrĕĕt, or Ancient Language of the Brāhmăns.* London: Nourse, 1785.

Wilks, Mark. Major Mark Wilks, Acting Resident of Mysore to George Buchan Esq., Chief Secretary to Government, Mysoor, March 4, 1807. Board's Collections. Vol. 280. 6426–6428. 1809–1810. IOR/F/4/280, ff. 89–95. British Library, Asia, Pacific, and Africa Collections, London.

———. *Historical Sketches of the South of India, in an Attempt to Trace the History of Mysoor; from the Origin of the Hindoo Government of That State, to the Extinction of the Mohammedan Dynasty in 1799.* Vol. I. London: Longman, Hurst, Rees, Orme, and Brown, 1810.

Wilson, David. "Paradoxes of Tourism in Goa." *Annals of Tourism Research* 24, no. 1 (1997): 52–75.

Wilson, H[orace] H[ayman]. *The Mackenzie Collection. A Descriptive Catalogue of the Oriental Manuscripts, and Other Articles Illustrative of the Literature, History, Statistics and Antiquities of the South of India; Collected by the Late Lieut. Col. Colin*

Mackenzie, Surveyor General of India. 2nd edition. Madras: Higginbotham and Co., 1882 [1828].

———. "Historical Sketch of the Kingdom of Pándya, Southern Peninsula of India." *Journal of the Royal Asiatic Society of Great Britain and Ireland* 3, no. 2 (1836): 199–242.

Windhausen, John D. "The Vernaculars, 1835–1839: A Third Medium for Indian Education." *Sociology of Education* 47, no. 3 (Spring 1964): 254–270.

Wolffhardt, Tobias. *Unearthing the Past to Forge the Future: Colin Mackenzie, the Early Colonial State and the Comprehensive Survey of India*. Translated by Jane Rafferty. New York and Oxford: Berghahn Books, 2018.

Woodward, Christopher. *In Ruins.* New York: Pantheon Books, 2001.

Worwick, Clark, and Ainslee Embree. *The Last Empire: Photography in British India, 1855–1911*. New York: Aperture, 1976.

"XXXII. An Account of Some Artificial Caverns in the Neighbourhood of Bombay: By Mr. William Hunter, Surgeon in the East Indies," "XXXIV. Account of a Curious Pagoda near Bombay, Drawn Up by Captain Pyke, Who Was Afterwards Governor of St. Helena. It Is Dated from On Board the Stringer East-Indiaman in Bombay Harbour 1712, and Is Illustrated with Drawings. This Extract Was Made from the Captain's Journal in Possession of the Honourable the East-India Company. By Alexander Dalrymple, Esq. F.R. and A.S. and Communicated to the Society, Feb. 10, 1780," and "XXXV. Extract by the Late Smart Lethieullier, Esq. from the Papers of the Late Charles Boon, Esq. Governor of Bombay, Giving an Account of the Great Pagoda on the Island of Salset," *Archaeologia, or, Miscellaneous Tracts Relating to Antiquity. Published by The Society of Antiquaries of London* 7 (1785): 286–302, 323–336, and 333–336 respectively.

Younger, Paul. *The Home of the Dancing Śivan: The Traditions of the Hindu Temple in Citamparam*. New York and Oxford: Oxford University Press, 1995.

Zastoupil, Lynn and Martin Moir, eds. *The Great Indian Education Debate: Documents relating to the Orientalist-Anglicist Controversy, 1781–1843*. Richmond, Surrey: Curzon Press, 1999.

Zhang, Li. "Private Homes, Distinct Lifestyles: Performing a New Middle Class." In *Privatizing China: Socialism from Afar*, edited by Li Zhang and Aihwa Ong, 23–40. Ithaca and London: Cornell University Press, 2008.

Zvelebil, Kamil V[eith]. *Companion Studies to the History of Tamil Literature.* Leiden and New York: E. J. Brill, 1992.

———. *Tamil Literature.* Wiesbaden, Germany: Otto Harrasowitz, 1974.

Index